UNDERSTANDING EU LAW

UNDERSTANDING EU LAW

Objectives, Principles and Methods of Community Law

NORBERT REICH

2nd amended and updated student edition
with references to the Draft Constitution
of 29 October 2004

intersentia

Antwerpen – Oxford

Distribution for the UK:
Hart Publishing
Salter's Boat Yard
Folly Bridge
Abingdon Road
Oxford OX1 4LB
UK
Tel: + 44 1865 24 55 33
Fax: + 44 1865 79 48 82

Distribution for Switzerland and Germany:
Schulthess Verlag
Zwingliplatz 2
CH-8022 Zürich
Switzerland
Tel: + 41 1 251 93 36
Fax: + 41 1 261 63 94

Distribution for North America:
Gaunt Inc.
Gaunt Building
3011 Gulf Drive
Holmes Beach
Florida 34217-2199
USA
Tel: + 1 941 778 5211
Fax: + 1 941 778 5252

Distribution for other countries:
Intersentia Publishers
Groenstraat 31
BE-2640 Mortsel
Belgium
Tel: + 32 3 680 15 50
Fax: + 32 3 658 71 21

Understanding EU Law
Norbert Reich

© 2005 Intersentia
Antwerpen – Oxford
http://www.intersentia.be

ISBN 90-5095-465-0
D/2005/7849/39
NUR 828

PREFACE

This book is not an introduction to EC law. Those already exist in plenty, and this book does not wish simply to add to the weight of literature. Nor, too, does this book deal with the complex interrelation between the various EU institutions involved in making and implementing the law. Indeed, it takes these for granted, even if subject to change once the results of the Draft Treaty Establishing a Constitution for Europe of 29 October 2004 (in the following: Draft Constitution)[1] are implemented. And if the approach might be criticized as positivistic – it would be preferable to call it realistic.

For this book is concerned with EU law in terms of its objectives, principles and methods. Its starting point is the famous wording of the European Court of Justice in *Costa v. ENEL*[2], that the *"EEC Treaty has created its own legal system which ... became an integral part of the legal systems of the Member States and which their courts are bound to apply"*. Was the Court being overly optimistic in pronouncing these words more than 40 years ago in a somewhat trifling setting?

Perhaps, but with hindsight it seems that in the meantime they have been accepted by the "old" Member States, although not without some difficulty. Moreover, the acceding new Member States have to integrate this important statement into their own legal orders. Certainly, that is no easy task. And so, this book aims to contribute to the process of *Europeanisation* in applying the law.

Understanding EU law means a number of things. It means, first of all, comprehending its legal peculiarities. These include its sources, instruments, methods of interpretation, effects, and the relationship between Community and national law (*Introductory Chapter*). It also means always respecting what case law and secondary legislation have already achieved, because these can only be modified at EU, not at national, level. This is the so-called *acquis communautaire*.

But that is only the starting point. For beyond it lies the field of personal application of EU law, now considerably widened. That is, from simply a law for market citizens EU law has become the law for *all citizens and residents* living in Member States. Thus,

---

[1]   [2004] OJ C310.
[2]   Case 6/64 Flaminco Costa v Enel [1964] ECR 585.

EU law determines their everyday rights and duties beyond existing national law (*Chapter I*). This is based on the principle of *equal treatment*.

The next step consists of the original liberal *esprit des lois* of EU law. This is about the opening of markets (*Chapter II*). However, the liberalizing process has now become *two-sided*, in that it is supplemented by an ever-growing set of what might be called *adequate standards* (*Chapter III*). At the same time, the process includes a concept of fundamental rights, as yet fragmented.

In addition, the generous grant of autonomy (*Chapter IV*) is sometimes applied against Member States, frequently also against privately-induced restrictions. This *liberalizing* force of EU law provoked substantial changes in legal application and thinking in new Member States.

To complete the picture, the first elements of governance and accountability appear (*Chapter V*), developed either by the case law of the Court or by legislation. However, this field remains incomplete and certainly subject to change in the future as legal integration continues.

Moreover, other areas are simply not included at all. This is due to sheer bulk of material, and incomplete participation by all Member States. A good example is the emerging *area of freedom, justice and security*.

Why is it, then, that the EU depends so heavily on its legal structures, principles, and methods? The short answer is that European integration is *integration by law* – indeed, law plays the leading role. This is because, whatever the outcome of the ratification process of the Draft Constitution, the EU is not and may never be a federal state with sovereign powers to implement the law. For its effectiveness depends crucially on co-operation with Member States, and notably with their courts of law. Indeed, it is in these very courts that the true *European judges* sit, in that it is they who must understand what EU law is all about. And it is lawyers, legal experts, and law students who must help them to fulfil this role or, even better, fulfil it themselves.

In doing so, they will keep in mind the main characteristic of European law. That is, the more it becomes an *integral part* of national law, the less it is visible as a distinct legal order. This, in turn, aids more effective integration of national law and European law. In that way, EU law is like the blueprint for a new house: the more the final building conforms to the blueprint, the less one needs to refer to it, but in some cases one must take a hard look at the blueprint to make sure the final building conforms!

This book introduces that blueprint both meaningfully and readably. To achieve this aim, it deliberately avoids a complete description of certain areas of EU law in full detail. Rather, it paints an impressionistic picture through characteristic examples. These consist of distinct concepts, methods and principles that EU law has developed, and that need to be kept in mind when working with questions of its application and interpretation. The examples chosen demonstrate the aspects of EU law that have often led to friction with existing national law. Indeed, the interfaces between national and EU law should always be remembered when working on the fault-lines between these two distinct yet interdependent legal orders.

It should also be kept in mind that EU law is an *incomplete legal order*, in that sometimes it only proposes broad principles but without telling us how these should be implemented. This is particularly true with regard to judicial protection as a mere *obligation de moyens* on the one hand, and a (still missing) theory of *legal duties* of citizens on the other. The effort to fill the gaps is central to understanding EU law. Hopefully, this book will contribute to the never-ending task of making EU law truly a system of its own, thus fulfilling the ambitious *Costa* pronouncement, also secure its acceptance in new Member countries, which will, after accession to the EU, fully participate in the European integration process.

The first edition had been prepared with the help of Christopher Goddard and Ksenija Vasiljeva while being Rector of the Riga Graduate School of Law. The student edition updates the original version. It refers in passing to the Draft Constitution, which, if ever entering into force, will only marginally modify the existing *acquis*. These potential changes have been mentioned, together with a Table of equivalences between the EU and EC Treaties in the Nice version (EU resp. EC) and the Draft Constitution (p. 389).

Bremen/Hamburg, Spring 2005

TABLE OF CONTENTS

INTRODUCTION: COMMUNITY LAW AS THE PATTERN OF A LIBERAL YET INCOMPLETE LEGAL ORDER

Table of Contents

Selected Bibliography

J. Basedow, "The Communitarisation of Conflict of Law Rules under the Amsterdam Treaty", *CMLRev* 2000, 687; J. Bengoetxea, *The legal reasoning of the European Court of Justice*, 1993; U. Bernitz (ed.), *General Principles of Community Law*, 1999; A. v. Bogdandy/J. Bast (eds.), *Principles of European Constitutional Law*, 2005; Brechmann,

Die richtlinienkonforme Auslegung, 1994; J. M. Broekman, *A Philosophy of European Law*, 1999; P. Craig/G. de Búrca, *EU Law – Texts, cases and materials*, 3ʳᵈ edition, 2002; G. de Búrca/J. Scott (eds.), *The EU and the WTO: Legal and Constitutional Issues*, 2001; N. Colneric, *Une Communauté de droit*, FS Rodrigues Iglesias, 2004; Dalloz (éd.), *Le Traité d'Amsterdam*, 1998; S. Douglas-Scott, *Constitutional Law of the EU*, 2002; C.D. Ehlermann, *Differentiation, Flexibility, Closer Cooperation*, 1998; U. Ehricke, "Die richtlinienkonforme und die gemeinschaftskonforme Auslegung nationalen Recht", *RabelsZ* 1995, 598; Th. Eilmannsberger, "The relationship between rights and remedies in EC-Law: The search of the missing link", *CMLRev* 204, 1199; E. Ellis (ed.), *The principle of Proportionality in the Laws of Europe*, 1999; E. Emiliou, "Subsidiarity – an Effective Barrier against the "Enterprises of Ambition"?", *ELRev* 1992, 383; A. Estella, *The EU Principle of Subsidiarity*, 2002; U. Everling, "Will Europe Slip on Bananas? The Banana Judgment of the Court of Justice and National Courts", *CMLRev* 1996, 401; U. Everling/W.-H. Roth (Hrsg.), *Mindestharmonisierung im Europäischen Binnenmarkt*, 1997; A. Furrer, *Die Sperrwirkung des sekundären Gemeinschaftsrechts*, 1994; W. van Gerven, *The European Union – A Polity of States and Peoples*, 2005; St. Grundmann, "Richtlinienkonforme Auslegung im Bereich des Privatrechts", *ZEuP* 1996, 400; T.C. Hartley, "International Law and the Law of the EU – A reassessment", *BYIL* 2001, 1; P.J.G. Kapteyn/P. VerLoren van Themaat/L. Gormley, *Introduction to the law of the European Communities*, 3ʳᵈ ed. 1998; A. Kellermann/J. De Zwaan/ J. Czuczai, EU *Enlargement. The Constitutional Impact at EU and National Level*, 2001; M. Kiikeri, *Comparative Legal reasoning in European law*, 2001; J. Kokott/A. Rüth, "The European Convention and its Draft Treaty Establishing a Constitution for Europe: Appropriate Answers to the Laeken Questions?", *CMLRev* 2003, 1315; L. Krämer, *EC Environmental law*, 5ᵗʰ edition 2003; P.J. Kuiper, "The evolution of the Third Pillar from Maastricht to the European Constitution", *CLMRev* 2004, 609; H. W. Micklitz, "The Maastricht Treaty, the principle of subsidiarity, and the theory of integration", *Lakimies* 1993, 508; H. W. Micklitz/St. Weatherill, *European Economic Law*, 1997; H.W. Micklitz/N. Reich/St. Weatherill, "EU-Treaty Revision and Consumer Protection", *Journal of Consumer Policy (JCP)* 2004, 367; A. Peters, "European Democracy after the 2003 Convention", *CMLRev* 2004, 37; Th. Pfeiffer, "Richtlinienkonforme Auslegung im Privatrecht", *Studentische Zeitschrift für Rechtswissenschaft Heidelberg (StudZR)* 2004, 171; Chr. Pitchas, *Die völkerrechtliche Verantwortlichkeit der EG und ihrer Mitgliedstaaten*, 2001; S. Prechal, "Does direct effect still matter?", *CMLRev* 1999, 1047; S. Prechal, *Directives in EC Law: A Study on EC Directives and their Enforcement by National Courts*, 1995; M. Radeideh, *Fair Trading in EC Law – Information and Consumer Choice in the Internal Market*, 2005; N. Reich, "Competition between Legal Orders", *CMLRev* 1992, 861; N. Reich, "The "November Revolution" of the ECJ", *CMLRev* 1994, 459; N. Reich, "Judge-Made 'Europe à la Carte'", *EJIL* 1996, 103; N. Reich, *Bürgerrechte in der EU*, 1999; N. Reich/R. Heine-Mernik (Hrsg.), *Umweltverfassung und nachhaltige Entwicklung in der EU*, 1997; N. Reich/H.-W. Micklitz,

Europäisches Verbraucherrecht, 4.A. 2003; U. Rörig, *Die Direktwirkung von Richtlinien in Privatrechtsverhältnissen*, 2001; J. Schapira/G. le Tallec/J.-B., Blaise, *Droit européen des affaires*, 5ème ed. 2000; A.-M. Slaughter/A. Stone Sweet/J. H.H. Weiler (eds.), *The European and National Courts*, 1998; R. Streinz, *Europarecht*, 6. A. 2004; A. Toth, "The principle of subsidarity in the Maastricht Treaty", *CMLRev* 1992, 1079; A. Toth, "Is subsidiarity justiciable?", *ELRev* 1994, 268; Chr. Vedder/W.H. v. Heinegg, *EU-Verfassung*, 2005; T. Tridimas, *General Principles of Community Law*, 1999; J. Usher, *Community Agricultural law*, 2001; St. Weatherill, "Beyond Pre-emption? Shared Competences and Constitutional Change in the EC", in: O'Keefe/Twomey (eds.), *Legal issues of the Maastricht Treaty*, 1994, 24; St. Weatherill, *Cases and Materials on EC Law*, 5th edition, 2000; St. Weatherill, "The European Commission's Green Paper on European Contract Law: Context, Content and Constitutionality", *Journal of Consumer Policy* 2001, 339; St. Weatherill/P. Baumont, *EC Law*, 3rd ed. 1999; F. Tuytsschaever, *Differentiation in European Union Law*, 1999; A. Verhoeven, The EU in search of a Democratic and Constitutional Theory, 2002; J. H. H. Weiler, "The State "über alles": Demos, Telos, and the German Maastricht Decision", in: O. Due *et al.* (eds.), *Festschrift Everling*, 1995, 1651; J.H.H. Weiler, *The Constitution of Europe*, 1999; G. Winter (ed.), *Sources and Categories of Community law*, 1996; O. Wicklund, *Judicial discretion in European Perspectives*, 2003; B. de Witte/D. Hauf/E. Vos (eds.), *The Many Faces of Differentiation in EU Law*, 2001; M. Zuleeg, "The European Constitution under Constitutional Constraints: The German Scenario", *ELRev* 1997, 19.

§ 1. LIBERAL ELEMENTS OF COMMUNITY LAW AND ITS COMPLEMENTARY PATTERNS

I. OVERVIEW: INTERNAL MARKET AS STARTING POINT

This book aims to promote an understanding of Community law. Indeed, its emphasis is on law, rather than on institutions. The starting premise is that Community law, in contrast to the law of most Member States, has a specific objective in mind. That is, here, an internal market – or a common market,[1] as the old version of the Treaty still calls it This overall objective is achieved by applying certain principles and methods. These are specific to Community law, and distinguish it from national or international legal systems.

The concept of *internal market* as used here is a broad one. It is of course mostly related to economic structures and performances, where the liberal elements of Community law are most clearly visible. This is especially true with regard to the basic objective of *open markets* (Chapter II). This is to be achieved in two main ways. Firstly, by the free movement of goods, persons, services and capital[2]. Secondly, by a system where competition is not distorted[3]. Community law is at its strongest and clearest where it follows this objective.

But even in this area Community law presents an incomplete legal regime. For it is only concerned with some aspects of opening markets. While these aspects are undoubtedly important, none the less Community law is *principle-oriented,* not *rule-oriented.* Certain principles, such as those relating to a system of *open markets,* have to be developed into legal rules. This can be achieved either by secondary law, or by detailed Court practice. These will be analysed here, in particular highlighting the most important tendencies and the techniques used, although not in every detail.

Open markets can only function if economic actors are guaranteed a wide margin of autonomy (Chapter IV). Surprisingly, Community law is somewhat silent on this point. However, a closer analysis reveals that autonomy stands implicitly as the basis of many Community measures. Indeed, it is here that Member States play an important complementary and supportive role. For EC law starts from the premise that Member State law, in different forms and instruments, guarantees this autonomy to private persons. That is so whether these be undertakings, associations, or natural

---

[1]   Per Art. 3 (1) lits a), c) g), h), m)-o), t)-u) of the Treaties establishing the European Communities, consolidated version [2002] OJ C 325/33 (hereinafter - EC).
[2]   (Art. 14 (2) EC).
[3]   (Art. 3 (1) lit g).

persons. Clearly, then, principles of Community law should not stand in fundamental contradiction with Member State law, and *vice-versa*. Moreover, any such contradiction requires Community law rules to resolve any potential conflict. This is especially so in respect of restrictions on autonomy, which have an influence on the functioning of the internal market.

We shall see that Community law has meanwhile developed a subtle system of conflict resolution. This relies on a highly legalized mechanism, in which Community and national courts co-operate (§§ 2/3). Confidence in the rule of law is one of the principles of a liberal order. However, this does not imply a rejection of *politics* but, rather, leaves conflict resolution to a separate set of rules and to independent institutions, namely courts of law. In the Community context, Member States have transferred part of their sovereignty to the Community. Further, they have voluntarily abandoned traditional mechanisms for conflict resolution under international law. And the reason they did so was for the sake of unity of the internal market, and uniformity of Community law.

This state of affairs was carefully stated by the Court as long ago as 1963 in the well known *Van Gend & Loos* decision[4]. Indeed, this has become part of the *constitutional acquis*[5] of the Community:

> ...the Community constitutes a new legal order of international law for the benefit of which the states have limited their sovereign rights, albeit in limited fields, and the subjects of which comprise not only Member States but also their nationals. Independently of the legislation of the Member States, Community law therefore not only imposes obligations on individuals but is also intended to confer rights upon them which become part of their legal heritage.

Such *juridification* of conflict resolution is seen as functioning in the best interests of all. This remains so, even if in some cases it leads to a reduction in autonomous decision-making by political or private actors in Member States. While the border lines of such transfer remain contested, these must be resolved on a case-by-case basis. The mechanism is part of a broader concept of *rule of law*, expressly mentioned in the preamble of the Treaty on European Union. Now established by the Treaty of Maastricht, this concept is one of the leading pillars of the Community and will be discussed throughout this book.[6]

---

[4]   Case 26/62 Van Gend en Loos v Nederlandse Administratie van Belastingen [1963] ECR 1.
[5]   Douglas-Scott, *Constitutional Law of the EU*, 2002 at 516-520.
[6]   Douglas-Scott at 374; Tridimas, *The General Principles of Community Law*, 1999 at 1, 163; van Gerven, *The European Union*, 2005, at 104-157.

II. DEVELOPING COMPLEMENTARY PATTERNS TO A LIBERAL CONCEPT OF COMMUNITY LAW

The liberal principles of open markets, autonomy, and rule of law cannot alone provide full democratic legitimacy to any regime. This is especially true of the EU, which intrudes so deeply into the lives of its citizens, residents, undertakings, associations, and political bodies.[7] As the internal market develops a regime of its own, the broader autonomy of players is respected. At the same time, as the rule of law is followed consequentially, complementary patterns develop more clearly. For if Liberalism tends to provoke abuses of freedom, then the task of law is to operate against such abuses. Moreover, Liberalism in its true sense also goes beyond recognizing individuals simply as economic actors.

The personal and individual element of action becomes visible with the European Union resolving[8] to establish *a citizenship common to the nationals of their countries*. Thus the citizen evolves as something more than a mere market agent, allowed to move freely for work and self-employed activity. As a result, in a broader context the values and rights of the citizen fall within the ambit of Community law. The concept is a dynamic one, potentially including:
– family members of citizens,
– persons permanently and legally resident in a Member State without necessarily being Union citizens, and
– citizens of countries on the verge of accession.

It therefore makes sense to begin a discussion of Community law with the concept of citizenship (Chapter I).

Markets are more than merely a mechanism of economic efficiency. Indeed, they are an instrument to improve the *living and working conditions of their people*[9], not an objective in themselves. They can only function with adequate standards (Chapter III). Moreover, these standards inevitably merge with the concept of citizenship, because they go beyond economic rationality to include such concepts as non-discrimination (§ 11), fundamental rights (§ 12), legitimate expectations (§ 13), and judicial protection (§ 14). For they do not contradict the basic liberal assumption, nor do they aim to regulate individual behavior for abstract goals. Significantly, however, they acknowledge that markets and autonomy can only work in a system of values and rules, where the freedom of one implicitly recognizes the freedom of the other.

---

[7]   Weiler, *The Constitution of Europe*, 1999 at 238-285.
[8]   Preamble of the EC.
[9]   Preamble of the EC.

Here, it should be kept in mind that Community law does not contain a complete set of adequate standards. Rather, it may only be seen in the context of existing Member State and other schemes, including self-regulatory schemes, to which Community law sometimes adds, but sometimes also stands in contradiction. Particularly with regard to setting standards, Community law should be seen as active *multi-functional* legislation[10], coordinating and combining different layers of existing and proposed rules. Usually, Community law will not give one clear answer on establishing and implementing a certain standard. It relies heavily on Member State law, at the same time modifying it in order to attain the objectives central to this book.

Finally, any legal order can survive only if a regime exists to sanction violations. Accountability and responsibility are core features of any legal order, and Community law is no exception (Chapter V). In the Community context, this problem requires analysis on four levels:
– accountability of the Community and its institutions as such (§ 18);
– responsibility of Member States, which in the original Treaty only existed *vis-à-vis* the Community[11], but not *vis-à-vis* its citizens and residents (§ 19);
– responsibility of undertakings, which Community law has established in competition but not in other matters (§ 20), and
– responsibility of citizens, which still remains a blind spot on the Community law agenda (§ 21).

However, from the outset the particular problem that Community law had to cope with is its *incompleteness*. It is here where the most striking difference to the law of any Member State can be found. The Community enjoys no jurisdiction in criminal matters. Moreover, only in exceptional cases – mainly in competition matters – may it impose financial sanctions upon private persons, in the shape of fines.[12] With regard to civil liability, no general regime exists in Community law to cover contract or tort liability. Instead, only fragments of responsibility are present. Moreover, these usually engage Member States rather than private persons. Administrative liability occurs only in those areas where private persons are directly subject to Community action. However, this is normally not the case at all, since Member States implement Community law – but in doing so may not violate the effectiveness of Community law itself.

---

[10]   Weatherill in: O'Keefe/Twomey, *Legal issues of the Maastricht Treaty*, 1994 at 24; Douglas-Scott at 171-172.
[11]   Per Art. 10 EC.
[12]   This has recently been reaffirmed by the new Regulation (EC) No. 1/2003 of 16.12.2002, *OJ* L 1 of 4.1.2003 implementing the competition rules.

III. AREAS EXCLUDED: ENVIRONMENTAL LAW, COMMON POLICIES, JUSTICE AND HOME AFFAIRS, "THIRD PILLAR"

As we have seen, Community law is not a coherent and comprehensive legal order. It focuses its attention *selectively* on legal problems that come within its competence. It has developed some general principles, but does not match Member State law in its aim for completeness. Community law is *function-oriented,* not *system-oriented.* It derives its functions from the objectives and principles already mentioned, and which we will examine in more detail in the following chapters. It therefore makes sense to exclude from this introduction four areas where the Community has developed principles and rules of its own:

1. Environmental law

In its early stages, environmental law featured as a corollary of internal market law.[13] Since then, it has freed itself from market orientation to become a policy on its own.[14,][15] However, it may still contain some internal market elements that justify Community action.[16] Another cause for the particular role of Community environmental law stems from its merger with international law and policy – for the simple reason that pollution does not stop at borders. On that basis, this book will look at environmental law only from the point of view of responsibility for environmental damage (§ 20 III 3).

2. Common policies in agriculture, fisheries, transport, foreign commerce

The Community has established common policies[17] in certain areas such as agriculture, fisheries, transport, and foreign commerce. These are characterized by a clear deviation from its liberal internal market objective. They therefore deserve special treatment, because the function of law is different, in that it serves to protect Community policy aimed at regulating markets, rather than opening them.[18] In the field of foreign commerce, the Community is not an autonomous actor but must respect the rules of the WTO. These will be treated only with respect to intellectual property rights (§ 10 I 1). It is true that much litigation on Community law has centred around these

---

[13]   Case 240/83 Procureur de la République v Association de Défense de Brûleurs de Huiles Usagers [1985] ECR 531.

[14]   Per Art. 3 lit l), 6 EC.

[15]   For an account cf. Krämer, *EC Environmental Law,* 5th ed. 2003.

[16]   Case C-300/89 Commission v. Council [1991] ECR I-2867 concerning titanium dioxide waste; a different approach was taken in case C-155/91 Commission v. Council [1993] ECR I-939 concerning the waste framework directive.

[17]   Per Art. 3 (1) lit b), e) and f).

[18]   Cf. Usher, *EC Agricultural Law,* 2001.

common policies. Indeed, many principles have been developed in this context, particularly on judicial protection (§ 12) and Community accountability and liability (§ 18). We therefore need to discuss how far these rules can be generalized into principles of Community law, or are specific to a certain regulated area.

3. Justice and Home Affairs (JHA)

The Treaty of Amsterdam introduced a new title, creating an *Area of freedom, justice and security*[19]. This has been separated from the former third pillar of the Maastricht Treaty, which only provided for international cooperation. Denmark has completely opted out of this title, while the UK and Ireland have an opt-in possibility which they have used selectively so far.

JHA really concerns two different sets of rules:
- Traditional internal affairs, such as migration, refugee and asylum policy, safeguarding the outer borders (the so-called *Schengen acquis*).[20]
- Cooperation in civil matters, integrated into EC law because of its *internal market* elements.[21, 22] This has resulted in a number of important regulations, including those on jurisdiction and enforcement in civil and commercial matters[23] (§ 14 II). This substitutes the former international law regime of the so-called 1968 Brussels Convention, which now applies only *vis-à-vis* Denmark.

The JHA still has some particularities concerning referral to the Court. This can only be done by courts against whose decisions there are no judicial remedies. The Court is barred from scrutinizing public policy and public order issues. This stands in total contrast to the *acquis* in the area of free movement. The voting procedure relies on unanimity in the Council with the Parliament's role decreased, but should be open to change after 5 years[24].

4. Police and judicial co-operation in criminal matters

The Amsterdam version of the EU[25] has singled out police and judicial co-operation in criminal matters from judicial co-operation in civil matters[26]. Community law, in

---

[19]   Its objectives are spelled out in Art 2 EC, its competences and procedures in Art. 62 *et seq.*
[20]   For an overview cf. S. Peers, *EU Justice and Home Affairs Law*, 2000; Hailbronner, *Immigration and Asylum law and Policy of the EU*, 2000; E. Guild, *Immigration Law in the EC*, 2001; Guild, *ELRev* 2004, 198.
[21]   Per Art. 65 EC.
[22]   Basedow, *CMLRev* 2000, 687; Remien, *CMLRev* 2001, 58.
[23]   Reg. (EC) No. 44/2001.
[24]   Art. 67 EC as amended by the Nice Treaty.
[25]   Title VI.
[26]   Craig/De Búrca at 39-41.

the sense described here, does not play a substantial role in this area[27]. The explanation is that Member States either stayed with the traditional international law concept of co-operation, or preferred less intrusive instruments of law-making called *common positions* and *framework decisions*[28], in contrast to Community law regulations and directives (§ 2).[29, 30] However, a certain Community involvement has been introduced into the so called *third pillar*. The Nice Treaty amendments have not changed the tendency towards co-operation. However, this should not be seen as being in serious conflict with integration.

The hybrid character of the third pillar can be seen in the following examples:
– Jurisdiction of the ECJ is not mandatory but depends on an autonomous decision of the Member State[31].
– The ECJ cannot review matters of internal security and the maintenance of law and order[32].
– Framework decisions[33] do not entail direct effect, contrary to the *acquis communautaire* with regard to directives (§ 2 II).
– Respect for fundamental rights is guaranteed only insofar as the ECJ has jurisdiction[34].

The existing *pillar structure*, on the one hand, and the special rules on JHA on the other, are not particularly well-placed for the development of the *acquis* in the exact sense as promised.[35] That is, to create a common European area of freedom, justice and security. Above all, it would appear desirable to discard the Protocols unilaterally favouring Denmark and (to a lesser extent) the UK and Ireland. Doing so would avoid different layers of law, even in such technical areas as competence of civil courts. References to the ECJ should be available to all courts, perhaps even in fast-track proceedings. This would be especially useful when questions of fundamental rights protection (asylum, family reunion) in the EU are at stake.

The Draft Constitution will abolish the pillar structure and entail a new Chapter IV in Part III on an "Area of Freedom, Security and Justice". By Protocols 19 and 20, it

---

[27]   Anderson/Apap (eds.), Police and Justice Co-operation and The New European Borders, 2002; Kuijpers, *CMLRev* 2004, 609; Douglas-Scott, *ELRev* 2004, 219.
[28]   Per Art. 34 (2) EU.
[29]   Per Art. 249 EC.
[30]   Douglas-Scott at 114.
[31]   Per Art. 35 EU.
[32]   Per Art. 35 (5) EU.
[33]   Per Art. 34 (2) lit b) EU.
[34]   Per Art. 46 d) EU.
[35]   Art. 2.

will continue the opt-out provisos for the UK, Ireland and Denmark, but modify the voting thresholds. It will contain four sections:
- Common policies on border checks, asylum and immigration;
- Judicial cooperation in civil matters;
- Judicial cooperation in criminal matters;
- Police cooperation.

§ 2. SOURCES AND METHODS OF COMMUNITY LAW

I. DIFFERENT SOURCES OF COMMUNITY LAW

1. Absence of hierarchy of Community legal acts

Community law, in contrast to Member State law, contains no clear hierarchy of sources.[36] Traditionally, the literature distinguishes between primary and secondary Community law, as follows:
- Primary law, in the shape of the Treaty and the instruments attached to it – Protocols, Accession Treaties.
- Secondary Community law[37]-regulations, directives and decisions.

The difference between these types of law lies not so much in their place in *a hierarchy of norms* as in their source. Thus, on the one hand primary Community law originates from the Member States in their role of *Masters of the Treaty*, with certain involvement of Community institutions.[38] Then on the other hand, secondary law originates directly from Community institutions. In this respect, suffice to say that procedures are characterized by different voting mechanisms and majority requirements in the Council and the European Parliament. However, these are not described in detail here. Moreover, as Community instruments, they usually require a proposal from the Commission, with some exceptions[39] on asylum, visa, and judicial co-operation in civil matters.[40]

Legal writers are unanimous that the Treaty[41] contain no *numerus clausus* of Community legal acts.[42] This is particularly true with acts of international law, in which the Community participates in different ways and which may have legal force within the Community legal order. Examples here would include association agreements.[43] Indeed, in its *ERTA* decision the Court affirmed that these acts are subject to jurisdictional control according to the relevant provisions of the Treaty.[44] Their legal effect in the Community legal order depends on criteria to be developed later (II).

---

[36]   Douglas-Scott at 115; Winter (ed.), *Sources and Categories of European Union Law*, 1996.
[37]   As described in Art. 249 EC.
[38]   Cf. Art. 49 EU concerning accession of new Member States.
[39]   In the new title IV.
[40]   Per Art. 67 (1) EC.
[41]   Specifically, Art. 249 EC.
[42]   Douglas-Scott at 113.
[43]   Per Art. 300 EC.
[44]   Case 22/70 Commission v Council [1971] ECR 263 at paras 38-41.

Community institutions make frequent use of *soft law* instruments. These are described[45] as *recommendations* and *opinions* with no binding force in the formal sense. However, they are not devoid of legal significance, as the ECJ declared in its *Grimaldi* decision.[46] Indeed, they should at least be observed when interpreting Member State law implementing them. In the meantime, so called "co-regulation" is used in certain areas such as free movement[47] and consumer protection[48], where Community institutions and market partners participate. In the field of social policy, labour and management may[49] conclude agreements. These may be transformed into legal acts by a Council decision upon proposal by the Commission. This method is particularly recommended as a new form of governance of Community institutions as being closer to the interests of those concerned (§ 18 II 1).

2. Observance of the law

The Treaty[50] goes beyond traditional sources of Community law when mandating the ECJ to "ensure that in the interpretation and application of this Treaty *the law*[51] is observed". This concept of *observance of the law* (in German: *Wahrung des Rechts*, in French: *respect du droit*) includes not only written and positive sources of law as described above, but also general principles common to the legal orders of the Member States. An example would be respect for fundamental rights (§ 12).[52]

Another interesting illustration concerns the principle of state liability in case of violations of Community law *vis-à-vis* private individuals. Even though this was not included in the Treaty (§ 14 II), it derives from such a general principle in the famous *Francovich* decision:[53]

> It follows that the principle whereby a State must be liable for loss and damage caused to individuals as a result of breaches of Community law for which the State can be held responsible is inherent in the system of the Treaty (para 35).

Since this broad principle has been recognized both by later Court practice and by Member State courts, it must be said to be part of the Community legal order. This remains so, even though it was never formally promulgated as an act of primary or

---

[45]   In Art. 249 EC.
[46]   Case C-322/88 Grimaldi (Salvatore) v Fonds des maladies professionelles [1989] ECR 4407.
[47]   Com (2001) 130of 7.3.2001.
[48]   Com (2002) 278of 5.6.2002.
[49]   Art. 139 EC.
[50]   Art. 220 EC.
[51]   Authors' italics (NR).
[52]   Per Art. 6 (2), 46 lit d) EU.
[53]   Cases C-6 and 9/90 Francovich and Others v Italy [1991] ECR I-5357.

secondary Community law. From this starting point a Community theory of *stare decisis*, or legal precedent, will be developed later (IV).

Other general principles concern legal certainty, protection of legitimate expectations, proportionality, and respect for principles of international law.[54] Indeed, the EC Treaty has given the Court a broad mandate to develop Community law and, above all, to fill existing gaps by Community-specific theories of interpretation. These comprise: the principle of autonomous interpretation, and the so-called *effet utile* doctrine (III). Thus, the *judicial activism* that has been the object of some criticism is not only inherent in the Treaty but also cannot be said to be going beyond the boundaries of the mandate of the ECJ.[55]

3. New terminology and structure of legal instruments according to the Draft Constitution

The Draft Constitution will – once ratified – substantially change the terminology of legal instruments of the EU. Regulations will be renamed "European laws"; directives will be called *"European framework laws"*, Art. I-33 (1) para 1. Their legal effects according to paras 2 and 3 will not be changed since the formulations used in Art. 249 (2) and (3) EC simply have been taken over by the Draft Constitution.

At the same time, the Draft Constitution tries to put some structure into non-legislative acts which are now called "European regulations", "European decisions", recommendations and opinions (as before). A European regulation is defined as a "non-legislative act of general application for the implementation of legislative acts and of certain provisions of the Constitution". Art. I-36 will contain constitutional requirements as to the delegation of powers via "European regulations", thus to some extent clarifying and codifying existing Community practice in the so-called "Comitology" area.[56] An "essential doctrine" theory similar to German constitutional law[57] is laid down in para (1) and will substantially modify Art. 202 3rd and Art. 211 4th indent EC:

> European laws and framework laws may delegate to the Commission the power to adopt delegated European regulations to supplement or amend certain non-essential elements of the laws or the framework law. The objectives, content, scope and duration of the

---

[54] Tridimas, *The General Principles of Community Law, passim* for more details; Craig/de Búrca at 371-396.

[55] For a critical opinion, cf. H. Rasmussen, *On Law and Policy of the ECJ*, 1986; more realistic, Douglas-Scott at 213-217 referring to "acceptable" judicial activism; Weiler, *supra* note 7 at 203-207.

[56] Craig/de Burca, at pp. 150-153.

[57] Streinz, *Europarecht*, 5th edition 2004, para. 456.

delegation of power shall be explicitly defined in the European laws and framework laws. The essential elements of an area shall be reserved for the European law or framework law and accordingly shall not be the subject of a delegation of power.

II. DIRECT EFFECT AND ITS LIMITS

1. Defining and contextualising direct effect

The theory of direct effect should for our purposes be accepted for what it is, or has become. That is, both a constituent element of the *acquis communautaire*, and part of the *law* whose observance the ECJ has to ensure. Therefore this book takes a somewhat positivist approach towards a development that has given rise to much controversy, both in Member State court practice and in legal writing. Most of this relates to the legal effect of directives[58]. The former Luxembourg ECJ Judge Pescatore[59] referred to it as an *infant disease* of Community law. We will not in detail repeat and evaluate this controversy, which indeed has outlived itself. For today, it is not the direct effect of Community law that is at stake, but rather its conditions, its scope, and its limits.

To find the justification for this approach, we need only look at the specifics of Community law itself. The Court already described this in its *Van Gend and Loos* judgment. That is, Community law as a legal order of its own contains rights and obligations not only of States *vis-à-vis* the Community and among each other, but also *vis-à-vis* individuals. The difference between Community and international law lies in the fact that the first aims to create individual rights as a regular part of its mandate, while the second does so only exceptionally.[60] The respect for these rights guaranteed by Community law, and the obligations imposed by it, are not so much a matter for Community courts but for the courts of *every Member State* (§ 12). The vital cooperation between Member State courts and the ECJ is secured by the reference procedure. This is the decisive interface between Community law and national law. It has a double objective. First, to ensure the uniformity of Community law, which is a consequence of its supremacy (§ 3). Second, to protect individual rights, while sanctioning individual obligations that result from its direct effect (§ 14 III 2).

---

[58] Cf. for modern accounts Prechal, *CMLRev* 2000, 1047; Tridimas at 164 (part of legal certainty); Reich, *Bürgerrechte in der EU*, 1999 at 101-108; Craig/de Búrca at 202-227; Douglas-Scott at 288-310.
[59] "The Doctrine of 'Direct Effect': An Infant Disease of Community Law", *ELRev* 1983, 155.
[60] The best example is the European Convention of Human Rights (ECHR) of 1950, extended by later Protocols.

If *Van Gend and Loos* was only concerned with the effects of primary Community law, later cases concerned secondary law, most notably directives. The leading case is *Van Duyn*[61] where the Court wrote in 1974:

> ...where the Community authorities have, by directive, imposed on Member States the obligation to pursue a particular course of conduct, the useful effect of such an act would be weakened if individuals were prevented from relying on it before their national court and if the latter were prevented from taking it into consideration as an element of Community law... (para 12)

In this context, three different principles, each in the form of a question, have clearly emerged in the *functional approach*, developed to allow for direct effect of Community legal acts:

1. In establishing rights and obligations, is the Community instrument sufficiently *clear and precise*? (Note: clarity may also be derived by way of interpretation.)[62]
2. Are these rights and obligations *self-executive*, that is, *unconditional*?
3. Are the rights invoked and obligations imposed *vertically* against the *state* (in a broad sense) or also horizontally against private individuals?

Direct effect therefore depends, not on the formal qualification of a legal act, but on the fulfilment of these three functional criteria, which must be met in every case. Of these, criterion 3 is particularly difficult and remains controversial.

2. Primary Community law

a. Direct effect of fundamental freedoms and individual rights

The direct effect of primary Community law depends on its place in the Community legal system as such. As a liberal system – as understood and analysed here – its aims are twofold: to protect individual freedoms and autonomy, and to contribute to the opening of markets. Therefore, the provisions on citizenship (Art. 17/18), on fundamental freedoms (Art. 28, 39, 43, 49, 56), on non-discrimination (Art. 12 and 141), and on competition (Art. 81/82, 88(3)), enjoy direct effect. Later, we will explore their importance.

Direct effect is not excluded by the mere fact that these rights and freedoms are granted in a limited way, even subject to restrictions,[63]. These include, for example, those on

---

[61]   Case 41/74 Van Duyn v Home Office [1974] ECR 1337.
[62]   As an example, take joined cases C-178/94 Dillenkofer *et al.* v Germany [1996] ECR I-4845.
[63]   This was reiterated by the decision of 17.9.2002 in case C-413/99 Baumbast & R/Secretary of State for the Home Department [2002] ECR I-7091 paras 84-85.

public policy, protection of certain social interests such as culture, environment, consumer interests, and social policy. A liberal concept of law can only work with recognition of adequate standards (Chapter III) as well as rules on accountability and responsibility (Chapter V). This remains so, even though this part of Community law is still considerably underdeveloped, so that Member States have to step in to ensure protection of important legal and possibly diverse social interests.

However, the fact that certain rights and freedoms need implementing measures – for example, recognition of diplomas and qualifications by secondary law – does not mean that the direct effect of primary law is excluded. Quite the contrary: we have to interpret and evaluate these instruments in the light of primary law. This implies a narrow interpretation of any restrictions on fundamental freedoms and individual rights.

On the other hand, certain provisions of primary Community law contain mere authority for Community action. An illustration would be certain aspects in the field of non-discrimination[64]. Only implementing measures (§ 11 IV) may be considered as having direct effect. This may change according to Art. II-81(2) of the Draft Constitution once ratified.[65]

b. Horizontal direct effect

The theory of direct effect was first developed against the *state*. The state should abstain[66] from any measure that might jeopardize attainment of Treaty objectives, in particular fundamental freedoms and individual rights. With one exception[67], no corresponding norm exists with regard to private individuals. In particular, German legal theory insists that where private parties can freely negotiate their contractual relationships, they may also restrict their freedoms and individual rights, within the limits of competition law. However, this view is formal, and, moreover, does not take into account that the private/public distinction does not hold true for Community law. On the other hand, Member States may use different legal approaches in solving a problem area. In practice, some leave this to self-determination and therefore to private law, while others prescribe certain behavior via public law. This is particularly true in the case of self-regulatory instruments with third party effect. Examples of these would include collective bargaining agreements, rules of associations, and general contract terms. The freedom of the weaker party – the worker, the member of an

---

[64]   Per Art. 13 EC.
[65]   Dorf, *Juristenzeitung (JZ)* 2005, 126 at 129.
[66]   Per Art. 10 EC.
[67]   Art. 81 (2) EG.

association or the consumer – to negotiate adequate terms is a mere fiction, and therefore cannot put aside the protection that Community law offers to private persons.

This principle was developed in the field of sex discrimination with regard to pay, which is forbidden[68]. In its famous *Defrenne II*[69] decision, the Court first implemented this principle of horizontal direct effect. Later cases concerned sports professionals, who had to be members of an association to be able to practice their profession. If the rules contained certain conditions on the exercise of their professional activity, then this amounted either to discrimination or to a restriction of the free movement principle. This applied, even if its origin lay, not in a rule of public law, but in the *autonomous* by-laws of a private law association. Thus, the restrictive effect on the freedom of the sport's professional was the same, whatever the origin of the restriction. Therefore the Court, in the *Bosman* case[70], allowed for horizontal direct effect. This was extended in *Angonese*[71] to all personal freedoms (§ 4 II). The *Wouters* case[72] summarized the existing case-law as follows:

> It should be observed, at the outset, that compliance with the rules of Art. 52 and 59 (now Art. 43 and 49 EC) is also required in case of rules which are not public in nature but which are designated to regulate, collectively, self-employment and provision of services. The abolition, as between Member States, of obstacles to freedom of movement of persons would be compromised if the abolition of State barriers could be neutralised by obstacles resulting from the exercise of their autonomy by associations or organisations not governed by public law.

3. Direct effect of directives

a. Vertical direct effect

The direct effect of directives – the draft Constitution will call them *framework laws* without changing their legal nature (*supra* I 3) – has been much more controversial in Community law. This can be explained by their difference from regulations, which are "binding in their entirety and directly applicable in the Member States."[73] In contrast, directives are addressed to Member States. Indeed, they are binding upon Member States "as to the result to be achieved, but shall leave to the national

---

[68] Art. 141 EC.
[69] Case 43/75 G. Defrenne/Sabena [1976] ECR 455.
[70] Case C-415/93 ASBL/Bosman [1995] ECR I-4921 at para 83-84.
[71] Vase C-281/98 R. Angonese v. Casa di Risparmio de Bolzano [2000] ECR I-4139 para 32.
[72] Case C-309/99 J.C.J. Wouters et al/Algemene Raad van de Nederlandse Orde van Advocaten [2002] ECR I-1577 at para 120.
[73] Per Art. 249 (2) EC.

authorities the choice of form and methods."[74] The wording appears to permit of no possibility to attach a direct effect to directives.

However, in its *Van Duyn* decision[75] the ECJ gave a different answer, arguing against *the effet utile* of Community law directives (*infra* III 5). Legal writing has pointed to the *estoppel* principle. That is, a Member State that has failed to correctly implement a directive, and thus violating its obligations[76], cannot impose upon individuals burdens that are contrary to its obligations under Community law.[77] Other authors[78] have taken issue with the function of Community law in guaranteeing certain rights to individuals. This may be done not only through primary law, but also through secondary law, insofar as the two relevant criteria are met. These criteria are that:
- they should be sufficiently precise and unconditional with regard to their legal content, and
- need no further implementing measures by the Community.

This approach has in mind the Member State which, in failing to implement directives as required under Community law, should not be allowed to frustrate rights of the individual as guaranteed under Community law. However, direct effect works here only "vertically". The Court has been called on to interpret the extent of this vertical direct effect. In doing so, it takes as a point of departure a wide notion of *state*. This is satisfied if self-governing institutions, such as communities, fail to fulfil Community law obligations, or if a private enterprise is regulated as a public utility.[79] A later case[80] allows direct effect against a private company which is under state control and performs a public service (financing and maintenance of motorways, including toll levying and collection). This theory does not help if private institutions, especially undertakings, have failed to respect individual rights, such as the right to non-discrimination (§ 11 II), because of missing or defective Member State implementation. Can they be caught by the direct effect of the directive itself?

b. Absence of positive horizontal effect

In its *Marshall I* case[81] the Court hinted that it was not willing to recognize the horizontal direct effect of directives. This doctrine was attacked by several

---

[74] Per Art. 249 (3) EC.
[75] *Supra* note 61.
[76] Per Art. 10 EC.
[77] Prechal, *CMLRev* 1999, 1047.
[78] Reich, *supra* note 58 at 101.
[79] Case C-188/89 Foster/British Gas [1990] I-3313.
[80] C-157/02 Riester International Transporte GmbH v Autobahnen- und Schnellstrassen-Finanzierungs-AG (Asfinag) [2004] ECR I-(5.2.2004).
[81] 152/84 Marshall/Southampton and Southwest Hampshire Health Authority [1986] ECR 723.

Advocates General[82] and in legal writing[83] for a number of reasons. These included:

- protection of individual rights,
- equality of citizens,
- mandatory character of directives with regard to *the result to be achieved*, which leaves Member States a tiny margin of appreciation in implementing directives, and
- the mandatory force of Community law *vis-à-vis* courts of law.[84]

However, the Court remained unconvinced by these arguments, denying horizontal direct effect in its well known *Dori* decision of 14.7.1994[85] with the following words:

> it would be unacceptable if a State, when required by the Community legislature to adopt certain rules intended to govern the State's relations – or those of State entities – with individuals and to confer certain rights on individuals, were able to rely on its own failure to discharge its obligations so as to deprive individuals of the benefits of these rights.... The effect of extending that case-law to the sphere of relations between individuals would be to recognise a power in the Community to enact obligations for individuals with immediate effect, whereas it has competence to do so only where it is empowered to adopt regulations" (paras 23-24).

This case law has been repeated and confirmed in several later decisions.[86] The main factor for the ECJ in denying horizontal direct effect concerns *enacting obligations for individuals.*[87] However, this term is open to interpretation, and especially so where existing obligations under Community law are only specified by directives. Or again, where Member State law has implemented a directive, even though incompletely, by reducing the rights the individual would have had under a directive. It is here that the discussion continues, *over declaratory or incidental horizontal effect of directives* (below), or on *directive-conforming interpretation* (§ 3 IV 2), in order to allow a (somewhat restricted) horizontal direct effect of directives.

---

[82]   AG Van Gerven in Marshall II Case C-271/91 [1993] ECR I-4367, AG Jacobs in case C-316/93 Veneetveld v SA Le Foyer [1994] ECR I-673 and AG Lenz in case C-91/92 Paola Faccini Dori v Recreb [1994] ECR-3325 at para 5.

[83]   Reich at 107; Douglas-Scott at 307-309.

[84]   Per Art. 10 EC.

[85]   *Supra* note 82.

[86]   Case C-97/96 Verband Deutscher Daihatsu Händler eV v Daihatsu Deutschland GmbH [1997] ECR I-6843.

[87]   For a detailed discussion cf. Rörig, *Die Direktwirkung von Richtlinien in Privatrechtsverhältnissen*, 2001.

c. Possibility of declaratory, negative *or* incidental horizontal effect?

A *declaratory horizontal direct effect* would exist where a directive concretises an obligation already inherent in Community law. An illustration might be concerning consumer information as an element of party autonomy[88] (§ 17 IV). Could it be said that a directive imposing information obligations on the supplier *vis-à-vis* the consumer merely affirms an existing right of the consumer, and a corresponding obligation on the supplier? Although the Court was hostile to this argumentation in its *El Corte Inglés* decision[89], the question seems far from finally settled.[90]

A *negative horizontal effect* would exist where a Member State has already implemented a directive imposing obligations on individuals, but (a) only incompletely and (b) denying the individual certain rights that the directive conferred upon them. This problem has arisen in particular with regard to the non-discrimination directive (§ 11 III). In several cases[91] the Court has declared that Community law is opposed to any reduction in the rights of the individual against the clear intention of the directive. Examples would include limiting the amount of damages to be recovered, or imposing time limits that the directive had not foreseen. Does this mean that, in setting aside the restriction, the national court is empowered to extend an employer's existing obligation? Can this be invoked in cases where the clear wording of the national implementing legislation violates the directive, requiring a *contra legem* application of national law? The Court has not given a final answer, but usually refers to the principle of directive-conforming interpretation (§ 3 IV), which seems to exclude a *contra legem* application.

Other authors have discussed an *incidental* horizontal effect.[92] Such a situation arises in private litigation, where one of the parties is banned from invoking a national law contrary to a directive which has not been implemented by the Member State.[93] The Court distinguished its case law from the *Dori* ruling and allowed the directive to modify existing contractual rights and obligations of the parties. This could be seen in the *Unilever* case[94], where an Italian importer of olive oil denied payment to the seller because the oil had not been packaged and labelled according to a new Italian

---

[88] Art. 153 EC.
[89] Case C-192/94 El Corte Inglés v Cristina Blasquez Rivero [1996] ECR I-1281.
[90] Reich/Micklitz, *Europäisches Verbraucherrecht*, 4. A. 2003 at para 1.35.
[91] Case 271/91 Marshall (II) v. Southampton and South West Hampshire Area Health Authority [1993] ECR I-4367; case C-180/95 Draehmpaehl v. Urania Immobilienservice [1997] ECR I-2195.
[92] Craig/de Búrca at 220-227; Douglas-Scott at 308.
[93] Case C-194/94 CIA Security International SA v Signalson SA and Securitel SPRL [1996] ECR I-2201.
[94] Case C-443/98 Unilever Italia SpA v Central Food SpA [2000] ECR I-7535.

regulation. Since this regulation had not been notified to the Commission, it could not be invoked in proceedings before the Italian court.

To some extent it is misleading to discuss when a directive *enacts obligations* and when it only *specifies* or *modifies* existing ones. At least it does do so in those cases where the legislator intended to transpose the directive into national law and thereby *enact obligations vis-à-vis* individuals. Put differently, it does so in fulfilling its Community law obligations[95]. Moreover, it is considered to have complied in full and not only partially. This theory recognizes the interpretive authority of the ECJ in defining the extent of obligations under Community law, and can be said to have faithfully transposed them into national law. The weight of these obligations, and the rights accruing from them, should be the same throughout the entire Union. Therefore, it seems reasonable that at least the *declaratory* and *negative horizontal effect of directives* should be accepted. In these cases the national judge has to interpret the directive as it is, using the instruments at hand to remedy potential defects of the national law transposing it.[96]

4. Direct effect of international agreements

Direct effect of agreements under international public law is usually discussed by referring to monist or dualist theories of national law. On the one hand, monist theories allow agreements to be directly effective once they are ratified, so long as they are "self-executive". However, dualist theories require additional national implementation regarding direct effect towards individuals. Community law, as a specific order of its own, could not adopt either of these theories. It had to develop criteria of its own. And these criteria are identical to those existing for other acts of Community law.

Thus the deciding issue is whether the agreement, once properly adopted by a Council decision[97], is precise and unconditional enough to allow for rights of individuals. The Court has denied this with regard to GATT/WTO, because in case of violations it is not "self-executive". That is, it installs a mainly international law conflict resolution mechanism allowing for a wide variety of remedies. The Court also pointed to the need for uniform application, which is not possible because some states, such as the US, have expressly excluded direct applicability. However, reciprocity remains an element of international trade law, and should not be avoided by the Community declaring unilaterally direct effect. Even if the new WTO agreement aimed to confer rights upon individuals, it does not do so unconditionally. There will be exceptions in those cases

---

[95]   Art. 10 EC.
[96]   Reich, *Bürgerrechte in der EU*, 1999 at 106.
[97]   Under Art. 300 EC.

where the Community instruments implement WTO measures or where they expressly refer to them.[98]

The TRIPS agreement on trade-related aspects of intellectual property rights may have an indirect effect on interpreting national law, in particular remedies to meet the principle of effective and speedy protection.[99, 100]

Other principles were developed with regard to association agreements. Although the 1963 agreement with Turkey did not as such have direct effect, the implementing decisions of the Association Council could be considered as having direct effect because they were sufficiently precise and unconditional in privileging Turkish migrants.[101]

The Europe Agreements with accession countries were said to have direct effect, at least with regard to establishment[102] and non-discrimination provisions.[103] They aim to give EA citizens directly enforceable rights when wishing to become established in the EU (§ 6 II) and when legally working in one of the Member States. These rights may also take horizontal direct effect under the same principles as in the *Bosman* case.[104] The Court, in a judgment in the *Simutenkov* case[105] has extended horizontal direct effect also to Art. 23 (1) of the EC-Russia Partnership Agreement on non-discrimination of Russian workers (football players) legally employed in the EU because of similar formulations as in the EU, even though Russia does not intend to become a member of the EU.

III.   METHODS OF INTERPRETATION

1.   Basis of interpretation in Community law

Classical interpretation theory of law usually distinguishes between four methods of interpretation of legal texts[106], namely:

---

[98]   Case C-149/96 Portugal v. Council [1999] ECR I-8395; C-377/02 Léon van Parys v BIRB [2005] ECR I-(1.3.2005). For a broader view see opinion of AG Alber of 15.5.2003 in case C-93/02P Etablissement Biret/Council [2003] ECR I-10497.

[99]   Art. 50 TRIPS.

[100]   Case C-89/99 Schieving/Nijstad-Groenveld [2001] ECR I-5851 at para 54.

[101]   Case C-192/89 Sevince/Staatssecretaris van Justitie [1990] ECR I-3461 distinguishing case 12/86 Demirel/Stadt Schwäbisch Gmünd [1987] ECR 3969.

[102]   Case C-63/99 The Queen and Secretary of State for the Home Dpt. *ex parte* Wieslaw and Elzbieta Gloszczuk [2001] ECR I- 6369 at para 33.

[103]   Case C-162/00 Land Nordrhein-Westphalen/Beata Pokrzeptowicz-Meyer [2002] ECR I-1049.

[104]   Case C-438/00 Deutscher Handballbund/Maros Kolpak [2003] ECR I-4135 at para 32.

[105]   Case C-265/03 Igor Simutenkov v Ministerio de Educación y Cultura et al. [2005] ECR I-(12.4.2005).

[106]   Douglas-Scott at 207-210; Bengoetxea, *The Legal Reasoning of the ECJ*, 1993 at 232-260.

- grammatical or literal interpretation;
- historical or/and comparative interpretation (reference to *travaux préparatoires*);
- systematic or contextual interpretation;
- teleological or dynamic interpretation.

The method of *analogy* extends the sphere in which a legal norm or principle applies to similar cases or problems. By contrast, *teleological restriction* narrows the sphere of applicable law where a norm is regarded as too wide.

Community law starts from similar principles. This is because both European Courts (the ECJ and CFI) and national courts have to interpret it when directly applying Community law. However, the ECJ has the final word in delivering Community-wide binding interpretations[107].

On the other hand, Community law is a specific legal order and has therefore developed its own criteria for interpretation. The Court already said as much in the landmark case of *Van Gend and Loos*[108], when referring to *the spirit, the general scheme and the wording of those provisions*[109]. To some extent, these Community methods specify traditional methods of interpretation and application, but in certain cases also contradict them. This will be briefly demonstrated in the following.

2. Literal interpretation – All language versions being equal

Law consists of texts. And interpreting texts involves finding out what they mean. The literal interpretation is therefore the starting point of any interpretation. Community law is no exception.

The problem specific to Community law consists in the fact that texts that need interpreting – primary law, secondary law, international agreements with Community involvement – are written not in one or two, but in *all* official languages. With new Member States there are now 20 official languages!

In its *CILFIT* decision[110] the Court declared that:

> ... Community legislation is drafted in several languages and that the different language versions are all equally authentic. An interpretation of a provision of Community law thus involves a comparison of the different language versions (para 18).

---

[107] Per Art. 234 EC.
[108] *Supra* note 1 at 12.
[109] I.e., of the then EEC Treaty, (NR) .
[110] Case 283/81 Srl CILFIT and Lanificio di Gavardo SpA v Ministry of Health [1982] ECR 3415.

The Court has repeated this pronouncement in later cases whereby:

> all the language versions must, in principle be recognised as having the same weight and this cannot vary according to the size of the population of the Member States using the language in question. According to settled case-law, the various language versions of a provision of Community law must be uniformly interpreted, and thus, in the case of divergence between those versions, the provision in question must be interpreted by reference to the purpose and general scheme of the rules of which it forms part.[111]

This means that a literal interpretation is only the beginning of a legal argument. If it leads to a clear result in all language versions – the famous *acte clair* – then usually no further interpretation is necessary by the ECJ. The national court may use all the classical interpretation methods to arrive at the meaning of a legal term. In case of divergence of language versions, additional criteria are necessary to establish the content of a Community law rule and its sphere of application. This is usually the task of the ECJ.

3. Autonomous, only exceptionally historical or comparative interpretation

Interpretation of rules of national law will usually refer to their origin, either historical or in comparative law. This may be rooted in publicly accessible documents, for example, those issued by national or regional governments, or by parliament, or both. Even if the legal traditions of Member States differ with regard to the importance of *travaux préparatoires*, it is established practice that parties may refer to them in pleadings and that the competent court may use them as an argument among others.[112]

Community law has been somewhat hostile to the principle of historical interpretation. This is based on several reasons:
- Community legal acts undergo lengthy and complex processes of preparation and adoption. Since this implies changes in meanings, it is hardly possible to single out one text which contains binding elements of interpretation.
- Community legal acts are a mixture of different legal traditions. This implies that the meaning of texts may differ according to the national law referred to.
- Declarations of the Council and/or the Commission in the process of adoption of a directive cannot be used in interpreting it against its wording or purpose.[113]

---

[111] Case C-257/00 Nancy Givane and Others v. Secretary of State for the Home Department [2003] ECR I-345.

[112] Douglas-Scott at 208.

[113] Case C-292/89 R v Immigration Appeal Tribunal *ex parte* Antonissen [1991] ECR I-745 para 16.

They may however be cited to support an interpretation within the context of a Community legal act.

- On the other hand, the Court will refer to the (published) recitals (preamble) of a directive or regulation for interpretation purposes.[114]

For these reasons, the ECJ has insisted on the principle of *autonomous interpretation* of Community law. In *CILFIT* it wrote:

> It must also be borne in mind even where the different language versions are entirely in accord with each other, that Community law uses terminology which is particular to it. Furthermore, it must be emphasized that legal concepts do not necessarily have the same meaning in Community law and in the law of the various Member States (para 19).

For instance, in *Levin* it held:[115]

> .... The terms "worker" and "activity as an employed person" may not be defined by reference to the national laws of the Member States but have a Community meaning. If that were not the case, the Community rules on freedom for workers would be frustrated, as the meaning of those terms could be fixed unilaterally, without any control by the Community institutions, by national laws which would thus be able to exclude at will certain categories of persons from the benefit of the Treaty (para 11).

Similar principles apply for interpretation of the other Community freedoms. This method of autonomous interpretation results from the principle of uniformity in applying Community law. That, in turn, implies that rules should have the same meaning, and should create the same set of rights and obligations throughout the entire Union. A reference to their historical or comparative law origin may undermine the unity of Community law and thereby create distortions of competition. But it has been used in exceptional circumstances, for instance in public procurement (§ 8 IV).[116] A single market needs rules that are interpreted uniformly. At the same time, all persons coming within the sphere of application of Community law should be treated equally – a consequence of the idea of Union citizenship (§ 5 II).

The method of autonomous interpretation is used for regulations and directives alike. However, this will be difficult where Community law contains no reference to interpreting certain terms. An illustration is the term *equitable remuneration* to be paid

---

[114]   Case C-481/99 Heininger v Bayr, Hypo und Vereinsbank [2001] ECR I-9945 para 39.
[115]   Case 53/81 Levin v. Staatssecretaris van Justitie [1982] ECR 1035.
[116]   Case 324/98 Telaustria Verlags GmbH v Telekom Austria AG [2000] ECR I-10745.

to performing artists and phonogram producers for broadcasting phonograms by radio and television[117, 118] In these cases, the Court restricted its role to:

> call upon the Member States to ensure the greatest possible adherence throughout the territory of the Community to the concept of equitable remuneration, a concept which must ... be viewed as enabling a proper balance to be achieved between the interests of performing artist and producers in obtaining remuneration for the broadcast of a particular phonogram, and the interests of third parties in being able to broadcast the phonogram on terms that are reasonable (para 36).

In other cases where the directive contains broad concepts such as *good faith*, or *reasonableness* the Court may refer to the recitals or to indicative lists of terms.[119]

The Court also applied the autonomous interpretation method for instruments much closer to international law than the acts listed[120]. However, this was where it has interpretative authority, namely the 1968 Brussels Convention on recognition and enforcement of judgments in civil and commercial matters (§ 14 II 1). The Court has consistently held that *classical* civil law concepts such as *contract, delict*[121] or *consumer*[122] should be interpreted autonomously. It had only allowed an exception for the concept of *place of performance* of contracts[123]. This, however, was partially abolished[124] (§ 14 II 2) because reference to the law of the Member State as determined by its conflict rules was proven to be impractical and complicated.

Exceptions may exist where Community law refers to applicable Member State law itself. This is true with regard to the concept of citizenship (§ 5), which is determined by Member States, not by Community law. In other cases, Community law may leave it expressly to Member States to determine a certain legal concept, such as compensation for non-material damage with regard to product liability (§ 20 III 2)[125].

---

[117]   Per Dir. 92/100.
[118]   Case C-245/00 Stichting ter Exploitatie van Naburige Rechten (Sena) and Nederlandse Omroep Stichting (NOS) [2003] ECR I-1251.
[119]   Case C-240-244/98 Océano Grupo Editorial v. Rocio Murciano Qintero [2000] ECR I-4941 at para 22.
[120]   I.e., in Art. 249 EC.
[121]   Case C-167/00 Verein für Konsumenteninformation/Karl Heinz Henkel [2002] ECR I-8111 at para 35.
[122]   Case C-96/00 Rudolf Gabriel [2002] ECR I-6367 at para 37.
[123]   Case 12/76 Tessili/Dunlop [1976] ECR 1473.
[124]   By the new Brussels Regulation 44/2001.
[125]   Per Art. 9 of the Product Liability Directive 85/374/EEC.

The method of autonomous interpretation as employed by the Court takes a sceptical view of using the comparative law argument.[126] Usually, comparative law studies result in a discrepancy of arguments, none of which can be regarded as binding for Community law. The Court refers to comparative law rather superficially and selectively, usually to support a certain preferred argument. Its Advocates-General may go deeper into comparative law where necessary.[127] In some exceptional instances, Community law expressly encourages comparative law arguments. A useful illustration would be with regard to Community non-contractual liability[128] (*infra* § 18 III), and in referring *to fundamental rights resulting from the constitutional traditions of the Member States* and the European Human Rights Convention (EHRC)[129] (§ 12 II 2).

4. Systematic-contextual interpretation

If Member State law has developed systematically by codification, consolidation or similar comprehensive approaches to law-making, then it is necessary to interpret rules within their systematic context. Interpretation should avoid contradictions Thus, a rule placed in a certain systematic context, such as a Civil code, needs interpreting uniformly within this context, unless otherwise required.

The requirement of systematic interpretation makes little sense in legal systems that do not rely on codification. This applies especially in common law and to some extent also in Scandinavian countries. Judge-made law, developed through the *stare decisis* doctrine, cannot aim to be systematic, since there is no theoretical reference point to which interpretation could turn. Legislation will usually define for itself the terminology used – which may be completely different in a neighbouring field.

However, Community law more closely resembles the common law than the civil law tradition. Community law is not systematized, but consists of numerous rules and principles that may even contradict one other. Legislative acts usually contain their own set of definitions, which then provide for interpretation. The systematic argument may be used in this limited context. In its *CILFIT* case the Court declared that:

> .... every provision of Community law must be placed in its context and interpreted in the light of the provisions of Community law as a whole, regard being had to the objectives

---

[126] For a discussion cf. Kiikeri, *Comparative Legal Reasoning and European Law*, 2001 at 148 with references.

[127] A good example is the careful comparative law study of AG Jacobs on the relationship between collective bargaining and competition law in case C-67/96 Albany International BV v Stichting Bedrijfspensioenenfonds Textielindustrie [1999] ECR I-5751; the Court did not refer to it, cf. Kiikeri at 222-240.

[128] Per Art. 288 (2) EC.

[129] Per Art. 6 (2) EU.

thereof and to its state of evolution at the date on which the provision in question is applied. (para 20).

This means that secondary law needs interpreting in the light of primary law. Thus, if a directive aims to open markets, then it must respect the free movement principles. Equally, if it aims to protect intellectual property, then it must keep to the case law of the Court.[130, 131]

The Court therefore developed an additional test: the interplay of *rules and exceptions*. The free movement rules may serve as a good example. That is, primary Community law contains a broad guarantee of fundamental freedoms, which directly apply in favor of individuals. Community law therefore has to defend the overall principle of free movement; any restriction is regarded with suspicion and should not be widened.

On the other hand, the fundamental freedoms are not granted without limits. Indeed, these limits are either spelled out in the Treaty itself (the public order proviso), or have been developed by case law (the general interest test, § 3 I 4a). Therefore, these limitations should be interpreted narrowly, nor should they be widened beyond their context. In *Boucherau*[132] the Court held that:

> the concept of public policy where it is used as a justification for derogating from the fundamental principle of freedom of movement for workers must be interpreted strictly, so that its scope cannot be determined unilaterally by each Member State without being subject to control by the institutions of the Community (para 33).

The Court used a similar, and somewhat formal, method of interpretation in its controversial *Kalanke* judgment[133]. This concerned exceptions to the principle of non-discrimination as to gender in access to work and job promotion (§ 11 III 4a). The provision of the relevant directive to some extent allowed affirmative action in favour of women. However, this was regarded as a derogation from the right to equal treatment, and thus subject to strict interpretation. In *Marschall*[134] the Court somewhat softened its approach by looking at the function of the rule (a so-called *savings clause*). This allowed an individual assessment of qualifications regardless of sex, at the same time attempting to give female candidates a certain priority in selection and promotion for work. This case-law clearly demonstrates that the method of systematic interpretation has only limited binding force. In other cases, the Court used it only

---

[130] Per Art. 30 EC.
[131] Case C-427/93 Bristol Meyers-Squibb v. Paranova [1996] ECR I-3457 at para 27.
[132] Case 30/77 R v Boucherau [1977] ECR 1999.
[133] Case C-450/93 Kalanke v Freie Hansestadt Bremen [1995] ECR I-3051 at paras 21/22.
[134] Case C-409/95 Hellmut Marschall v Land Nordrhein Westfalen [1997] ECR I-6363 at para 33.

together with other methods of interpretation. For example, in *Berliner Kindl*[135] it did
so to determine whether the consumer credit directive[136] also protected guarantors.

5. Teleological interpretation – The effet utile

The method of interpretation attracting greatest attention among writers has been the
teleological or dynamic interpretation, also called the *effet utile* doctrine.[137] This links
the interpretation of a specific rule with a broader Community law principle, for
example, free movement or effective judicial protection (see below at para 6). It has
been used in very different contexts:
- It makes an incomplete rule effective, for example by providing for remedies where
  a Member State breaches its obligations under Community law (§ 19 II).[138]
- It curbs attempts to limit protection of workers against retaliatory measures by
  a mere literal interpretation of the relevant directive (§ 11 II).[139]
- It looks at the function of compensation in the context of the competition rules.[140]
- It also applies to interpretation of Association Agreements, for example the right
  of entry and residence as *corollaries of the right of establishment* of a person it
  protects.[141]

However, it is not always easy to distinguish the borderline between *interpreting* an
existing rule and *applying* a broad principle. As we have seen, the principle of vertical
direct effect of directives was developed from the *effet utile* doctrine. This was so, even
though an interpretation of the Treaty[142] should have led to a contrary result by an
argumentum e contrario. This is because direct applicability is foreseen for regulations,
not for directives. Thus, inserting the vertical direct effect of directives into Community law posed some difficulty. It could only be achieved by imposing upon
Member States the broad obligation to make Community law effective, and not to
excuse non-performance by breach of Community law obligations. This derived from
their guarantee function[143] and involved the *estoppel –* or *venire contra factum proprium*
– principle mentioned in *Van Duyn* (*supra* II 3a).

---

[135]   Case C-208/98 Berliner Kindl Brauerei AG v Andreas Siepert [2000] ECR I-1741 at para 24;
        particularly interesting in this respect is the opinion of AG Léger.
[136]   87/102.
[137]   For a discussion Tridimas at 276-277.
[138]   Joined cases C-6 + 9/90 Francovich and Others v. Italian Republic [1991] ECR I-5357 at para 33.
[139]   Case C-185/97 Belinda Jane Coote v. Granada Hospitality Ltd. [1998] ECR I-5199 at para 27.
[140]   Case C-453/99 Courage Ltd v Crehan [2001] ECR I-6297 at paras 26-27.
[141]   Case C-257/99 The Queen v Secretary of State for the Home Department *ex parte* Julius Barcosi and
        Marcel Malik [2001] ECR I- 6557 at para 50; comment Reich/Harbacevica, *Europarättslig Tidskrift*
        2002, 411 at 423.
[142]   Art. 249 EC.
[143]   Per Art. 10 EC.

6. Principle orientation, not rule orientation

In reality, the Court goes far beyond traditional methods of interpretation when applying Community law to unresolved factual situations. It has developed certain written and unwritten rules into broad principles, which allow reference in case of doubt. These principles are the core of the following chapters. In linking the interpretation of a text with such broad principles as *fundamental freedoms, effective judicial control, protection of fundamental rights*, and *non-discrimination in the field of application of EC law*, the Court is able to develop *intermediate interpretation guidelines*. These help in closing gaps left by existing legal rules. Thus, to some extent the borderlines between *interpreting* law and *making* policy are becoming blurred.[144]

This can be demonstrated by referring to the controversial *Carpenter* case:[145] British immigration authorities wanted to expel Mrs. Carpenter, as was possible under the English law on aliens that applied at that time. Mrs. Carpenter was a Philippines national, married to a British national, Mr. Carpenter, and took care of her stepchildren. Mrs. Carpenter was not protected by EC law because she was not a Union citizen. Originally, she was also not protected as Mr. Carpenter's wife. This was because Mr. Carpenter himself did not come into the protective ambit of Community law. In turn, that was because he was a British national living and working in the UK and not a national from another EU country (§ 4). In order to overcome these protective gaps left by Community law, the Court used a three-step interpretation to allow Mrs. Carpenter protection against deportation:

- Mr. Carpenter still came into the sphere of application of EU law at the time of the court decision. The reasoning here was that, even though a British national, he was offering his advertising services as a self-employed person not only in the UK, but also in other Member countries, and therefore the Treaty[146] applied in his favor.
- As an EU citizen, he is entitled to protection of his family life[147], which the Community must respect[148].
- Expelling Mrs. Carpenter would interfere in his freedom to provide services, because it would disrupt his family life. He would either have to leave the UK and follow her to the Philippines, giving up his profession, or stay home separated from his family. The Court found this consequence disproportionate and unjustified. Thus, Mrs. Carpenter was allowed to stay with her husband. She was therefore an *indirect beneficiary* of the freedom, enjoyed by her husband, to provide services.

---

[144] Douglas-Scott at 210-217 with a discussion of the controversies in literature.
[145] Case 60/00 Mary Carpenter v Secretary of State for the Home Department [2002] ECR I-6279.
[146] Art. 49 EC.
[147] Per Art. 8 ECHR.
[148] Per Art. 6 (2) EU.

Methodologically, the decision seems to be flawed because it stretches the concept of *restriction of the freedom to provide services* beyond economic activity, to cover any interference with family life.[149] From a legal policy point of view, the decision should perhaps be welcomed, even though the accent might have been put on the personal element of protecting the family relationship between Mr. and Mrs. Carpenter, rather on Mr. Carpenter's cross-border economic activity. For the wife is treated as a mere chattel, connected with the economic activity of her husband, rather than as an autonomous person deriving Community law rights from her family status, as suggested in the opinion of AG Stix-Hackl.

7. Teleological restrictions

This method of restricting the sphere in which a Community rule applies is also well known to the case law of the European Court. Again, it is not always clear whether a methodological or a legal policy argument was decisive. Three examples will illustrate:

– In its well-known and highly controversial *Keck* judgment[150] (§ 7 II 3) the Court restricted the Treaty's[151] sphere of application on measures whose effect equated quantitative restrictions on the free movement of goods – *contrary to what has previously been decided* – to product-related regulations of Member States and not to

> certain selling arrangements .... provided that those provisions apply to all affected traders operating within the national territory and provided that they affect in the same manner, in law and in fact, the marketing of domestic products and of those from other Member States (para 16).

– Community competence to legislate under the internal market provision,[152] aimed at approximating measures for the establishment or functioning of the internal market, was used almost without limits in law-making.[153] It fell to the *tobacco advertising* judgment of 5.10.2000[154] to severely narrow down this competence, by restrictively interpreting these criteria, which do not give the Community a general power *to regulate the internal market*. However, newer case law is content

---

[149] Cf. differing comments by Reich/Harbacevica, *CMLRev* 2003, 615 at 635; Editorial, *CMLRev* 2003, 537; Spaventa, *CMLRev* 2004, 743.
[150] Case C-267 + 268/91 Bernhard Keck and Daniel Mithouard [1993] ECR I-6097.
[151] Art. 28 EC.
[152] Art. 95 EC.
[153] Barents, *CMLRev* 1993, 85 at 106.
[154] Case C-376/98 Germany v. EP and Council [2000] ECR I-8419 at para 83.

to justify restrictive legislation on the basis that Member States are likely to introduce divergent rules on tobacco consumption and advertising.[155]
- Discrimination with regard to sexual orientation[156] was regarded as falling outside the relevant Community law on prohibiting workplace discrimination on the ground of sex. This situation was partially remedied by legislation[157] (§ 11 IV 3).

IV. A COMMUNITY STARE DECISIS DOCTRINE?

The above discussion shows that Community Courts employ a wide variety of instruments in making Community law effective. However, from a strictly legal point of view a decision is only binding upon the parties to the proceedings *(res iudicata)*. Judgments cannot be formally binding upon third parties, because they have not participated in the hearings – a fundamental principle of a government of laws, which the Community embraces.

On the other hand, a decision of the ECJ, and to a lesser extent the CFI, certainly has *persuasive authority*. This is particularly true in preliminary proceedings[158] (§ 14 III). Here, the ECJ (not the CFI) is approached by a Member State court – not by the parties – to give a binding interpretation of Community law, or to decide on the validity of a Community act. In both cases, the result of the decision goes far beyond the specific litigation:
- In interpreting a Community law provision, the Court uses an abstract formula that can be applied to similar later cases involving the same question of interpretation.
- In doing so, the Court usually refers to its own case-law. It may distinguish the case before it from earlier decisions, or simply follow its *settled case-law*. Only under narrowly-defined circumstances will it *overrule* its former case law – as indeed it did in *Keck*.
- If a national court wishes to challenge an interpretation given by the ECJ on Community law, it should refer the question once again to the ECJ before adopting its own contrary interpretation. If not, then the uniformity of Community law would be impaired, contrary to the Treaty[159].
- If the ECJ voids a Community legal measure, then that measure cannot be applied anywhere in the Union, whether by national or by European courts.

---

[155]   Case C-491/01 R.v. Secretary of State for Health *ex parte* British American Tobacco (Investment) Ltd. *et al.*, [2002] ECR I-11453 at para 67.
[156]   Case C-249/96 Grant v South West Trains Ltd. [1998] ECR I-621 at paras 47-48.
[157]   Specifically, adoption of Directive 2000/78.
[158]   Per Art. 234 EC.
[159]   Art. 10 EC.

- If a national court has doubts regarding the validity of a Community act, then it cannot declare this act void, but is obliged to refer the question to the ECJ; under certain circumstances it may suspend the application of this act (§ 14 III 2), but has to respect existing ECJ case law.[160]
- The ECJ enjoys discretion to limit the time consequences of a decision with *ex nunc* effect. The best known examples are *Defrenne II*[161] and *Barber*[162]. However, this corrective mechanism should be used only rarely. Indeed, it was rejected in *Heininger*[163], concerning annulment of a doorstep consumer real estate credit contract, voiding thousands of contracts and involving banks in serious losses.

These examples show that the case-law of the ECJ goes far beyond the concrete case at hand, at least in reference proceedings, which form the bulk of its jurisprudence. Bengoetxea[164] appears to summarize the position neatly and accurately in writing:

> It could be argued that considering such *"jurisprudence constante"* as a should-source is in line with the principle of legal certainty and protection of legitimate expectations: citizens can plan their actions according to the practical information drawn from the knowledge that there is a series of Court decisions in the same sense on a given point of law, and that therefore it is very likely that future relevantly similar cases will be treated in a like manner. Besides, consistency in judicial decisions increases the legitimacy of the Court. But it is not an ought-source …. It is always possible to make a reference to the ECJ for a preliminary ruling on a question of Community law that has been previously raised….

---

[160] Case C-466/93 Atlanta Fruchthandelsgesellschaft v Bundesamt für Ernährung und Forstwirtschaft [1995] ECR I-3799.

[161] Case C-43/75 Defrenne/Sabena [1974] ECR 455.

[162] Case C-262/88 Barber/GRE [1990] ECR I-1889; cf. also the Barber Protocol attached to the Maastricht Treaty.

[163] Case C-481/99 Heininger v. Bayr. Hypo und Vereinsbank [2001] ECR I-9945.

[164] *Supra* note 105 at 69.

§ 3. COMMUNITY AND MEMBER STATE LAW

I. THE SUPREMACY DEBATE – DISCONTINUED

1. *The original approach of the ECJ*

The relationship between Community and Member State law has in the past been characterized by two principles developed by the ECJ in its early case-law, to some extent challenged by certain Member State courts. These principles are:
- supremacy of Community law over Member State law;
- uniformity of application of Community law in all Member States, to be achieved by the ECJ's interpretative authority.

In the words of the ECJ in its 1964 *Costa v ENEL* decision[165], supremacy of Community law derives from its *specific character*. That is, neither from Member State (constitutional) law, nor from international law:

> By creating a Community of unlimited duration, having its own institutions, its own personality, its own legal capacity and capacity of representation on the international plane and, more particularly, real powers stemming from a limitation of sovereignty or a transfer of powers from the States to the Community, the Member States have limited their sovereign rights, albeit within limited fields, and have thus created a body of law which binds both their nationals and themselves.

This argument was repeated and extended to Member State law adopted *after* relevant Community legislation;[166] the *lex posterior* principle does not apply in relations between Community and Member State Law. It was applied against Member State constitutional law[167] and fundamental rights.[168] The supremacy doctrine does not depend on the hierarchy of a norm in Member State legal order. Otherwise it would be possible for any Member State to avoid the effects of Community law on states' and citizens' rights and duties, by placing their own law on a *higher* level of validity. This would infringe uniformity in applying the law throughout the Community, and be at odds with the non-discrimination principle[169] (§ 11 II).

---

[165]   Case 6/64 [1964] ECR 585.
[166]   Case 106/77 Amministrazione delle Finanze v Simmenthal [1978] 629.
[167]   Case C-213/89 R v. Secretary of State for Transport *ex parte* Factortame Ltd. and others [1990] ECR I-2433.
[168]   Case 11/70 Internationale Handelsgesellschaft GmbH v. Einfuhr- und Vorratsstelle für Getreide und Futtermittel [1970] ECR 1125.
[169]   Art. 12 EC.

2. The original criticism – overcome

The doctrine of supremacy did not go uncontested. Indeed, the constitutional courts of several Member States, in particular Germany and Italy, uttered reservations to this new doctrine, which seemed to be in conflict with national constitutional and with international law.[170] The debate was to some extent highlighted by the well known *Maastricht* judgment of the German Constitutional Court of 12 October 1993.[171] This on the one hand allowed ratification of the Maastricht Treaty by the German government, but on the other imposed two important and problematic qualifications on a far-reaching transfer of sovereignty to the EU/EC. These were:

– Fundamental rights protection must be guaranteed by European jurisdictions. If the indispensable standard of rights protection were not generally guaranteed by the Community, then the *Bundesverfassungsgericht* seemed willing to step in and apply a sort of *reserve control.*
– Community acts must remain strictly within Union competence and not allow any *ultra vires* extension; any future legal acts exceeding the competence of the EC would not be binding on Germany. *The German state organs would be prevented, for constitutional reasons, from applying them in Germany.*

The reach of these provocative pronouncements was tested in German administrative law in the so-called *Banana* litigation.[172] That occurred after the ECJ had rejected a claim that the banana regulation[173] was unconstitutional.[174] This litigation was unsuccessful. Indeed, the German Constitutional Court, without overruling its *Maastricht* judgment in its later case law, put nearly insurmountably high barriers on proving insufficient protection of fundamental rights, and on *ultra vires* action by Community institutions.[175] However, the question of *Kompetenz-Kompetenz*, to which Weiler[176] refers, was never formally settled.

Therefore, at the time of writing, the debate has changed direction. Community law has developed a set of fundamental rights *iure praetoris* of its own, and the ECJ has to ensure respect for this[177] (§ 12). Differences may certainly exist in the levels of

---

[170]   The debate is documented in A.-M. Slaughter/A. Stone Sweet/J.H.H.Weiler, *The European Courts and National Courts*, 1998; review by Reich, *EJIL* 1999. 154; cf. also the documentation by Craig/de Búrca at 285-315.
[171]   Brunner *et al.* v EU 89 BVerfGE 155; English translation [1994] 1 CMLR 57; critique by Weiler, *Festschrift Everling*, 1995, 1651; Herdegen, *CMLRev* 1995, 1369; Douglas Scott at 266-273.
[172]   Reich, EJIL 1996, 103.
[173]   404/93.
[174]   Case C-280/93 Germany v. Council [1994] ECR I-4973; critique Everling, *CMLRev* 1996, 401.
[175]   Cf. the review article by Hofmeister, *CMLRev* 2001, 791.
[176]   The Constitution of Europe at 298.
[177]   Per Art. 6 (2), 46 d) EU.

control (*Kontrolldichte*) and in access to courts by individuals. But this difference is acceptable in a government of laws such as the Community, where judicial control is available to ensure that "the law" is observed, per Art. 221 EC[178].

Control of *ultra vires* Community acts is a matter of competence. Under Community law, only Community courts may declare a Community act void. Indeed, this constitutional rule has become part of the *acquis communautaire*. Member State courts may not avoid Community acts; Community courts cannot annul Member State acts. There is no *Kompetenz-Kompetenz*, but rather a division of competences. This state of the law would only differ if no judicial control at all were available at Community level, which is not the case[179].

The reason for this reconciliation can be found in the fact that the ECJ seems to be more willing to review Community legal acts in response to arguments, either on competence, or on fundamental rights. While differences may still exist in the depth of review, or in the results achieved, none the less this difference cannot be avoided in a multi-level system of judicial control such as the Community's.

In the meantime, Art. I-6 of the Draft Constitution has explicitly recognized the supremacy of Union law over national law with the following words:

> The Constitution and law adopted by the institutions of the Union in exercising competences conferred on it shall have primacy over the law of the Member States.

This article restates the existing *acquis* and extends it to all "law" (not only legislative acts in the formal sense of Art. I-34, but also delegated European regulations in the sense of Art. I-36) of the Community, see § 2 I 3. This supremacy also extends to the constitutions of Member states. Member state courts have no power to control the legality of legal acts of the Community; this is the exclusive competence of the ECJ and the CFI.

3. Supremacy and uniformity

In today's practice, the question of supremacy is not one of hierarchy but of *uniformity*. Community law is a separate legal order with its own sources, specific effects on states and individuals, and methods of interpretation and review. In its sphere of application, it aims at guaranteeing to, and enforcing against, Union citizens and residents a similar and equally effective set of rights and duties. Member States must cooperate in the rea-

---

[178]   Van Gerven, *supra* note 6 at 110.
[179]   As Art. 230/234 EC clearly shows.

lization of this aim and must abstain from any measure that would jeopardize attaining Treaty[180] objectives.

This duty of cooperation in achieving equal rights protection is the basis for the supremacy doctrine. Even in 1970 the ECJ, in its *Internationale Handelsgesellschaft* judgment,[181] maintained that:

> (r)ecourse to the legal rules or concepts of national law in order to judge the validity of measures adopted by the Institutions of the Community would have an adverse effect on the uniformity and efficacy of Community law.

Supremacy is not an objective in itself, but a means of attaining uniformity in application and interpretation. It makes clear the ECJ's final authority both to interpret and to avoid Community acts, as already explained.

4. Flexibilisation of supremacy and uniformity

On the other hand, the Community legislator may *waive* uniformity, thus reducing supremacy. Indeed, supremacy and uniformity are not an absolute goal. Rather, they should be seen in the ever-precarious balance of competences between the Union and its Member States in achieving Community objectives as laid down in the Treaty. Several mechanisms for a flexible doctrine of supremacy have been developed. In addition, a more differentiated approach towards supremacy characterizes the area of law harmonization.[182]

a. The public policy and general interest provisos

The best known and most important exceptions to a uniform application of Community law are the express public policy provisos. These limit the scope and extent of the fundamental freedoms[183]. However, certain limitations attach to this:
– The public policy proviso is subject to control by the ECJ.
– The proviso as an exception must be narrowly interpreted, and measures must comply with the proportionality principle.
– Secondary Community law may always pre-empt Member State measures.
– Certain measures may only be adopted if a prior Community notification or authorization procedure has been followed.

---

[180] Per Art. 10 (2) EC.
[181] *Supra* note 167, at para 3, case C-473/93 Commission v. Luxembourg [1996] ECR I-3207 at paras 37-38.
[182] An overview is given by de Witte/Hauf/Vos (eds.), *The Many Faces of Differentiation in EU Law*, 2001.
[183] Per Art. 30, 39 (3), 46, 55 EC.

In addition, Court practice has developed a general interest test to legitimise Member State restrictions on free movement that are not overtly discriminatory. These relate to such matters as Member State social, environmental and consumer policy, cultural heritage, fairness of commercial practices, creditor protection in non-harmonized areas. They have to respect the proportionality principle and are under control of the ECJ.

b. Special exceptions granted or permitted by primary Community law

The "Masters of the Treaty" may also waive uniformity of Community law themselves. This occurs through Protocols attached to the Treaty, or in Accession Treaties with new Member countries. It is particularly true of the free movement of persons provisions, which apply to new Member States only after certain transition periods (§ 6 III). This amounts to a problematic infringement of the principle of uniformity and equal protection of citizens.[184]

Other examples concern opt-out rules granted to Denmark and the UK with regard to Monetary Union and to the relevant part of the Amsterdam Treaty[185] establishing an area of freedom, security, and justice. In particular, the last exception is highly problematic because it contradicts the very objective of the title. It creates arbitrary differences in legal protection, which stand in contradiction to the very idea of Community law.

The Treaty of Nice has extended the title on *Enhanced cooperation* in the Union Treaty to be used by not less than eight Member States. However, the conditions are highly restrictive and usually exclude legal measures:
-   Enhanced cooperation may not impair the internal market, nor may it create distortions of competition.
-   It will not become part of the *acquis*.

II. BROAD YET LIMITED COMPETENCES

1. Express competences

The Treaty[186] contains the basic rule on Community competence:

> it shall act within the limits of the powers conferred upon it by this Treaty and of the objectives assigned to it therein.

---

[184]   Cf. Reich/Harbacevica, *Europarättslig Tidskrift* 2002, 411 at 427-432.
[185]   The new Title IV.
[186]   Art. 5 (1) EC.

Unlike Member States, the Community only enjoys those powers that Member States, as "Masters of the Treaty" were willing to transfer to it. These powers mostly concern legislation, and to a lesser extent implementation and judicial protection, which are usually left to Member States. Their extent and degree have varied in the course of time, and have seen extensions – in some cases also a restriction – of powers.

The most important power conferred upon the Community[187] is the one to adopt:

> the measures for the approximation of the provisions laid down by law, regulation or administrative action in Member States which have as their objective the establishment and functioning of the internal market.

These broad powers conferred upon the Community[188] have formed the basis of most regulations and directives analysed in this book, and follow the co-decision procedure[189]. Before the enactment of the Single European Act, similar powers[190] required unanimity of voting in the Council.

However, this power is not without limits, and the Court exercises a control mandate. It therefore maintains that the choice of enabling norm should be based on objective criteria, to be scrutinized by the European judiciary.[191] This control is even stricter than any control under fundamental rights aspects, which so far remains quite undeveloped in Community law (§ 12).

The conflict over competences was highlighted in the Court's *tobacco advertising* judgment of 5.10.2000,[192] a case we met when examining teleological restrictions. Later case law tried to be more explicit on this point. If the relevant part of the Treaty[193] is to be taken as a basis for Community action, then the measures referred to in that provision must satisfy two conditions, according to the Court in its later *tobacco manufacture* judgment of 10.12.2002.[194] Firstly, the measures should aim to improve conditions for the establishment and functioning of the internal market. Secondly, they must genuinely have that objective, actually promoting elimination of obstacles to the free movement of goods, or to the freedom to provide services, or to the removal

---

[187] Per Art. 95 (2) EC.

[188] By the Single European Act of 1987.

[189] Art. 251 EC.

[190] Based on Art. 94 EC.

[191] Cf. the cases cited in note 16.

[192] Case C-376/98 Germany v EP and Council [2000] ECR I-8419 at para 84.

[193] Art. 95 EC.

[194] Case C-491/01 The Queen v Secretary of State for Health *ex parte*: British American Tobacco (Investments) Ltd. *et al.* [2002] ECR I-11453.

of (appreciable?)[195] distortions of competition. A mere disparity of Member State law is not enough to justify Community action. The Community may not use its internal market power to avail itself of competences (e.g., health policy) it does not enjoy by express Treaty provision[196]. The later *tobacco manufacture* judgment clarified the Court's earlier hostility to internal market powers used for health purposes. Indeed, the Court was satisfied that:

> obstacles to the free movement of tobacco products would arise by reason of the adoption of Member States of new rules reflecting that development[197] and intended more effectively to discourage consumption of those products by means of warnings and information appearing on packaging or to reduce the harmful effects of tobacco products by introducing new rules governing their consumption (para 67).

These rules could aim to safeguard *the general interests recognized by the Treaty, such as public health* (para 77). However, they should ensure that such products may freely circulate in the internal market. The Court seems to take the view that a mere minimal harmonization, as in the annulled tobacco advertising directive[198], fails to satisfy the internal market proviso (*infra* III).

In its practical consequences for the Community legislature, the case law of the ECJ is not always easy to understand and follow.[199] This is not only true in the vertical Community-Member States relationship, but also horizontally concerning the Community's different competences and procedures in legislating. For example:

- Art. 12 EC concerning discrimination based on nationality.
- Art. 13 EC allowing combat against discrimination based on sex or sexual orientation, racial or ethnic origin, religion or belief, age or disability.
- Art. 18 (2) and (3) as amended by the Nice treaty concerning citizenship and free movement.
- Art. 67 concerning JHA measures.
- Art 133 EC on common commercial policy, also amended by the Nice Treaty.
- Art. 141 (3) EC concerning equal opportunities for men and women in access to and treatment in employment or occupation.
- Art. 153 (3) EC on supporting measures for consumer protection.
- Art. 175 EC concerning environmental protection.

---

[195] The tobacco advertising judgment insisted in para 106 on this appreciability element, which was not, however, repeated in para 60 of the more recent tobacco manufacture judgment.
[196] (Art. 152 (4) lit b) EC).
[197] *E.g.*, increased public awareness of health hazards posed by smoking (NR).
[198] 98/43.
[199] For a discussion in the legal literature, Craig/de Búrca at 533; Weatherill, *JCP* 2001, 339 at 368-371.

The different bases of competence will only be important where the Treaty provides for different procedures and majority requirements of legislation. This makes a combination of enabling provisions difficult. If recourse to a twofold legal basis, each incompatible with the other, does not affect the actual outcome of the act, then the Court will avoid its annulment.[200]

2. Implied competences?

The theory of implied competences was much debated in the founding years of the EEC, when the Court seemed willing to stretch the rather general competence norms to their extreme. The best known example in relation to external competences is perhaps the *ERTA* judgment.[201] There, the Court deduced from harmonization that external relations with third countries also fell under Community competence, in order to avoid disparities between internal and external regulation. Later judgments and opinions have been much more cautious.[202] Only areas of exclusive competence, in particular relating to the internal market, are subject to Community treaty-making powers. In other areas, such as intellectual property, the Community has to share competence with Member states.[203] The Amsterdam and Nice Treaties have tried to clarify the shared competences by amending the original Treaty[204, 205]

Another provision used as a basis for an extensive reading of Community competences was Art. 308 EC.[206] This requires unanimity of voting in the Council, an extension severely criticized in the Maastricht judgment of the German *Bundesverfassungs-gericht.*[207] Many early directives, for example those relating to non-discrimination between the sexes in access to employment[208] (§ 11 III 2), were based on the broad competence of Art. 308. Since the basis was never challenged before the ECJ, and since action required unanimity by the Council, it could not be tested legally how far the implied competence of the Community really went. This extensive reading of Art. 308 is no longer necessary, because special competence norms added to the Treaty allow the Community to legislate in these matters.

---

[200]   Case C-491/01 *supra* note 193 at 110.
[201]   Case 22/70 Commission v. Council [1971] ECR 263 at para 19.
[202]   Opinion 1/94 on the WTO [1994] ECR I-5267; C-476/98 Commission v. Germany [2002] ECR I-9855 para 103-112.
[203]   Case C-13/00 Commission/Ireland [2003] ECR-I 2943.
[204]   Art. 133 EC.
[205]   Craig/de Búrca at 130.
[206]   Ex-Art. 235 EEC.
[207]   *Supra* note 170.
[208]   *E.g.* Dir. 76/207.

The Court[209] was therefore right in substantially limiting the legislative powers of the Community under the broad provisions of Art. 308 – in response to the question whether the Community could adhere to the ECHR by unanimous decision of the Council. Indeed, it rejected such an *implied power* with the following remarks:

> Respect for human rights is therefore a condition of the lawfulness of Community acts. Accession to the Convention (ECHR, NR) would however entail a substantial change in the present Community system for the protection of human rights in that it would entail the entry of the Community into a distinct international institutional system as well as the integration of all the provisions of the Convention into the Community legal order. Such a modification of the system for the protection of human rights in the Community with equally fundamental institutional implications for the Community and the Member States would be of constitutional significance and would therefore be such as to go beyond the scope of Art. 235 (now Art. 308, NR). It could be brought about only by way of Treaty amendment (paras 34-35).

Today's practice only invokes Art. 308 when attaching institutional regulations to Community instruments, such as trade marks and designs (§ 10 IV), or to supplement existing Community jurisdiction. The requirement of unanimity ensures that every Member State can veto the establishment of a new Community institution, and that it is therefore necessary to negotiate their regional distribution respecting Member State interests.

3. Subsidiarity

It was the Maastricht Treaty that introduced the subsidiarity principle into EC law, as an element limiting extension of Community competence, and against encroachment on Member State powers. The Amsterdam Treaty attached a particular protocol where some basic principles of subsidiarity were formulated.

Art. 5 (2) of the Treaty reads:

> In areas which do not fall into its exclusive competence the Community shall take action, in accordance with the principle of subsidiarity, only if and insofar as the objectives of the proposed action cannot be sufficiently achieved by the Member States and can therefore, by reason of their scale or effect of the proposed action, be better achieved by the Community.

---

[209] Opinion 2/94 [1996] ECR I-1759.

An intense legal debate, particularly in legal literature[210], along with the minimal legal output of the subsidiarity principle, results from the ambiguous wording of the Treaty itself:

– Subsidiarity does not apply in areas of exclusive Community competence, especially the internal market, in order to eliminate barriers to trade.
– Subsidiarity only concerns the *exercise* of existing competences. It does not call into question the powers conferred on the Community as interpreted by the Court[211].
– Subsidiarity cannot be invoked to restrict the rights that individuals enjoy under Community law.[212]
– Subsidiarity leaves a broad margin of discretion to Community institutions to decide on the necessity, level and degree of action.
– Subsidiarity does not have direct effect in favour of individuals challenging the legality of a Community act.[213]

The ECJ, when asked to rule on a Community measure under the subsidiarity principle, usually takes a "light" judicial approach.[214] That is, it will allow the Community legislator a wide margin of discretion. Its pronouncement in the *tobacco manufacture* judgment of 10 Dec. 2002[215] made clear that the Community does not have exclusive competence as to avoiding distortions of competition under the internal market proviso. Nevertheless, the directive was justified by avoiding different rules for the marketing of tobacco products and at the same time achieving a high level of health protection:

> Such an objective cannot be sufficiently achieved by the Member States individually and calls for action at Community level ... (para 182).

4. Proportionality

The principle of proportionality developed in justifying restrictions by Member States on free movement under the public policy or general interest proviso.[216] The Court summarized the basic principles in *Gebhard*:[217]

---

[210] Toth, *CMLRev* 1992, 1079; Emiliou, *ELRev* 1992, 383; de Búrca, *Reappraising subsidiarity's significance after Amsterdam*, 1999; Estella, *The EU principle of subsidiarity and its critique*, 2002; Callies, *Subsidiariäts- und Solidaritätsprinzip in der EU*, 1996; Nörr/Oppermann (eds.), *Subsidiarität: Idee und Wirklichkeit*, 1997; Merten, *Die Subsidiarität Europas*, 1994. The German Federal government regularly published so-called *Subsidiaritätsberichte* (reports on the subsidiarity principle) which, however, had no practical effect in Community law-making and law implementation.
[211] Per Art. 3 of the protocol.
[212] Case C-415/93 ASBL/Bosman [1995] ECR I-4921 at para 81.
[213] Toth, *ELRev* 1994, 268.
[214] Craig/de Búrca at 137 with references to ECJ cases.
[215] *Supra* note 193.
[216] Tridimas at 89.
[217] Case C-55/94 Gebhard v. Consiglio dell'Ordine degli Advocati e procuratori di Milano [1995] ECR I-4165.

It follows, however, from the Court's case law that national measures liable to hinder or make less attractive the exercise of fundamental freedoms guaranteed by the Treaty must fulfil four conditions: they must be applied in a non-discriminatory manner; they must be justified by imperative requirements in the general interest; they must be suitable for securing the attainment of the objective which they pursue; and they must not go beyond what is necessary in order to attain it (para 37).

Thus, the proportionality principle applies on a case-by-case basis. In some cases, the Court takes the necessary value-judgment itself, while in others it leaves the matter to Member State courts, usually providing them with some guidance on the application of the proportionality principle in the case at hand. As a general rule, the more severe the restriction to free movement appears to be, and the less it is justified,[218] the more readily will the Court intervene.

Later developments of Community law have extended the proportionality principle to the control of Community acts. It has become part of positive Community law in Art. 5 (3) EC which reads:

> Any action by the Community shall not go beyond what is necessary to achieve the objectives of this Treaty.

Unlike subsidiarity, it allows a relatively precise test to challenge and evaluate the legality of, for example, Community directives. It was used extensively in the *tobacco advertising* judgment as an argument for annulment[219]. In its later *tobacco manufacture* judgment, the Court took a more cautious approach, insisting on the broad discretion of the legislature:

> Consequently, the legality of a measure adopted in that respect can be affected only if the measure is manifestly inappropriate having regard to the objective which the competent institution is seeking to pursue (para 123).

The Court will use additional tests to define the proportionality of a Community measure:

- Will it improve the free movement of goods or services, e.g. by a corresponding internal market clause[220] or by avoiding double controls?[221]
- Can information rules achieve the same objective with less restrictive means as a complete ban on a marketing activity?

---

[218]   Reich/Harbacevica, *CMLRev* 2003, 615 at 629.
[219]   *Supra* note 154 at paras 98-104.
[220]   Case C-376/98 *supra* note 191 at para 104.
[221]   Case 37183 REWE Zentrale v Landwirtschaftskammer Rheinland [1984] ECR 1229.

- Can objective information requirements, even though strict, imposed on manufacturers avoid misleading descriptions?
- Will the measure at hand allow enough flexibility to actors to adapt their behavior accordingly?

5. New catalogue of Union competences according to the Draft Constitution

The Draft Constitution has not changed the principles of "conferral", "subsidiarity" and "proportionality" in the exercise of Union competences, but has restated them expressly in Art. I-11. It has created new definitions in order to distinguish between areas of "exclusive competence" and "shared competences", as well as special rules on "coordination" in the areas of employment and economic policy, competence to define and implement a common foreign and security policy, and competence in supporting Member state action in certain areas.

Within the subject matters covered by this book, it is worth mentioning the exclusive competence of the Union in the area of the "customs union" and "the establishing of the competition rules necessary for the functioning of the internal market", per Art. I-13. Shared competences concern most of all the internal market, certain areas of social policy, environment, consumer protection, area of freedom, security and justice, and certain safety concerns in public health matters, Art. I-14.

III. PRINCIPLES OF LAW HARMONIZATION

Harmonization measures are available to the Community according to its legislative powers under the different enabling provisions. They usually define their relationship to Member State law by themselves. This is most notable relating to internal market competence. It is therefore a question of interpretation how far Member State law can be maintained or adopted in areas already harmonized. The Community legislature has developed three different techniques of harmonization:
- *Complete harmonization*: Member States are prevented from adopting diverging measures in the area harmonized, as the Court ruled with regard to the product liability directive 85/374/EEC (§ 20 III 2).[222] The trade-mark directive 89/104/EEC (§ 10 IV) was interpreted as containing complete harmonization in the areas of exhaustion and confusion – two central concepts of trade mark law in the internal market. It is therefore decisive to determine the area in order to judge whether Member State law conforms to Community law. If the latter is not caught by a

---

[222] Case C-52/00 Commission v. France [2002] ECR I-3827.

harmonization measure, it must always be scrutinized under the free movement rules.

- *Minimum harmonization*: This is used in certain areas where the Community legislature sets adequate standards, for example in non-discrimination, social, and consumer policy matters. Member State protection may go further, even if that seems to be in opposition to the harmonization principle itself. This principle, sometimes called *flexible integration*, and first recognized by the Court in consumer protection,[223] has been expressly recognized, although with certain limitations on social policy[224], consumer policy[225], and on environmental policy[226]. In certain areas close to the internal market, especially consumer protection, the Commission wants to abandon minimum harmonization in favour of complete harmonization,[227] a highly problematic approach.
- *Country of origin principle*: This harmonization principle developed in the area of free movement of goods. It was later applied to other fundamental freedoms and developed by the Community as a general principle to attain the objectives of the internal market. It states as a rule that goods, services and capital should be able to freely circulate in the Community once they respect the rules of the country where the provider has its main place of business. The receiving state may not impede free movement for reasons which fall in the harmonized area, but it may still impose stricter standards for products and services originating there. Community law allows a certain "competition between legal orders".[228] As a result, the minimum Community standards, with which products or services must comply in the country of origin, are usually the general standards, because normally no Member State will impose stricter standards on its business if they do harm to its competitive position (§ 8 III).

The different techniques may be combined in a legislative act. Frequently, Community acts provide for safeguard clauses or for secondary implementing legislation to adapt a directive to technical or scientific progress. A special flexibility regime has been provided[229], allowing Member States to opt out of internal market measures under certain limited conditions, strictly controlled by the Commission and the ECJ.

---

[223] E.g., Case 382/87 Buet et al/Min. Public [1989] ECR 1235; C-361/89 Criminal proceedings against Mr. Di Pinto [1991] ECR I-1189.
[224] Art. 137 (2) EC.
[225] Art. 153 (5) EC.
[226] Art. 176 EC.
[227] Micklitz/Reich/Weatherill, *JCP* 2004, 367 at 386.
[228] Reich, *CMLRev* 1992, 861, Radeideh, *Fair Trading in EC Law*, 2005 at 105.
[229] By Art. 95 (4-7) EC.

IV. COMMUNITY-CONFORMING INTERPRETATION OF NATIONAL LAW

1. The principle

The duty to mutual cooperation and respect[230] is not limited to legislating and implementing Community law, but also applies to the judicial branch. This duty becomes particularly important when Community and Member State Law differ. An example would be cases of insufficient or incorrect implementation of directives that aim to create rights in favour of individuals, but which do not have horizontal direct effect (§ 2 II 3b). As a second best solution – leaving state liability outside our discussion (§ 19 II) – the Court has developed the principle of *Community* – or *directive – conforming interpretation* of national law. This is a duty flowing from the supremacy and uniformity doctrines, and not out of (different) Member state law theories of interpretation.[231]

This technique was first used in *Von Colson*[232], concerning the inadequate implementation of Dir. 76/207 by German labour law (§ 11 III). The Court wrote:

> However, the Member States' obligation arising from a directive to achieve the result envisaged by the directive and their duty under Art. 5 (now Art. 10 EC, NR) of the Treaty to take all appropriate measures, whether general or particular, to ensure the fulfilment of that obligation, is binding on all the authorities of the Member States, including, for matters within their jurisdiction, the courts. It follows that, in applying the national law and in particular the provisions of a national law specifically introduced in order to implement directive 76/207, national courts are required to interpret their national law in the light of the wording and the purpose of the Directive in order to achieve the result referred to in the third para of Art. 189 (now 249 EC) (para 26).

The obligation of Member State courts is incomplete, because Community law cannot monitor it. Community courts have no authority to interpret and apply Member State law. Moreover, no guarantee exists that uniformity of Community law application will be achieved in this way.

2. Limits and extensions

This obligation is also not absolute, because Member State courts are not required to interpret their law *contra legem*. In *Marleasing*[233] the Court found the following formula

---

[230]   Art. 10 EC.
[231]   Grundmann, *ZEuP* 1996, 400 against Ehricke, *RabelsZ* 1995, 598.
[232]   Case 14/83 Von Colson and Kamann v. Land Nordrhein-Westfalen [1984] ECR 1891.
[233]   Case C-106/89, Marleasing SA v La Comercial Internacional de Alimentación SA [1990] ECR-4135.

to reconcile Community law imperatives with Member State autonomy in law application:

> ... in applying national law, whether the provisions in question were adopted before or after the directive, the national court called upon to interpret it is required to do so, *as far as possible (italics NR)*, in the light of the wording and the purpose of the directive in order to achieve the result pursued by the latter and thereby comply with the third para of Art. 189 (249 EC) (para 8).

In his opinion, AG van Gerven made clear that this obligation should be fulfilled by choosing the interpretation method of national law "which enables [the national court] to construe the national provision concerned in a manner consistent with the directive".[234]

This formula *as far as possible* was repeated in later cases.[235] It clearly shows the limits of directive-conforming interpretation. In criminal matters it will reject an interpretation extending the sphere in which penal liability applies beyond the wording of the law in opposition to the human rights principles of *nulla poena sine lege*. This was written into the ECHR, which must also be respected by Community law.[236] In administrative law, state action against an individual requires a legal basis in national law. This cannot be substituted by a directive, because it creates no obligations on the individual. On the other hand, in cases favoring the position of an individual, the method of Community-conforming interpretation may well be used, even if it imposes an indirect burden on third parties.[237]

By contrast, in civil liability matters, analogy and teleological restriction are well-established methods of interpreting and applying the law. This may, on the one hand, lead to an extension of civil liability,[238] on the other to restricting the application of a broad provision of national law in conformity with the directive. The national judge is confronted with an increased responsibility in applying its law in conformity with Community law requirements. In using these powers of interpretation, the judge may at the same time avoid liability of their Member State for breaching Community law.

---

[234] At 4146 para 8.

[235] Case C-355/96 Silhouette International Schmied GmbH & Co KG v. Hartlauer Handelsgesellschaft GmbH [1997] ECR I-4799 at para 36; case C-63/97 Bayrische Motorenwerke (BMW) and BMW Nederland BV v. Ronald Karel Dseenik [1999] ECR I-905 at para 22.

[236] Joined cases C-74 + 129/95 Criminal proceedings against X [1996] ECR I-6609.

[237] Case 103/88 Fratelli Costanzo SpA/ Comune di Milano [1989] ECR 1839.

[238] Cf. in this sense AG Jacobs in case C-456/98 Centrosteel v. Adipol [2000] ECR I-6007 at para 35 of his opinion.

In the recent DRK-Case[239] the Court insisted

> that …, if the application of interpretative methods recognised by national law enables, in certain circumstances, a provision of domestic law to be construed in such a way as to avoid conflict with another rule of domestic law or the scope of that provision to be restricted to that end by applying it only in so far as it is compatible with the rule concerned, the national court is bound to use those methods in order to achieve the result sought by the directive. In such circumstances, the national court, … must, when applying the provisions of national law specifically intended to implement the directive, interpret those provisions so far as possible in such a way that they are applied in conformity with the objectives of the directive (paras 117-118).

The principle of Community law conforming interpretation is therefore to be understood as an obligation of the national judge to use the full range of interpretation possibilities – including those of a teleological restriction as in the case at hand – to make sure that national law conforms to EU directives taking direct effect, even if this amounts to imposing a burden on a private party. Therefore, the original distinction between denying (§ 2 II 3b) horizontal effect of directives and imposing a Community conforming interpretation of national law looses much of its importance, at least in relations governed by civil and commercial law.

To summarize the approach chosen by the Court, Community-conforming interpretation has been widely accepted in order to ensure the supremacy of Community law without attaining uniformity. It remains a second best solution to horizontal direct effect of directives in cases where implementation has been insufficient. It is certainly not a substitute for Member State obligations to guarantee their full compliance with Community law.[240] It should only be used in areas where direct effect cannot otherwise be assured. If the fundamental freedoms are at stake, there is no need for directive-conforming interpretation.

---

[239]   Case C-397/01 et al. Bernhard Pfeifer et al. v Deutsches Rotes Kreuz [2004] ECR I-(5.10.2004).
[240]   Case C-144/99 Commission v. Netherlands [2001] ECR I-3541.

51

CHAPTER I. CITIZENSHIP AND FREE MOVEMENT

Table of Contents

Selected Bibliography

J. Apap (ed.), *Freedom of Movement of Persons*, 2002; A. Bocker, "The Establishment Provisions of the Europe Agreements", *ZERP-Diskussionspapier* 1/2002; G. Borchardt, "Der sozialrechtliche Gehalt der Unionsbürgerschaft", *NJW (Neue Juristische Wochenschrift)* 2000, 2057; J. Broeckman, *A Philosophy of European Law*, 1999; A. Castro Oliveira, "Workers and other persons: Step-by-step from movement to citizenship", *CMLRev* 2002, 77; C. Closa, "Citizenship of the Union and Nationality of Member States", *CMLRev* 1995, 487; P. Craig/G. de Búrca, *EU Law*, 3rd ed. 2002, 701-754; W.R. Davies, "Citizenship of the Union – rights for all?", *ELRev* 2002, 121; G. Davies, ""Any place I hand my hat"? or: residence as the new nationality?", *ELJ* 2005, 43; M. Dougan/E. Spaventa (ed.), *Social Welfare and EU-Law*, 2005; S. Douglas-Scott, *Constitutional law of the EU*, 2002, 479-514; K. Famira, *Der freie Personenverkehr in Europa – Schengen nach Amsterdam*, 2004; Gardner (ed.), *Citizenship – The White Paper*,1997; M.J. Garot, *La citoyenneté de l'Union européenne*, 1999; M. Hedemann-Robinson, "An overview of recent legal developments at Community level in relation to third country nationals within the EU", *CMLRev* 2001, 525-586; K. Inglis, "The Europe Agreements compared in the light of their pre-accession orientation", *CMLRev* 2000, 1173-1210; K. Inglis, "The Union's fifth accession treaty", *CMLRev* 2004, 937; Y. Jorens/B. Schulte (eds.), *European Social Security Law and Third Country Nationals*, 1998; K. Kruma, *EU citizenship: unresolved issues. RGSL Working papers* No. 22, 2004; P.J. Kuijper, "Some Legal Problems associated with the Communitarization of Policy on Visas, Asylum and Immigration under the Amsterdam Treaty and Incorporation of the Schengen Acquis", *CMLRev* 2000, 345; Mouton, *La citoyenneté de l'Union*,

Europa-Institut des Saarlandes, 1996 at 5; S. O'Leary, "The Relationship between Community Citizenship and the Protection of Fundamental Rights", *CMLRev* 1995, 519; S. O'Leary, *The Evolving Concept of Community Citizenship*, 1996; C. Nowak, "EU-Osterweiterung, Personenfreizügigkeit und staatliche Schutzpflichten", *EuZW* 2003, 101; H.U.J. d'Oliveira, "European Citizenship: Its Meaning, Its Potential", in: Dehousse (ed.), *Europe after Maastricht*, 1994, 126; A. Ott/K. Inglis, *Handbook on European Enlargement*, 2002; N. Reich, *Bürgerrechte in der EU*, 1999, 208-261; N. Reich, "Union citizenship – Metaphor or source of rights?", *ELJ* 2001, 4-23; N. Reich, *Union Citizenship – Yesterday – today – tomorrow*, RGSL Working paper No. 3, 2000; N. Reich in collaboration with S. Harvacevica, "Citizenship and family on trial", *CMLRev* 2003, 615; N. Reich/S. Harbacevica, "The Stony Road to Brussels", *Europarättslig Tidskrift* 2002, 411; N. Reich, *The European Constitution and New Member Countries: The Constitutional Relevance of Free Movement and Citizenship*, RGSL Working Papers No. 19; Sauerwald, "Die Unionsbürgerschaft, 1996; J. Shaw, Citizenship of the Union: Towards Post-National Membership?", in: European University Institute (ed.), *Collected Courses of the Academy of European Law*, Vol. VI-1,1998, 237; N. Shuibhne, "Free movement of persons and the wholly internal rule: Time to move on?", *CMLRev* 2002, 731; K. Sieveking, "EU Agreements with the CEEU", *European Jounal of Social Security* 2003, 38; H. Staples, *The Legal Status of third country nationals resident in the EU*, 1999; E. Spaventa, "From *Gebhard* to *Carpenter*: Towards a (Non)-Economic European Constitution", *CMLRev* 2004, 743; T. Tridimas, *The General Principles of EC Law*, 1999; J. Weiler, *The Constitution of Europe*, 1999; F. Weiss/F. Wooldbridge, *Free Movement of Persons within the EC*, 2002.

§ 4. THE ECONOMIC ORIGIN OF CITIZENSHIP: MARKET CITIZEN

I. THE NATURE OF FREE MOVEMENT OF CITIZENS, ITS DEVELOPMENT, SCOPE AND LIMITATIONS

Free movement of Member State nationals is one of the foundations of the EC/EU. The ECJ has often called it a *fundamental principle of the Community*[1]; later cases have extended it[2] to a right ensuring protection of the family[3]. The relevant Council Regulation[4] on freedom of movement for workers within the Community, supplemented by a further Council Directive[5] *on the abolition of restrictions on movement and residence within the Community for workers of Member States and their families*, characterizes its liberal origin in sweeping words:

> ...freedom of movement constitutes a fundamental right of workers and their families....; mobility of labour within the Community must be one of the means by which the worker is guaranteed the possibility of improving his living and working conditions and promoting his social advancement, while helping to satisfy the requirements of the economies of the Member States;... the right of all workers in the Member States *to pursue the activity of their choice within the Community* should be affirmed (recital 3).

This fundamental right enjoys special status in the directly applicable rules of primary Community law on mobility of workers[6], establishment for self-employed persons[7] and freedom to provide services[8]. It is therefore linked to economic activity of *the market citizen*, a concept that includes activities relating to sports or culture.[9] Later directives have extended it to:

– those in the pre-work phase, that is, students[10];
– students' right of residence;

---

[1] Case 222/86 Unctef/Heylens [1987] ECR 4097.
[2] In combination with Art. 8 ECHR.
[3] Case C-459/99 MRAX v Belgium [2002] ECR I-6591 at para 53.
[4] Regulation (EEC) No 1612/68 of the Council of 15 October 1968 on freedom of movement for workers within the Community [1968] OJ L 257/2, in the following: Reg. 1612/68.
[5] Council Directive 68/360/EEC of 15 October 1968 on the abolition of restrictions on movement and residence within the Community for workers of Member States and their families [1968] OJ L 257/13.
[6] Art. 39 EC.
[7] Art. 43 EC.
[8] Art. 49 EC.
[9] Case 36/74 Walrave v Union Cycliste Int. [1974] ECR 1405.
[10] Council Directive 93/96/EEC of 29 October 1993 on the right of residence for students [1993] OJ 317/59.

- those phased out of work, that is, retired workers[11];
- right of residence of otherwise non-employed persons[12].

The relevant directives will be discussed below, together with the primary Community law applying (III).

An abundant case law exists as to how to interpret and apply these fundamental rules. The ECJ's *effet utile* doctrine (§ 2 III) has extended existing rights to ancillary entitlements where the wording of the Treaty, or of secondary law, was silent. The ECJ's interpretation, and to a lesser extent Community legislative activity, show a clear paradigm change. That is, from economic liberalism to a civil society concept of free movement of Member State nationals. This is achieved by separating the right to free movement from economic activity. The final and most ambitious recognition of free movement as a fundamental right of EU citizens occurred with creation of a separate Union citizenship[13]. The legal importance of the concept of citizenship, still somewhat vague, will be treated separately (§ 5).

The tension between economic and personal components inherent in free movement is particularly evident in the status of nationals of Europe Agreement countries. These have become members of the EU from 1st May 2004 on. The specifics will have to be treated in a broader context of transition rules (§ 6).

Above all, free movement protects its beneficiaries against discrimination based on nationality. This remains true whether discrimination is direct or indirect, indeed even if it comes from private entities exercising collective power (§ 11 II). As an example, the denial of a length of service increment for 15 years of activity as a professor in Austria to a professor who served part of his activity in another Member State (Germany) amounts to an indirect discrimination and is therefore forbidden by Art. 39 EC (ex-48 EEC).[14] Free movement has been extended, against the seemingly narrow wording of the Treaty, to include the *prohibition of restrictions*. Moreover, going beyond existing legislation, Court practice has developed a rather narrow approach on how these limitations can still be justified; the decisive test has been the test of proportionality as a general principle of Community law (§ 2 III).

Free movement includes certain positive rights, in the shape of social and tax advantages. However, these are limited to certain groups of persons, most notably

---

[11]   Per Council Directive 90/365/EEC of 28 June 1990 on the right of residence for employees and self-employed persons who have ceased their occupational activity, [1990] OJ L 180/28.
[12]   Per Council Directive 90/364/EEC of 28 June 1990 on the right of residence [1990] OJ L 180/26.
[13]   Per Art. 8/8a of the Maastricht Treaty, later Art. 17/18 of the EC-Treaty in the Amsterdam version.
[14]   Case C-224/01 Gerhard Köbler v Republik Österreich [2003] ECR I-10239.

workers in the sense of Reg. 1612/68 and their family members. These have to be treated separately, because here the great differences between Member State social systems become apparent. Moreover, the principle of solidarity among EU citizens has its limits, if only to avoid a migration to the most generous social protection regime. Other nationals such as self-employed persons, students, and retired persons are usually denied access to these benefits. Instead, they have to provide proof that they are able to cover their own living expenses and sickness insurance. A new area of conflict has arisen in the discussion on how far citizenship also includes social rights. This is due to its legal link with the principle of non-discrimination, which also enjoys special status in the Treaty.[15]

In evaluating the dynamics of the free movement rules, it is important to remember that EU law also functions as a principle of exclusion.[16] Usually, EU law only protects nationals. As a result, non-nationals only enjoy protection if they come under some other instrument extending protection to them. This might apply to:
- family members of nationals;
- migrant workers from countries with which the EU has special agreements;
- persons protected by international law, which the EU respects.

The following description can only give an overview of the many facets of free movement of persons.

II. FREE MOVEMENT OF WORKERS

1. Protection ratione personae: the concept of worker

Primary Community law does not define the concept of *worker* as beneficiary of free movement. The relevant Regulation[17] gives a first hint of a definition, by extending this right not only to permanent workers, but also to seasonal and frontier workers, indeed even to those who carry on their activities with the aim of providing services.

The case law of the ECJ is characterized by the search for an independent, autonomous concept of *worker*. Member States should not be entitled to set up a restrictive definition of worker in order to limit free movement. In *Levin*[18] the Court had to decide whether a part-time worker, whose income was below the national minimum

---

[15]   Art. 12 EC (§ 5 V).
[16]   Cf. the critique by Douglas-Scott, *Constitutional Law of the EU*, 2001, at 489-493.
[17]   Recital 4 of Reg. 1612/68.
[18]   Case 53/81 Levin v Staatssecretaris van Justitie [1982] ECR 1035.

required for subsistence, would fall within the ambit of the Treaty. The Court declared, somewhat ambiguously:

> ... the concepts of "worker" and "activity as an employed person" must be interpreted as meaning that the rules relating to freedom of movement for workers also concern persons who pursue or wish to pursue an activity as an employed person on a part-time basis and who, by virtue of that fact obtain or would obtain only remuneration lower than the minimum guaranteed remuneration in the sector under consideration... (para 16)

The Court went on to exclude *purely marginal and ancillary activities*. The distinction is not always easy to draw, for example with students working part-time to finance their studies (§ 5 V). It should be noted that the search for employment, and vocational training, are included in the concept of worker.[19] The same is true for persons seeking employment.[20]

Another implicit requirement in the concept of worker relates to dependent, in contrast to self-employed, activity. That is, workers are subject to an employer's powers of direction; they cannot determine the time and scope of their work on their own. In *Martínez Sala*[21] the Court gave the following definition of worker:

> In the context of Art. (39 EC) and Regulation 1612/68, a person who, for a certain period of time, performs services for and under the direction of another person in return for which he receives remuneration must be considered to be a worker. Once the employment relationship has ended, the person concerned as a rule loses his status of worker, although that status may produce certain effects after the relationship has ended....

The Court will usually give only guidelines to national courts that have to apply this concept to the case at hand. The mere fact that a football player may receive a high income does not exclude the status of worker, because it is the club, not the player autonomously, that decides issues on playing, and transfer to other clubs.[22]

2. Protection ratione materiae: sphere of application

A cross-border element must always be inherent in the protection a worker is claiming under EU law. This is a fundamental requirement for the free movement rules to apply. EU law does not catch *purely internal situations*, because it does not aim to interfere

---

[19]   Case 66/85 Lawrie-Blum v Land Baden-Würtemberg [1986] ECR 2121.
[20]   Case C-292/89 R v Immigration Appeal Tribunal *ex parte* Antonissen, [1991] ECR I-745.
[21]   Case C-85/96 Maria Martínez Sala v Freistaat Bayern [1998] ECR I-2691 at para 32.
[22]   Case C-415/93 URBSFA ASBL v Bosman [1995] ECR I-4921 at para 73.

with the internal order of any Member State.[23] This does not mean that nationals of Member States do not enjoy the protection of EU law, but to the extent that they have such a problem, then it must relate to their activity as a migrant worker or citizen. As in other areas, the Court prefers a broad interpretation of the Treaty in this respect. However, Community legislation on freedom of movement in any case only applies to situations presenting a link to the situations envisaged by Community law. As a result, the situation of persons who have never exercised those freedoms would be excluded.[24]

The type of activity is not decisive. Employment in public administration only creates an exception to the concept of economic activity if the conditions of *employment in the public service*[25] are met. As an exception to the general rule on free movement, the ECJ has interpreted this proviso restrictively, to comprise only such activities where nationality is a decisive factor. This might include, for example, activities involving the exercise of powers conferred by public law, or safeguarding the general interests of the State.[26] Member States may not monopolize certain activities for their own nationals by invoking reasons of public service. Therefore, the teaching profession,[27] employment in security services,[28] or training of future state officials or lawyers governed by public law, must be opened up to all EU nationals, even if they have acquired the status of a public official.

To some extent even illegal activities, or those said to be against public order, such as prostitution, are protected by the Treaty, provided the Member State concerned does not outlaw them entirely for its own citizens as well. But this is more a question of the permitted public policy exception than of the economic nature of the activity itself.[29]

3. The concept of restriction and its possible justifications

The extensive case law of the Court forbids not only direct and indirect discrimination, such as "conditions imposed by national law ... where, although applicable irrespective of nationality, they affect essentially migrant workers..."[30], but also *any* restriction. An

---

[23]   Case C-332/90 Steen v. Deutsche Bundespost [1992] ECR I-341; for a critical discussion cf. Shuibhne, CMLRev 2002, 731; Reich/Harbacevica, *CMLRev* 2003, 615 at 634.
[24]   Case C-459/99 MRAX *supra* note 3 at para 39.
[25]   Art. 39 (4) EC.
[26]   Case 225/85 Commission v Italy [1987] ECR 2625 at para 10.
[27]   Case C-4/91 Bleis v Ministère de l'éducation nationale [1991] ECR I-5627.
[28]   Case C-114/97 Commission v Spain [1998] ECR I-6717.
[29]   Joined cases 115 + 116/81 Adoui and Cornuaille v Belgium [1982] ECR 1665.
[30]   Case C-237/94 O'Flynn v Adjudication Officer [1996] ECR I-2617 at para 18, also naming some other criteria for indirect discrimination.

exception exists when applying a public interest test that meets the criteria of proportionality and that specifically justifies discrimination. This approach was clearly developed in *Bosman*[31], which concerned both the nationality clauses and the transfer rules of European professional football. The nationality clauses were a clear discrimination. The transfer rules made the cross-border exercise of professional football activities as a worker more difficult, even if applying these rules to nationals playing for the club and to players from other EU countries alike. These rules provided that a professional footballer may only perform his activity with a new club established in another Member State if the new club has paid the former club a transfer fee agreed upon between the two clubs. Without this payment, the player is not free to play for the new club. The Court carefully scrutinized the transfer rules for possible justifications for these inherent restrictive elements, in the end rejecting them by a proportionality test. This led to the finding that they were not necessary, nor were they proportionate in reaching the alleged objective, namely to recruit and train young players, to recover investment, and to allow for an equal share of revenues in the professional football league. The Court noted, laconically:

> The same aims can be achieved as efficiently by other means, which do not impede freedom of movement for workers (para 110).

A restriction also occurs in relation to employment of posted workers, if they are subject to the regulations and collective bargaining agreements of the host country. However, such restrictions may be justified by social policy reasons, namely to protect the posted worker.[32] On the other hand, requiring teachers and other officials in Ireland to know the Irish language amounted to both a disguised discrimination and a restriction. However, it could be justified on cultural policy grounds, provided all candidates had an equal chance to pass an Irish test.[33]

4. *Access to social advantages*

Migrant workers are granted[34] the *same social and tax advantages as national workers*. This generous extension of the non-discrimination principle to a positive right of access to social benefits has given rise to considerable litigation and controversy. The Court had to strike a balance between two competing factors. The one was certain benefits based on social security systems financed by contributions and not by taxes. The other was benefits based on social assistance schemes that are supposed to help

---

[31] *Supra* note 22.

[32] Case C-113/89 Rush Portuguesa v Office national d'immigration [1990] ECR I-1417.

[33] Case 379/87 Groener v Ministry of Education and the City of Dublin Vocational Committee [1989] ECR 3967.

[34] Art. 7 (2) of Reg. 1612/68.

the poor and the needy and that are not the result of activity as a worker. In a recent case[35] the Court restricted the concept of worker with regard to access to social advantages. It is only applicable to those persons who have already entered the employment market, not to those who are seeking employment and therefore don't have "a sufficiently close connection" with the employment market of the country where they ask for the benefits.

The case law of the Court has preferred a broad reading of *social advantages*. The main criterion for distinguishing these from other benefits is how they relate to a worker's position, even if an employment relationship does not (yet) exist, or has ceased to exist. It must directly or indirectly benefit the worker and their mobility, for example reductions in fares for large families.[36] The Court justifies this extension with the argument that granting social and tax advantages will increase mobility in the Community.[37] The advantage must in any case benefit the worker as such, and not just a family member.[38] Craig/de Búrca mention *rights of families parasitic on the worker's rights*.[39] On the other hand, in *Reina* the Court went so far as to include in this category an interest-free childbirth loan granted under German law to German nationals in order to stimulate the birth rate of the population. Thus an Italian couple in Germany, one of whom was a worker, was also eligible for the loan.[40]

5. Extension of free movement rights ratione materiae and ratione personae

A number of secondary acts[41], which cannot be referred to in detail here, extend the free movement rights *ratione materiae*, in particular against public law restrictions on entry, stay, and residence. The Court has made clear in several judgements that Member States may require a migrant worker to possess a residence permit or some similar document, but that this document as such does not grant rights flowing from directly applicable Community law. It merely serves to prove the individual's position. Therefore, failure to apply for or prolong such a document does not lead to an automatic refusal of free movement rights.[42] If an administrative fine is attached as a sanction, it must be equivalent to that demanded of nationals and not restrict the substance of the Community law right. In any case, effective judicial protection must

---

[35] Case C-138/02 Brian Francis Collins v Secretary of State for Work and pension [2004] ECR I- (23.3.2004); comment Davies, *ELJ* 2005, 43 at 54.
[36] Case 32/75 Christini v Société Nationale des Chemins de Fer Francais [1975] ECR 1085.
[37] Case 207/78 Criminal proceedings against Even [1979] ECR 2019.
[38] Case 316/85 Centre public d'aide sociale de Courcelles v Lebon [1987] ECR 2811.
[39] At 739.
[40] Case 65/81 Reina v Landeskreditbank Baden-Württemberg [1982] ECR 33.
[41] *E.g.*, Dir. 68/360/EEC *supra* note 5.
[42] Case C-459/99 *supra* note 3 at para 74.

be available for the migrant worker, along with family members, to defend their rights (§ 14).

Community Law[43] extends protection *ratione personae* to the spouse and offspring under the age of 21 years. They can install themselves with the worker provided sufficient housing is available. Family members may also take up any activity as employed persons, even if they are not nationals of any Member State[44]. Children of a Member State national who is or has been employed in the territory of another Member State must be admitted to that State's general educational and vocational system[45].

Community law has in mind a certain concept of family and migrant work. That is, the husband who is a national of one EU country works in another country. His spouse and children live with him in a common household. Indeed, they may also look for work or education, which is accepted by Community law even if they are not EU nationals. Community law respects the unity of the family, which is superior to nationality and thus in accordance with the ECHR[46]. The family concept of the Treaty,[47] however, is a *static* concept. That is, Community law does not take into account problems when parents separate[48], when one of the spouses loses their status as a migrant worker, when other forms of partnership arise, and/or when children move out of their parents' home.

In his opinion of 5 July 2001 to the *Baumbast* case[49], AG Geelhoed pointed to the social changes in family relations and to the inadequacy of Community law to cope with them:

> ... the Community legislature has failed to have regard to cases where the family or working situation changes after entry into the host country....In other words the legislation is in need of overhaul (para 87).

The case concerned a couple consisting of Mr. Baumbast, a German national, and Mrs. Baumbast, a non-national. Their family consisted of one common daughter and one daughter of Mrs. Baumbast. Originally the family had installed itself in the host

---

[43]   Art. 10 - 12 of Reg. 1612/68.
[44]   Per Art. 11 of Reg. 1612/68.
[45]   Per Art. 12 of Reg. 1612/68.
[46]   Art. 8 ECHR.
[47]   Art. 10-12 of Reg. 1612/68.
[48]   In case 267/83 Diatta v Land Berlin [1985] ECR 567 the Court held that the spouse lost protection only after formal divorce, not because of separation of accommodation.
[49]   Case C-413/99 Baumbast and R v Secretary of State for the Home Department [2002] ECR I-7091; comment Reich/Harbacevica, CMLRev 2003, 615.

Member State (the UK) with Mr. Baumbast only as a migrant worker. However, circumstances changed later when Mr. Baumbast started working in a third country. The mother was taking care of the couple's daughters, who were under 21 years of age and wanted to continue their education in the UK. By literal interpretation of Reg. 1612/68, none of them would be protected:

- Mr. Baumbast, because he was working outside the EU and therefore no longer a migrant worker.
- Mrs. Baumbast was not a national.
- Their children did not come under the ambit of protection of Community law.

In the parallel "R" case the parents had in the meantime been divorced, but the husband continued his work in a EU Member country.

The Court maintained that children do not lose protection by the mere fact that one of their parents is no longer a migrant worker, or is now divorced from the caring mother. The Court based its judgment on fundamental rights considerations, namely:

> ... it must be borne in mind that the aim of Regulation No. 1612/68, namely freedom of movement for workers, requires, for such freedom to be guaranteed in compliance with the principles of liberty and dignity, the best possible conditions for the integration of the Community worker's family in the society of the host Member State (para 50).

The Court rejected any restrictive interpretation of Reg. 1612/68. The right to residence was extended to the *primary carer* of the children, in both cases the mother, even if she is not a EU national. This is justified by reference to Art. 8 of the ECHR (§ 12 II). Thus, the new concept of *carer* of the children of a EU national opens the door to a broader understanding of non-traditional partner relationships, which as a result come indirectly under Community law protection.

The right of residence of Mr. Baumbast himself derives from his status as EU citizen (§ 5 VI).

A right of return of the Moroccan spouse of an EU/UK national who was deported from the UK and lived legally in Ireland was discussed in the *Akrich* case[50], clarifying an earlier ruling in *Singh*[51]. Art. 10 of Reg. 1612/68 is not applicable because the spouse was not legally admitted to the UK. A right of return might however accrue on the basis of Art. 8 ECHR if the EU national moves from Ireland to the UK and the marriage is genuine.

---

[50]   Case C-109/01 Secretary of State for the Home Department v Hacene Akrich [2003] ECR I-9607.
[51]   Case C-370/90 Secretary of State for the Home Department v Singh [1992] ECR I-4265.

III.   FREE MOVEMENT OF OTHER ECONOMIC PLAYERS

1.   Self-employed persons

Self-employed persons and members of liberal professions enjoy freedom of establishment under Art. 43 EC, supplemented by a number of directives concerning recognition of diplomas, which we will not deal with here. The original content of these rights was economic, as with other Community rights. Gradually this has changed into a citizen's right. However, this does not have the same value as the freedom to work. As with other free movement rights, there should always be a cross-border element. This is fulfilled if a national from one country is applying in their home state for recognition of a diploma or other qualification from another EU State.[52]

Community law was again concerned with extending these rights *ratione materiae* and *personae*, and with developing a test for justifying still possible restrictions.

The most important ancillary right to the freedom of establishment has been the directly applicable right to residence.[53] This extended to the spouse of a Member State national and their children, according to Directive 73/148/EEC[54]. In these situations, too, the *Baumbas*t reasoning should apply to extend family rights related to establishment. This would be especially so when one family member takes over the care of the children, or if the children want to continue education even though establishment has lapsed.

The Court has developed a number of additional rights, for example:
–   The right to establishment includes the right of access to a regulated profession. This is so, even if EC recognition directives do not cover the profession concerned. For example, in *Vlassopoulou*[55] the Court held that a Greek lawyer, who had studied law in Germany, should have the opportunity to submit his equivalent qualifications for examination in the host state (Germany). Moreover, that state was required to develop a procedure where equivalence of diplomas might be fairly assessed.
–   The *Morgenbesser*-case[56] concerns the recognition of a French law diploma for entry into the stage of *practicanti* in Italy, which is the requirement for practising as a

---

52   Case C-19/92 Kraus v Land Baden-Württemberg [1993] ECR I-1663 at para 15.
53   Case 48/75 Royer [1976] ECR 497.
54   Council Directive 73/148/EEC of 21 May 1973 on the abolition of restrictions on movement and residence within the Community for nationals of Member States with regard to establishment and the provision of services {1973} OJ L 172/14.
55   Case C-340/89 Vlassopoulou v. Ministerium für Justiz, Bundes- und Europaangelegenheiten des Landes Baden-Würtemberg [1991] ECR I-2357.
56   Case C-313/01 Christine Morgenbesser v Consiglio dell'Orinde degli avvocati di Genova [2003] ECR I-13467.

lawyer. Italian law required a diploma from an Italian law school or recognised by it. In referring to the free movement of workers or establishment rules and to its prior case law in *Vlassopoulou*, the Court insisted on the establishment of an examination procedure by the host country where the candidate can show knowledge and qualification in law equivalent to a national diploma.

- *Kraus*[57] concerned a German LLM student who had obtained his diploma in Scotland and applied for recognition in Germany. The practice of rejecting recognition or submitting it to a separate assessment procedure was judged to be contrary to Community law. This was so, even if the diploma was not a formal requirement of access to a regulated profession. Nevertheless, the diploma eased access to a professional career by certifying certain qualifications. The receiving state can only examine whether the diploma has been correctly awarded.
- On the other hand, self-employed persons are denied access to social advantages[58]. These are limited to migrant workers in the traditional sense. However, if the host Member State also extends these advantages to self-employed persons, it cannot deny them to nationals of other Member States in a similar position. The legal basis here arises under the non-discrimination principle (*infra* § 11 II).

Restrictions on the freedom to establishment must meet the proportionality test, clearly developed by the Court in *Gebhard*:[59]

> It follows, however, from the Court's case law that national measures liable to hinder or make less attractive the exercise of fundamental freedoms guaranteed by the Treaty must fulfil four conditions: they must be applied in a non-discriminatory manner; they must be justified by imperative requirements in the general interest; they must be suitable for securing the attainment of the objective which they pursue, and they must not go beyond what is necessary in order to attain it (para 37).

2. Service providers, recipients and consumers

In exceptional cases, a service provider may also fall within the protection of a personal free movement right. According to Art. 50(2) EC, the service provider may *temporarily pursue his activity in the state where the service is provided, under the same conditions as are imposed by that State on its own nationals.* In contrast to the establishment provisions, providing a service relates to a mere temporary activity in another Member State. This does not require full integration into the social and legal order of the receiving state. Therefore, the position of the service provider is weaker than that of

---

[57]   Case C-19/92 *supra* note 52 at para 19.
[58]   Art. 7(2) of Reg. 1612/68.
[59]   Case C-55/94 Reinhard Gebhard v Consiglio dell'Ordine degli Avvocati e Procuratori di Milano [1995] ECR I-4165.

a person wanting to become established. Indeed, the right of residence is limited to the period during which services are provided[60].

In *Carpenter*[61], the grant of entry and residence rights to family members[62] was extended to the spouse of a national of a country that the national provided services from. By a literal reading of Art. 49 EC and Dir. 73/148, Community law did not apply here. This was because the dispute concerned a purely internal situation, and Mrs. Carpenter was not a EU citizen. However, the Court went beyond the narrow wording of Community law to uphold protection of family life. The Court reasoned that, in order for Mr. Carpenter effectively to exercise his fundamental freedom to provide services in other Member countries from his country of residence (the UK), his wife should have a derivative right of residence to make these freedoms effective. The Court went on to say:

> It is clear that the separation of Mr. and Mrs. Carpenter would be detrimental to their family life and, therefore, to the conditions under which Mr. Carpenter exercises a fundamental freedom. That freedom could not be fully effective if Mr. Carpenter were to be deterred from exercising it by obstacles raised in his country of origin to the entry and residence of his spouse (para 39).

An altogether different situation arose in *Cowan*.[63] This case also concerned freedom to provide services, but from the standpoint of the recipient – here, a consumer of tourist services. As such, the consumer enjoys the right to free movement in order to receive these services.[64] If a Member State attaches certain rights to such a – primarily economic – position, then the tourist from another EC country should not be discriminated against in the exercise of these rights. That is, the tourist should be treated in the same way as nationals. The Court went on to say:

> When Community law guarantees a natural person the freedom to go to another Member State the protection of that person from harm in the Member State in question, on the same basis as that of nationals and persons residing there, is a corollary of that freedom of movement... (para 17).

The next case concerned discriminatory regulations for entry to (local) museums in Italy[65]. The Court rejected rules allowing free entry to state museums for EU citizens of pension age, but for local museums limiting this right only to Italian citizens or local

---

[60]   Art. 4 (2) of Dir. 73/148 *supra* note 54.
[61]   Case C-60/00 Mary Carpenter v Secretary of State for the Home Department [2002] ECR I-6279.
[62]   Art. 1 (1) of Dir. 73/148.
[63]   Case 186/87 Cowan v Trésor public [1989] ECR 195.
[64]   Case 286/82 + 26/83 Luisi & Carbone/Ministerio del Tesoro [1984] 377.
[65]   Case C-388/01 Commission v Italy [2003] ECR I-721.

residents of pension age. Such differentiation amounted either to direct discrimination based on nationality, or indirect discrimination based on residence. In both cases, this would affect foreign tourists more seriously than local ones. The discrimination could not be justified because it was based on purely economic reasons.[66]

This case law combines the economic right of free movement (here the freedom to provide and receive services) with other fundamental rights such as protection of family life (Carpenter) or the right to non-discrimination (Cowan/Italian tourists). In doing so, it comes close to transforming the position of economic citizen into that of Union citizen. We will be examining this more closely in § 5. Before that, however, we should briefly look at secondary Community law creating a general right of residence for citizens *before* or *after* they are market citizens. That is, students on the one hand, and retired or other persons on the other.

IV. RESIDENCE OF "PRE"- AND "POST" MARKET CITIZENS

1. Students

Primary Community law already protects certain rights of students, so long as these relate in some way to economic activity, or may be seen as preparation for some future professional activity. In *Gravier*[67] the ECJ regarded a special inscription fee for foreign students as discrimination based on nationality. Since this came within the sphere in which the Treaty applied, it was therefore forbidden (§ 11 II 2). On the other hand, with certain exceptions in relation to their work, students have no right to participate in state grant or maintenance systems, whether under primary law or under relevant legislation[68] – an approach now partially overruled by the *Bider* case.[69]

Students who are nationals of EU countries have a residence right of their own.[70] This right is guaranteed to every student enrolled in a "recognized educational establishment for the principal purpose of following a vocational training course". The wording of the directive is broad enough to encompass nearly any type of studies, including,

---

[66]   Critique Davies, *ELJ* 2005, 43 because the rule also concerned non-resident Italian tourists, there was no proof of an "indirect discrimination" by using the residence criteria for granting free entry.
[67]   Case 293/83 Gravier v City of Liège [1985] ECR 593.
[68]   Art. 7 (2) of Reg. 1612/68; Case 39/86 Lair v Universität Hannover [1988] ECR 3161.
[69]   Case C-209/03 The Queen (on application of Dany Bider) v London Borough of Ealing, Secretary of State for Education and Skills, [2005] ECR I-(15.3.2005).
[70]   According to Council Directive 93/96/EEC *supra* note 11.

for example, post-graduate studies such as the LL.M. program covered by the *Kraus* judgment.[71]

Moreover, the right extends to the spouse and dependent children. However, the student must assure the national authority that "he has sufficient resources to avoid becoming a burden on the social assistance system of the host state". The student must also be covered "by sickness insurance in respect of all risks in the host Member State". A simple declaration without evidence of means is sufficient.[72]

The right of the student to payment of maintenance grants is excluded[73]. Moreover, the right of residence continues[74] for as long as the beneficiaries of that right fulfil the conditions laid down[75]. However, these limitations are supplemented by Community rules on citizenship (*infra* § 5 V).

2. Retired and other persons

Retired persons enjoy a right of residence[76]. Other persons, especially those carrying on self-employed activity, enjoy similar rights[77]. In both cases, the right depends upon proof of sufficient resources, to avoid becoming a burden on the social assistance system.

The beneficiaries and their families must be covered by sickness insurance covering all risks in the host state. A residence right also exists for spouses, along with dependent offspring and dependent relatives in the ascending line of the holder of the right of residence and their spouse. Spouses and dependent offspring also have a right to take up any employed or self-employed activity, even if they are not nationals of a Member State.

---

[71] *Supra* note 52 Kraus.
[72] Case C-424/98 Commission v Italy [2000] ECR I-4001 at para 44.
[73] Art. 3 of Dir. 93/96/EEC.
[74] Art. 4 of Dir. 93/96/EEC.
[75] Art. 1 of Dir. 93/96/EEC.
[76] Council Directive 90/365/EEC *supra* note 11.
[77] Directive 90/364/EEC *supra* note 12.

§ 5. THE CONCEPT OF UNION CITIZENSHIP: PRESENT POSITION

I. SOME UNCERTAINTIES

Union citizenship – is it a "flag which fails to cover its cargo", as Laurence Gormley suggests[78]? Or can it be regarded, as Joe Shaw[79] has concluded, as "a positive contribution to the legitimacy of the European Union, which an active and participatory concept of social citizenship may make"? In a broader sense, is citizenship a mere metaphor "as creation of another type of expressiveness", perhaps even "a fiction as the creation of another type of semantic reality" in the sense of the Flemish legal philosopher Jan Broekman[80]? Or can it be regarded as a source of rights extending the scope of citizens' rights in the European Treaties?

A first reading of the concept of citizenship, as introduced by the Maastricht Treaty and reinforced by the Amsterdam Treaty, seems to suggest its character as a metaphor. The Maastricht Treaty[81] simply affirms that "citizenship of the Union is hereby established. Every person holding the nationality of a Member State shall be a citizen of the Union". The Amsterdam Treaty added the following sentence: "Citizenship of the Union shall complement and not replace national citizenship".

The Treaty makes it clear that citizens of the Union enjoy the rights it confers, and are subject to the duties it imposes. The most important rights relate to:
- free movement[82];
- the right to vote and to stand as a candidate for municipal elections and elections to the European Parliament[83];
- rights of diplomatic and consular protection[84], and
- the right of petition to, and protection by, an ombudsman of the EP[85].

Nothing is said about corresponding duties and responsibilities (§ 21).

---

[78] In: Kapteyn/VerLoren van Themaat, Introduction to the Law of the European Communities, 3rd Ed. 1999 at 157.
[79] Shaw, in: Collected Courses of the European Academy VI-1, 1998 at 346.
[80] A Philosophy of European law, 1999 at 142.
[81] Art. 17 EC.
[82] Art. 18 EC.
[83] Art. 19 EC.
[84] Art. 20 EC.
[85] Art. 21 EC.

It is also well known that some of the rights included in Union citizenship have already been developed by ECJ practice, in its extensive interpretation of the fundamental freedoms of the EC Treaty (§ 4), and rights to non-discrimination based on nationality and gender (§ 13). The combination of these developments was highlighted by the *Cowan* case of 1989[86] (§ 4 II 2). What did the Treaty[87] add to this established right of the European citizen in the role of consumer? Has a paradigm change taken place? That is, a move from granting rights not only to the market citizen (*bourgeois*) but also to the "Union citizen" *stricto sensu* not playing an economic role (*citoyen*)?[88]

II. THE LEGAL CORE OF UNION CITIZENSHIP

From the very wording of the Treaty[89] and the history of its drafting, one is tempted to conclude that Union citizenship is nothing more than a corollary of nationality of one of the Member States. As the German author Kluth has expressed it: " This (citizenship) always attaches to Member State nationality."[90] This is in accordance with the ECJ's *Micheletti* judgment[91] handed down in 1992, parallel to the adoption of the Maastricht Treaty. In this judgment the Court made it clear that Member States, and Member States only, may create and abolish nationality. However, they may not put restrictions on it if another Member State has already granted nationality. The Court said:

> (...) it is not permissible for the legislation of a Member State to restrict the effects of the grant of the nationality of another Member State by imposing an additional condition for the recognition of that nationality with a view to the exercise of the fundamental freedoms provided for in the Treaty[92].

Closa[93] therefore comes to the conclusion that citizenship of the Union might be characterized as "a [derived] condition of nationality". The Union, or Community, has no competence to establish criteria of its own on granting citizenship as a corollary of nationality.

---

[86]   See Case 186/87 Cowan v Trésor Public [1989] ECR 195 *supra* 63.
[87]   Art. 18 EC.
[88]   O'Leary, *CMLRev* 1995, 519 at 524.
[89]   Art. 17 EC.
[90]   in: Chr. Callies/M. Ruffert (Hrsgs.), Kommentar zum EUV, 1999, Art. 17 Rdnr. 45.
[91]   Case C-369/90 Micheletti v Delegación del Gobierno en Cantabria, [1992] ECR I-4239; case C-192/99 R v Secretary of State for the Home Dpt. ex parte Mangjit Kaur [2001] ECR I-1237.
[92]   At para 10.
[93]   Closa, *CMLRev* 1995, 487 at 510.

The mutual recognition principle of Member State nationality is established by international law, not Community law. This involves both a positive and a negative side. That is, once a Member State has recognized a citizen as its national, this decision should be respected Union-wide, even in the case of dual nationality, as shown in *Micheletti*. By contrast, mutual recognition in the negative sense means that once a Member State has revoked nationality according to its own law and procedural requirements, then this decision has to be respected by every other Member State, unless a new bond of nationality to another state has been established.

III. OTHER CRITERIA FOR ESTABLISHING RIGHTS AND DUTIES IN THE UNION

Union citizenship does not of course exclude rights of (natural) persons under EC law being established by other criteria, especially those based on the concept of residence. This is particularly true, as we shall see in Chapter III, with fundamental rights, as well as rights of workers and consumers. The Amsterdam Treaty, following its predecessor to that extent, has created different subjective rights. These are not based on the formula *nationality = Union citizenship*, but on other criteria, especially residence.

The Treaty:
- provides that "each Member State shall ensure that the principle of equal pay for male and female workers for equal work or work of equal value is applied" (§ 11 III). This right to equal pay clearly does not depend on the nationality of the worker, but rather on work done in the Union;[94]
- contains[95] a "right of consumers to information, education and to organize themselves in order to safeguard their interests" without any reference to citizenship or even residence (§ 17);
- gives[96] "any citizen of the Union, and any natural or legal person residing or having its registered office in a Member State, the right to address individually or in association with other citizens or persons a petition to the European Parliament;"
- grants[97] a right of access to European Parliament, Council and Commission documents to any citizen of the Union and any natural or legal person residing or having a registered office in a Member State (§ 18);

---

[94] This was recognized by Art. 5 (1) of the Brussels Convention as amended (§ 14 II), cf. for an interpretation case C-383/95 Petrus Wilhelmus Rutten v Cross Medical Ltd. [1997] ECR I-57.
[95] Art. 153 para 1 EC.
[96] Art. 194 EC.
[97] Art. 255 EC.

– declares[98] that from "1 January 1999 on, Community acts on the protection of individuals with regard to the processing of personal data and the free movement of such data shall apply to the institutions and bodies set up by, or on the basis of this Treaty".

Secondary Community law, for instance Directives on worker, consumer, health, and safety protection (§ 13), contain many subjective rights of citizens that depend not on nationality but on other criteria, such as residence. The same is true with international or European conventions, for example on jurisdiction, or on conflict of laws. The concept of residence supplements – and in certain cases supersedes – the traditional concept of nationality/citizenship as a basis for granting subjective rights to individuals. Only a rather limited number of rights depend on citizenship. These, though, are important – especially free movement and voting rights.

IV. VERTICAL ADDED VALUE TO CITIZENSHIP

How is the concept of citizenship important in the development of EC law after Maastricht? Has it given a new impulse to creating, extending or safeguarding citizens' rights? Or has it merely given new rhetoric to old concepts of free movement (§ 4)?

In *Skanavi*[99], its first judgment dealing with citizenship, the Court refused to discuss application of the then Art. 8, which it considered to be residual. The first express use of citizenship by the Court to extend the rights of Union citizens was prepared from earlier obiter dicta by its AGs Léger and Ruiz-Jarabo Colomer[100]. The Court applied it in the *Sala* judgment of 12.5.1998.[101] The case concerned a Spaniard, resident in Germany, unemployed, and claiming a German child-raising allowance. Under German social security law, her application was refused because she did not possess a valid residence permit. The Court did not accept this limiting condition upon access to child allowance. A reading of Art. 17 on Union citizenship, in conjunction with Art. 12 EC on non-discrimination, put her under protection of the Treaty, which could not be denied by absence of a permanent residence permit.

---

[98]   Art. 286 EC.

[99]   Case C-193/94 Criminal proceedings against Skanavi Chryssanthakopoulos [1996] ECR I-929.

[100] See AG Léger in his opinion in C-214/94 Boukhalfa v Bundesrepublik Deutschland [1996] ECR I-2253 at para 63 (where the status of a Belgian national working in the German embassy in Algiers had to be treated under the free movement rules); and AG Ruiz-Jarabo Colomer's opinion in C-65 & 111/95 R v. Secretary of State for the Home Department ex parte Shingara and Radion, [1997] ECR I-3343 at para 34.

[101] Case C-85/96 Maria Martínez Sala v Freistaat Bayern [1998] ECR I-2691.

In continuing the tradition as developed in *Cowan*, the Court used Art. 8/8a (now Art. 17/18 EC) to extend protection against discrimination based on nationality to every Union citizen; the former somewhat construed connection with one of the free movement rights is abandoned, so extending the scope of persons protected.

The Court followed the same approach in the *Bickel and Franz* judgment of 4.11.1998[102]. Both persons, Mr. Bickel being a lorry driver of Austrian nationality, Mr. Franz a German tourist, violated Italian law while in the province of Bolzano, where German is spoken. By special regulation based on an Italian-Austrian agreement concluded well before their membership in the EU, the German language is to have the same status as Italian in the Alto Adige region. This means that German-speaking Italian citizens are entitled to a court hearing in German. Could this also be extended to the defence of Mr. Bickel and Mr. Franz before a local court in the province of Bolzano? Both AG Jacobs and the Court were willing to extend the prohibition against discrimination[103] to all nationals coming under the free movement rules[104]. AG Jacobs referred to *Cowan* and extended it to the right of a Union citizen accused in criminal proceedings. Both the Advocate General and the Court agreed that in refusing to allow German-speaking citizens from Austria or Germany to use their mother language in the province of Bolzano, where this was allowed to German-speaking Italians, amounted to a discrimination based on nationality. The Court said[105]:

> In that regard, the exercise of the right to move and reside freely in another Member State is enhanced if the citizens of the Union are able to use a given language to communicate with the administrative and judicial authorities of a state on the same footing as its nationals.

This statement by the Court appears rather sweeping. However, two later judgments – *Calfa*[106] and *Wijsenbeek*[107] – were somewhat more restrictive in applying the concept of citizenship. Indeed, the Court used rather traditional approaches, even though the referring Greek and Dutch courts expressly mentioned citizenship as a basis for supplementary free movement rights, disregarding the economic status of the persons involved.

---

[102]   Case C-274/96 Criminal proceedings against H.O. Bickel und U. Franz [1998] ECR I-7637; comment Bulterman *CMLRev* 1999, 1325.
[103]   Art. 12 EC.
[104]   Per Art. 18 EC.
[105]   Para 16 of the judgment.
[106]   Case C-348/96 Criminal proceedings against Donatella Calfa [1999] ECR I-11; comment Costello *CMLRev* 2000, 817.
[107]   Case C-378/97 Criminal proceedings against Florus Ariel Wijsenbeek [1999] ECR I-6207.

V. EXTENSION OF CITIZENSHIP *RATIONE MATERIAE*

The analysis of the Court's early jurisprudence reveals some hesitancy in fully applying the concept of citizenship by extending citizens' rights. This is especially so in the area of free movement. The opinions of the Advocates General seem to go much further, at least in rhetoric, although perhaps to a lesser extent in substance. The *Grzelczyk* case[108] demonstrates the dynamism inherent in citizenship. The case concerns student benefits refused to a French national studying in Belgium. During the first three years, he earned money to pay for his studies. In the final year he wanted to concentrate on his exams, rather than spend time jobbing around. He therefore asked for a special benefit called *minimex*, available to Belgian students under similar conditions. However, the relevant statutory basis[109] (§ 4 III 1) expressly excludes entitlement to payment of maintenance grants. Could this limitation be overcome by directly applicable Community law, in the shape of *social citizenship* as a corollary to Union citizenship[110] as already suggested by Borchardt[111]? AG Alber took the traditional approach of linking Community rights to free movement of workers, as in *Calfa*. That is, he did not make the link with an autonomous concept of citizenship. According to his opinion, a student as citizen might very well be entitled to non-discriminatory treatment concerning student benefits such as the minimex. However, the Member State is entitled to revoke these if the status of a resident is in doubt. The right of residence of the student would therefore not be absolute, but would, rather, be subject to reasonable limitations imposed by the host state.

The Full Court judgment[112] is not concerned with whether or not Mr. Grzelczyk is a worker. Instead, the Court widens the path opened by *Sala* in developing a right of its own, namely of the Union citizen being entitled to non-discriminatory treatment with regard to social benefits. Moreover, it expressly rejects the submission that "the concept of citizenship has no autonomous content" (para 21), as proposed by several Member States,[113] including Belgium and Denmark. Instead the Court maintains that:

> Union citizenship is destined to be the [fundamental status of nationals of the Member States], enabling those who find themselves in the same situation to enjoy the same

---

[108] Case C-184/99 Rudy Grzelczyk v. le Centre public d'aide sociale d'Ottignies-Louvain-la-Neuve [2001] ECR I-6193; cf. Borchardt, *NJW* 2000, 2057.
[109] Art. 3 of the Dir. 93/96.
[110] Per Art. 17 EC.
[111] Borchardt at 2060.
[112] *Supra* note 108 Grzelczyk.
[113] For presentation of the different Member States' opinions, see Grzelczyk, *supra* note 108 at paras 21-25.

treatment in law irrespective of their nationality, subject to such exceptions as are expressly provided for (para 31).

Grzelczyk is an important judgment insofar as it recognizes for the first time that citizenship contains a positive element, in that it allows nationals of other Member States access to social benefits beyond existing secondary Community law. A new judgment[114] extends the non-discrimination principle to assistance (subsidised loans or grants) provided to students lawfully resident in the host Member State to cover their maintenance costs, thus indirectly overruling the earlier *Lair* case (§ 4 IV 1). The country of residence may impose certain time limits (e.g. 3 years of residence) without however making the exercise of this right impossible, provided that the student has established a genuine link with this state.

More recent case-law[115] allows Member States to impose a residence requirement for EU citizens before receiving social advantages under the non-discrimination principle of *Grzelczyk* if based on objective considerations that are independent of the nationality of the persons concerned. This is to avoid a potential abuse of access to non-contributory social benefits by persons who don't have a sufficiently close link with the country where they apply.

VI. EXTENSIONS *RATIONE PERSONAE*

In *D'Hoop*[116], the Court extended its reasoning to migrant nationals of one Member State. Here, a student seeking first employment was denied a certain social benefit called "tideover allowance" because she had received her secondary education in another Member State. Normally the free movement rules do not apply to a Member State's own nationals. Thus, the issue was whether Ms. D'Hoop, a Belgian national who had completed her *baccalauréat* in France, could be excluded from a benefit that was both available to Belgians having studied in Belgium and to foreigners under the same conditions. The Court wrote:

> The situations falling within the scope of Community law include those involving the exercise of the fundamental freedoms guaranteed by the Treaty, in particular those involving the freedom to move and reside within the territory of the Member States, as conferred by Art. 18 EC ... By linking the grant of tide-over allowances to the condition of having obtained the required diploma in Belgium, the national legislation thus places at a

---

[114] Case C-209/03 The Queen (on application of Dany Bider) v London Borough of Ealing, Secretary of State for Education and Skills, [2005] ECR I-(15.3.2005).

[115] Case C-138/02 Brian Francis Collins v Secretary of State for Work and Pensions [2004] ECR I-(23.3.2004).

[116] Case C-224/98 Marie-Nathalie D'Hoop v Office national de l'emploi, [2002] ECR I-6191.

§ 6. CITIZENSHIP, FREE MOVEMENT, NEW MEMBER STATES AND BEYOND

I. EUROPE AGREEMENTS AS A PRELIMINARY STAGE AND THEIR DIRECT EFFECT

Since citizenship depends on nationality, the nationals of accession countries will only be EU citizens after accession. This means that nationals of these countries could not invoke the fundamental rights of free movement and residence granted to EU citizens[122] and by the specific provisions on free movement of persons, that is on workers, on establishment, and on provision of services[123]. Thus, nationals of accession countries were in a similar position to that of any third country national. Only after accession will citizenship be extended to nationals of new member countries – with several transitional restrictions and limitations. These will be referred to later (IV).

It is of course legally possible to extend rights to third country nationals in the EU by international treaties. The most important instruments in this respect have been association agreements between the EU and third countries. The latest round of treaties under international law has been the Europe Agreements between the EU and accession states. This includes the Europe Agreement concluded with Latvia[124], which will provide the basis for further discussion in the following paragraphs.

The Europe Agreements (EA), today relevant in relation to Bulgaria, Romania and, recently, Croatia,[125] aim to prepare accession states for EU membership, and to help them take over the *acquis communautaire*.[126] Although this corresponds to an extension of the rights of nationals and residents of these countries, it does so in a limited way. That is, in an EC context, these rights have direct effect only in those cases where they are specific and unconditional enough to be invoked before national and European jurisdictions. However, with regard to accession countries their enforceability depends on the status of international law in the respective jurisdictions.

The Europe Agreement deals with movement of workers, establishment, and supply of services. However, in contrast to normal EC terminology, it says nothing about

---

[122]   Per Art. 18 EC.
[123]   Art. 39, 43 and 49 EC.
[124]   Europe Agreement establishing an Association between the European Communities and their Member States, of the one part, and the Republic of Lativa, of the other part [1998] OJ L 26/1. The other Europe Agreements with candidate countries contained nearly identical provisions.
[125]   [2005] OJ L 26 (Stabilisation and Association Agreement of 28.1.2005).
[126]   For a discussion cf. Hedemann-Robinson, *CMLRev* 2001, 525 at 570-576.

freedom of movement. At once it becomes clear how the difference in both spirit and content affects EU nationals seeking access to the EU labour market, and residence in EU Member States.

The EA grants EA citizens legally employed in a member country the right to non-discrimination. Legally resident spouses and children of a legally employed worker will have access to the labour market during the period of the worker's authorized stay of employment.

The EA make an important distinction. That is, it is up to individual Member States to grant an employment permit to nationals of accession countries. The Member State determines access to the labour market[127]. As yet, no Community authority to do so exists. Once a permit is granted, Community law foresees upgrading the legal status of workers and their family members. Direct effect cannot be denied, because the provision is sufficiently precise and self-executive to be invoked before courts of law.[128] Thus, it does not need to be concretised by decisions of the Association Council as foreseen in the Europe Agreements. Under existing European law, the right of non-discrimination on the basis of nationality, gender, and race enjoys a broad sphere of application (§ 11). In particular, it forbids both direct and *indirect discrimination*, and can be invoked not only against the state but also against private parties, such as employers.[129]

The judgment in *Pokrzeptowicz-Meyer*[130] confirmed the direct effect of the non-discrimination provision of the EA with Poland. The Court held this provision to be clear, specific and unconditional enough to be applied directly, without further implementing legislation. Any other interpretation would deny the *effet utile* of the provision. Even if such interpretation leads to an imbalance in rights and obligations between the EU on the one hand and EA countries on the other, this does not exclude direct effect because such imbalance is an express aim of the EA. In the opinion of the Court, the non-discrimination provision should be interpreted in the same sense as the similar provision in Art. 39 EC concerning free movement of workers. This means that both direct and indirect discrimination is forbidden.

The case in point concerned a Polish lecturer in the Polish language at the University of Bielefeld. According to German legislation in force at the time the contract was entered into, he had a fixed-term employment contract for teaching. Generally, such

---

[127] Case C-438/00 Deutscher Handballbund v Maros Kolpak [ECR] 2003 I-4135.
[128] In this sense Hedemann-Robinson at 573.
[129] Case C-281/98 R. Angonese v Cassa di Rispaarmio di Bolzano [ECR] 2000 I-4139.
[130] Case C-162/00 Land Nordrhein-Westphalen v Beata Pokrzeptowicz-Meyer [2002] ECR I-1049.

contracts had to be individually justified by objective grounds specifically listed in the legislation. Moreover, these grounds were held to exist regularly for foreign-language assistants. Since such differentiation typically occurred with lecturers of foreign origin, this amounted to indirect discrimination, which is forbidden.[131] At the end of the day, the Court was not convinced by the argument that this discrimination occurred before the EA between Poland and the EU entered into force. Even though the EA could not be applied retroactively, it nevertheless had continuing legal effects on the employment contract; therefore, the clause on its termination without individual objective grounds was ineffective.

This judgment substantially strengthens the position of EA nationals *legally* employed in one of the EU Member States. However, it clearly does not imply rights to free movement and non-discrimination for workers as such, which can only be guaranteed by the accession treaties (sub III 3). But what it does mean is that the many EA nationals already in an employment situation based on national or international law can now directly invoke their right to non-discrimination. Therefore, they are protected against employment conditions that differ without good reason from those of EU nationals.[132]

In her opinion in the *Kolpak* case[133], AG Stix-Hackl also applied the direct effect of a similar provision in the EA with Slovakia. In this case the relevant provision, which appeared in the rules of the German professional handball league, limited the number of third-country players in an official championship tournament. In the AG's opinion, the argument in *Bosman*[134] can be transferred in full to the situation of legally resident nationals from EA countries. In its judgment of 8 May 2003, the Court took a similar view.

II. ESTABLISHMENT: A NEW WAY TO FREE MOVEMENT AND CITIZENSHIP?

Persons coming under the establishment rules may enjoy certain supplementary rights. Several cases before the European Court recognize that the right to non-discrimination

---

[131]   The Court referred expressly to its former case law concerning teachers of foreign language, e.g., case C-272/92 Maria Chiara Spotti v Freistaat Bayern [1993] ECR I-5185.
[132]   See Reich, *The European Constitution*, RGSL Working Paper 18, 2004 at 25.
[133]   C-438/00 Deutscher Handballbund/Maros Kolpak [2003] ECR I-4135 supra 127.
[134]   Case C-415/93 *supra* note 22.

has direct effect.[135] Even more importantly, in its *Barcosi* judgment the Court – against the opinion of its Advocates General – developed a derivative right of entry and stay:

> The right of a Czech national to take up and pursue economic activities not coming within the labour market presupposes that the person has a right to enter and remain in the host country ... Art. 45 (3) of the Europe Agreement with the Czech Republic, in wording similar or identical to that of Art. 43 EC, does indeed mean that a right of entry and residence are conferred as corollaries of the right of establishment (paras 44 and 50).

As a result, the Court applies the principles of the *Royer* case law[136] to the Europe Agreements. That is, the right of establishment requires a right of entry and stay. The two are linked, and are a consequence of the four freedoms directly guaranteed by the EC. However, practice in Member States can differ quite substantially from this generous, though (arguably) theoretical, advance.

The Europe Agreements still allow certain restrictions on entry, stay and establishment "provided that – in so doing – they do not apply them in a manner as to nullify or impair the benefits accruing to any party under the terms of a specific provision of the Agreement". Although the importance and scope of this proviso was extensively discussed in the above litigation, clarity in the questions concerned did not result.[137] The Court, again unlike its AGs, tries to avoid a mere formalistic attitude, which would exclude from establishment persons who only apply for a residence permit at the border, or in the host country, rather than in their home state. The picture differs if nationals of EA countries enter a EU country under false pretences, for example claiming to be a tourist, a student or limited time worker, but in reality intending to become established. Indeed, this may be a reason to expel them, but the national authority still has to accept applications in "another state" and respect fundamental rights.[138]

In the *Panatova* case[139] the Court had to decide about a Dutch system which linked a permanent resident permit for persons from EA countries to establish themselves in the Netherlands with a prior temporary permit received in the home country. In distinguishing its *Barcosi* judgment and against the opinion of AG Poiares Maduro

---

[135]   Cases C-257/99 R v Secretary of State for the Home Dpt. *ex parte* Julius Barkoci and Marcel Malik, C-63/99 ex parte Wieslaw and Elzbieta Gloszczuk, C –235/99 *ex parte* Eleanova Ivanova Kondova [2001] ECR I-6557, 6369, 6427.
[136]   Case 48/75 Royer [1976] ECR 497.
[137]   This is criticized by Weiss in his annotation to the above-mentioned judgments in *EuZW* 2001 696 at 704.
[138]   Para 85 of the *Gloszczuk* and 90 of the *Kondova* judgments *supra* note 136.
[139]   Case C-327/02 Lili Georgieva Panatova et al. v Minister voor Vreemdelingenzaken en Integratie [2004] ECR I-(16.11.2004).

the Court found justification of such a system of prior entry control with the need to avoid "easy circumvent(ions)" of the national rules of entry and stay by persons coming to a Member country as tourists and then applying for residence as self-employed persons, thereby eliminating the "practical effect" of the relevant provisions of the EA (para 33).

The main restriction to establishment lies in the limited nature of the right itself. For it excludes any access to the labour market and any social benefits or similar entitlements. Any attempt to evade this restriction can indeed be rejected and sanctioned by national authorities. The right to establishment is therefore limited to persons who, by becoming established, can earn a living by themselves, for example as gardeners (*Barkoci*), cleaning personal (*Gloszczuk*) or even Amsterdam prostitutes (*Jany*).[140] Immigration authorities can therefore monitor whether applicants from EA countries can prove that their financial means, or business plans to establish themselves as self-employed persons, are sufficiently viable.

Access to regulated professions coming under EU recognition directives cannot be automatically granted, because this depends on a decision of the Association Council. No decision is available in this respect.

III. CITIZENSHIP AND FREE MOVEMENT IN THE ACCESSION REGIMES

1. Controversies

At the insistence of the German and Austrian governments, full citizenship rights will only be extended to nationals of acceding member countries after a seven-year transition period. However, it is doubtful whether this arrangement conforms to the spirit of creating a greater Europe after the fall of the Soviet regime. For a new European or Communitarian spirit should surely be based on the fundamental freedoms and equal rights of all its citizens. If citizenship is linked to nationality of Member States, then the fact of becoming a member of the EU should automatically confer on a country's nationals the full ambit of rights foreseen, and the corresponding free movement rights. Indeed, the European Charter of Fundamental Rights confirms this position. Thus, all union citizens have the right to look for work, to work, to establish themselves, and to provide services, in every Member State, Art. II-75(2) Draft Constitution. This is subject, of course, to legally imposed restrictions meeting the proportionality and essence of rights tests.

---

[140] Case C-268/99 Aldona Malgorzata Jany and others v Staatssecretaris van Justitie [2001] ECR I-8615.

On the other hand, it has to be admitted that restrictions on citizens' rights to free movement and residence do exist, Art. 18. This may in practice result from secondary law, and, even more important, from accession treaties themselves. A similar observation is true with regard to the provision on free movement of workers. Consequently, the accession treaties may in effect legally restrict and/or postpone the wide range of rights guaranteed under this provision. These include the abundant and citizen-friendly case law of the Court (§ 4), and specific positive rights. However, this is nothing new: it all happened before in the case of Greece, Spain and Portugal.

2. Compromises

In the result, agreement has been achieved in accession negotiations between the Community institutions, the Member States and the Accession countries. That is, the accession treaties[141] foresee a transition period. Detailed provisions negotiated with Latvia annexed to Art. 24 of the Act of Accession, which are similar to other new Member States, provide for a differentiated transition regime. This consists of a two-year period after accession, where free movement of Latvian workers depends on the autonomous decision of the respective Member State. These measures are to be reviewed by the Council before the end of the second year, on the basis of a report from the Commission. On its completion, the "old" Member States can notify the Commission whether they intend to continue to apply national measures; this is possible till the fifth year after accession. Latvia (and the other new Member States) may request one further review. Member States can invoke an additional two-year period of restrictions on free movement, after notification to the Commission in case of "serious disturbances of the labour market or threat thereof".

Additionally, a safeguard clause will enable a EU country already applying the *acquis* to restrict free movement until the end of the seventh year after accession. This would be in cases "undergoing or foreseeing disturbances on its labour market which could seriously threaten the standard of living or level of employment in a given region or occupation". This, in normal cases, will require a request to the Commission, and its decision. "In urgent and exceptional cases", the member states may decide on their own, "followed by a reasoned *ex- post* notification to the Commission".

Consequently, free movement of workers as a Community right of its own will only come into full effect after a period of seven years. There are serious doubts as to how these vague concepts allowing a restriction of this "fundamental" Community right of free movement can be effectively controlled by the Court. These restrictions are somewhat "sweetened" by the introduction of a *préférence communautaire*, with

---

[141]   Published in [2003] OJ L 236.

Member States introducing a preference for nationals from new Member States over non-EU nationals in access to their labour markets. On the other hand, new Member states will have the same rights *vis-à-vis* those countries applying "national measures".

With regard to freedom to provide services, for example by posted workers, there will be no general transition regime. However, Austria and Germany will be authorized to apply restrictive national measures in certain sensitive areas after notifying the Commission. In Germany, these concern the construction business and industrial cleaning. In Austria, the list is extended also to cover horticultural services, manufacture of metal structures, security activities, home nursing, and other social work and activities without accommodation.

Even if primary and secondary EC law may impose restrictions on free movement and residence, such restrictions must always respect the principle of proportionality. On that basis alone, it would appear that the optional "2 + 3 + 2" regime by far exceeds what is necessary to achieve harmonious integration of EA nationals into the EU's free movement regime[142]. Moreover, the ECJ's interpretation of the respective provisions of the EA, namely on non-discrimination and establishment, should be taken into account in preparing Member States for access to their territory of EA nationals. These already enjoy substantial rights under the EA, which should prepare and ease full integration, a point on which the ECJ has particularly insisted in its latest case law concerning the direct effect of the EAs. Therefore, if nationals of new Member countries are admitted to the labour market, they enjoy the same rights and protection as its own nationals.[143]

IV. CITIZENSHIP FOR NON-NATIONALS: CAN IT EXIST BEYOND THE NATION STATE?

1. Permanent legal residence as a substitute for nationality?

The question of citizenship, the rights attached to it, and the particular problems which EA countries face before and after accession have so far only been discussed with regard to nationals. However, it is also relevant to discuss the status of long-term residents in the context of the present EU. The European Parliament has recommended abolition of differentiation between Member State nationals and other residents of the Union.[144] Moreover, the European Council's Tampere summit of 15 and

---

[142] For a critique, see Reich/Harbacevica, *Europarättslig Tidskrift* 2002, 411 at 429.
[143] Inglis, *CMLRev* 2004, 937 at 967, 970; Reich *supra* note 132.
[144] Cf. Kingston, "Citizenship in the EU", in: Gardener, *Citizenship*, 1997 at 315.

16 October 1999 addressed the issue of legally resident third country nationals, stressing the need to develop a common approach to ensure integration of third country nationals lawfully resident in the EU. In particular, the summit advocated a "more vigorous integration policy" concerning economic, social and cultural issues. This should aim at granting them rights and obligations comparable to those of EU citizens. These would include the right of residence, education rights, economic rights and non-discrimination *vis-à-vis* nationals of the host country.[145] Such a move would imply that a third country national, once legally entitled to work and reside in one Member State, can then do so in all Member States. This would, of course, include family members. In this way, the concept of citizenship would be superseded by the concept of (legal and permanent) residence.

However, the *Charter of Fundamental Rights in the EU* (§ 12 III) has not taken up these tendencies. It provides[146] that "freedom of movement and residence may be granted, in accordance with the Treaty establishing the EC, to nationals of third countries legally resident in the territory of a Member State." The explanations refer expressly to the relevant Treaty provisions[147], thus leaving the Community legislature to decide on this status.

As the next step in the direction of extending rights of third country nationals living legally in the Union on a long-term basis, the Commission Communication of 22 Nov. 2000[148] should be mentioned. The Commission discusses measures "to ensure fair treatment of third country nationals residing legally on the territories of the Member States through an integration policy aimed at granting them rights and obligations comparable to those of EU citizens[149]."

2. New orientations in legal literature

An interesting study on European citizenship by Marie José Garot[150] has developed an intriguing new theory, which tries to separate nationality and citizenship. She bases her analysis on French and US experiences, where residence has historically been regarded as a substitute to formal nationality, at least if certain criteria of time and permanent integration are met. If residence is taken as a central criterion for citizenship, then it is important to define it exactly. Here, an autonomous Community

---

[145]   Editorial comment, *CMLRev* 1999, 1119 at 1122.
[146]   Art. 45(2)=Art. II-105(2) of the Draft Constitution.
[147]   Art. 18 and 63 (4) EC.
[148]   Communication from the Commission to the Council and the European Parliament on a Community immigration policy Com (2000) 757 final.
[149]   At p. 9.
[150]   *La citoyenneté de l'Union européenne*, 1999.

law interpretation is required, distinguished from the concept of nationality, or citizenship. Garot suggests that this concept be formalized so as to extend the basic community law principle of mutual recognition to persons, as well as goods, services, and capital (§ 8 IV), adding nationality by relying on *Micheletti* and Art. 17 EC. As a result, rights that now only attach to market citizens could be extended to non-market citizens from third countries.[151]

The study by Helen Staples[152] comes to similar conclusions, after first having analysed the existing unsatisfactory state of Community law. She proposes a separation of nationality and Union citizenship for a number of reasons:
- Third country nationals contribute in the same way as nationals to the social policies of the states where they legally reside, and therefore contribute towards the economic aims of European integration.
- Decision-making in the European polity affects third country nationals legally residing in the Union in nearly the same way as nationals.
- Globalisation has brought about a plurality of citizenship, and has separated ("decoupled") democratic governance from nationality.

She proposes an amendment to the Amsterdam Treaty that would read:

> Citizenship of the Union is hereby established. A person holding the nationality of a Member State *or who has been lawfully resident in the territory of a Member State for five years* shall be a citizen of the Union.

This author has voiced strong support for a new such concept of citizenship based on residence. However, this would imply a new impetus in Community immigration policy.[153]

3. The status of "long-term resident" – Directive 2003/109

In dealing with these different developments, the Commission has proposed a directive to create the status of long-term resident under EC law.[154] Under the proposal, a third country national would be entitled to nearly the same free movement rights as an EU citizen, including equal treatment and the right to take up residence in any Member State, after 5 years of legal residence. The administrative machinery would involve

---

[151] At 340.
[152] *Legal Status of Third Country Nationals Resident in the EU*, 1999 at 335-349.
[153] Reich, *Union Citizenship*, 2001; ibid. *supra* note 132.
[154] Proposal for a Council Directive concerning the status of third-country nationals who are long-term residents Com (2001) 127 final [2001] OJ C 240/79. It would not apply to the UK, Ireland and Denmark.

issuing a specific document, the EC residence permit. Art. 12 grants them equal treatment rights, including:
- access to employment and self-employed activity;
- education and vocational training;
- recognition of diplomas;
- social protection, social assistance, and social and tax benefits.

This would imply that they benefit from nearly the same *acquis* as EU citizens (§ 4 II 4).

The right of residence in other Member States is guaranteed, subject to certain conditions and restrictions. The proposal requires "exercise of an employment in an employed or self-employed capacity". This does not as such guarantee access to the labour market, unless they fall under some other provisions. To that extent, third country nationals' status would be lower than that of EU citizens. Family members enjoy a right to accompany or join them. However, election rights are exempted, unless Member States individually decide otherwise.

The Commission proposal concretises the resolutions of the Tampere summit and the Recommendation of the Committee of Ministers of the Council of Europe of September 2000. The debates in the Council have advanced so far that there has been political agreement to adopt a "Council Directive concerning the status of third country nationals who are long term residents", though with some additional restrictions and conditions.

In the meantime, Directive 2003/109/EC has been adopted on 25 November 2003.[155] Art. 2 (a) defines a 'third country national' as "any person who is not a citizen of the Union within the meaning of Art. 17 (1) EC". According to Art. 11 (4) equal treatment in respect of social assistance and social protection may be limited to "core benefits", thus departing from the more generous proposal of the Commission. These persons have the right to receive a residence permit, conditional on sufficient resources in order not to become a burden on the social assistance system, and sickness insurance. They may be required to take language courses. Family members according to Dir. 2003/86/EC[156] may accompany or join the long-term resident. The definition of family members is contained in Art. 4 and may be extended to unmarried partners with a third-country national "with whom the sponsor is in a duly attested stable long-term relationship", subject to evidence under Art. 5 (2). With regard to residence in other

---

[155] Council Directive 2003/109/EC of 25 November 2003 "concerning the status of third-country nationals who are long-term residents" [2004] OJ L 16/44.
[156] Council Directive 2003/86/EC of 22 September 2003 on the right to family reunion, [2003] OJ L 251/12. It is based on Art. 63 and therefore does not apply to the UK, Ireland, and Denmark.

Member States, long-term residents will be allowed access to the labour market, but there may be safeguard clauses attached to that. These rights will be extended to family members. These persons have the right to receive a residence permit. The Directive must be implemented by 23 January 2006.

CHAPTER II. OPEN MARKETS

Table of Contents

§ 7. FREE MOVEMENT (1) – THE MEMBER STATES' TRUST AND SUPPORT MISSION

Selected Bibliography of § 7

M. Andenas/W.-H. Roth (eds.), *Services and Free Movement in the EU*, 2002; A. Biondi *et al.* (eds.), *The Law of State Aid in the EU*, 2004; Chr. H. Bovis, "Financing Services of General Interest in the EU: How do Public Procurement and State Aids Interact to Demarcate between Market Forces and Protectionism", *ELJ* 2005, 79; A. Epiney, *Umgekehrte Diskriminierungen*, 1995; A.P. den Exter, "Legal Consequences of EU Accession for Central and Eastern European Health Care Systems", *ELJ* 2002, 556; K. Erhardt, *Beihilfen für öffentliche Dienstleistungen*, 2003; L. Flynn, "Coming of age: The free movement of capital case law", *CMLRev* 2002, 773; L. W. Gormley, "Reasoning Renounced? The Remarkable Judgement of Keck and Mithouard", *EBusLRev* 1994, 63; Halbhuber, "National doctrinal structures and European company law", *CMLRev* 2001, 1385; L. Hancher *et al.*, *EC Law of State Aid*, 2nd ed. 1999; K. Hopt/E. Wymeersch, *European Company and Financial Law*, 3rd ed. 2003; Th. Kingreen, *Die Struktur der Grundfreiheiten des Europäischen Gemeinschaftsrechts*, 1999; G. Marenco, "Pour une interprétation traditionelle de la notion de mésure d'effet équivalent à une restriction quantitative", *CDE* 1984, 291; A. Mattera, *Le marché unique*, 2ème éd. 1990; E. Mestmäcker/H. Schweitzer, *Europäisches Wettbewerbsrecht*, 2, A. 2004; H.-W. Micklitz/N. Reich, *Legal Aspects of European Space Activities*, 1989; S. Mohamed, *EC Law on Free Movement of Capital and the EMU*, 1999; K. Mortelmans, "Towards convergence in the application of the rules on free movement and competition", *CMLRev* 2001, 613; P. Oliver (with M. Jarvis), *Free Movement of Goods in the EC*, 4th ed. 2003; P. Oliver/W.-H. Roth, "The internal market and the four freedoms", *CMLRev* 2004, 407; M. Poiares Maduro, *We the Court*, 1997; N. Reich, "Europäische Wirtschaftsverfassung und bremische Landesverfassung", in: V. Kröning u.a., *Handbuch der bremischen Verfassung*, 1991, 689 ff.; N. Reich, "The November Revolution of the ECJ", *CMLRev* 1994, 459; N. Reich/C. van Aken, *The Evolution of Community Law on Financial Services*, 1995; N. Reich/H.-W. Micklitz, *Europäisches Verbraucherrecht*, 4. A. 2003; O. Remien, *Zwingendes Vertragsrecht und Grundfreiheiten des EG-Vertrages*, 2003; W.-H. Roth, "From *Centros* to *Überseering*: Free movement of companies, private international law, and Community law", *ICLQ* 2002, 177; J. Snell, *Goods and services in EC Law*, 2002; E. Steindorff, *EG-Vertrag und Privatrecht*, 1996; J. Stuyck, "Libre circulation et concurrence", *Mélanges M. Waehlbroeck*, 1999, 1477; D. Verse/W. Wurmnest, "Zur Nichtigkeit von Verträgen bei Verstößen gegen das EG-Beihilferecht", *Archiv für die zivilistische Praxis (AcP)* 2004, 855; St. Weatherill, "Recent case law concerning the free movement of goods: Mapping the frontiers of internal market deregulation", *CMLRev* 1999, 51; S. Weatherill, "The Internal market", in: Ward & Peers (eds.), *The EU Charter of Fundamental Rights*, 2004, 183-210; J. Winter, "Re(de)fining the notion of State aid in Art. 87 (1) EC", *CMLRev* 204, 475; J. Wouters, "Private International Law and companies' freedom of establishment", *EBOR* 2001, 101; E. Wymeersch, "The transfer of the company's seat in European company law", *CMLRev* 2003, 601.

I. CONCEPT AND NATURE OF FREE MOVEMENT

1. Importance of free movement rules in the economic and legal order of the EU

In the overall context of free movement rules, those on free movement of persons appear to be losing their purely economic content and orientation. As we have seen from the developing model of citizenship, they have become part of the citizenship concept given special status in the Treaty[1]. They take direct effect *vis-à-vis* Member States and also – with certain limitations – as to private collective entities (§ 2 II 2b). In addition, they may under certain circumstances be extended to legal residents who are not citizens *stricto sensu,* especially family members (§ 5 III).[2]

This stands in contrast to the other freedoms of the Treaty – free movement of goods, services, and capital. These have maintained their purely economic content, even though the case-law of the ECJ has insisted on their "fundamental" character for the economic constitution of the EU[3]. They take direct effect against Member States – a legal consequence which has been recognized by primary Community law for the free movement of capital only since the Maastricht Treaty.[4] Usually they will not have "horizontal direct effect" – the principle of autonomy (§ 15) prevails over the free movement rules.

The establishment rules, with their hybrid content, are situated between free movement of persons on the one hand, and freedom of economic transactions in the internal market on the other. They have a personal element insofar as they protect self-employed persons in their economic activities, grant them ancillary rights of residence, and encourage their mobility. They also allow all EU citizens to set up and manage undertakings. Those "formed in accordance with the law of a Member State and having their registered office, central administration or principal place of business within the Community" are themselves protected by the establishment rules per Art. 48 EC. These make clear the mainly economic context of freedom of establishment of and for undertakings, whereby the concept of "company" or "firm" expressly excludes those that are non profit-making.[5] It remains to be seen how far these undertakings themselves enjoy "free movement" in the sense of transferring their business from one Member State to another seat without undue restrictions (sub V).[6]

---

[1]   Art. 17/18 EC.
[2]   Reich/Harbacevica, *CMLRev* 2003, 615 at 637.
[3]   In the sense of Art. 4 and 98 EC.
[4]   Cf. case 203/80 Criminal proceedings against Casati [1981] ECR 2595. Dir. 88/361/EEC of 24 June 1998 for the implementation of Article 67 of the Treaty OJ L 178/5 introduced freedom of capital through secondary law.
[5]   They may be protected by other provisions of the Treaty, eg. Art. 12 EC, § 11 II 2.
[6]   For an overview cf. Roth, ICLQ 2003, 176.

2. Interplay of free movement guarantees and their limitations

Guaranteeing and protecting free movement of economic goods takes three directions. These are not clearly spelled out in the Treaty, but have developed in later case law:
- Protection against *direct discrimination* (different *treatment* of "domestic" and "foreign" products, services, capital, and undertakings).
- Prohibition of *indirect discrimination* (different *effects* on foreign products, services, capital and companies by seemingly neutral rules).
- General protection against *restrictions* imposed on free movement by measures originating from Member States. The concept of restriction is a broad one; it is sufficient that a Member State rule makes an economic activity protected by Community law less attractive or more onerous.

No right – not even a fundamental one – is guaranteed without limitations. These limitations, which may be inherent in the right itself, will be debated within the context of free movement of goods, services, capital, and undertakings. As a general rule, free movement has something to do with *cross-border activities* and does not concern "purely internal matters" – a concept subject to debate and elaboration.

External limitations, in the sense of discrimination and restrictions that Member States impose or encourage, must be justified. The case law of the ECJ has developed a hierarchy of justifications due to this interplay between rule and exception. That is, free movement is the rule and must be broadly interpreted, while limitations are the exception and must therefore be restrictively construed (§ 2 III 4). This scheme of justification applies in principle to all economic freedoms, and has been substantially modified and refined by case law. The present state of the law can be summarized as follows:
- Open discrimination can only be justified on public policy grounds spelled out expressly[7], subject to strict monitoring by the ECJ.[8]
- Indirect discrimination and other restrictions must be justified by a general interest test, which excludes merely economic grounds.[9] The catalogue of justified general interests in Community case law is open-ended, and includes, for example, consumer and environmental protection, safeguarding the cultural heritage, social policy, and fairness in commercial transactions.
- Every act of discrimination or restriction that passes the public policy and/or general interest tests must still meet the proportionality principle as defined in *Gebhard* (§ 3 II 4).

---

[7]   In Art. 30 (1), 46 (1), 55 (1), 58 (1) b) EC.
[8]   Cf. for a recent account case C-476/98 Commission v Germany [2002] ECR I-9855 at para 157.
[9]   Case 72/83 Campus Oil v Minister for Industry and Energy [1984] ECR 2727; C-398/95 SETTG v Ypourgos Ergasias [1997] ECR I-3091.

– As a general guide, the Court has been more willing to accept restrictions on the freedom to provide services than on the free movement of goods. For example, it has accepted such imprecise criteria as the "coherence of the tax system" to deny tax deductions for payments to funds established abroad,[10] "social and cultural considerations" in forbidding the marketing of foreign lotteries,[11] "maintaining a balanced medical and hospital service open to all"[12] to justify a prior authorization requirement for treatment in foreign hospitals, if authorization is dependent on objective, transparent and non-discriminatory criteria.

– The *Gambelli*-case[13] concerned an Italian prohibition of commercial betting by internet via unlicensed agents established in Italy. Art. 49 EC was applicable to the prohibition, which could be justified under the proportionality principle only to protect consumers from fraud, not in order to generate income for the state.

– Special rules apply to restrictions imposed by intellectual property rules (§ 10).

3. Scope of overview of free movement

The following sections give an overview of the general ambit and sphere of application of the different economic free movement principles. We will not evaluate the abundant case-law with regard to (justified, proportional) limitations. We show that the different free movement guarantees contain structural differences, despite their common origin. These differences have so far prevented construction of one all-encompassing free movement principle. The EU lawyer must get used to the distinctions – not always clear because of overlapping applications – between the different free movement rules, and be sure to apply the correct one in cases of doubt.

As to possible justifications of limitations, this task is much easier because the test to be applied is the same for all limitations, whatever the specific free movement right concerned. The closing section is devoted to special rules on State aid which have a considerable impact on open markets and indirectly on free movement.

---

[10]   Case C-204/90 Bachmann v Belgium [1992] ECR I-249.

[11]   Case C-275/92 HM Customs and Excise v Schindler [1994] ECR-I 1039.

[12]   Case C-157/99 Geraets-Smits v. Stichting Ziekenfonds *et al.* [2001] ECR I-5473 at para 73; cf. den Exter, *ELJ* 2002, 556 at 563 n. 34 referring to the fact that at the same time the Court insisted that reimbursement must be at least the same as the amount which would have been granted if the insured person had received hospital treatment in the Member State in which he is insured. In the case of higher tariffs in the country in which he is insured this could mean a profit for the insured! See now Case I-385/99 V.G. Müller-Fauré/ Onderlinge Waarborgmaatschappij *et al.* [2003] ECR I-4509.

[13]   Case C-243/01 Piergiorgio Gambelli *et al.* [2003] ECR I-13031.

II. FREE MOVEMENT OF GOODS

1. *The Member State as actor*

The Treaty[14] sets out in plain terms:

> Quantitative restrictions on imports and all measures having equivalent effect shall be prohibited between the Member States.

It also contains the same rule with regard to quantitative restrictions on exports[15].

They will be merged after ratification of the Draft Constitution.[16]

The Treaty addresses only Member States (and other state bodies), not private persons or undertakings. If undertakings restrict trade, by agreement or by abuse of a dominant position, the competition rules apply. That remains so even though a certain overlap is conceivable in the case of public undertakings or state measures distorting competition (*infra* § 9 VI). This does not rule out both relevant provisions[17] having the same objective, that is, to open national markets and to allow competition to function effectively in the internal market.[18] This can be seen particularly with regard to the case law on parallel imports.

The concept of state action, although not expressly written into the Treaty[19], follows from its systematic place and is a broad one. To give some examples:
–   The British *Royal Pharmaceutical Society* exercises a disciplinary power over its members which has been delegated by the state[20, 21]
–   A marketing campaign sponsored and supported by the state or a marketing organization created by law and financed by contributions from producers is a state measure .[22] In its *"Buy Irish"* judgment the Court wrote:[23]

> Whilst it may be true that the two elements of the programme which have continued in effect, namely the advertising campaign and the use of the "Guaranteed Irish" symbol, have

---

[14]   Art. 28 EC.
[15]   Art. 29 EC.
[16]   Art. III-153.
[17]   Namely Art. 28/29 and 81/82 EC.
[18]   Case 103/84 Commission v Italy [1986] ECR 1749 at para 19; Mortelmans, *CMLRev* 2001, 613.
[19]   Arts. 28/29 EC.
[20]   Art. 28 applies.
[21]   Case 266/87 R. v Pharmaceutical Society ex parte API [1989] 1295.
[22]   Case C-325/00 Commision v Germany [2002] ECR I-9977 ("CMA" quality mark).
[23]   Case 249/81 Commision v Ireland [1982] ECR 4005.

not had any significant success in winning over the Irish market to domestic products, it is not possible to overlook the fact that regardless of their efficacy, those two activities form part of a government programme which is designed to achieve the substitution of domestic products for imported products and is liable to affect the volume of trade between Member States (para 25).

–   A State also has a negative obligation in the sense of preventing private collective action against free movement of goods (§ 19 III 1),[24] unless justified by a proportionate defence of fundamental rights such as freedom of assembly (Art. 11 EHRC) and free speech (Art. 10 EHRC).[25]

2. Measures having an effect equivalent to quantitative restrictions of import (MEE)

The concept of MEE is a broad one. It was first spelled out by the ECJ in its seminal *Dassonville* case:[26]

> All trading rules enacted by Member States which are capable of hindering, directly or indirectly, actually or potentially, intra-Community trade are to be considered as measures having an effect equivalent to quantitative restrictions (para 5).

From its origin, the formula was mostly applied against restrictive Member State rules preventing parallel imports, for example medicines, plant protection products, and cars. In its *de Peijper* case[27] the Court criticized a Member State rule limiting distribution of a medicinal product to an authorized importer and excluding parallel importers from market access. Similar principles were developed in competition law against restrictive practices (the *Grundig* doctrine (§ 9 I 3), and against the use of intellectual property rights beyond their "substance matter" (§ 10 I) with the object or effect of hindering parallel imports.

This wide definition makes it clear that the Treaty[28] prohibition catches not only direct or indirect discrimination. It also catches other indirect restrictions – so *called equally applicable measures* – with a potential negative effect on intra-Community trade. This was later confirmed by the famous *Cassis de Dijon* case.[29] Here, the Court said:

> ... the concept of (MEE) .... is to be understood to mean that the fixing of a minimum alcohol content for alcoholic beverages intended for human consumption by the legislation

---

[24]   Case C-265/95 Commision v France [1997] ECR I-6959.
[25]   Case C-112/00 Eugen Schmidberger v Austria [2003] ECR I-5659.
[26]   Case 8/74 Procureur du Roi v Dassonville [1974] ECR 837.
[27]   Case 104/75 v Adriaan de Pijper [1976] ECR 613.
[28]   Art. 28 EC.
[29]   Case 120/78 Rewe Central AG v Bundesmonopolverwaltung für Branntwein [1979] ECR 649.

of a Member State also falls within the prohibition laid down in that provision where the importation of alcoholic beverages lawfully produced and marketed in another Member State is concerned (para 15).

This case has played a central role in Community law of free movement of goods:

- The Treaty[30] also applies to seemingly neutral measures that catch domestic and imported products alike, such as fixing a minimum alcohol content of certain alcoholic beverages. Note, however, that the Court was concerned with rules directly relating to the product composition and content, not to its marketing or distribution.
- The Court conceived the so-called *country of origin* principle. That is, a product legally marketed in one Member country should be admitted to the market of any other Member State without restrictions. This principle became the basis of later Community internal market legislation (§ 8).
- The Court developed the *general interest* test as an imminent justification of restrictions to trade *as being necessary to satisfy mandatory requirements relating in particular to the effectiveness of fiscal supervision, the protection of public health, the fairness of commercial transactions and the defence of the consumer* (para 8).

All three elements of *Cassis* have been subject to a lively debate in legal writing. This is echoed by controversies in application of the law, both by Member State courts and the ECJ itself. Although a full follow-up is beyond the scope of this book, it may be fair to comment that the main problem of the *Dassonville/Cassis* formula was its sheer limitless applicability. It seemed to suggest that every Member State rule having the slightest potential effect[31] on intra-Community trade would be caught[32] and needed a particular justification. As a result, the rule-exception principle was placed upside down. This operated to the detriment of Member States, severely impairing their legislative autonomy.[33] In determining whether a state measure was justified, courts were obliged to undertake difficult policy choices for which they are not really qualified.

---

[30] Art. 28 (ex-Art 30 EEC).
[31] Contrary to suggestions by several writers and Advocates General (*e.g.* AG Jacobs in case C-412/93 Société d'importation Edouard Leclerc-Siplec v TF1 Publicité [1995] ECR I-179), the Court denied a *de minimis* test, cf. case 16/83 Criminal proceedings against Prantl [1984] ECR 1299), but excluded mere hypothetical restrictions of trade from the application of Art. 28, cf. case 75/81 Blesgen v Belgium [1982] ECR 1211.
[32] By Art. 28.
[33] Cf. the account by Poiares Maduro, *We the Court*, 1997 and the review by Reich, *OxfLJ* 1998, 337.

3.   MEE (2): the Keck formula

Litigation after *Cassis* was concerned both with classic restrictive state regulations and with more general rules on the marketing of products, for example:
– advertising for alcoholic products in a certain region,[34]
– information about product guarantees,[35]
– shop opening hours,[36]
– price regulations[37], and
– distribution of pornographic products[38].

The issue was whether the Treaty[39, 40] was to be regarded as a general rule of a liberal economic constitution in the EU and its Member States, combating whatever restrictions to trade unless specifically justified. Alternatively, was it to be limited to intra-community trade in the classic sense? That is, was state action which had no specific discriminatory or restrictive effects on imports to remain outside its field of application? The Court decided the issue in the highly controversial *Keck* case:[41]

> In *Cassis*... it was held that, in the absence of harmonisation of legislation, measures of equivalent effect prohibited by (Art. 28 EC) include obstacles to the free movement of goods where they are the consequence of applying rules that lay down requirements to be met by such goods (such as requirements as to designation, form, size, weight, composition, presentation, labelling, packaging) to goods from other Member States where they are lawfully manufactured and marketed, even if those rules apply without distinction to all products unless their application can be justified by a public-interest objective taking precedence over the free movement of goods. However, contrary to what has previously been decided, the application to products from other Member States of national provisions restricting or prohibiting certain selling arrangements is not such as to hinder directly or indirectly, actually or potentially, trade within the Member States ..., provided that those provisions apply to all affected traders operating within the national territory and provided that they affect in the same manner, in law and in fact, the marketing of domestic products and of those from other Member States (paras 17/18).

---

[34]   Cf. C-1 + 176/90 Aragonesa de Publicidad [1991] ECR I-4151.
[35]   Case C-93/92 CMC-Motorradcenter v Pelin Basiciogullari [1993] ECR I-5009.
[36]   Case 145/88 Torfaen Borough Council v B & Q plc.[1989] ECR 3851 and later cases.
[37]   Joined cases 16-20/79 Criminal proceedings against Danis [1979] ECR 3327 where the Court insisted on a discrimination test.
[38]   Case C-23/89 Quietlynn and Richards v Southend Borough Council [1990] ECR I-3059.
[39]   Art. 28 EC – unlike Art. 29, which was always interpreted much more narrowly.
[40]   Case 155/80 Summary proceedings against Oebel [1981] ECR 1993.
[41]   Joined cases C-267 + 268/91 Keck and Mithouard [1993] ECR I-6097, prepared by AG Tesauro in case C-292/92 Hünermund v. Landesapothekerkammer Baden-Württemberg [1993] ECR I-6787.

4. Applying the Keck criteria

The *Keck* decision has been subject of an extended controversy[42, 43], which will not be followed up here. However, analysis of later case law more than ten years after the landmark *Keck* decision allows a clearer understanding of what the Court really meant[44]. It is useful to distinguish recent case-law between product regulations and selling arrangements:

a. Product regulations

Product regulations similar to those of the *Cassis* case are, in effect, Member State rules on the composition, denomination, and labelling of products. These still play a significant role in the case law of the Court. Indeed, it is here that the country-of-origin principle plays a dominant role. That is, a product marketed legally in one country should be allowed to circulate freely without further changes in its composition, labelling, or packaging unless mandatory requirements impose modifications. Such requirements might include those on consumer protection. These rules must always respect the proportionality principle, also developed in the *Cassis* case. Information rules will usually be preferable to rules on product composition.[45]

The Court prefers a broad reading of *product regulations*:
- The case of *Mars + 10%*[46]. German law on unfair trade practices attempted to restrict marketing of pre-packaged ice cream products, on the ground that their labelling and advertising was exaggerated and potentially misleading. The Court was not concerned with the character of the law as selling arrangements, but with the direction of the ban, which concerned the product as such and not merely its advertising. The *Cassis* criteria were applied in full.
- The *Familiapress* case[47] concerned advertising for a prize competition – illegal under Austrian law. This regulation was not regarded as a mere selling arrangement but concerned the product as such, that is, a news magazine which could not be distributed without eliminating the advertising. The ban had to be justified under the general interest and proportionality tests. Among these, freedom of the press as guaranteed by Art. 10 EHRC had to be respected.[48]

---

[42]   A good overview is given by Weatherill, *CMLRev* 1999, 91; Barnard, *ELRev* 2001, 35.
[43]   Reich, *CMLRev* 1994, 451.
[44]   Oliver, *Free movement of goods*, 4th ed. 2003 at 124-133.
[45]   Case 178/84 Commission v Germany [1987] ECR 1227 at para 30 concerning the so-called purity laws of beer in Germany.
[46]   C-470/93 Verein gegen Unwesen im Handel v Mars GmbH [1995] ECR I-1923.
[47]   C-368/95 Vereinigte Familiapress Zeitungsverlags- und Vertriebs GmbH v. Heinrich Bauer Verlag [1997] ECR I-3689.
[48]   Craig/de Búrca at 345; Jacobs ELRev 2001, 331 at 337.

- A ban on the denomination *Clinique* as misleading for a cosmetic product was regarded as a product rule. The reason was because this impeded its marketing in the country of destination on the same terms as in the country of origin.[49]
- Language regulations concerning the labelling of a product are caught by the Treaty[50]. These must be justified either by mandatory requirements or by specific EC labelling directives.[51]
- In the case concerning the German Verpackungsverordnung[52] requiring producers of soft drinks to change waste disposal from a collection to a deposit and return system, coupled with the charging of a deposit, the Court applied the *Keck* criteria because it makes the placement of imported products on the German market more difficult, even though this hindrance is slight and even though it is possible that the product may be marketed in other ways (para 68). It can be justified by environmental concerns because the payment of a deposit will encourage consumers to collect waste instead of throwing it away. But the transfer to such an "environmental friendly" system must leave producers a "reasonable transitional period to adapt thereto" (para 81).

b. Selling arrangements

Selling arrangements are not *per se* caught by the ban[53], but only where a discriminatory element is inherent. The complainant against a Member State rule must show that the rule makes access to the market more difficult in law or fact. This test has been used by the Court in a number of cases concerning product advertising and marketing:
- *De Agostini*[54] concerned an outright ban on children's advertising on television. This is only covered by the Treaty if it can be shown that it does not affect the marketing of national products and of products of other Member States in the same way, in fact and in law. This must be established by the national court.
- Austrian law limited sales on rounds by bakers to those established in a certain district.[55] This made market access by potential competitors from abroad more difficult than for local bakers. The reasoning here was that the first had to get established in a particular district before starting their sales on rounds, while the second were more likely to be already established there.

---

[49]   Case C-315/92 Verband sozialer Wettbewerb v Clinique Laboratories SNC [1994] ECR I-317.
[50]   Art. 28 EC.
[51]   Case C-366/98 Criminal proceedings against Geoffrey [2000] ECR I-6579.
[52]   C-309/02 Radlberger Getränkegesellschaft mbH & Co *et al.* v Land Baden-Württemberg [2004] ECR I-(14.12.2004).
[53]   I.e., of Art. 28.
[54]   Joined cases C-34-36/95 Konsumentenombudsmannen (KO) v De Agostini (Svenska) Forlag AB and TV Shop Sverige AG [1997] ECR I-3843 at para 44.
[55]   Case C-254/98 Schutzverband gegen unlauteren Wettbewerb v. TK Heimdienst Sass GmbH [2000] ECR I-151 at para 29.

– The *Gourmet* case[56] concerned a Swedish ban on advertising of alcoholic drinks, said to be more detrimental to foreign producers than to local ones. As a result, the relevant Treaty provision[57] applied, so that the national court had to determine whether this was justified under the general interest (health protection) and proportionality tests.

– The *Doc Morris* case[58] concerned the cross-border marketing of medicinal products via e-commerce. The German prohibition was regarded as a "measure of equivalent effect". As far as the marketing of prescription drugs was concerned, this could be justified by public health reasons in the sense of Art. 30 EC, but not for non-prescription medicines.

III. FREE MOVEMENT OF SERVICES

1. Importance and forms of free movement of services

The original focus of Community law on free movement was on products. Later technology developments made cross-border provision of services ever more important. These would include, for example, broadcasting, communication and information services. Under Community law, services can be provided in three different forms, namely:

– the provider moves to the recipient without becoming established, in the sense of becoming permanently integrated into another jurisdiction;

– the recipient moves to the provider, for example to a clinic, to get treatment in the country where treatment is available;

– the service moves cross-border like a product. This would include a radio or TV broadcast, offering securities via internet, and providing documentation services from data bases established in one Member country.

The first and second forms of providing services are closely linked to the free movement of persons and have been treated in this context (§ 4 III). The third is closer to the free movement of goods rules and will be discussed in the following.

---

[56] Case C-405/98 Konsumentenombudsmannen (KO) v Gourmet International products [2001] ECR I-1795 at para 21.

[57] Art. 28 EC.

[58] Case C-322/01 Deutscher Apothekenverband v Doc Morris NV and Jacques Waterval [2003] ECR I-14887.

2.   Concept of service

The concept of service is only defined negatively in the Treaty by reference to the rules on the free movement of goods, capital and persons. Some examples are given[59] of services protected by the Treaty. The concept is a very broad one and includes such "unusual" services as lotteries.[60]

To illustrate, in *Sacchi*[61] the Court held that the transmission of TV signals and advertising constitutes a service, while the free movement of goods covers only videos and sound tapes. As later cases made clear,[62] the cultural element inherent in them does not exclude the applicability of the service rules because they also contain an economic element. However, cultural policy reasons may justify certain restrictions on the freedom to provide services. On the other hand, the economic element is absent where a genuine state activity is concerned. This would include management of and access to public schools.[63]

The concept of service requires some sort of *remuneration* as consideration for the service provided. Therefore, information about abortion clinics in the UK provided free-of-charge by an Irish student organization was not protected by the Treaty[64], even though the service advertised was itself against remuneration. This was the ECJ's ruling in its highly-contested *Grogan*[65] decision against AG van Gerven.[66] On the other hand, it is not necessary that the service is directly paid by users as in broadcasting, which is financed via the transmission of advertisements or by sponsorship. Therefore, in *Bond van Adverteerders*[67] the Court distinguished two markets that both come under the freedom to provide service rules. The one is the market for broadcasting services *vis-à-vis* the spectator. The other is the market for advertising between the broadcaster and the advertising companies.

---

[59]   Art. 50 (2).

[60]   Case C-275/92 HM Customs & Excise v Schindler [1994] ECR I-1039; C-124/97 Läärä [1999] ECR I-6067, however allowing the country of destination a wide discretion in forbidding the entry or regulating the marketing of such services and therefore retaining strict control of their distribution for fiscal or public policy reasons.

[61]   Case 155/73 Sacchi [1974] ECR 409.

[62]   Cases C-288/89 Collectieve Antennevoorziening Gouda v Commissariaat voor de Media [1991] ECR I-4007.

[63]   Case 263/86 Belgium v Humbel [1988] ECR 5365 at para 18.

[64]   Art. 49 EC.

[65]   Case C-159/90 Society for the protection of Unborn Children (SPUC) v Stephen Grogan [1991] ECR I-4685.

[66]   See his opinion at 4713, allowing however justification on constitutional grounds prohibiting abortion, and the discussion by Weiler/Lockhardt, *CMLRev* 1995, 51; O'Leary, *CMLRev* 1995, 548.

[67]   Case 352/85 Bond van Adverteerders v Netherlands [1988] ECR 2085.

The service rules do not apply where the provider is established more or less permanently in the receiving country, as by setting up branches, agencies or subsidiaries in the sense of the relevant Treaty provision[68, 69] The difference is important, not so much with regard to the general guarantee of the freedom to provide services, but rather in relation to justified restrictions. Indeed, case law recognizes that an economic actor established in the receiving country may be subject to its professional and prudential rules. However, this is not necessarily the case for a service provider, which is sufficiently controlled by its country of origin. In order to combat a circumvention of these rules, the Court early on, in *Van Binsbergen*[70], allowed restrictions on the freedom to provide services in order to make its professional rules effective:

> ... a Member State cannot be denied the right to take measures to prevent the exercise by a person providing services whose activity is entirely or principally directed towards its territory of the freedom guaranteed by (Art. 49 EC) for the purpose of avoiding their professional rules of conduct which would be applicable to him if he were established within that State; such a situation may be subject to judicial control under the provisions of the chapter relating to the right of establishment and not that on the provision of services (para 13). .

This case law was later developed with regard to TV services where the broadcasting operator chose its business seat in a country with a more liberal policy. The aim was to avoid stricter regulation in the country of destination, and the service was such as to be wholly or principally directed to that country.[71] On the other hand, Community law forbids imposing a requirement of establishment where this would amount to negating the freedom to provide services.[72]

As with free movement of goods, the Treaty forbids not only direct or indirect discrimination, but also all restrictions, even if they apply without distinction to both foreign and national service providers.[73]

As to possible justifications of a restriction on the provision of services, the Court seems to allow a more generous approach of Member States, if the criteria of proportionality are met. This is particularly true in relation to social policy objectives

---

[68] Art. 43 (1) 2 EC.
[69] Case 205/84 Commission v Germany [1986] ECR 3755 at para 23.
[70] Case 33/74 Van Binsbergen v Bestuur van de Bedrijfsvereniging voor de Metaalnijverheid [1974] ECR 1299 at para 13.
[71] Case C-23/93 TV 10 v Commissariaat voor de Media [1994] ECR I-4795.
[72] Case 205/84 Commission v Germany [1987] ECR 3755 at para 52.
[73] Case C-76/90 Säger v Dennemeyer & Co Ltd. [1991] ECR I-4221 at para 12.

such as protecting posted workers[74] where a special directive exists.[75] Due to the non-material character of services, a mere information rule as in the free movement of goods may not be enough to attain the objective justified by Member State law. On the other hand, the Court seems to be hostile to double controls, in that an activity which has undergone state control or monitoring in one country should not have to follow the same or a similar procedure in the country where the service is provided. It is here that the country of origin principle has its main importance.[76]

3. Cross border element inherent in the free movement provisions

Similarly to the free movement of persons, the provisions on the freedom to provide services only apply if there is a cross-border element inherent in the activity to be protected by Community law. The Court has been rather generous in finding a cross-border element, which can result from an activity itself that is directed across borders, and from those involved residing in different countries.[77]

It is sufficient that the service provider directs its activities both at local residents and to customers abroad. The *Keck* rule does not apply to services, as the Court made clear in *Alpine Investments*, where a ban on "cold calling" on potential customers of financial services was at issue.[78] The cross-border element was seen in the following:

> A prohibition such as that at issue is imposed by the Member State in which the provider of services is established and affects not only offers made by him to addressees who are established in that state or move there in order to receive services but also offers made to potential recipients in another Member State. It therefore directly affects access to the market in services in the other member State and is thus capable of hindering intra-Community trade in services (para 38).

On the other hand, where all relevant elements of service provision are confined within a single Member State, the relevant Treaty provision[79] will not apply.[80] Community law does not aim to interfere in the internal affairs of Member States, even if this provokes *reverse discrimination* (§ 11 II 2).

---

[74] Case C-113/89 Rush Portuguesa v Office National d'immigration [1990] ECR I-1417; C-369 + 376/96 Criminal proceedings against Arblade [1999] ECR I-8453.
[75] Directive 96/71/EC of the EP and the Council of 16 Dec. 1996 concerning posted workers, [1997] OJ L 18/1.
[76] Joined cases 110 + 111/78 ASBL v Van Wesemael [1979] ECR 35; case 279/80 Criminal proceedings against Webb [1981] ECR 3305 at para 20 and later cases.
[77] Case C-158/96 Kohll v Union des Caisses de Maladie [1998] ECR I-1931.
[78] Case C-384/93 Alpine Investments BV v Minister van Financiën [1995] ECR I-1141 at para 36.
[79] Art. 49 EC.
[80] Case C 52/79 Procureur du Roi v Debauve [1980] ECR 833 at 9.

IV. FREE MOVEMENT OF CAPITAL

1. *Scope of application*

The freedom of capital provisions as introduced by the Maastricht Treaty have a particularly wide scope of application. According to the Treaty[81], "all restrictions on the movement of capital between Member States *and between Member States and third countries* (author's italics) shall be prohibited." As the only freedom under Community law, it is extended to third countries (subject to a special safeguard clause[82]), while free movement of persons is strictly limited to EU citizens (§ 5). The EU demonstrates its openness to world capital markets, parallel to the introduction of the *euro* as part of the EMU (Economic and Monetary Union). At the same time, it demonstrates its exclusiveness with regard to the privileged position of its citizens. However, the following discussion will briefly concentrate on the internal market aspects of the free movement of capital without reference to EMU and third countries[83].

According to the Treaty[84], free movement is extended to payments thus conforming to a situation that existed prior to the Maastricht Treaty.[85] It is clear that the free circulation of persons, goods and services can only function alongside the ancillary freedom of payments to fulfill contractual obligations (§ 15 II).

Free movement of capital implies access to all markets:
- for equity and finance capital,
- for direct investment[86],
- for purchase of real property without prior authorization,[87] and
- for all transactions with securities and financial derivatives.

This freedom includes ancillary rights such as reception and transfer of dividends, and profits on invested capital without discrimination by tax authorities. Limitations to grants on State interest rate subsidies on home construction to local banks are an obstacle to the free movement of capital.[88]

---

[81] Art. 56 (1) EC.
[82] In Art. 57.
[83] For an overview Flynn, *CMLRev* 2002, 773.
[84] Art. 56 (2) EC.
[85] Case 286/82 Luisi & Carbone v Ministero del Tesoro [1984] ECR 377.
[86] Case C-54/99 Eglise de Scientologie v The Prime Minister [2000] ECR I-1335.
[87] Case C-423/98 Albore [2000] ECR I-5965.
[88] Case C-484/93 Swensson & Gustavsson v Ministre du Logement et de l'Urbanisme [1995] ECR I-3955.

It may be difficult to determine what rules apply in cases of doubt, for example as to services, establishment, or capital. Therefore, reference can be made to the non-exhaustive list of capital transactions.[89, 90]

2. Controversies about the case of "golden shares"

The economic importance to a liberal economy of the free movement of capital rules can be shown in the litigation concerning so-called "golden shares", brought by the Commission against several Member States.[91] Further litigation has been undertaken. It will also play a major role in regard to new Member countries, where the liberalisation process of capital markets is still in the offing.

The term "golden shares" relates to limitations on shareholder ownership of privatised companies. It can take different forms, depending on the company law of the Member State in question, for example:
– right to restrict the acquisition of shares by third persons,
– right to appoint company directors,
– right to veto important company decisions, and
– limitations on the number of foreign company directors.

By enjoying these privileges, the former owner – notably the state or other state-like institution – aims to retain some control over a privatised company. They can be foreseen in the agreement with investors and then transposed into law, into regulation or into the statutes of companies under state control. One could argue that these privileges are not a matter of EU law, but of "the rules in Member States governing the system of property ownership"[92]. However, the Court has not accepted this argument, insisting that the relevant Treaty provision[93]:

> does not have the effect of exempting the Member States' system of property ownership from the fundamental rules of the Treaty[94].

This reading of Art. 295 EC conforms to the ECJ's method of interpreting exceptions strictly, and fundamental freedoms as a rule broadly (§ 2 III 6). As a consequence, the free movement of capital rules apply in full to the holding of golden shares by Member

---

[89]   In Dir. 88/361, *supra* note 4.
[90]   Case C-222/97 Proceedings brought by Trummer and Mayer [1999] ECR I-1661 at para 21.
[91]   Case C-483/99 Commission v France [2002] ECR I-4781, C-503/99 Commission v Belgium [2002] ECR I-4809 and C-367/98 Commission v Portugal, [2002] ECR I-4731; for a comment cf. Camara, *EBOR* (European Business Organisation Review) 2002, 503.
[92]   Per Art. 295 EC.
[93]   Art. 295 EC.
[94]   Para 44 in cases C-483 + 503/99, *supra* note 91.

States. Their restrictive effect lies in making investment in privatised companies less attractive than in normal companies. However, the Court was only concerned with the vertical direct effect of these restrictions. On the other hand, it was not concerned with a potential horizontal direct effect which would conflict with the freedom of contract and association principles recognized by Community law as a fundamental right (§ 15 IV)[95].

The case law of the Court turned on possible justifications of golden shares. These must meet three criteria:
- they must be non-discriminatory;
- they must be proportionate;
- they must be non-discretionary.

The first two criteria are well-known from the discussion of justified restrictions of Community freedoms. The third one is new, in that the Court requires that the basis on which a golden share right is to be exercised must be made known publicly. It is not sufficient that the administrative decisions on which this exercise is based be reasoned.[96] In this way, the Court seems eager to develop criteria on regulating capital markets for investment in privatised companies. It seems to be worried that intransparant practices on how golden shares are exercised by Member States prevent effective functioning of capital markets and protect national *niches*.

V. FREE MOVEMENT OF COMPANIES

1. National or Community law as decisive?

The free movement rules enjoy a broad personal and substantive scope of application. However, they seemingly do not include the right of a company established in one Member State to move freely to another without restrictions. The reasons for such activities may be diverse, for example avoiding tax burdens in the country of establishment, using arbitrage in labour costs, getting rid of investor-unfriendly co-determination rules. Great differences exist in tax and company legislation of Member States. These have not been overcome by harmonization, which makes such border crossing activities attractive. Indeed, AG La Pergola in *Centros*[97] suggested that, "in the absence of harmonization, competition among rules must be allowed free play in

---

[95]   Flynn *supra* note 83 at 786.
[96]   For a discussion cf. Camara at 507.
[97]   Case C-212/97 Centros Ltd. v Erhyervs og Selskabsstryrelsen [1999] ECR I-1459 at 1479.

corporate matters." Restrictive rules on company transfer must be seen as an impediment to the functioning of competition in this field.

The starting point of EU law is clear enough: it is up to Member States to determine the property regime in their jurisdictions, including company law. Rules on transfer of the business seat are subject to conflict of law rules. Again, these are a matter for Member States and not the Community, unless harmonized. The Treaty[98] leaves the "retention of legal personality in the event of transfer of their[99] seat from one country to another" not to harmonization but to the adoption of an agreement between Member States under international law. New competence under the Amsterdam Treaty[100] allows measures in the field of judicial cooperation to promote compatibility of the rules of conflict of laws insofar as necessary for the proper functioning of the internal market. So far, these rules have not been adopted[101].

The different Member State laws on companies and their corresponding conflict rules are without doubt a serious impediment to the free movement of companies. As an example, German law with its traditional "seat-theory" required a company wishing to transfer its business seat to liquidate its assets in one country and to re-establish itself in another.[102] As a second best solution, under the establishment rules a company can always set up branches, agencies or subsidiaries in another country. Alternatively, under the free movement of capital rules, it can invest freely in companies already established there, form holding companies and joint ventures – always of course respecting the limits of European merger law. But it cannot remove its entire business without risking substantial losses in autonomy and corporate assets.

2. Evolution of ECJ case-law as to transfer of companies

a. The restrictive approach in *Daily Mail*

As with frequent developments in Community law, it was left to the ECJ to take over the role of quasi-legislator in an area where Member States could not reach consensus. To the disappointment of followers of a radically liberal theory on transfer of undertakings, the Court took a deeply cautious view on this question in its *Daily Mail*

---

[98] Art. 293 EC third indent.
[99] The companies' (NR).
[100] New Art. 65 (b) EC.
[101] Neither under Art. 293 nor under Art. 65 EC.
[102] For an overview Halbhuber, *CMLRev* 2001, 1385: Roth, ICLQ 2002, 177; but see the new case law of the Bundesgerichtshof judgment of 13.3.2003 in *Juristenzeitung* 2003, 825.

decision.[103] A company resident in the UK wished to transfer its business seat to the Netherlands and set up a subsidiary in the UK. It had to get permission from the treasury, which was conditional on prior liquidation of assets. The Court held that "companies are creatures of law and, in the present state of Community law, creatures of national law". Therefore, in the eyes of the Court:

> the problems related to the transfer of undertakings cannot be resolved by the rules concerning the right to establishment but must be dealt with by future legislation or conventions (para 15).

The *Daily Mail* judgment was a severe blow to those who advocated free movement of companies in the internal market. This appears to be justified by the difference between natural persons on the one hand and legal persons on the other.

That is, a natural person has an inherent mobility. It follows that restrictions imposed on it are external and to some extent artificial. In any event, restrictions would certainly need justification in an *area without internal frontiers in which the free movement of goods, persons, services and capital is ... ensured*[104]. By contrast, a company or other legal person cannot exist without rules, such as those on its foundation, management, capital, and winding-up. The very existence of a company implies a much closer tie to the underlying legal order than is the case with natural persons. It is therefore clear that this legal order may determine rules on transfer of its business seat. This is independent of the conflict of law rules governing the internationally applicable legal order, be it the company seat (Germany) or incorporation (UK) principle. It is also not sure that the incorporation theory of the UK is investor-friendlier than the German seat theory, as the *Daily Mail* case clearly shows. It is not up to Community law to decide on the applicable conflict rules unless its powers[105] have been used. It must strive to avoid unjustified restrictions on free establishment. Later case law went precisely in this direction.

b. *Centros* and its liberalizing effects

The *Centros* case concerned the requirement of registration and proof of capital of the subsidiary of a company established under liberal English law. This is not conditional on minimal capital. It was clear from the outset that the company was to do business exclusively in Denmark, and that registration in the UK served to avoid stricter rules on minimum capital in Denmark. Could registration in Denmark be refused and be

---

[103] Case 81/87 R v the Queen v Treasury and Commissioners of Inland Revenue *ex parte* Daily Mail and General Trust [1998] ECR 5483.
[104] Per Art. 14 (2) EC.
[105] Under Art. 65 EC.

conditional upon fulfilling the stricter Danish capital requirements? The Court flatly rejected the applicability of the Danish registration rules and insisted on freedom of establishment, which also includes the right to set up branches, agencies, or subsidiaries[106]. It did not find any abuse in the simple use of a Community-guaranteed freedom – a conclusion that is surely open to criticism (§ 21 III). Even if creditor protection was a legitimate objective under Community law justifying restrictions on the freedom of establishment, it could be achieved by less restrictive means and not by imposing the company law standards of the country of business activity (Denmark) on a company legally set up under the law of the incorporation state.

The *Centros* decision certainly has a liberalizing pathos and effect. However, it does not deviate from Member State authority to impose its rules on the establishment and management of a company. These are only limited in cases where fundamental freedoms are at stake. In the case at hand, that means the secondary freedom to set up branches and subsidiaries. However, it was surely arguable that the subsidiary was really the main business seat, and under the seat theory this company-subsidiary should fulfil the requirements of the state where it has its main business activity. Therefore, several authors have argued that *Centros* gave the death-blow to the seat theory.[107] However, this view can be challenged on the basis that the Court seems to insist only on the country of origin principle. This would imply that a company established in one state according to its provisions and in compliance with Community law enjoys all the fundamental freedoms of the Treaty, including the right of secondary establishment. This right can only be restricted according to the general rules of Community law, which apply to all fundamental freedoms.

c.   *Überseering* and beyond

The recent *Überseering* case[108] concerned a somewhat strange consequence of the German seat theory. Here, a company formed according to the law of one state (NL) and whose ownership was transferred to another (Germany) had to be re-established in the country of residence of its owners in order to have standing in civil litigation matters. It is a debated question under German law whether this consequence of the seat theory is really imposed by German law or not.[109] The ECJ clearly cannot decide this question. In a carefully-worded decision, it repeated its insistence on the country-of-origin principle, whereby the company did not cease to be validly incorporated

---

[106]   Per Art. 43 (1) 2 EC.
[107]   Behrens, IPRax 1999, 323; for a discussion cf. Roth *CMLRev* 2000, 147.
[108]   Case C-208/00 Überseering BV v Nordic Construction Company Baumanagement GmbH (NCC) [2002] ECR I-9919. See the discussion bij Wymeersch, *CMLRev* 2003, 661.
[109]   Roth, ICLQ 2003 at 198, 207 concerning *Statutenwechsel*. The Bundesgerichtshof has meanwhile modified its restrictive case law by judgment of 13.3.2003, *supra* note 102.

under Dutch law. It discussed the *Daily Mail* judgment at length and found a difference. This consisted in the fact that the litigation did not concern a voluntary transfer of a business seat from the country of incorporation to another country, but an imposed transfer by the law of the receiving country against the very intention of the company owners. Therefore, the Court aptly stated:

> The requirement of re-incorporation of the same company in Germany is therefore tantamount to outright negation of freedom of establishment... It is not inconceivable that overriding requirements relating to the general interest, such as the protection of the interests of creditors, minority shareholders, employees and even the taxation authorities may, in certain circumstances and subject to certain conditions, justify restrictions on freedom of establishment... (paras 81, 93).

In limiting its dicta to the case at hand, the Court did not prejudice the rules of applicable law of Member States, nor did it outlaw restriction on the freedom of movement of companies justified by taxation purposes (*Daily Mail*), or to protect the German co-determination by being evaded. The Court seems to suggest that these questions will eventually have to be settled by harmonization, and not by applying the freedom of establishment rules.

The latest *Kamer van Koophandel* case[110] concerns restrictive Dutch laws that aimed to combat *Centros*-like abuses by imposing strict labelling and publicity requirements on subsidiaries of "Delaware"-type companies. AG Alber regarded the Dutch law as a restriction on the freedom of (secondary) establishment and found no justification for it. The use of Community freedoms could only *per se* be regarded as an abuse if specific individual circumstances justified such a condemnation. The case has been decided by mostly following the opinion of AG Alber. The additional disclosure requirements were said to be contrary to Council Directive 89/666/EEC of 21.12.1989 (11th company directive).[111]

The main thrust of these cases is the liberalizing effect on Member State company law. However, they remain restricted to cross-border activities of companies. They do not introduce a "preference rule"[112] nor do they concern the structure of company law as such. This remains subject to harmonization, or to establishment of a genuine Community company law via the Council Regulation[113] on the European Economic

---

[110]   Case C-167/01, Kamer van Koophandel v. Inspire Act [2003] ECR I-10155.
[111]   [1996] OJ L 395/36.
[112]   Roth *supra* note 102 at 190-193.
[113]   Council Regulation (EC) No. 2137/85, OJ L 199/1.

Interest Grouping of 1985 or the Council Regulation[114] on the Statute for a European company (SE).

VI. STATE AID

1. Principles of EU regulation on state aid

Member States may restrict or falsify market access and thereby impede the building of a true internal market in the sense of Art. 14 (2) EC not only by "negative measures" concerning the free movement of goods, services, capital, and undertakings, but also by "positive measures" that grant certain undertakings financial benefits and thereby distort competition.[115] These "positive measures" – which may be examined in litigation against Member States parallel with the free movement rules[116] – are caught by the section on "*Aids granted by States*", Art. 87 EC et seq. These provisions are placed immediately after the competition rules, which are directed at undertakings and which we will discuss in § 9. This demonstrates the hybrid character of the rules on state aids: on the one hand, they relate to state activities, on the other, they are based not so much on the negative effect of aids on free movement (an aid given to an undertaking may on the contrary enhance its capacity to engage in cross-border business!), but rather its impact on the level playing field in a market economy in the sense of Art. 4/109 EC, namely that all undertakings should have the same chances on a competitive market (principle of *per conditio concurrentium*), and that states should not interfere to distort this game of market forces by granting special benefits or subsidies to certain undertakings.

At the same time, the EC rules on state aids recognise that there may be certain justifications to support undertakings, e.g. for regional or structural purposes in the sense of Art. 87 para. 3, which allows for a "flexible" handling and therefore declares state aids only to be "incompatible" with the common market under certain conditions, and not simply *per se* forbidden as provided in the rules of free movement or on competition between undertakings, subject to narrowly defined exceptions. This explains the central role of the Commission to monitor and regulate state aids through a detailed system of notifications and authorisations, written into Art. 88 and

---

[114]   Council Regulation (EC) No. 2157/2001, [2002] OJ L 294/1.

[115]   The interrelation between Art. 87 and Art. 28 EC has been stressed in case 18/84 Commission v France [1985] ECR 1139 para 13.

[116]   See for a recent example case C-379/98 PreußenElektra v Schleswag [2001] ECR I-2099. For a discussion of the somewhat changed case law see Craig/de Búrca at 1163-1164; Winter, *CMLRev* 2004, 475.

implemented under the detailed rules of Reg. 659/99[117]. This power of the Commission is directed against Member States, which, as was said in the well-known *Alcan*-case[118], have to "merely give effect to the Commission's decision". This is sanctioned by the interdiction of Member States to put the "proposed measures into effect" before a final decision of the Commission is taken, per Art. 88 (3) EC last sentence, and by a strict obligation of Member states to enforce repayment of illegally paid out state aids (§ 8 V).

2. Concept of state aid

The concept of state aid is not defined in the EC Treaty and therefore had to be clarified by a steady flow of case law and of Commission decisions. The main principles are quite clear, but there are still some borderline cases, which will be discussed in the next section.

The main elements of the concept of state aid are:[119]
–   The aid must be granted by Member States or through state resources in any form whatsoever.
–   The aid must be granted selectively to individual undertakings or to a group of undertakings, not to the economy or to consumers at large, e.g. as measures of economic policy in the sense of Art. 109 or social policy which the "*ius reservatum*" of States.
–   The aid must give a gratuitous advantage to these undertakings.
–   The aid must distort or threaten to distort competition.
–   It must affect trade between Member States.

The elements have been broadly interpreted in order to cover indirect measures like tax benefits, exemptions, or reductions, waivers of social security payments,[120] preferential tariffs approved or initiated by the State,[121] State loans and guarantees otherwise not available at market conditions. The concept of "State resources" is a broad one to include any system of public financing in what form so-ever, whether ruled by public or by private law. If the State injects capital into a company in

---

[117]   Council Regulation (EC) No. 659/99 of 22 March 1999 laying down detailed rules for the application of Art. 93 (now Art. 87) of the EC Treaty, [1999] OJ L 83/1.
[118]   Case C-24/95 Land Rheinland-Pfalz v Alcan [1997] ECR I-1591 at para 34; the German Constitutional Court in its decision of 17.2.2000 did not object to this strict view, see Hofmeister, *CMLRev* 2001, 791.
[119]   Hancher/Ottervanger/Slot, *EC State Aids*, 2nd edition 1999 at 2-059-2-086.
[120]   Case C-75/97, Belgium v Commission [1999] ECR I-3671.
[121]   Cases 67/85 et al., Kwekerij Gebroeders Van der Koy BV v Commission, [1988] ECR 219 para 35.

economic trouble, the ECJ has developed the *"private investor test"*, i.e. "whether the undertaking could have obtained the amounts in question on the capital market".[122]

The concept of state aid is, in the words of the Court[123],

> "wider than that of a subsidy, because it includes measures which, in various forms, mitigate the charges which are normally included in the budget of an undertaking and which, without therefore being subsidies in the strict meaning of the word, are similar in character and have the same effect."

An aid, however, always requires a transfer of State resources. This will also be the case where the undertaking from which resources are transferred to other undertakings is subject to state control, e.g. in situations where the authorities are able by exercising their dominant influence over undertakings to direct the use of the undertaking's funds.[124]

The mere conferral of an advantageous legal position is not enough to constitute an aid, even though this may be prohibited by the free movement rules. Therefore, the obligation imposed on private electricity supply undertakings to purchase electricity produced from renewable energy sources at fixed minimum prices does not involve any direct or indirect transfer of State resources to undertakings that produce that type of electricity.[125]

The distortion of competition needs not to be substantial; any lowering of the production costs in a certain sector of the economy, e.g. the Italian textile industry by granting family allowances reducing temporarily and partially social charges, have been qualified as state aid.[126] The trade between Member states may be affected by an aid that aims to strengthen the export position of an undertaking, if a high percentage is destined to other Member states.[127]

3. Available *"defences"* to States

The rules on state aids do not contain a *per se* interdiction, but allow certain "defences", the most important of which are inserted in para. 2 of Art. 87. These

---

[122] Case C-142/87 Re Tubemeuse: Belgium v Commission [1990] ECR I-959 para 26. For details see Mestmäcker/Schweitzer, *Europäisches Wettbewerbsrecht*, 2. A. 2004, pp. 1066 ff.
[123] Case C-53/00 Ferring SA v Agence centrale des organismes de sécurité sociale (ACOSS) [2001] ECR I-9067 at para 15.
[124] Case C-482/99 France v Commission [2002] ECR I-4397 (Stardust Marine).
[125] Case C-379/99 PreußenElektra supra note 116 at para 59; critical comments by Winter at p. 483.
[126] Case 173/73 Italian Republic v Commission [1974] ECR 709.
[127] Case 730/79 Phillip Morris Holland BV v EC Commission [1980] ECR 2671 para 11.

exceptions to the general rules concerning the incompatibility of state aids with the common market must, as is generally accepted in Community law, be interpreted strictly (§ 2 III 4). This is true for instance for Art. 87(2)(c) containing a provision for the special position of Germany, resulting from the division of the country, in order to compensate for the economic disadvantages caused by that division. It does not however allow full compensation for the new *Länder*.[128]

The provisions of para. (3) depend on a prior decision of the Commission, which enjoys a certain discretion in this field,[129] and which will be discussed in the following § 8 V.

Recent case law has developed two more defences available to states, one based on Art. 86 (2) EC (see § 9 VI), the other on developing a more functional concept of aid relating to the support of undertakings charged with services of general economic interests in the sense of Art. 16 EC.

The *Ferring* case[130] concerned state measures (tax benefits) intended to offset the costs which an undertaking incurs in discharging a public service obligation. The Court implicitly recognised that, insofar as the tax advantage does not exceed the additional costs that this undertaking bears as imposed by national law, it is justified by Art. 86(2) EC (§ 9 VI 2). Only "to the extent that it exceeds the additional costs ... this cannot be regarded as necessary to enable them to carry out the particular tasks assigned to them."

The *Altmark* case[131] concerned subsidies given to an undertaking responsible for discharging regional transportation obligations. The Court gave a very sweeping statement on the conditions when such payments would be caught by the state aid rules resp. be exempted from the notification requirements:

> "... if a state measure must be regarded as compensation for the services provided by the recipient undertakings in order to discharge public service obligations, so that those undertakings do not enjoy a real financial advantage and the measure thus does not have the effect of putting them in a more favourable competitive position than the undertakings competing with them, such a measure is not caught by Article 92(1) (now Art. 87(1) EC, NR) of the Treaty.

---

[128]   Cases T-132 & 143/96, Freistaat Sachsen v Commission [1999] ECR II-3663, confirmed on appeal by case C-57/ooP [2003] ECR I-9975.

[129]   Case 730/79 footnote 126 at para 17.

[130]   Case C-53/00 Ferring SA v Agence centrale des organismes de sécurité sociale (ACOSS) [2001] ECR I-9067 at para 32; for a critique K. Erhardt, *Beihilfen für öffentliche Dienstleistungen*, 2003.

[131]   Case C-280/00 Altmark Trans et al. v Nahverkehrsgesellschaft Altmark [2003] ECR I-7747; critical comment by Bovis, *ELJ* 2005, 79 at 107.

However, for such compensation to escape classification as State aid in a particular case, a number of conditions must be satisfied.

– First, the recipient undertaking must actually have public service obligations to discharge, and the obligations must be clearly defined. In the main proceedings, the national court will therefore have to examine whether the public service obligations which were imposed on Altmark Trans are clear from the national legislation and/or the licences at issue in the main proceedings.

– Second, the parameters on the basis of which the compensation is calculated must be established in advance in an objective and transparent manner, to avoid it conferring an economic advantage which may favour the recipient undertaking over competing undertakings. Payment by a Member State of compensation for the loss incurred by an undertaking without the parameters of such compensation having been established beforehand, where it turns out after the event that the operation of certain services in connection with the discharge of public service obligations was not economically viable, therefore constitutes a financial measure which falls within the concept of State aid in the meaning of Article 92(1) of the Treaty.

– Third, the compensation cannot exceed what is necessary to cover all or part of the costs incurred in the discharge of public service obligations, taking into account the relevant receipts and a reasonable profit for discharging those obligations. Compliance with such a condition is essential to ensure that the recipient undertaking is not given any advantage which distorts or threatens to distort competition by strengthening that undertaking's competitive position.

– Fourth, where the undertaking which is to discharge public service obligations, in a specific case, is not chosen pursuant to a public procurement procedure which would allow for the selection of the tenderer capable of providing those services at the least cost to the community, the level of compensation needed must be determined on the basis of an analysis of the costs which a typical undertaking, well run and adequately provided with means of transport so as to be able to meet the necessary public service requirements, would have incurred in discharging those obligations, taking into account the relevant receipts and a reasonable profit for discharging the obligations" (paras. 87-93).

4. Direct effect

As mentioned above, Art. 88(3), last sentence, forbids Member states to pay out (new) aid before a final decision of the Commission has been taken. According to Art. 3 Reg. 659/99, there is a standstill obligation to Member states not to put a notifiable aid into effect before the Commission has taken a decision authorising such aid.

What about the consequences of non-notification or breach of the standstill obligation? Does it imply *per se* nullity, which national courts of law and administrative agencies have to respect and thereby impose on undertakings the unconditional duty to repay the aid, or would this interfere with the discretion of the Commission to authorise the payment of the aid later? In an earlier case, the ECJ had decided in the last sense[132].

It later substantially modified this ruling in order to effectively protect competitors against illegally paid out state aid. This is realised by the doctrine of "direct effect", which the Court, in distinguishing earlier case-law, developed in its subsequent *FNCE* case[133], where it was held:

> "National courts must offer to individuals in a position to rely on such breach the certain prospect that all the necessary inferences will be drawn, in accordance with their national law, as regards the validity of measures giving effect to the aid, the recovery of financial support granted in disregard of that provision and possible interim measures".

It also made clear that a later decision of the Commission declaring the aid compatible with the common market did not *ex post* legalise the payment in violation of Art. 88(3).

This direct effect in the sense of the immediate enforceability of the prohibition on implementation referred to in Article 88(3) EC extends to all aid that has been implemented without being notified as well as to the means of financing this aid, e.g. by a specific tax imposed on competitors.[134] Competitors may rely on the direct effect of this provision before national courts to ask for an injunction to freeze the aid, or an action to enforce repayment.[135] It is up to national law to determine standing, but it should not undermine the principle of effective judicial protection (§ 14 I).[136]

This doctrine of direct effect follows developments of Community law in other fields. It reinforces the position of the Commission in monitoring state aid (§ 8 V). It puts upon Member states the burden to strictly comply with Community law, unless one of the "defences" can be invoked, which the Court seems to broaden in respect of the public service obligations of Member states which are protected by Art. 16/86(2) EC.

The German Federal Court (Bundesgerichtshof – BGH) has concluded that contracts in violation of Art. 88(3) EC are void under German civil law and cannot be enforced. The aid has to be paid back, including interest.[137]

---

[132]   Case C-307/87 France v Commission [1990] ECR I-307.
[133]   Case C-354/90 Fédération nationale du commerce extérieur des produits alimentaires et Syndicat national des négociants et transformateurs de saumon v Commission [1991] ECR I-5505 para 12.
[134]   Cases C-261 + 262/01 Belgische Staat v Van Calster et al. [2003] ECR I-12249.
[135]   Hancher et al. para 21-062.
[136]   Case C-172/02 Streekgewest Westelijk Noord-Brabant v Staatssecretaris van Financiën [2005] ECR I-(13.1.2005) para 18.
[137]   BGH *EuZW* 2003, 444; 2004, 252; comment by Verse/Wurmnest AcP 2004, 855.

§ 8. FREE MOVEMENT (2) – THE EC AND ITS LEGISLATIVE AND SUPERVISORY MISSION

Selected Bibliography of § 8

H. Abbott/M. Tyler, *Safer by Design*, 2nd ed. 1997; S. Arrowsmith, *The Law of Public and Utilities Procurement*, 1996; S. Arrowsmith, "An assessment of the new legislative package on public procurement", *CMLRev* 2004, 1277; R. Bieber/R. Dehousse/J. Pinder/J. Weiler, *1992: One European market*, 1988; A. Biondi et al., *The law of State Aid in the EC*, 2004; Chr. Bovis, "Recent case law relating to public procurement: A beacon for the integration of public markets", *CMLRev* 2002, 1025; P. Cecchini, *The European Challenge: 1992, the Benefits of a Single Market*, 1988; D. Dingel, *Public Procurement*, 1999; C. Ehlermann, "The internal market following the Single Act", *CMLRev* 1987, 361; U. Ehricke, "Dynamischer Verweis in EG-Richtlinien auf Regelungen privater Normungsgremien", *EuZW* 2003, 746; D. Esty/B. Geradin (eds.), *Regulatory Competition and Economic Integration*, 2001; A. den Exter, "Legal Consequences of EU Accession for Central and Eastern European Health Care Systems", *ELJ* 2002, 556; L. Hancher, *Regulation for Competition*, 1989; G. Howells, *Consumer Product Safety*, 1998; Ch. Joerges/J. Falke/H.-W. Micklitz/G. Brüggemeier, *Die Sicherheit von Konsumgütern und die Entwicklung der Europäischen Gemeinschaft*, 1988; Th. Klindt, "Der "new approach" im Produktrecht des europäischen Binnenmarktes: Vermutungwirkung der technischen Normung", *EuZW* 2002, 133; A. Lopez-Teruella, "A European Community Regulatory Framework for Electronic Commerce", *CMLRev* 2001, 1337; H.-W. Micklitz (ed.), *Post-market control of consumer goods*, 1990; H.-W. Micklitz, *Internationales Produktsicherheitsrecht*, 1995; H.-W. Micklitz/Th. Roethe,/St. Weatherill, *Federalism and responsibility*, 1994; H-W. Micklitz/N. Reich, *Legal Aspects of European Space Activities*, 1989; H.-W. Micklitz/N. Reich, *Public Interest Litigation before European Courts*, 1996; P. Oliver (with M. Jarvis), *Free Movement of Goods in the EC*, 4th ed. 2003; N. Reich, "Competition between legal orders", *CMLRev* 1992, 861; N. Reich/A. Halfmeier, "Consumer Protection in the Global Village", *Dickinson Law Rev.* 2001, 111; N. Reich/H.W. Micklitz, *Europäisches Verbraucherrecht*, 4. A. 2003; C. Röhl, *Akkreditierung und Zertifizierung im Produktsicherheitsrecht*, 2000; S. Weatherill, "Pre-emption, Harmonisation and the Distribution of Competences to Regulate in the Internal Market", in: C. Barnard/D. Scott, *The Law of the Single European Market*, 2002, 41; P. Sutherland, *1 Janvier 1993 – ce qui se va changer en Europe*, 1988; E. Vos, *Institutional Frameworks of Community Health and Safety Regulation*, 1999.

I. CONTROL MECHANISMS: PRINCIPLES, METHODS, LIMITATIONS

As we have seen, the free movement of goods, persons, services and capital is already guaranteed by primary Community law with direct effect. It has been written into Art. 14(2) EC, where the Single Act of 1987 defines the internal market as:

> an area without internal frontiers where the free movement of goods, persons, services and capital is ensured in accordance with the provisions of this Treaty.

However, this provision does not have direct effect.[138]

On the other hand, Community law allows Member States to maintain restrictions to free movement . This is either under the public policy or the general interest tests. In turn, these tests are subject to observing the proportionality criteria, supervised by the European Court. Although farreaching, this control of Community law over Member State restrictions on free movement cannot guarantee uniform or harmonized conditions of marketing in the internal market. The reasons for this are as follows:

- The free movement provisions are limited to economic activities with a "Community" element. This has been defined differently for goods on the one hand (the *Keck* criteria, *supra* § 7 II 3), and for persons and services on the other (the cross-border element, §§ 4 II 2, 7 III 3). Purely internal situations are not caught by primary law and may lead to reverse discrimination, thereby undermining the unity of the internal market.[139]
- Even if exceptions to free movement provisions are strictly controlled by Court practice, this can only be done on a case-by-case basis. This is time consuming, unpredictable and inefficient. It is only to a limited extent capable of setting common standards, which all market partners have to observe in the EU.
- In granting generous liberal rights of free movement, the Community must at the same time take care that adequate standards of production and marketing are set. This would include, for example, the area of product safety, truth in advertising, and fairness in commercial and consumer transactions. Since Member State regulations may differ considerably, these have to be coordinated by mechanisms of rules on jurisdiction and conflict of laws. Since these mechanisms themselves clearly lack harmonization, they may create additional impediments to free movement, thus lacking preventive effect.

---

[138] Case C-378/97 Criminal proceedings against Florus Ariel Wijsenbeek, [1999] ECR I-6207.
[139] For a discussion of recent tendencies of a more restrictive reading on permitting reverse discriminations cf. Oliver, *supra* note 44 at 146-154.

In achieving its mission to create an internal market, the Community has at its disposal a wide range of instruments. The classic instruments were harmonization measures by directives, namely unanimous voting in the Council (Art. 94 EC), or by Commission supervision under the infringement proceedings (Art. 226 EC). Both instruments are cumbersome. For example, the first not only requires unanimity in the Council but also excludes equal participation of the European Parliament in the law making process. As for the second, this focuses on the wrongdoing of an individual Member State that has maintained or introduced impediments to free movement.

The Single Act of 1987 and the following Community measures have introduced new approaches both to legislation and to supervision. These will be briefly examined by giving typical examples, although without attempting an exhaustive approach:
- Measures may be adopted for the approximation of Member State provisions whose object is the establishment or functioning of the internal market, Art. 95 EC. This is done by the co-decision procedure of Art. 251 EC, which puts Parliament and Council on an equal footing. It also allows for (qualified) majority voting in the Council. In this way, it avoids veto rights of individual Member States. However, veto rights are still possible with regard to free movement of persons and direct taxation.
- The competence of the EC has been interpreted broadly, even though it is not unlimited and is controlled by the ECJ (§ 3 III).
- Member States may opt out if Community legislation fails to meet certain standards, Art. 95(4)-(9) EC.

The liberalizing thrust of Community law began with the Commission preparing an intensive legislative program in its 1985 White Paper on the internal market[140]. This was followed up and pushed through by a number of legislative and supervisory measures after the enactment of the Single Act:
- The principle of country of origin and mutual recognition, developed in the *Cassis* case of 1979 for product standards (§ 7 II). That is, a product put legally into circulation in one EU country should be able to circulate freely within the entire internal market without additional controls or other impediments. In this field, legislative action of the Community would not be necessary.[141]
- Next, areas involving *public interests*, namely health, safety, environmental protection and consumer protection. Where these were at stake, Community directives would establish certain general safety requirements. However, details would be left to technical standards elaborated under the auspices of Community

---

[140] Com (1985) 310 final.
[141] For details, cf. Oliver, *Free movement of goods*, 4th ed. 2003, 133-138.

institutions (*infra* II). At the same time, a system of post-marketing surveillance had to be established Community-wide (§ 13 II).

–   In the area of *services,* primary law could not simply impose the country of origin principle. Instead, additional Community measures were needed, as will be shown in the area of television and electronic commerce (*infra* III).

–   Member States can indirectly manipulate free movement as purchasers of goods or services. They can do so through preferential or intransparant *procurement practices*. Legislation and Court practice in this area have been particularly active in opening public markets to suppliers from the entire Community, thereby stimulating competition (*infra* IV).

–   Establishing governance rules of Member States with direct effect could result in de-centralizing Commission supervision of the functioning of the internal market. At the same time, the system would operate more efficiently if market actors participate (§ 19 III 2).

–   Special rules exist for the supervision of state aid (V) They are supported by the direct effect of illegally paid out aid according to Art. 88(3) EC (§ 7 VI 4).

The following sections cannot give a complete analysis of the impressive bulk of Community regulation and case law. Rather, they will take a look at some typical and relevant examples where the directions and objectives of Community law can be seen most clearly. This is in line with the functional approach of this work towards an understanding of Community law.

II. "NEW APPROACH" – THE IMPORTANCE OF TECHNICAL STANDARDS

The so-called "old approach" to technical harmonization aimed to establish detailed standards for every product so that it could circulate freely in the common market. This led to a highly cumbersome and lengthy harmonization process. The "new approach" introduced after the *Cassis* decision and the 1985 program on the internal market is much more efficient: The legislative instrument used here is a combination of framework directives setting out the essential requirements, and a reference to (European) technical standards including the procedures for evaluating conformity, and the introduction of the "CE" marking. Free circulation is ensured by a Community system of certification, with the position of the "CE" mark guaranteeing unhampered access to all Member State markets, subject to a safeguard clause. Business and industry have the choice as to how to comply with these obligations. Within this framework, the European standards organizations have the task of drafting technical specifications, which would offer one way (amongst others) of complying with directives.

The "new approach" directives apply to products to be placed (or put into service) on the Community market for the first time. They accordingly apply to new products manufactured in the Member States and to new, used, and second-hand products imported from third countries. The Commission, in "Improving and simplifying the regulatory environment"[142], describes the main features of this type of internal market legislation as follows:

- Legislative harmonization is limited to the essential requirements to which products placed on the Community market must conform in order to benefit from freedom of movement on the EC market.
- Technical specifications of products reflect the essential requirements, as defined in the relevant directives. These are established by harmonized standards.
- Applying harmonized standards remains voluntary. The manufacturer can always apply other technical specifications to meet essential requirements.
- Products manufactured in conformity with harmonized standards are presumed to conform with essential requirements.

Since 1987, some 20 "new approach" directives have been adopted by the Council and the European Parliament.[143] Their application ranges from medical instruments[144] to machinery[145] and toys.[146]

This work does not undertake an in-depth analysis of the sometimes highly technical directives, or the standards adopted to make them conform to essential safety requirements. They have so far not given rise to substantial litigation. It should be mentioned that as early as 1980, the Court approved this type of internal market regulation concerning the so-called Low Voltage Directive 73/23/EEC of 23.2.1973[147]. It did so by delegating functions to private bodies. That is, once a conformity mark had been put on a product according to Community law, judicial authorities could not prevent its marketing in the country of destination. This was only possible under the specific safeguard procedure as foreseen in the directive.[148]

Clearly, the problem of consumer product safety remains in relation to rules which aim primarily to ease market access. The Community has also created two supplementary instruments to guarantee a high level of consumer protection with regard to product safety, per Art. 153(1) EC, namely:

---

[142]   Communication of 7.3.2001 Com (2001) 130 final at 12.
[143]   Details Reich/Micklitz, *Europäisches Verbraucherrecht*, 4. Auflage, 2003, paras 25.27-25.34.
[144]   Dir. 93/42/EC of 14.6.1993 [1993] OJ L 169.
[145]   Dir. 98/37/EC of 22.6.1998 [1998] OJ L 207.
[146]   Dir. 88/378/EEC of 3.5.1988 [1988], OJ L 187.
[147]   [1977] OJ L 77/29.
[148]   Case 815/79 Criminal proceedings against Cremonini and Vrancovich [1980] ECR 3583.

– Directives on post-marketing surveillance with a Community ambit (§ 13 II) to protect the legitimate expectations of consumers.
– Rules on product liability as a safety net of last resort (§ 20 III 2).

III. "COUNTRY OF ORIGIN" – TV AND E-COMMERCE

1. *"TV without frontiers"-Directives 89/552 and 97/36*

a. TV as a "service"?

In the early years of EC law it was not clear whether TV could be regarded as a service. The cause of uncertainty stemmed from the general structure of the organization of radio and TV broadcasting. This was either done by a public monopoly, or was put under strict public regulation. Moreover, the system usually excluded foreign providers. The *Sacchi* case[149] indeed recognized that the transmission of TV signals should be regarded as a service. However, at the same time it accepted that the service could be monopolized by the State.

Later technological and economic developments made possible the commercial cross-border transmission of broadcasts via cable or satellite. The following questions then arose:
– Whether such activities would come under the freedom to provide service provisions.
– Whether and how far restrictions on transmission and on advertising were compatible with Community law.
– Whether broadcasters could evade stricter rules of the receiving country – for example, the Netherlands – by changing their business seat and transmission activities to a country with less strict standards – for example, Luxembourg.
– Whether the Community had power to regulate, or rather to liberalize, cross-border TV transmission and reception – with the possible result of undermining the traditional public monopoly existing in a given Member State.

The Court, after some hesitation,[150] took an active stand in its case law and particularly its *Bond van Adverteerders* judgment (§ 7 III 2). It did so by two routes. Firstly, by insisting that cable TV financed by advertising was a cross-border service against remuneration. Secondly, by maintaining that rules of national law that attempt to

---

[149] *Supra* note 61.
[150] Case 52/79 Procureur du Roi v Debauve [1980] ECR 833 where restrictions of advertising in cross-border cable transmissions were regarded to be justified by the public interest test.

monopolize advertising revenues to a state controlled body are a discrimination prohibited by EC law. It should also be mentioned that during the eighties a general trend towards a more commercial concept of TV services won support in the EC. This paved the way for the adoption of Directive 89/552/EEC of 3.10.89[151].

b. The *country of origin* principle of Dir. 89/552 and its limitations

Directive 89/552, based on the internal market and freedom to provide service provisions, is only concerned with cross-border TV. It does not deal with regulating TV in general, in order not to interfere in Member State competences. It tries to balance the requirements of Community law – which are mostly linked to economic considerations – with Member State regulation of broadcasting as a public service with a cultural mission, as recognized by the case law of the ECJ. The country of origin principle as regulatory mechanism of the directive sought to balance these conflicting objectives as follows:

– Requiring that all broadcasts emanating from the Community must comply with the legislation of the originating Member State[152].
– Requiring Member States to ensure freedom of reception and not to impede retransmission on their territory of TV broadcasts from other Member States for reasons which fall within the field coordinated by the directive[153].
– Allowing Member States where the service provider has its business seat to adopt more stringent provisions on content and advertising than foreseen in the Directive[154].
– Providing for a safeguard procedure to prevent the transmission of clearly illegal broadcasts, especially pornography[155].
– Forbidding advertising for tobacco products and for prescription medicines[156].
– Restricting advertising for alcoholic beverages[157], and advertising to children[158].
– There is no specific rule prohibiting misleading advertising in TV. This is left to the general provision of Dir. 84/450/EEC.[159]

---

[151]   [1989] OJ L 298/23.
[152]   Art. 2 (1) of Dir. 89/552.
[153]   Art. 2 (2) of Dir. 89/552.
[154]   Art. 3 of Dir. 89/552.
[155]   Art. 22 of Dir. 89/552.
[156]   Art. 13/14 of Dir. 89/552.
[157]   Art. 12 of Dir. 89/552.
[158]   Art. 16 of Dir. 89/552.
[159]   [1984] OJ L 250/17.

The *de Agostini* litigation[160] concerned, amongst other issues, whether the country of origin principle applied to the Swedish ban on TV advertising to children against a broadcaster or advertiser established in the UK. The advertising had been presented in the Swedish language to attract Swedish children. The Consumer Ombudsman based the prohibition on the special rules of Swedish TV advertising legislation and on the general clause of the Act against unfair practices. AG Jacobs applied the country of origin principle both to the special rules on TV advertising and to the prohibition contained in the general clause. This would have meant that only British authorities are competent to control whether the broadcast violated British rules on children's advertising[161], and on deceptive advertising, not having regard to the fact that the British authority did not understand Swedish. The Court preferred a more differentiated approach:

– Since the Directive only attempts a partial harmonization, the country of origin principle is limited to the harmonized field. Here, this was TV advertising to children. Swedish authorities are prohibited from applying their (stricter) rules.
– The Directive does not in principle preclude application of national rules with the general aim of consumer protection. However, this is on condition that they do not involve a second control of TV broadcasts in fields already controlled by the country of origin. Therefore, the general ban on misleading and unfair advertising is not caught by the country of origin principle, and may be enforced by the Ombudsman according to Swedish legislation.

The *Bacardi* case[162] concerned the interdiction of indirect alcohol advertising by the French "Loi Envin" arising from the appearance on screen of hoardings during the transmission of sporting events and its effects on bi-national cross-border TV broadcasts. The Court found that indirect advertising is not caught by the country of origin-principle of Dir. 89/522. A possible restriction of cross-border marketing of services is justified under health aspects: "... it is for the Member States to decide on the degree of protection which they wish to afford to public health and on the way in which that protection is to be achieved" (para 33). They must of course observe the principle of proportionality.

c. Dir. 97/36

The *de Agostini* decision, which is clearly a compromise between different principles, allows a flexible reading of the country of origin principle. The *Bacardi* case seems to reverse this doctrine. Its ambit therefore depends on the area harmonized. This may

---

[160] Joined cases C-34-36/95 Konsumentombudsmannen v De Agostini Forlag AB and TV Shop i Sverige AB [1997] ECR I-3843.
[161] That is, in implementing Art. 16 of Dir. 89/552.
[162] Case C-429/02 Bacardi-France v TF1 et al. [2004] ECR I-(13.7.2004).

be broader or narrower, depending on the regulatory technique of the directive at hand. The later amendment of Dir. 89/552 by Dir. 97/36/EC of 30.6.1997[163] did not change the substance of the country of origin principle, but extended it to sponsoring activities. It also clarified the concept of establishing a broadcasting company, and improved the safeguard procedure of Art. 22.

Litigation was particularly concerned with calculating the 45-minute period for the purpose of determining the amount of advertising interruptions[164], where the Court, in its *Pro-Sieben* decision[165] opted for the most liberal solution. This was the gross principle, where the time for advertisements is added to this period, against the more restrictive net principle. However, Member States may impose the net principle for broadcasters under their jurisdiction.

2. The e-commerce Directive 2000/31

a. Issues of applicable law in e-commerce

E-commerce evolved first as a technological possibility and than as an economic activity with the spread of the internet. It allows a "de-territorialisation" of trading hitherto unknown. Providers of internet services, and suppliers of goods or services offer distance purchases via the internet. Since business (B2B) clients or private (B2C) consumers may reside in different areas, the question of applicable law in a cross-border situation becomes important. Traders may become subject to a multitude of jurisdictions and laws when offering their services, marketing their goods, and enforcing potential claims (§ 12 II, 16 III). Consumers, on the other hand, may be confronted with jurisdictions and laws that are foreign to them. At the same time, service providers and service recipients may not know about the place of residence of their counterparts because of either wrong assumptions or of wilful misleading. The result might be either to abstain from using the internet for their purchasing decisions, or have their legitimate expectations (§ 13) frustrated. At the same time, Member States may be tempted to enact restrictions on business activities via the internet. This would apply especially to commercial communications, to imposing licensing requirements, or to subjecting providers to unjustified risks of liability.

Against this background and despite legislation on distance contracts (§ 17 II 2),[166] in April 1997 the Commission issued a communication on "A European initiative in

---

[163] [1997] *OJ* L 202/60.
[164] According to Art. 11 (3) of Dir. 89/552.
[165] Case C-6/98 [1999] ARD v Pro Sieben Media AG ECR I-7599 at para 30.
[166] In the meantime, the Community had enacted Dir. 97/7/EC of 20.5.1997 on the protection of consumers in respect of distance contracts, [1997] OJ L 144/19, excluding however financial services.

electronic commerce". This was followed in November 1998 by a proposal for a "Directive on certain legal aspects of electronic commerce in the internal market."[167] After following the co-decision procedure in Parliament and Council with surprising speed, the Council adopted the "E-commerce directive" on 8 June 2000.[168]

b. Internal market and *country of origin* principle

The country of origin principle is laid down in Art. 3 under the heading of "Internal market", similar to the TV Directive. The most important provision is para (2) which reads:

> Member States may not, for reasons falling within the coordinated field, restrict the freedom to provide information society services from another Member State.

This rule is supposed to liberalize E-commerce within the EU. It is supplemented by a provision expressly excluding prior authorization procedures. This stands in contrast to radio and TV broadcasting. Its legal content and importance is subject to controversies. These can briefly be summarized as follows:

–   It is not clear whether the country of origin principle must be understood as a conflict-of-law rule determining the applicable law in cross-border conflicts as the law of the information society service provider. This seems to contradict another of its provisions (Art. 1 (4)), according to which the Directive does not establish "additional rules on private international law nor does it deal with the jurisdiction of courts". Yet again, it is unclear whether it creates a "most-favoured-regulation" principle, allowing the supplier from one EU country always to rely on its country of origin, but also relates to the country of service provision when this is more favourable.[169]

–   The country of origin principle depends on the "coordinated field", Art. 1 (h). In this way, it specifically exempts requirements applying to goods as such, to the delivery of goods, and to services not provided by electronic means. These distinctions are not always easy to understand in practice, since they may lead to the applicability of different laws depending on what aspect of the supply of goods or provision of services is involved.

–   The Directive does not apply to certain services, such as gambling, representation of clients before the courts, and taxation. As a general rule of Community law, these exceptions have to be construed narrowly, thereby allowing lawyers to offer their services cross-border without being subjected to restrictive rules of the

---

[167]   COM (1998) 586 final [1999] C 030/4.
[168]   [2000] OJ L 178/1.
[169]   Reich/ Halfmeier, *DickLR* 2001, 111 at 133.

receiving country. These may, for instance, forbid advertising on websites of lawyers for reasons of professional ethics.

– The Annex contains express derogations from Art. 3, in particular copyright and other industrial property rights, "contractual obligations concerning consumer contracts", the permissibility of forbidding unsolicited commercial communications by electronic mail, and others.

– The Directive is without prejudice to existing Community law protecting "in particular public health and consumer interests, as established by Community acts and national legislation implementing them in so far as this does not restrict the freedom to provide information society services", Art. 1 (5). The latter qualification is again subject to doubt, since rules on health and consumer protection can only operate to restrict the freedom to provide services, but are usually justified by the general interest.

– A special safeguard procedure is provided to combat, for example, pornography on the internet, similar to the procedure of the TV Directive.

– The country of origin principle only applies to information society service providers established in the EU. Service providers established in third countries (including association countries) have to follow the general rules on jurisdiction and conflict of laws.

– Competent authorities of the country of origin are obliged to protect not only citizens of their own country but *all* Community citizens. Although an extension of the principle of territoriality of control, this is not reflected in the provisions of the directive itself, for example on information exchange between competent authorities.[170]

The importance of Dir. 2000/31 is most substantially felt in the area of advertising and commercial communication. Here, the liberalizing effect of the country of origin principle will encourage traders to shop for the "best" (that is, the most liberal and least restrictive) regulatory environment. In this way, they undermine higher standards in the receiving country. To avoid such a "race to the bottom", the Directive also contains minimum requirements on information, transparency, and contracting. The aim here is to increase the autonomy of contracting partners, most notably consumers (§ 17 II 2). On the other hand, it exempts certain service providers from liability for mere conduit, caching and hosting, without however establishing rules on liability of its own but only duties of cooperation.[171]

---

[170]   The constitutional and economic problems involved in this extension of the principle of home country control are discussed by Weatherill, in: Barnard/Scott, *The Law of the Single European Market*, 41 at 66-69.

[171]   Lopez-Teruella, *CMLRev* 2001, 1337 at 1350.

No Court practice exists with regard to applying and interpreting the e-commerce directive. The exceptions to, and controversies around, the country of origin principle shed doubt on whether its intention, as expressed in recital (7), can really be achieved:

> In order to ensure legal certainty and consumer confidence, this Directive must lay down a clear and general framework to cover certain legal aspects of electronic commerce in the internal market.

3. Proposal on services

The proposal for a "Directive of the European Parliament and of the Council on services in the internal market" of 5.3.2004[172] wants to introduce the country of origin-principle to all services offered in the internal market. Art. 16 (1) insists that

> "Member States shall ensure that providers are subject only to the national provisions of their Member State or origin which fall within the coordinated field. Para 1 shall cover national provisions relating to access to and the exercice of a service activity, in particular those requirements governing the behaviour of the provider, the quality or content of the service, advertising, contracts and the provider's liability".

Art. 16 (3) contains a "blacklist" of forbidden requirements, Art. 17 a list of general derogations covering *i.a.* "contracts concluded by consumers", Art. 18 a list of temporary derogations, Art. 19 a list of case-by-case derogations. Section 2 imposes detailed rules on rights of recipients of services, in particular a prohibition of discriminatory treatment based on nationality or residence, Art. 21. Chapter IV is concerned with quality of services, e.g. transparency, professional insurance, after-sales guarantees, dispute settlement. The final destiny of the far-reaching "horizontal" proposal, which covers many different services and has great repercussions on contract law, remains to be seen.

IV. STIMULATE COMPETITION – THE CASE OF PUBLIC PROCUREMENT

1. The need to liberalize public procurement

Traditionally, public procurement in Member States had been an area for national, regional or social policy objectives. These were to be achieved not by regulatory, but by economic measures. If other EU nationals or companies were openly or indirectly

---

[172] COM [2004] 2 final.

banned from participating in tenders for public procurement, such measures amounted to a violation of either Art. 28 or 49 EC, depending on the type of business. Moreover, because of their purely economic nature they could usually not be justified (§ 7 I 2). As a result, even in its early case law the Court condemned those Member State practices that preferred home suppliers because only home suppliers could fulfill them[173] – for example, by imposing technical standards on tenders for pipelines. Thus, Community law banned industrial policy objectives through procurement rules in national or international law.[174]

However, this "negative" aspect did not suffice to make procurement practices open, transparent and objective. This was first done by a directive on public work[175] and on public supplies.[176] These were amended several times and codified[177] to meet the requirements of the internal market. Their sphere of application was extended to the supply of public services.[178] The so-called exempted areas concerning procurement in the public utility sector were abandoned.[179]

Directives 2004/17 and 18/EC of the EP and the Council of 31 March 2004[180] codified and amended the procurement procedures of entities operating in the water, energy, transport and postal services sector, and for the award of public works, supply and service contracts.

In addition to the substantive law on public procurement, the Community also enacted the so-called remedies Directive[181] This obliged Member States to establish effective review procedures for decisions taken by contracting authorities and to provide for interim relief. This allowed the possibility to set aside decisions contrary to the procurement directives in the interest of competitors, and potentially allow for compensation in case of economic loss.[182]

The Court, under the principle of effective judicial protection (§ 14 I), prefers a broad reading of the remedies to be provided by Member states. They must be granted also

---

[173] E.g. case 45/87 Commission v Ireland [1988] ECR 4929 (Dundalk).
[174] For an overview cf. Micklitz/Reich, *Legal Aspects of European Space Activities*, 1989.
[175] Dir. 71/305/EEC, [1971] OJ L 185/5.
[176] Dir. 77/62/EEC, [1997] OJ L 13/1.
[177] In Dir. 93/36 and 93/37 EEC, [1993] OJ L 199/1.
[178] Via Dir. 92/50/EEC, [1992] OJ L 209/1.
[179] Via Dir. 93/38/EEC, [1993] OJ L 199/84.
[180] [2004] OJ L 134; comment Arrowsmith *CMLRev* 2004, 1277.
[181] Dir. 89/665/EEC [1989] OJ L 395/33, supplemented by Dir. 92/13/EEC [1992] OJ L 76/14.
[182] Cf. the discussion by Arrowsmith in Micklitz/Reich, *Public Interest Litigation before European Courts*, 1996 at 125; cases C-76/97 Tögel v Niederösterreichische Gebietskrankenkasse [1998] ECR I-5357 and C-327/00 Santex v Unito Socio Sanitaria [2003] ECR I(27.12.2003).

against decisions taken by contracting authorities outside a formal award procedure and a decision prior to a formal call for tenders.[183]

2. Procurement decisions: purely economic or social and environmental criteria, too?

Since then, the case law on interpreting the procurement directives has become quite substantial, and cannot adequately be analysed here.[184] The most controversial discussion has centred around the question whether other than merely economic criteria could be taken into account for decisions on selection of participating undertakings and award of contracts. How far can objectives of structural, social and environmental policy be achieved by procurement decisions? Should one regard this as a contradiction to the mostly competitive objective of the directive, or could the general interest criterion which allows restriction on free movement also be read into procurement decisions?

The Court's answer is two-fold. On the one hand, in its *Swoboda* decision[185] it insisted that:

> Dir. 92/50 pursues fundamentally the same objective as the directives on the coordination of the procedures for the award of public work and supply contracts, which is, according to the settled case-law of the Court, to avoid the risk of preference being given to national tenderers or candidates whenever a contract is awarded by the contracting authorities and the possibility that a body financed or controlled by the State, regional or local authorities, or other bodies governed by public law may choose to be guided by considerations other than economic ones.

This seems to apply a purely economic, market-oriented approach, as is confirmed by the Directive that an award should be given to the economically "*most advantageous tender*".

On the other hand, in its *Beentjes* decision[186] the Court maintained that social policy reasons – awarding the contract to a bidder privileging long-term unemployed persons – were permissible, provided there was no direct or indirect discrimination. However, such criteria cannot be used for selecting candidates, but for awarding the contract – and then only if stated clearly in the tender offer.

---

[183] Case C-26/03, Stadt Halle, RPL Recyclingpark Lochau GmbH v Arbeitsgemeinschaft Thermische Restabfall- und Energieverwertungsanlage TREA Leuna, [2005] ECR I-(11.1.2005).
[184] For an overview, Bovis, *CMLRev* 2002, 1025.
[185] Case C-411/00 Felix Swoboda v Österreichische Nationalbank [2002] ECR I-10567 at para 45.
[186] Case 31/87 Gebroeders Beentjes v Netherlands [1988] ECR 4635 at para 30; Bovis at 1051.

The *Concordia Bus* decision[187] was concerned with ecological criteria. In this case, preference was given to tenders for an urban bus system to operators with low NOx emissions to avoid pollution in Helsinki. This could only be achieved by buses operating on natural gas. The Court stated that *economically most advantageous tender* was not limited to merely economic criteria, but could establish other criteria too. These included environmental quality. In this respect, the commitment of the Community to improve environmental standards[188] could be used as an argument in public procurement decisions.

In order to avoid abuses or a hidden discrimination against competitors, the Court developed a number of criteria to be fulfilled by public procurement authorities:
–   Criteria must be linked to the subject-matter of the contract.
–   The authority must apply all procedural rules as laid down in the directive.
–   Criteria must be made known in advance and must be expressly mentioned in the contract documents.
–   Criteria must comply with the fundamental principles of Community law, especially the principle of non-discrimination.

The Court also discarded the argument that the ecological criteria of the tender could only be fulfilled by a small number of bidders, including the contracting entity's own fleet and that this amounted to discrimination. It was sufficient that the award criteria were objective and applied without distinction to all bidders.

V.   MONITORING OF STATE AID BY THE COMMISSION

1.   The pivotal role of the Commission

Within the rules on state aids, the Commission plays a central role in a double direction:
–   A *supervisory role* insofar as it controls the legality of state aid, which differs whether it relates to existing aid or to newly granted ones. For "new" aid, this role is reinforced by the direct effect of Art. 88(3) last sentence (§ 7 VI 4), where Member State courts and the Commission share jurisdiction. In order to safeguard the powers of the Commission, Member States are subject to strict notification requirements with certain exceptions for so-called *de minimis* aids.[189]

---

[187]   Case C-513/99 Concordia Bus Finland Oy Ab v Helsingin kaupunki and HKL Bussiliikenne [2002] ECR I-7213.
[188]   Per Art. 6 EC.
[189]   Commission Reg. (EC) 69/2001 of 12.1.2001 on *de minimis* aids, [2001] OJ L 10/30.

- A *regulatory role* insofar as the Commission has discretion, subject to control by the CFI and finally the ECJ, to declare certain aid compatible with the internal market, Art. 87(3). Art. 89 EC authorises the Council to adopt exemption regulations for certain categories of state aid and to delegate this power to the Commission.[190]

The supervisory role of the Commission has been laid down in the already mentioned Reg. 659/1999 (§ 7 VI 1). The regulatory practice has been implemented in several binding or non-binding instruments concerning regional aids,[191] environmental aids[192], aid to employment,[193] training aid,[194] aid to support SMU[195], research and development,[196] risk capital.[197] Aids to rescue or restructure failed companies are allowed under strictly controlled circumstances: they must be limited in time, undertakings have to submit a realistic restructuring plan (which must usually reduce capacity, including workforce), and the aid must not become a permanent subsidy to an undertaking or a group of undertakings. States have a reporting and monitoring obligation to avoid abuses.[198]

2. Recovery of illegally paid out state aid

Under Art. 88(2) EC illegally granted state aid must be abolished or altered according to a time period determined by the Commission. In Court practice, later taken up by Art. 14 of Reg. 659/1999, this leads to an obligation of the Member state to recover illegally paid out aid.[199] Art. 15 provides for a 10-year limitation period. The procedure is performed in two steps: the Commission takes a "recovery decision"; the Member state, according to its own procedural rules, which must however comply with the Community law principle of effectiveness, obligates the recipient of the aid to pay it back to the institution that has granted the aid. This obligation also extends to reimburse illegally raised taxes in order to finance the aid[200].

---

[190] By Council Regulation (EC) No. 994/98 of 7 May 1998 on the application of Articles 92 and 93 of the Treaty to certain categories of horizontal state aid, [1998] OJ L 142/1. For the policy issues involved, see Caig/de Búrca at 1138-1140.

[191] Guidelines on National Regional Aid [1998] OJ C 74/9; Craig/de Búrca at p. 1164.

[192] L. Krämer, *EC Enviromental law*, 5th ed. 2003, pp. 113-114.

[193] Commission Regulation No. 2204/2002 of 23 Dec. 2002 [2002] OJ L 337/3.

[194] Commission Regulation No. 68/2001 of 12.1.2001 [2001] OJ L 10/20.

[195] Commission Regulation No. 70/2001 of 12.1.2001, [2001] OJ 10/33, amended by Reg. 364/2004 of 28.2.2004, [2004] OJ L 63/22 extending its scope to include aid for research and development.

[196] Communication of 27.1.1995 [1996] OJ C 45, amended on 8.5.2002, [2002] OJ C 111.

[197] Commission notice of 21.8.2001, [2001] OJ C 235.

[198] Commission guidelines of 1.10.2004, [2004] OJ C 244/2; comment Nicolaides/Kekelekis, *ECLR* 2004, 578; for prior law see Hancher et al. supra note 134 at 3-022-3-071.

[199] Mestmäcker/Schweitzer supra note 122 at 1141-1154.

[200] Cases C-261/ + 262/01 Belgische Staat v Van Calster et al. [2003] ECR I-12249 para 54.

The Court has developed very strict rules regarding the obligation of an undertaking to pay back the illegally paid aid. Even if recovery takes place in accordance with the relevant procedural provisions of national law, these provisions must be applied in such a way that the recovery is not rendered "practically impossible", as the Court insisted in its *Alcan* decision.[201] This has a number of far-reaching consequences on Member state law and on the position of an undertaking that has received illegally paid out aid:

- Time-limits for repayment under national law must be disapplied if they make recovery impossible.[202]
- The undertaking cannot rely on its "legitimate expectation" not to pay back the aid; the obligation of repayment cannot depend on the conduct of state authorities.
- There is no "good-faith" defence as far as receiving the aid is concerned because "a diligent businessman should normally be able to determine whether that procedure (under the Community aid rules, NR) has been followed".[203]
- The undertaking cannot argue that the aid was "used up" and does not appear anymore in its balance sheets. It is sufficient that the aid benefits its overall good-will and position in the market.[204]
- In the same spirit, the undertaking cannot invoke any "impossibility" or "financial difficulties" to pay back the aid. Eventually it must be liquidated, unless there is a case of "*force majeure*", which must be construed strictly. This is not the case if some undertakings will go bankrupt in the case of an illegally granted structural aid to a group of undertakings.[205]

Member state law on recovery must comply with these Community obligations under the general rules of supremacy and uniformity (§ 3 I). These rules may seem harsh and rigid at first glance and put a considerable burden on undertakings that receive state means, but must be explained by the effort of the Court to safeguard the *per conditio concurrentium* in the internal market, and by the fact that the Community rules on state aids have been developed for a long time and seem to be quite settled now, even if in individual cases there may be doubt as to the existence of (illegal) aid. But this risk of wrong legal interpretation is put on the receiving undertaking (and the state institution granting the aid), not on the Community. On the other hand, the Court seems to be prepared to consider the special role and function of undertakings delivering services of general economic interest in the sense of Art. 16 EC (§ 7 V 3).

---

[201] Case C-24/95 Land Rheinland-Pfalz v. Alcan GmbH [1997] ECR I-1591 para 24.
[202] Para 37 of the *Alcan*-judgment.
[203] Para 25 of the *Alcan*-judgment.
[204] Para 51 of he *Alcan*-judgment.
[205] Case C-75/97 Commission v Belgium [1999] ECR I-3671 para 89.

§ 9. SAFEGUARDING FREE AND FAIR COMPETITION (1) – RULES FOR UNDERTAKINGS

Selected bibliography of § 9

A. Amato, *Antitrust and the Bounds of Power*, 1997; J. Basedow, "Who will protect competition in Europe", *EBOR* 2001, 443; J. Basedow, *Weltkartellrecht*, 1998; K. Becker-Schwarze, *Steuerungsmöglichkeiten des Kartellrechts bei umweltschützenden Unternehmenskooperationen*, 1997; Bellamy & Child/P. Roth (ed.), *EC Law of Competition*, 5th ed. 2001; Bishop & Walker, *The Economics of EC Competition Law*, 2001; R. H. Bork, *The Antitrust Paradox – A Policy at War with itself*, 1978/1993; D. Edward/M. Hoskins, "Art. 90 – Deregulation and EC Law", *CMLRev* 1995, 7; C. Ehlermann/I. Atanasiu (eds.), *The Modernisation of EC Antitrust Law, European Comp. Law Annual*, 2000; C. Ehlermann, "The Modernisation of EC Antitrust Policy – A Legal and Cultural Revolution", *CMLRev.* 2000, 537; J. Faull/A. Nikpay, *The EC Law of Competition*, 1999; D. Geradin (ed.), *The Liberalization of State Monopolies in the EU and Beyond*, 1999; D. Gerber, *Law and Competition in the 20th Century – Protecting Prometheus*, 2000; A. Gleiss/M. Hirsch, *Europäisches Kartellrecht*, 1998; L. Gormley (ed.), *Current and Future Perspectives of EC Competition Law*, 1997; D. Goyder, *EC-Competition Law*, 4th ed. 2004; J. Goyder, *EC Distribution Law*, 3rd ed. 2000; D. Hildebrand, *The Role of Economic Analysis in the EC Competition Rules*, 2nd ed. 2002: Ch. Joerges (ed.), *Franchising and the law*, 1991; Ch. Jones, *Private Enforcement of Antitrust-Law in the EU, UK and USA*, 1999; M. Kenny, *The Transformation of Public and Private in EC Competition Law*, 2002; C. Kerse, *EC Antitrust Procedure*, 4th ed. 1998; M. Kiikeri, *Comparative Legal Reasoning and European law*, 2001; A. Komninos, "New prospects for private enforcement of EC Competition Law: Courage v. Creehan and the Community right to damages", *CMLRev.* 2002, 447; V. Korah, *An Introductory Guide to EC Competition Law*, 8th ed. 2004; E.-J. Mestmäcker/H. Schweitzer, *Europäisches Wettbewerbsrecht*, 2. A. 2004; H.-W. Micklitz/St. Weatherill (eds.), *European Economic Law*, 1997; Monopolkommission, "Kartellpolitische Wende in der EU?", *Sondergutachten* 28, 1999, 32, 2001; K. Mortelmans, "Towards convergence in the application of the rules on free movement and competition", *CMLRev.* 2001, 613; C.M. v. Quitzow, *State Measures Distorting Free Competition in the EC*, 2002; R. Posner, *Antitrust Law*, 2nd ed. 2001; N. Reich, "The November Revolution of the European Court", *CMLRev.* 1994, 459; N. Reich, "Competition between Legal orders – A New Paradigm in EC Law?", *CMLRev.* 1992, 861; N. Reich, "The "Courage"-doctrine: Encouraging or discouraging compensation for antitrust injury?", *CMLRev* 2005, 35; L. Ritter *et al.*, *European Competition Law – A Practitioner's Guide*, 2nd ed. 2000; J. Rivas/Horspool (eds.), *Modernisation and Decentralisation of EC Competition Law*, 2000; J. Rivas/F. Stroud, "Developments in EC Competition Law in 1999/2000", *CMLRev.* 2001, 935; W. Sauter, *Competition Law and Industrial Policy in the EU*, 1998;

D. Seeliger, "EG-kartellrechtliche Probleme in Vertikalverhältnissen beim Vertrieb über das Internet", *WuW* 2000, 1174; Y. Serra/J. Calais-Auloy, *Concurrence et consommation*, 1994; P. Slot, "A view from the mountain: 40 years of developments in EC competition law", *CMLRev* 2004, 433; J. Stuyck, "EC Competition Law after Modernisation: More than ever in the Interest of Consumers", *Journal of Consumer Policy (JCP)* 2005, 1; J. Stuyck/H. Gilliams (eds.), *Modernisation of European Competition Law*, 2002; I. Van Bael/J.-F. Bellis, *Competition Law of the EC*, 4th ed. 2005; I. G. van Gerven/E. Navarro Varona, "The Wood pulp case", *CMLRev.* 1994, 575; W. van Gerven, "Of rights, Remedies and Procedures", *CMLRev.* 2000, 501; R. Wesseling, *Modernisation of EC Antitrust Law*, 2000; R. Whish, *Competition Law*, 5th ed. 2003; R. Whish, "Regulation 2790/99: The Commision's New Style Block Exemption for Vertical Agreements", *CMLRev* 2000, 887.

I. IMPORTANCE OF THE COMPETITION RULES IN THE LIBERAL EU REGIME

1. Objectives of EU Competition law

The competition rules have certainly been one of the central points of EC law ever since its beginning. This is no surprise, in a liberal concept of law and economy.[206] For in the absence of state manipulation or supranational regulation of the economy – certain sectors excluded will not concern us here – it is the free play of autonomous actors that determines market behavior and results. This play must work without distortion, namely:

– by the state – which explains the importance of the free movement and state aid rules;
– by competitors themselves, tempted to employ restrictive practices or abuse of their market dominating power – this is the objective of Art. 81, 82 of the Treaty.

The importance of the competition rules is already present in the very objectives of the EC Treaty[207], and within the framework of the European Economic Constitution[208]. Open markets become the central catchword of competition law and policy. Indeed, EC law and practice has done much to assure its working. The objective of this system is twofold:

– in the interest of *individuals*, namely competitors, but also traders up- and downstream, parallel importers as well as consumers;[209]

---

[206] Gerber, *Law and Competition in 20th Century Europe*, 2000; Kenny, *The Transformation of Public and Private in EC Competition Law*, 2002.
[207] i.e., Art. 3 (g) EC.
[208] Per Art. 4, 109 EC.
[209] Stuyck, *JCP* 2005, 1 at 10.

- in the interest of the *Community and its Member States* as a whole, to provide for efficient allocation of resources, adequate provision of goods and services, and optimal diffusion of technology.

The competition rules therefore protect individuals through the theory of *direct effect* and through a compensation system of their own (§ 20 II). They also protect the Community interest at large, thus allowing broad powers of intervention, both by the Commission and also by national agencies and courts in the case of non-compliance by undertakings. These powers have been shaped by Court practice and in secondary law. Indeed, primary law was incomplete, only foreseeing the sanction of annulling restrictive practices[210]. However, the abuse of market dominating power still remains without any sanction in primary law!

Different theories are advocated to defend or criticize the predominance of competition law in the EU. This work will not go into that discussion. Although the Court once insisted on the theory of "workable competition", usually it makes no pronouncement on the economic theory it follows.[211] Whether competition law increases concentration or is an effective instrument against it – this is an empirical question for economists, and not to be decided by lawyers. How much monopoly may be efficient, what is the threshold where it begins to have damaging effects – this is debated by proponents of the economic analysis of law, who usually take a more generous approach towards monopolization.[212] Whether competition is a precondition to efficiency or an incentive to economic and ecological waste needs welfare analysis foreign to a lawyer. Whether individual preferences or collective goods should be at the centre of the value system of competition law depends on individual philosophy. Whether consumers profit directly or indirectly from competition still remains a debated question.[213] It may depend on the income bracket to which a person belongs.

The approach taken here is more modest: it is based on the liberal prerequisites of a system of an open market economy. It should allow entry into markets when they do not work efficiently, avoiding a segregation of the internal market along national frontiers[214]. The principal objectives of the free movement and competition rules are identical.[215] However, their means and instruments are quite different. In addition, competition law contains strong guarantees for individual and economic autonomy. This will be debated later (§ 15 III).

---

[210] Art 81 (2) EC.
[211] Case 26/76 Metro-SB-Grossmärkte GmbH & Co KG v Commission[1977] ECR 1875 at para 2.
[212] Posner, *Antitrust Law,* 2nd, 2001, at p. 236.
[213] Reich/Micklitz, *Europäisches Verbraucherrecht,* 4. A. 2003 at 4.5.
[214] Art. 14 (2).
[215] Mortelmans, *CMLRev* 2001, 613.

2. Implementation: Reg. 1/2003

It is impossible to give an overview of the many sources of EU competition law. The original Treaty was limited to a *"traité cadre"*:[216]
- A ban on restrictive practices and abuse of market dominating power[217].
- Authorization to the Council (or Member States) to get the competition rules to work[218].

The most important regulation in this context, adopted in 1962[219, 220] provided for direct effect[221]. At the same time, however, it installed a complicated and wasteful notification and authorization system for exempted agreements in the exclusive hands of the Commission[222].

This was only recently modified by adopting the new regulation 1/2003[223, 224] according to which the relevant provisions both with regard to prohibiting restrictive agreements and allowing an exemption under specially defined circumstances[225] take direct effect, even though in different directions and with different burdens of proof[226]. Indeed, it is clearly stated[227] that national courts are empowered to apply the relevant provisions[228] of the Treaty.

Although the theory of direct effect was never in doubt in this context[229], it was rarely applied. However, its general recognition in para 3 of Art. 81 EC means a radical departure from former ways of implementing EU competition law. Instead of one principal and central actor, now these will be counted in their hundreds. The Commission aims to impose a certain priority of its decisions even over courts of law[230] in the interest of uniformity – a somewhat doubtful proviso!

---

[216] Kenny, *supra* note 205 at p. 34.
[217] Art. 81/82 EC.
[218] Art. 87 EEC/83 EC.
[219] As so called "Regulation (EC) No. 17".
[220] Special English edition 1956-1962 at 87.
[221] I.e., of Art. 81 (1).
[222] According to para 3.
[223] Reg. (EC) 1/2003 of 16 Dec. 2002 on the implementation of the rules on competition laid down in Art. 81 and 82 of the Treaty, OJ L 1/1.
[224] For an overview of the discussion leading to Reg. 1/2003 cf. Craig/de Búrca at 1063-1087, Stuyck/Gilliams (eds.), *Modernisation of European Competition Law*, 2002.
[225] Art. 1 (1) and (2) of the Reg. 1/2003, Art. 81 (1) and (3).
[226] Art. 2 of the Reg. 1/2003.
[227] Art. 6 of the Reg. 1/2003.
[228] Articles 81 and 82 EC.
[229] I.e., with regard to Art. 82 EC.
[230] In Art. 16 of the Reg. 1/2003.

3. General trends in EU competition law – An overview

a. The *Grundig* doctrine

The introduction of a separate set of competition rules among the six countries of the original common market should be seen as a truly legal experiment, whose consequences were demonstrated only later. The first cases, most notably the famous *Grundig* litigation of 1964/1966,[231] are still characterized by an important and significant broadening of application of Art. 81 (1) and a narrow reading of Art. 81 (3). The case concerned the establishment of an exclusive distribution system of Grundig, a German producer of radio and TV hardware, in France by an independent distributor, Consten. Grundig wanted to assure Consten absolute territorial protection by excluding parallel imports. It did so by using instruments which at that time were quite common in commercial transactions in the EEC. In a bold interpretation of Art, 85 EEC/81 EC, the Court held:

- Art. 81 (1) applies not only to horizontal, but also to vertical agreements. As the Court declared: "The principle of freedom of competition concerns the various stages and manifestations of competition".
- Art. 81 (1) protects not only the traditional inter-brand competition between undertakings on a market, but also the internal competition within one group of undertakings of similar products which are marketed in different outlets and may therefore, if purchased by independent dealers (also called parallel importers or "free-riders"), provoke *intra-brand competition.*
- Distribution contracts between undertakings in a different market position are void if they have as their objective or effect to segregate the common market artificially, for example by provisions on absolute territorial protection.
- Where an explicit "object" by the participating undertakings to segregate the market is proven, no further economic considerations are necessary as to the "good" or "bad" effect of this behavior on competition (the so called *per se* rules).
- Ancillary clauses such as those on use and defence of trade marks, honouring of guarantees, resale price imposition, are also caught by this absolute ban.
- Art. 81 (3) does not give the Commission a free hand to exempt whatever agreement, but excludes what is later called "hardcore restrictions" such as price maintenance clauses, absolute territorial protection, and export bans.

---

[231] Joined cases 56 + 58/64 Etablissements Consten SARL and Grundig-Verkaufs GmbH v Commission [1966] ECR 299.

b. Narrowing the sphere of application of Art. 81 (1)

The *Grundig* doctrine shows a surprising optimism in the philosophy of competition to achieve the basic aim of the EC: *an integrated market*. Even if at the time of writing the concept of "internal market" was not yet known, it certainly lies behind the philosophy of *Grundig* and later cases.[232] Its main importance related to vertical distribution systems such as exclusive selling and buying arrangements, selective distribution, and franchising. It is here that the battles of the following years were waged, and where as a result the *Grundig* doctrine was considerable narrowed by what might be called a "*rule of reason approach*". If this did not work through primary law, the Commission was quickly at hand to adopt so called "group exemption regulations". These defined in an abstract way the conditions under which certain agreements could be exempted according to para 3 of Art 81, and the "black list" of restrictions which under no circumstances could be exempted. More recent experience attempted even greater flexibility by setting up lists of "grey clauses" which could be exempted under a simplified procedure. This approach was also used for horizontal and sectoral agreements, which are not examined here.

The most important cases concerned selective distributions systems, licensing and franchising agreements:
–   If a manufacturer or importer distributes goods via a selective system, it is willing to do business only with a carefully selected group of distributors either on the wholesale or on the retail level, or on both. Sales to retailers outside the system are forbidden, unless they are end-consumers. Selective distribution systems restrict intra-brand competition, but at the same time create an incentive for the manufacturer to establish a viable and quality-geared network. This is important for the consumer, particularly in the case of after-sales service. On the other hand, the tighter and more intransparant the selection criteria are, the closer the system comes to *Grundig*, provoking an intervention[233]. In its *Metro-Saba I* decision of 1977[234], the Court opted for a compromise. That is, if the resellers are chosen on the basis of qualitative objective criteria, this does not fall under the prohibition of Art. 81 (1) and does not need an exemption. This might include, for example, criteria relating to technical qualifications of the reseller and its staff in order to guarantee a high level of after-sales service. The Court was ready to accept a decrease in price competition by maintaining that this was not the only form of competition protected by Art. 81 (1) EC and did not take priority over other forms

---

[232]   Case C-70/93 BMW v ALD Auto-Leasing [1995] ECR I-3439.
[233]   I.e., of Art. 81 (1) EC.
[234]   Case 26/76 Metro-SB-Grossmärkte GmbH & Co KG v Commission and SABA [1977] 1875 at para 20.

of competition. On the other hand, if the manufacturer applies quantitative and/or subjective criteria, then such a system must be specifically exempted under Art. 81 (3). This might be the case, for example, in the sense of a *numerus clausus* of authorised dealers.

– Licensing of patents, know-how, and other intellectual property rights is usually part of the very "essence" of the protection which Community law accepts (§ 10 I). However, clauses on territorial exclusivity of the use of the licensed property right may come under the prohibition of Art. 81 (1). In its *Maize seed* decision of 1982[235] the Court struck a balance: it allowed exclusivity with regard to territorial protection of the production of the licensed product itself, but voided absolute territorial protection which would ban any type of parallel trading on the distribution level. The case law has been consolidated into the Technology Transfer Regulation 240/96[236], now replaced by Regulation 772/2004 of 27 April 2004[237] (§ 10 III 1).

– Franchising systems, originating in the US, became popular in the EU in the eighties. These differ from selective systems insofar as the franchiser is not itself a producer or service provider, but markets a package of know-how and goodwill to franchisees, who then sell the product or service at their own risk. They usually have to pay considerable entrance and license fees to participate in the system. They profit from the know-how, the prestige, the marketing success of the franchiser. In its *Pronuptia* case of 1986[238], the Court was quite welcoming to these systems, indeed excluding them from Art. 81 (1) insofar as the restrictions were necessary to diffuse and protect the know-how, and to preserve the identity and reputation of the network. Qualifying examples here might include quality standards, price recommendations or exclusive purchasing obligations. However, the Court did not exempt place of business clauses. These exist where the franchisee may only open one business outlet, and therefore a territorial restriction is imposed. The Commission was quick to fill the gap by a block exemption regulation[239, 240], which was only recently replaced[241] (sub III).

c. Widening the sphere of application: the double face of public interventions

The emergence of a rule-of-reason approach with regard to vertical restrictions shows the Court's openness in adapting the competition rules to changing market conditions.

---

[235] Case 258/78 L.C. Nungesser KG and Kurt Eisele v Commission [1982] ECR 2015.
[236] [1998] OJ L 31/2.
[237] [2004] OJ L 123.
[238] Case 161/84 Pronuptia de Paris GmbH v Pronuptia de Paris Irmgard Schillgallis [1986] ECR 353.
[239] Commission Regulation 4087/88.
[240] [1998] OJ L 359/46.
[241] By Commission Regulation (EC) 2790/1999 [1999] OJ L 336/21.

This approach was continued by adopting broad block exemption regulations. We will look at these later.

This surprisingly liberal approach stands in seeming contrast to the increasingly critical practice of both the Commission and – in particular – the Court regarding restraints of competition induced by public law. However, within the liberal philosophy of competition law itself, this comes as no surprise: state intervention is viewed with scepticism and hostility because it distorts the free play of market forces. On the other hand, EU law leaves Member States wide discretion to:
- follow their own economic policy[242],
- provide for public services, which to some extent are placed outside competition[243], or
- determine their property regime[244], which may be more or less open to competition and which differs considerably among Member States.

Put simply, though, no consensus exists among the States as "Masters of the Treaty" that only a liberal model of the economy is viable for the EU – even if Art. 4 EC is a strong indicator in that direction.

Such ideological ambiguities explain the incremental and somewhat intransparant approach of the Court to these truly delicate questions. Every case cited finds a counter case which seemingly challenges the premises of the first. The interpretation of the Court is frequently blurred and imprecise. The Commission, as the EU's liberal watchdog, tends to exaggerate the case law, which itself submits public intervention in the market place to increasing scrutiny. In certain areas, secondary legislation has taken over the task of deregulation and liberalization of former state activities, especially in electronic communication.[245]

The following remarks will suffice to give an overview of existing trends:
- One battleground has been public undertakings and monopolies[246]. This will be mentioned later.
- Another area of conflict has been the so called 'INNO-ATAB'[247] doctrine. Here, the Court held that a Member State violated its duties under the Treaty[248] if it

---

[242] Art. 89/99 EC.
[243] Art. 16 EC.
[244] Art. 295 EC.
[245] For a critical overview see Kenny *supra* note 206.
[246] In the sense of Art. 86 EC.
[247] Case 13/77 GB Inno-BN v ATAB [1977] ECR 2115.
[248] Under Art. 10 EC.

supported, exempted or induced anti-competitive behavior by undertakings.[249] One instance of this, and its consequence, will illustrate: the German rule on exempting the insurance sector from the (German) competition rules could not be upheld against Community law.[250]

-   If Member States authorize *professional bodies* to self-regulate their internal affairs and professional standards, this may easily conflict with the competition rules. The state cannot completely abandon its control – otherwise a price scheme by a professional association will be caught[251, 252]. The Court was more friendly towards a regulation of the Dutch Bar Association[253] forbidding partnerships of lawyers with accounting firms. Even though this amounted to a restraint of competition, it could be justified by considerations of "professional ethics, supervision and liability, in order to ensure that the ultimate consumers of legal services and the sound administration are provided with the necessary guarantees in relation to integrity and experience."[254]

II. ART. 81 (1): BASIC CONCEPTS

1. *Three elements of restrictive practices*

Art. 81 (1), whose wording has never been changed during the nearly 50-year history of the E(E)C and has found its place in Art. III-161 of the Draft Constitution, contains three different elements. These must be present cumulatively in order to include a practice under Art. 81 (1) under the head "prohibited as incompatible with the common market". The three elements are:
-   a *functional* element, namely the concept of undertaking or association of undertakings;
-   an *intellectual* element, namely agreements or concerted practices between undertakings, or decisions by associations;
-   an *economic* element, whereby these agreements or decisions "may affect trade between Member States and have as their object or effect the prevention, restriction or distortion of competition within the common market".

---

[249] Cf. The limits of the case-law were spelled out in Case C-2/91 Criminal proceedings against Meng [1993] ECR I-5751; for a critique cf. Reich *CMLRev* 1994, 451.

[250] Case 45/85 Verband der Sachversicherer v Commission [1987] ECR 405.

[251] By Art. 81 (1) EC.

[252] Case C-35/96 Commission v Italy [1998] ECR I-3851 "CNDS".

[253] Case C-309/99 J.C.J. Wouters *et al.* v Algemene Raad van de Nederlandse Orde van Advocaten [2002] ECR I-1577.

[254] Id, para 97.

The exact legal content of these concepts has been elaborated by an active ECJ case law, which will be summarized in brief.

2. A functional concept of undertaking

It was clear from the very outset of applying the Community competition rules that the concept of undertaking could not be defined by having recourse to the very different Member State laws, but must be interpreted autonomously. This has been done by the so-called "functional theory", which was defined in *Höfner*[255] in very broad terms:

> In the field of competition law, the concept of an undertaking covers any entity engaged in an economic activity, regardless of its legal status and the way in which it is financed.

The Court added that any activity consisting of offering goods and services on a given market is an economic activity.[256]

This broad definition includes:
– Any private law company, whether it makes a profit or not, whether is has legal personality or not.
– Private persons engaged in an economic activity. This includes liberal professions, brokers and commercial agents, working at their own risk.[257]
– Holding companies, concerns, *groupements d'intérêt économique* and the like.
– However, subsidiaries within an economic unit are not undertakings if they have no real autonomy and only carry out the instructions of the parent company.[258]

Special rules exist for public undertakings (*infra* VI).

Employees and agents working exclusively under the instruction of one company are not undertakings.

3. The intellectual element: concertation

Unlike Art. 82 EC, Art. 81 (1) is not directed against unilateral action by one or a group of undertakings, but against a concertation between different undertakings that are – at least in theory – economically and legally independent. The classic form concerned so-called cartels, but the concepts of Art. 81 (1) are much broader, covering softer

---

[255] Case C-41/90 Höfner and Elser v Macroton [1991] ECR I-1979 at para 21.
[256] Case C-309/99 Wouters, *supra* note 253 at para 47.
[257] Commission guidelines on vertical restraints, [2000] *OJ* C 291/4.
[258] Case C-73/95P Viho Europe v Commission [1996] ECR I-5457 at para 15.

forms of coordination. After *Grundig*, it does not matter whether the concerting under-takings are competitors on the same (horizontal) markets or are active on different levels of the production and/or marketing chain. But there must always be some intellectual element of concertation of market behavior – merely unilateral or so-called parallel actions do not qualify under Art. 81 (1). Frequently, the question remains one of proof. Moreover, it is up to the competition authorities to prove the existence of a concertation in the sense of Art. 81 (1), unless a *prima facie* case can be made for an agreement or a concerted practice.

Out of the abundant case-law, the following highlights concerning the concept of agreement should be mentioned:
- A gentlemen's agreement is an agreement in the sense of Art. 81 (1).[259]
- A selective or exclusive distribution system should be regarded an agreement. This is so, even if the anti-competitive behavior follows after its conclusion, for example by illegally excluding price active distributors from the system or imposing supply quotas to avoid parallel imports.[260]
- However, there is no agreement where a producer autonomously limits the delivery of medicines of its distributors in one country to such a scale as to avoid re-exportation. On appeal the Court[261] insisted that in order to be an agreement in the sense of Art. 81 (1) EC, "it is necessary that the manifestation of the wish of one of the contracting parties to achieve an anti-competitive goal constitute an invitation to the other party, whether express or implied, to fulfil that goal jointly ..." (para 102). A mere quota system of delivery of the drug manufacturer (Bayer) imposed on its national wholesalers in order to avoid parallel trade does not amount to an agreement but is a unilateral measure caught only by Art. 82. Such behaviour may be judged differently if happening within a selective distribution system (para 141).
- Share acquisition by competing companies may indicate the existence of an agreement between merging companies.[262] In the meantime, Merger Regulation 4069/89, now replaced by Regulation 139/2004[263], would have exclusive jurisdiction in such cases.

---

[259] Cases 45/69 AFC Boeringer Mannheim v Commission [1970] ECR 769.
[260] Cases 228 + 229/82 Ford v Commission [1984] ECR 1129; C-338/00P Volkswagen AG/Commission [2003] ECR I-9189 para 62.
[261] Joined cases C-2 + 3/01 P Bundesverband der Arneimittel-Importeure et al v Bayer-AG, [2004] ECR I-(6.1.2004).
[262] Cases 142 & 158/84 British American Tobacco Ltd. and R.J. Reynolds Industries v Commission [1987] ECR 4487.
[263] Council Regulation (EC) No. 139/2004 of 20 January 2004 on the control of concentrations between undertakings, [2004] OJ L 24/1.

With regard to concerted practices, the Court gave a now classic definition in the *dyestuffs* cases:[264]

> Art. 81 draws a distinction between the concept of "concerted practices" and that of "agreements between undertakings"…; the object is to bring within the prohibition of that Article a form of coordination between undertakings which, without having reached the stage where an agreement properly so-called has been concluded, knowingly substitutes practical cooperation between them for the risks of competition (para 64).

The Court went on to discuss at length the difference between mere parallel behavior in an oligopoly – which is not caught by Art. 81 (1) although perhaps by Art. 82 – and concertation, which can be inferred from circumstances such as timing and level of price increases

4. The economic element: appreciable distortion of competition

As the Court stated in *Grundig,* where the parties to an agreement or a concerted practice intend to restrict competition, there is always a case for a distortion of competition. This is especially so where it is in the form mentioned in Art. 81 (1) paras 1-4. Indeed, economic arguments become irrelevant, especially as to whether the parties intended a "good cartel" or not. In cases of doubt, they had to rely on the old notification and exemption procedure of Reg. 17. Today, with the direct applicability of Art. 81 (3), they have to decide themselves whether the practice is caught by the competition rules.

Things are more difficult when such intent (or "object")[265] is absent or cannot be proven. In order to avoid bans on a minor agreement having no substantial effect on trade between Member States, the Court developed the so-called *appreciability* doctrine.[266] This *de minimis* principle has been put into several notices by the Commission regarding agreements of minor importance. The aim is to develop objective criteria based on market share: 15% for non-competitors, 10% for competitors.

Therefore, the overall *effect* of such agreements on competition has to be studied and proven by an analysis of the relevant product and regional market. The Court of First Instance[267] has developed this test with regard to exclusive purchasing agreements that,

---

[264] Case 48/69 ICI v Commission [1972] ECR 619.
[265] As required by Art. 2 of Reg. 1/2003.
[266] Case C-234/89 St. Delimitis v Henninger Brau [1991] ECR I-935; case C-180/98 Pavlov v Stichting Pensioenefonds Medische Specialisten [2000] ECR I-6451.
[267] Case T-7/93 Langnese Iglo GmbH v Commission [1995] ECR II-1533.

taken in isolation, would have no appreciable effect on competition but may do so when taken in aggregate:

> As to whether the exclusive purchasing agreements fall within … Art. 81 (1) … it is appropriate….to consider whether, taken as a whole, all the similar agreements entered into the relevant market and the other features of the economic and legal context of the agreements at issue show that those agreements cumulatively have the effect of denying access to that market for new and foreign competitors… (para 99).

III. "NEW STYLE" BLOCK EXEMPTION REGULATION FOR VERTICAL AGREEMENTS: 2790/99

1. Objectives and sphere of application

Regulation (EC) No. 2790/99 of 22 December 1999[268] results from the Commission's new approach towards vertical restraints. It abolishes the somewhat detailed and specific former regulations on exclusive distribution, purchasing, and franchising. Its scope of application is particularly wide, including selective distribution systems with quantitative elements of selection which in earlier practice needed an individual exemption. It has therefore been called an "umbrella" regulation.[269] It allows generous thresholds of application: the market share of the supplier (in the case of exclusive purchasing agreements: the buyer) should not exceed 30%[270].

Art. 2 (1) contains a broad exemption for vertical restraints:

> …. Art. 81 (1)shall not apply to agreements or concerted practices entered into between two or more undertakings each of which operates, for the purposes of the agreement, at a different level of the production or distribution chain, and relating to the conditions under which the parties may purchase, sell, or resell certain goods or services ("vertical agreements"). This exemption shall apply to the extent to which such agreements contain restrictions of competition falling within the scope of Art. 81 (1) ("vertical restraints").

Art. 2 (3) makes the block exemption applicable where intellectual property rights are ancillary to the main purpose of the vertical agreement.

---

[268] [1999] *OJ* L 336/21; the Commission has published detailed Guidelines on Vertical Restraints, [2000] *OJ* C 291/1; for details cf. Craig/de Búrca at 986-990.
[269] Whish, *CMLRev* 2000, 887.
[270] Art. 3 of Reg. 2790/99.

2. Hardcore restrictions

Art. 4 contains a fairly detailed black list of clauses – now called hardcore restrictions – which do not profit from the exemption. These include price maintenance, absolute territorial protection and the like. End users cannot be restricted in their choice of outlets. In exclusive distribution systems, active sales outside the protected territory may be banned. Examples here would include personalized advertising. However, passive sales must always be allowed. Examples there would include interactive websites.[271] In selective distribution systems, active and passive sales at the retail level may not be restricted, but a quantitative dealer selection is allowed, thus broadening the *Metro* judgment's *rule of reason* (*supra* I 3a).

It is permissible for a buyer operating at the wholesale level to restrict sales to end users, and for members of a selective distribution system to restrict sales to unauthorized distributors. The regulation allows selective and exclusive distribution systems[272] to combine, for example by place of establishment clauses. It also contains rules for franchising.

IV. "NEW STYLE" REGULATION FOR MOTOR VEHICLES: REG. 1400/2002

1. From Reg. 123/85 to Reg. 1475/95 to Reg. 1400/2002

Motor vehicles as the "consumer's preferred and most expensive toy" have from the very beginning played a central role in EC law. It is therefore helpful to discuss the importance of the competition rules in this sector as an example, and as a guide to understanding their function. The specific place of the car sector in EU competition law can be explained by the following reasons:
- Substantial price differentials for cars led to arbitrage and to an incentive for parallel imports which the manufacturers and their franchised dealers tried to stop. Here, the free movement of goods and competition rules under the *Grundig* doctrine played a central role in avoiding illegal boycotts, refusals to supply, and the like.
- Technical standards for cars were only slowly harmonized in the EU. This created artificial segregation of markets. Tax differentials which could not be overcome provoked price differentiation by manufacturers in order to be present in all national markets.

---

[271] Commission Guidelines at para 51.
[272] Craig/de Búrca at 989.

- Cars are service-intensive goods needing a border crossing system of after-sales service. This was provided by the big car manufacturers in using a network of dependent dealers and repair shops, to the exclusion of competing suppliers and service providers. That amounted to a restriction of competition which, in turn, tended to keep price levels high and inelastic.

The Commission's original approach started with individual exemptions granted to tight dealer systems of car manufacturers. This led to the first block exemption regulation 123/85.[273] It allowed a combination of a quantitative selective distribution system with elements of exclusive distribution. In that way, it guaranteed dealers an *exclusive sales territory* limited to one product or brand. This was justified by the investment needed for a high level after-sales service. Although exclusivity was extended to "original" spare parts, in theory the dealer was permitted to use parts of the same quality if the consumer insisted. In order to allow some intra-brand competition, a so-called *intermediary clause* was inserted[274]. That is, a customer could authorize an agent outside the system to buy a car for him in another EC country where prices were lower. This intermediary clause gave rise to much litigation;[275] it was a toothless instrument because no dealer could be obliged to honour the prior written authorization. Car manufacturers quite openly defied this parallel outlet and were heavily fined by the Commission for anti-competitive behavior.[276]

After ten years, Reg. 123/85 was substituted by Reg. 1475/95[277]. This was somewhat more open in allowing multi-brand distribution by the dealer, but only with separate premises and legal personality. Active sales continued to be banned outside the territory. This raised the question how far the internet could be used by the trader to attract new clients: was it a forbidden active form, or an allowed passive form, of sales?[278] As a general tendency, it was felt that the old approach had outlived itself and that a more competitive approach was needed. At the same time, this left intact the main purpose of the original regulation, namely to ensure a high level of after-sales service to the consumer.

2. Objective and scope of application of Reg. 1400/2002

The Commission Regulation[279] "on the application of Art. 81 (3) ... to categories of vertical agreements and concerted practices in the motor vehicle sec-

---

[273]   [1985] *OJ* L 15/16.
[274]   In Art. 3 (11) of Reg. 123/85.
[275]   Cf. case C-322/93P Peugeot v Commission [1994] ECR I-2727 (Eco-System).
[276]   Case T-62/98 VW/Commission [1998] ECR II-2707. Confirmed on appeal by case C-338/00P *supra* note 260.
[277]   [1995] *OJ* L 145/25.
[278]   Cf. Commission study on the implementation of Reg.1475/95, Com (2000)743of 15.11.2000.
[279]   Commission Regulation (EC) No 1400/2002.

tor"[280] is *lex specialis* to the umbrella regulation[281]. Thus, it covers only vertical agreements with regard to the sales and servicing of new motor vehicles[282], as well as the servicing of "original spare parts"[283].

In order to open up the rigidity of the distribution system, the regulation allows manufacturers to choose – but not to combine – either an exclusive or a selective distribution system. The exclusive system (market share threshold: 30%) will, as before, allow territorial protection of dealers. However, passive sales to the exclusive territory, including via internet sites[284] cannot be prevented[285]. A quantitative selective distribution system, with a threshold of 40%, will channel sales within the network. On the other hand, this will not allow any restriction of passive or active sales to end-users[286], including leasing companies who do not sell the products[287]. Dealers may not be prevented from establishing additional sales or delivery outlets at other locations[288]. However, this highly contested location clause was suspended for three years to allow for adaptation of the parties to a contract[289].

3. Hardcore restrictions

Following the example of Reg. 2790/99, Art. 4 contains a detailed list of hardcore restrictions. These aim to avoid the abuses which the Commission had been facing in implementing the prior regulations[290]. The types of behavior banned are described in detail. The Commission's aim here is also to catch *indirect restrictions*, or those that are effective only in combination with other clauses of the contract. However, it is not clear what is meant by the term "have as their object"[291]: Does this exclude an effects test, or is *prima facie* evidence of a restriction sufficient to prove the "object"?

The former intermediary clause is substituted[292] by a ban on any restriction of the distributor's freedom to sell any new motor vehicle corresponding to a model within its contract range. However, it does not create an obligation to contract. The regulation

---

[280] [2002] *OJ* L 203/30.
[281] Reg. 2790/99.
[282] As defined in Art. (1) n)-p) of Reg. 1400/2002.
[283] In the sense of Art. 1 (1) t) of Reg. 1400/2002.
[284] Recital 15 of Reg. 1400/2002.
[285] Per Art. 4 (1) b) (i) of Reg. 1400/2002.
[286] Per Art. 4 (d) of Reg. 1400/2002.
[287] Per Art. 1 (1) w) of Reg. 1400/2002.
[288] Per Art. 5 (2) b) of Reg. 1400/2002.
[289] Art. 12 (2) and recital 37 of Reg. 1400/2002.
[290] I.e., Reg. 123/85 and Reg. 1475/95.
[291] In Art. 4 (1) of Reg. 1400/2002.
[292] Art. 4 (f) of Reg. 1400/2002.

also aims[293] to open the market for spare parts and service facilities to competitors outside the system. The manufacturer and its franchisees are to enjoy no after-service monopoly. Particularly important is the article[294] forbidding:

> the restriction of the sale of spare parts for motor vehicles by members of a selective distribution system to independent repairers which use these parts for the repair and maintenance of a motor vehicle.

This clause amounts to a duty to contract (*Kontrahierungszwang*), because there is no reason conceivable under which such restrictions could be justified in normal commercial activities if sufficient stock is available.

The regulation also[295] concerns protection of independent repair and maintenance operators. These should be able to access technology and know-how in a "non-discriminatory, prompt and proportionate way, and the information must be given in a usable form. If the relevant item is covered by an intellectual property right or constitutes know-how, access shall not be withheld in an abusive manner". This formula is reminiscent of the *Magill* test for essential facilities (§ 10 III 2).

Sanctions in case of violations of these obligations are foreseen[296] in the shape of withdrawal of the benefit of the Regulation. Since the hardcore restrictions enjoy direct effect, they may be sanctioned by injunctions and claims for compensation according to the new case law of the Court under the *Courage* doctrine (§ 20 I 2).

V. ABUSE OF MARKET POWER

1. Conceptual and legal characteristics

Art. 82 is the (uneven) twin brother to Art. 81 EC and has the same objective – promoting competition by forbidding distortions through the abuse of power. However, it shows a number of important conceptual and legal differences. These explain its relatively restricted field of application:

---

[293] Art. 4 (h) to (l) of Reg. 1400/2002.
[294] Art. 4 (i) of Reg. 1400/2002.
[295] Art. 4 (2) of Reg. 1400/2002.
[296] In Art. 6 of Reg. 1400/2002.

- Art. 81 is directed at concertation among independent undertakings, while Art. 82 concerns *unilateral* behavior of one undertaking (or several undertakings under the theory of collective dominance)[297].
- Art. 81 (3) allows for exemptions, which is not the case with Art. 82.
- Art. 81 provides a sanction in the shape of the (partial) annulment of an anti-competitive agreement, while Art. 82 attaches no specific sanction to abusive behavior.
- The threshold of application of Arts. 81 (1) and 82 with regard to distorting competition is different. That is, while Art. 81 (1) is satisfied with an appreciability test (about 10-15% share of the relevant product market), on the other hand Art. 82 requires a "market dominating position" (share usually above 50%).
- With the exception of Reg. 1/2003, Art. 82 is not accompanied by a body of secondary law. Merger control, even though taking as its starting point the creation or strengthening of a market dominating position, has completely moved out of Art. 82.
- However, both provisions are undoubtedly *directly applicable*. Indeed, they can be invoked before national jurisdictions and administrations. Both are paralleled by new Community rules on compensation (§ 20 II) and the possibility of injunctions.
- The concept of "undertaking" as subjective addressee of the prohibition is identical, in that it takes on special importance with public enterprises and monopolies[298] (VI).

2. Market dominance

Even in its early case law, the Court defined market dominance as the possibility for the undertaking in question to behave *"to an appreciable extent independently of its competitors, customers and ultimately of its consumers"*.[299] This was qualified in *Hoffmann-la-Roche*[300] insofar as an *appreciable influence* on competition conditions is sufficient.

This independence or dominance must be established regarding a particular market characterized by:
- the substitutability of products (or services), and by
- a certain geographical area where the undertakings do, or do not, compete.

---

[297] Cases C-395-396/96P Compagnie Maritime Belge Transports SA et al v Commission [2000] ECR I-1365 at para 45. We will not go into the details of the highly controversial discussion, cf. Craig/de Búrca at 1026-1029; Kenny *supra* note 205 at p. 207.
[298] Per Art. 86 EC.
[299] Case 27/76 United Brands Company and United Brands Cont. BV v. Commission [1978] ECR 207 at para 65.
[300] Case 85/76 Hoffmann-La Roche AG v Commission [1979] ECR 461 at para 39.

Rich Court practice – and literature, particularly in economics – exist on how to define product and regional markets. As a general rule, one can say: the smaller the market, the easier the proof of dominance, or vice versa; the larger the market, the smaller the risk of an undertaking being accused of dominance. "Smaller markets" were usually advocated by the Commission while undertakings under investigation usually insisted on the bigger size of the market. In many cases, the Court preferred a narrow market definition, for example;

- for spare[301] and substitute parts,[302]
- bananas as differentiated from other fresh fruit,[303]
- different user profiles for spare tyres.[304]

In other cases, the Court was not satisfied with the market definition of the Commission and quashed the complaint.[305] In studying these cases, it should be remembered that every market definition is relative, and depends on the circumstances. In many cases it may in reality only be justified by hindsight. The dominating result orientation of market definition is one of the main criticisms of economic analysis towards antitrust law.

Unfortunately, EU law contains no concept of dependence or "relative market power". Therefore, the market definition in some of the cases cited above (*Hugin, Hilti*) is rather narrow for bringing behavior felt to be anti-competitive into the ambit of Art. 82 EC. A more convincing approach may look at the "hardcore restrictions" in exemption regulations and, due to their direct effect[306], define violations as a *per se* infringement of Art. 81 (1) EC which is sanctioned by a claim for compensation under the *Courage* doctrine (§ 20 I 3).

Even if the relevant market has been established, the undertaking in question (or the oligopoly if joint dominance is accepted as a theory) must still enjoy dominance. A number of factors are debated, each of which in itself is not conclusive without further proof:

---

[301] Case 22/78 Hugin Kassaregister AB and Hugin Cash Register Ltd. v Commission [1979] ECR 1869.
[302] Case T-30/89 Hilti v Commission [1991] ECR II-1439.
[303] Case 27/76 *supra* note 299.
[304] Case 322/81 Nederlandsche Banden-Industrie Michelin v. Commission [1983] ECR 3461.
[305] A typical example is case 6/72 Europemballage Corporation and Continental Can Inc. v Commission [1973] ECR 495 where the Court applied Art. 82 to structural changes in undertakings by takeovers enhancing an already market-dominating position, but did not decide on the merits because it was not satisfied with the (narrow) market definition of the Commission, cf. for a comment Vogelenzang, *CMLRev* 1976, 61.
[306] In the sense of Reg. 1/2003.

- *Market share:* the critical threshold is about 50%[307]. However, this is a mere indicator, not sufficient proof as such. A high market share may exist only temporarily; moreover, it may also indicate a particular competitiveness of the undertaking in question, for example through its intellectual property rights portfolio.
- *Barriers to entry:* these may be natural or artificial and are subject to a case-by-case analysis. Special attention must be given to legal regulations creating or reinforcing monopolies through awarding exclusive or special rights to (public) undertakings. This will be studied separately in the context of Art. 86 (1) EC.
- *Vertical integration,* especially where a "normal" position on one market can be compensated by a dominating position on another to allow cross-subsidization strategies.[308]

3. Abuse of market power

The mere existence of a market-dominating position is not forbidden under EU law, but only an abuse of such a position. Such a theory easily becomes circular, insofar as dominance creates a likelihood of abuse, while a liberal theory of competition always insists on power-control through antitrust law. Is there a presumption of abuse on the part of market conduct of dominating undertakings? Does this mean that a dominating undertaking owes a special responsibility to the public, and that certain forms of competition are forbidden which would be allowed under "normal market conditions"?

The Court has not gone so far, preferring a case-by-case approach in developing specific types of abusive behavior without really explaining the philosophy or economy behind it. Certain examples can be summarized as follows:
- *Refusal to supply* normally does not constitute an abuse. That is, in a market economy no business – not even a market-dominating undertaking – is under a duty to contract. But certain circumstances may make such a refusal abusive. One example might be a strategy to deny complete access to a secondary market where a competitor was active before refusal.[309]
- Refusal to provide so called *essential facilities*, which will be discussed in the context of intellectual property rights (§ 10 III 2).
- Rebates are a commercial form of marketing and are therefore not abusive. This may be different when *fidelity rebates* are used to tie customers to the market-dominating undertaking and to prevent entry of potential competitors.[310]

---

[307] Craig/de Búrca citing several cases at 1002.
[308] Case 85/76 Hoffmann-la Roche *supra* note 300.
[309] Cases 6 and 7/73 Istituto Chemioterapico Italiano SpA and Commercial Solvents v Commission [1974] ECR 223.
[310] Case 85/76 Hoffmann-la Roche at para 90.

- *Price differentiation* may be an expression of lively competition on the market. This may amount to an abuse when used by a market-dominating undertaking to segregate markets.[311]
- *Predatory pricing* can be abusive if the market-dominating undertaking sells below variable costs to prevent entry of a competitor.[312]
- *Excessive prices* may be abusive if they grossly exceed normal market rates, and where this can only be explained by the power of the undertaking imposing these prices.[313]

VI. PUBLIC UNDERTAKINGS AND MONOPOLIES

1. The starting point: Art. 86 (1) and (2) EC

It is useful to remember the exact wording of Art. 86:

1. In the case of public undertakings and undertakings to which Member States grant special or exclusive rights, Member States shall neither enact nor maintain in force any measure contrary to the rules contained in this Treaty, in particular to those rules provided for in Art. 12 and Art. 81 to 89.
2. Undertakings entrusted with the operation of services of general economic interest or having the character of a revenue-producing monopoly shall be subject to the rules contained in this Treaty, in particular to the rules on competition, in so far as the application of such rules does not obstruct the performance, in law or in fact, of the particular task assigned to them. The development of trade must not be affected to such an extent as would be contrary to the interests of the Community....

The two paragraphs of Art. 86 seem to be contradictory. That is, the first posits as a general principle the submission of public undertakings and of those with special and exclusive rights to the competition rules. On the other hand, the second allows for certain exceptions, but unlike Art. 81 (3) does not attach any type of procedure or control by the Commission – it seems to take direct effect without any further legislative act such as Reg. 1/2003.

For reasons of analysis, a three-step test is proposed:
- First, the concept of undertaking has to be focused in the particular setting of Art. 86 (1).

---

[311] Case 27/76 UBC *supra* note 299 at para 232.
[312] Case C-62/86 Akzo Chemie BV v Commission [1991] ECR I-3359 at para 71.
[313] Case 210, 241, 242/88 Lucazeau et al v Commission [1989] ECR 2811.

- Second, the type of abusive behavior under the applicable Art. 82 must be defined; Art. 81 will be left aside.
- Third, possible justifications under the criteria named in para 2 will be elaborated.

The critical reader should now be warned: the ECJ case law is of surprising confusion and singularity; and legislation provides no guide.

2. The concept of public undertaking

In reality, Art. 86 (1) distinguishes three types of undertakings. These are united under the somewhat blurred heading of public undertakings:
- Public undertaking in the narrow sense, such as a city transportation system in the form of a private limited company with the shares held by the community.
- Undertakings to which Member States have granted exclusive rights, for example, the right to job placement services,[314] or universal services of different kinds, such as postal services.
- Special rights exist where, for example, a private association is empowered to certify conformity with technical standards, which is shared with other competitors.

In any case, the general concept of "undertaking" in the broad, functional sense applies here (*supra* II 3). Only in cases where genuine state activity is organized in public law form, like schools of secondary higher education[315] or flight control institutions,[316] is the concept of undertaking not applicable. The same is true with institutions providing health, age or workplace insurance, where this is based on the principle of solidarity, so that every risk is insured despite its costs, length or amount of premiums paid.[317]

Groups of sickness funds based on the principle of solidarity are not "associations of undertakings" in the sense of Art. 81 EC.[318] The imposition of fixed minimum amounts for medicines following criteria laid down by the legislature cannot be regarded as an economic activity.

The Court applies the concept of undertaking autonomously. It is not concerned with Member State organizational and legal structures. Indeed, these differ considerably in this area. It is of no importance whether the public agency – such as the German

---

[314] Case C-55/96 Job Centre coop arl. [1997] ECR I-7119.
[315] Case 263/86 Belgium v Humbel an Edel [1988] ECR 5365.
[316] Case C-364/92 SAT Fluggesellschaft GmbH v Eurocontrol [1994] ECR I-43.
[317] Case C 159 + 160/91 Poucet and Pistre [1993] I-637.
[318] Joined cases C-264/01 et al., AOK Bundesverband et al. v Ichtyol-Ges. Cordes, Hermani & Co et al. [2004] ECR I-(16.3.2004).

Bundesanstalt für Arbeit – offers its services without remuneration and that it implements a social policy mandate of international and national constitutional law.[319] Such a tendency in the case law of the ECJ is not without problems. This can be explained on the basis that it implies the mandate to completely reshuffle the organizational and administrative structures of Member States and put them on a competitive level; however, the democratic mandate to do so is lacking. Art. 86 (1) was not meant to be a rule on privatization and deregulation. Indeed, liberalism seems to go somewhat too far in this area.

3. The concept of abuse

Art. 86 (1) is a reference norm without a legal consequence of its own. The central reference point is Art. 82. Market power will usually be present in the case of undertakings that have been granted exclusive or special rights. This may not be the case with other public undertakings, unless their position is reinforced by some additional exclusionary or preferential arrangements.

Therefore, the central interface for the legal debate is the concept of "abuse". One has to keep in mind that the mere granting of special or exclusive rights cannot as such be regarded as an "abuse".[320] Some additional element has to exist, showing that the undertaking in question did not use exclusivity in the way defined, but that it somehow exceeded the limits intended with the grant.[321]

The traditional criteria which had already been developed for clarifying "abuse" can also be used here (V 3). Two specific criteria have been particularly important:
– The privileged undertaking tries to extend its exclusivity to neighbouring markets, to the detriment of competitors.[322]
– Exclusivity as such induces an abuse. One example might be where the undertaking in question extends its over-broad legal competence for job placement services to leading managerial positions but without really being able to provide the service, even though there is an urgent demand and other (specialized) providers are willing to do the job – one could call this the "Superman" syndrome.[323]

---

[319] Case C-41/90 Höfner *supra* 254; for a critique Reich, *CMLRev* 1992, 887; Shaw, *ELRev* 1991, 501.
[320] Cf. the most convincing discussion by Craig/de Búrca at 1127.
[321] For a discussion Edwards/Hoskins, *CMLRev* 1995, 179.
[322] Case 311/84 Telemarketing (CBEM) v SA CLT and IPB [1985] ECR 3261.
[323] This is the essence of the Höfner case; it is a typical example of *venire contra factum proprium*.

4. Justification of abuse

Under Art. 82, once abusive behavior is established, then this is regarded automatically as an illegal practice prohibited and sanctioned under EU law. Not so in the case of Art. 86 (1). Here, the abuse can still be justified under the three-tier test of para 2. In this respect, the Court has become much more generous in recent years. To some extent it has tried to limit the liberalizing effect of its own doctrine, returning to more traditional public service concepts which had found their place in Art. 16 of the Amsterdam Treaty. Again it needs to be stressed that open value judgments are replacing strict legal argumentation, and that the outcome of a contested case can never be predicted.

Justification operates on three levels:
- Not every public undertaking is privileged, but only those that are entrusted with the operation of *services in the general economic interest*. It is not clear whether this is an autonomous concept, or one defined by Member States themselves. It seems more likely that it is up to Member States how they organize these services. Most public undertakings, including those to whom exclusive or special rights have been granted, will qualify. Universal service obligations are also included.
- The application of the competition rules should not, in law or in fact, *obstruct* the fulfilment of these tasks. In early ECJ case law, the threshold of "obstruct" was put very high and identified with "to make impossible".[324] In more recent case law, the test is satisfied if fulfilment is simply made *more difficult*, so that the survival of the undertaking need not be under threat.[325] This is a question of balancing, a task that the Court will usually refer to Member State courts.[326] It is not yet clear how far proportionality criteria[327] can be used here, as in other areas concerned with restrictions on economic freedoms.
- At a third level, the Community interest must be taken into account.

Recent Court practice shows a widening application of Art. 86 (2), similar to the state aid rules (§ 7 VI 3):
- Postal services in the traditional sense as universal services can be protected against "cherry picking" of one profitable service by a private provider. On the other hand, postal services may cross-subsidize loss-generating universal services. They may do so by introducing and marketing value-added special services, even to the

---

[324] Case 155/73 Sacchi [1974] ECR 409.
[325] Case C-157/94 Commission v Netherlands [1997] ECR I-5699; C-159/94 Commission v France [1997] ECR I-5815.
[326] Cf. Case C-320/91 P Procureur du Roi v Paul Corbeau [1993] ECR-2533.
[327] Case C-179/90 Merci Convenzionale Porto di Genova SpA v Siderurgica Gabrielle SpA [1991] ECR I-5889 para 19 could be read in this direction.

detriment of potential private competitors. Art 86 is not meant to put a cap on the expansion of public undertakings.[328]

– Re-mailing services for mail deposited in one country and to be delivered in another must not be done at a loss by the monopoly provider; it has a right to reimbursement of its actual re-mailing costs.[329]

– A compulsory insurance scheme set up by social partners could only work efficiently to the exclusion of private insurers to avoid a wandering out of "good risks" (young and healthy workers) to the detriment of older workers who would not find private insurance.[330]

---

[328] Case C-320/91 P Corbeau.
[329] Case 147-148/97 Deutsche Post AG v Gesellschaft für Zahlungssysteme and Citicorp Kartenservice [2000] ECR I-825.
[330] Case C-67/96 Albany Int. BV v Stichting Bedrijfspensioenfonds Textielindustrie [1999] ECR I-5751.

§ 10. UNDISTORTED COMPETITION (II): PROTECTING INTELLECTUAL PROPERTY RIGHTS

Selected Bibliography of § 10

St. A. Anderman, *EC Competition Law and Intellectual Property Rights*, 2000; U. Bath, "Access to Information v. Intellectual Property Rights", *EIPR* 2002, 138; W. Baumol, *The Free-Market Innovation*, 2002; L. Bently/B. Sherman, *Intellectual Property Law*, 2001; L. Boehmer-Nessler, *Cyber Law*, 2001; B. Doherty, "Just what are "essential facilities"", *CMLRev* 2001, 38; M. de Cock Bruning/E. Hondius/C. Prines/M. de Vries, "Consumer@Protection.EU. An Analysis of European Consumer Legislation in the Information Society", *Journal of Consumer Policy*, 2001, 287; P. Craig, G. de Búrca, *EU Law*, 3rd ed. 2002, 1088-1121; J. Davis, "A European Constitution for IPRS? Competition, trade marks, and culturally significant signs", *CMLRev* 2004, 1005; P. Drahus, *A Philosophy of Intellectual Property*, 1996; R. C. Dreyfuss/D. L. Zimmerman/H. First (eds.), *Expanding the boundaries of Intellectual Property*, 2000; M. Franzosi (ed.), *European Community Trade Mark*, 1997; I. Govaere, *The use and abuse of intellectual property rights in EC Law*, 1996; F. Gioia, "Alicante and the harmonisation of intellectual property law in Europe", *CMLRev* 2004, 975; P. Goldstein, *International Copyright*, 2001; P. B. Hugenholz (ed.), *Copyright and e-commerce*, 2000; D. S. Karjala, "The Future of Copyright in the Digital Age", in: *FS N. Horn*, 1997, 470; D. Kitchen et al., *Kerlys Law of Trademarks and Tradenames*, 13th ed. 2001; B. de Nayer, "Droit d'auteur et protection des intérêts des consommateurs dans la société d'information", *Revue européenne de droit de la consommation* 1998, 3; T. Pinot, "The influence of the European Convention on Human Rights on Intellectual Property Rights", *EIPR* 2002, 209; R. Prime, *European Intellectual Property Law*, 2000; N. Reich, "Brevet pharmaceutique et accessibilité au médicament – le droit communautaire", *Revue internationale de droit économique (RIDE)* 2000, 83 = Special English edition 2001, 83; J. Reinbote/S. V. Lewinski, "The WIPO Treaties 1996: ready to come into force", *EIPR* 2002, 199; P. Rott, *Patentrecht und Sozialpolitik unter dem TRIPS-Abkommen*, 2002; P. Samuelson, "Author's rights in cyberspace: are new international rules needed?", *UNESCO Copyright Bulletin* 1996 Vol. XXX N. 2, 3; H. K. S. Schmidt, "Article 82's "Exceptional Circumstances" that restrict intellectual property rights", *ECLR* 2002, 210; F. Siiriainen, ""Droit d'auteur" contra "droit de concurrence"", *RIDE* 2001, 413; J. Stuyck, *Product differentiation – the legal situation*, 1983; G. Tritton, *Intellectual property in Europe*, 2nd ed. 2002; H. Ullrich, "Patent protection in Europe : Integrating Europe into the Community or the Community into Europe?", *ELJ* 2002, 433; I. Van Bael/J.-F. Bellis, *Competition Law of the EC*, 4th ed. 2005, 583-727.

I. FREE MOVEMENT VS. EXCLUSIVITY OF INTELLECTUAL PROPERTY RIGHTS

1. Recognition of intellectual property rights by Member States

Intellectual property – patents, trade marks, designs and models, copyright and the like – reward the inventive, artistic and literary activity of persons, and protect the goodwill of businesses. They may come into existence by creative activity (e.g., copyright of an artist, a writer or a composer, performance right of a musician), by registration (patents, trade marks, designs) or by commercial marketing (trade names, know-how, goodwill). They are protected by Member States – and other countries, notably in the industrialized world – as rights giving the beneficiary exclusivity of use, disposal and income. They are goods in commerce and may be exploited by the right holder himself by outright sale or by simple or exclusive licences. Individual rights may be bundled in the hands of exploitation associations, which is particularly the case with copyright and related (*e.g.*, performance or film) rights. Non-authorized exploitation of intellectual property rights is usually a violation of Member State law, which contains a raft of remedies in order to sanction violations, to skim off profits and to make good the damage to the right holder. Acts of counterfeiting and piracy may also be sanctioned by criminal law.

International Treaties will provide national treatment of right holders and may in addition allow for uniform minimum standards for certain rights (e.g., the Paris Convention for the Protection of Industrial Property of 1883 with amendments, the Bern Convention for the Protection of Literary and Artistic Works of 1886 with amendments, the Rome Convention for the Protection of Performers, Producers of Phonograms and Broadcasting of 1961). Lately, the World Industrial Property Organization (WIPO) has been active in proposing the Copyright (WCT) and Performances Treaties (WPPT) of 1996 to adapt the earlier Conventions to the requirements of the "information society". These entered into force on March 6 and May 20, 2002 respectively.[331]

This impressive system of rights is constitutionally protected by the European Human Rights Convention,[332] by the Charter of Fundamental Rights of the EU (§ 12 III), by the Constitutions of the Member States and indirectly by the EC, which respects their "systems of property ownership"[333]. The Agreement on Trade Related Aspects of Intellectual Property Rights (TRIPS), to which both EU Member States and the EU

---

[331]   Reinbothe & Lewinski, *EIPR* 2002, 199.
[332]   Pinto, *EIPR* 2002, 203.
[333]   Per Art. 295 EC.

itself adhere[334], contains rather strict rules on the effective protection of different intellectual property rights by the adhering partners. Under EC law, the question of direct effect has been debated with regard to provisional measures[335]. The ECJ has denied direct effect (§ 2 II 4). But Member State courts are required to implement these remedies "as far as possible in the light of the wording and purpose of the …TRIPS".[336]

2. The basic conflict

The exclusivity of intellectual property rights has an undeniable effect on free movement of goods and services. One of the origins of this conflict is the *territoriality* principle of intellectual property law: protection is limited to the country where the right originated; protection in other states demands a repetition of the same or similar procedures for coming into effect. In its "classic" pre-EC reading, territoriality works "the other way round": That is, the right holder can prevent importation of a product or service protected by his intellectual property right for the simple reason that he does not want marketing in the relevant territory, even if it has been put on another market with his consent. The right holder may use this territorial effect to segregate markets – an activity contrary to the *Grundig* doctrine of the ECJ (*infra* III 1).

The basic conflict between protection of intellectual property and free movement is inherent in Art. 30 EC itself. The relevant provision reads:

> The provisions of Art. 28 … shall not preclude prohibitions or restrictions on imports, exports or goods in transit justified on grounds of …. the protection of industrial and commercial property. Such prohibitions or restrictions shall not, however, constitute a means of arbitrary discrimination or a disguised restriction on trade between the Member States.

To a somewhat smaller extent, a similar conflict can be seen in applying the freedom to provide services, and the competition rules: Activities involving the licensing of intellectual property are within the exclusive power of the licensor and therefore cannot freely be commercialised across borders without his consent. Exclusivity limits intra-brand competition and gives the right holder a quasi-monopoly position on the territory of the state where the right has originated – a position which may and (as case-law shows!) has been abused by imposing discriminatory or excessively restrictive conditions on licensees.

---

[334]   The issue of joint competence was decided by the ECJ in its opinion 1/94 [1994] I-5267; adoption by Council decision 98/800/EC [1994] *OJ* L 336/1.

[335]   Per Art. 50 TRIPS.

[336]   Case C-89/99 Schieving-Nijstad *et al* v Robert Groenevold [2001] ECR I- 5851 at para 54 relating to Art. 50 (6).

In its early case law, the Court took quite a negative position *vis-à-vis* the exercise of intellectual property rights in EU commerce. Trade marks should not be protected against unauthorized use when they originated from the same source, as the Court ruled in its highly controversial *Hag I* decision.[337] Conflicts between trade marks of different origin had to be resolved, according to *Terrapin*[338], by a balancing test:

> In the particular situation the requirements of the free movement of goods and the safeguarding of industrial and commercial property rights must be so reconciled that protection is ensured for the legitimate use of the rights conferred by national laws, coming within the prohibitions on imports "justified" within the meaning of Art. 36 of the Treaty (now Art. 30 EC), but denied on the other hand in respect of any improper exercise of the same rights of such a nature as to maintain or effect artificial partitions within the common market (para 7).

The ECJ reacted negatively against attempts to restrict parallel imports in (ab)using the territoriality principle inherent in intellectual property rights protection. This was first developed with regard to patents and trade marks and repeated with regard to copyright of musical works under control by a management society (GEMA):[339]

> The argument put to the Court .... that in the absence of harmonisation in this sector the principle or territoriality of copyright laws always prevails over the principle of freedom of movement of goods within the common market cannot be accepted. Indeed, the essential purpose of the Treaty, which is to unite national markets into a single market, could not be attained if, under the various legal systems of the Member States, nationals of those Member States were able to partition the market and bring about arbitrary discrimination or disguised restrictions on trade between Member States.

3. The distinction between existence and exercise of intellectual property rights

The Court tried to resolve inherent tension between intellectual property rights on the one hand, and the free movement and competition rules on the other. It did so by the somewhat deductive approach of defining the "specific subject matter", "existence" or "essence" of intellectual property rights as against their mere "exercise". This essence was to be protected by Community law[340], while the exercise had to stay within the limits of Community law and not allow a "disguised restriction" or "arbitrary discrimination" in the free movement of goods. In the famous

---

[337]   Case 192/73 Van Zuylen v Hag [1974] 731.
[338]   Case 119/75 Terrapin Overseas v Terranova [1976] ECR 1039.
[339]   Joint cases 55 + 57/80 Musik-Vertrieb Membran v GEMA – Gesellschaft für musikalische Aufführungsrechte, [1981] ECR 147 at para 14.
[340]   According to Art. 30, para 1, 295 EC.

Centrafarm/Sterling Drug case of 1974[341], the Court defined the subject matter of patents as

> the guarantee that the patentee, to reward the creative effort of the inventor, has the exclusive right to use an invention with a view to manufacturing industrial products and putting them into circulation for the first time, either directly or by the grant of licences to third parties as well as the right to oppose infringements

A similar definition was given for trade marks in the parallel litigation *Centrafarm/Winthrop*.[342]

Later cases took a more functional approach to intellectual property rights and did so explicitly with regard to trade marks, designs, copyright and performance rights. With regard to trade marks it is the *control function*, for the latter the *reward function*, that allows for the exclusivity which Community law has to respect. In trade mark law, the Court in *Hag II*[343], in following a detailed review by AG Jacobs of former controversial case law and in departing from the common origin doctrine pronounced in *Hag I*, said:

> Trade marks are ... an essential element in the system of undistorted competition which the Treaty seeks to establish and maintain. Under such a system, an undertaking must be in a position to keep its customers by virtue of the quality of its products and services, something which is possible only if there are distinctive marks which enable customers to identify those products and services. For the trade mark to be able to fulfil this role, it must offer a guarantee that all goods bearing it have been produced under the control of a single undertaking which is accountable for their quality (para 13).

This quality function does not mean that the trade mark owner guarantees to the customer a certain quality of his product or service which has been marked by him, but that he can control its first marketing and can oppose any changes in the marking of the product or its quality which may impair this function. This concept is closely linked to the question of consent. It is decisive for exhaustion of exclusivity and its limits, and will be discussed later.

With regard to copyright and performance rights, the Court recognized both the economic function and the moral right as being protected by Community law. In *Phil Collins*[344] it wrote:

---

[341]   Case 15/74 Centrafarm BV et Adriaan de Peijper v Sterling Drug Inc. [1974] ECR 1147 at para 9.
[342]   Case 16/74 Centrafarm BV et Adriaan de Peijper v Winthorp BV [1974] ECR 1183.
[343]   Case C-10/89 SA CNL-SUCAL NV v HAG GF AG [1990] I-3711; repeated in case C-9/93 IHT Internationale Heiztechnik GmbH v Ideal Standard GmbH [1994] ECR I-2789.
[344]   Joined cases C-92 + 326/92 Phill Collins v Imarat and Patricia v EMI Elelctrola [1993] ECR I-5145.

The specific subject-matter of those rights, as governed by national legislation, is to ensure the protection of the moral and the economic rights of their holders. The protection of moral rights enables authors and performers, in particular, to object to any distortion, mutilation or other modification of a work which would be prejudicial to their honour or reputation. Copyright and related rights are also economic in nature, in that they confer the right to exploit commercially the marketing of the protected work, particularly in the form of licences granted in return for payment of royalties (para 20).

Other rights, such as designs[345], are determined by national law. In the meantime, many of these rights have been harmonized by Community directives or even transformed into an (optional) Community regime[346].

4. Effective protection – requirement of Community Law

Directive 2004/48/EC of the EP and the Council of 29 April "on the enforcement of intellectual property rights"[347] obliges Member States to provide for a bundle of remedies and procedures to protect intellectual property rights and trade marks, including rules on standing, evidence, information, provisional and precautionary measures, injunctions, compensation, and codes of conduct. The directive must be implemented by 29 April 2006.

II. THE PRINCIPLE OF EXHAUSTION AND ITS LIMITS

1. Basis of the exhaustion doctrine: consent

The most striking development of Community law has been the development of the Community-wide exhaustion principle. This is based on the doctrine of consent first developed in the *Centrafarm* cases:

> ... a derogation from the principle of the free movement of goods is not ... justified where the product has been put onto the market in a legal manner, by the patentee himself or with his consent, in the Member State from which it has been imported, in particular in the case of the proprietor of parallel patents (para 11).

---

[345] Case 53/87 Consorzio italiano della componentistica di ricambio per autoveicoli and Maxicar v Regie nationale des usines Renault [1988] ECR 6039 at para 12.

[346] Directive 98/71/EC of the EP and the Council of 13 October 1998 on the legal protection of designs [1998] OJ L 289/28; Council Regulation (EC) 6/2002 of 12.12.2001 on Community designs, [2002] OJ L 3/1.

[347] [2004] OJ L 157/45.

The Court deliberately disregards the territoriality principle inherent in the protection of intellectual property rights and sacrifices it on the altar of the unity of the common, or later internal, market. Later cases make clear that consent is not a factual but a legal concept; the right holder can therefore not limit consent to one Member State. On the other hand, where the placing of the product has been imposed upon him, e.g., by compulsory licence, there is no consent and therefore no exhaustion.[348] However, a mere moral obligation to market the product does not preclude exhaustion.[349] The overall issue was particularly discussed in the "repackaging" case law and gave rise to a rather detailed and complex case law.

The theory of consent is only relevant with regard to products, not to services. In *Coditel I*[350] the Court said:

> … the problems involved in the observance of a film producer's rights in relation to the requirements of the Treaty are not the same as those which arise in connection with literary and artistic works the placing of which at the disposal of the public is inseparable from the circulation of the material form of the works, as in the case of books or records, whereas the film belongs to the category of literary and artistic works made available to the public by performances which may be infinitely repeated and the commercial exploitation of which comes under the movement of services, no matter whether the means whereby it is shown to the public be the cinema or television (para 11).

2.   Limits to consent: the repackaging debate

A special case law has evolved in the so-called repackaging debate. This relates particularly to the marketing of proprietary medicines by parallel importers. Since the licensing and labeling requirements of medicines are still separate in the Member States despite Community harmonization, the trade mark holder can easily provoke market segregation by placing different packages with different labelling and different trade marks onto national markets. This restricts parallel imports because products purchased in one country cannot be marketed without repackaging or re-labelling in another market. However, this manipulation of the original product is regarded as an infringement of the trade mark right of the proprietor. Here, the doctrine of exhaustion in its traditional reading does not help because the consent is deemed to exclude these manipulations.

---

[348]   Case 19/84 Pharmon BV v Hoechst AG [1985] ECR 2281.
[349]   Joined cases C-267+ 289/95 Merck & Co Inc. et al. v Primecrown *et al.* [1996] ECR I-6285 against the opinion of AG Fenelly.
[350]   Case 62/79 Coditel et al v Cine-Vog Films [1980] ECR 881.

In its case law, beginning with *Hoffman-La Roche*[351], the Court had to develop criteria on how to balance free movement on the one hand with the right of trade mark owners on the other. Originally a distinction was made between a "mere" repackaging on the one hand and, in *AHP*,[352] a replacement of the original trade mark of the country of origin by the mark used in the country of distribution on the other. Here, the first was concerned with the market-segregating *effects* of product differentiation on the marketing of medicines, while in the second case *"intent"* to segregate was required.

Recent case law has clarified the issues and allowed far-reaching interventions of the parallel importer into the packaging and labelling of the medicine to make it marketable in the country of destination. In *Bristol-Meyers Squibb*[353] the Court maintained:

> If the repackaging is carried out in conditions which cannot affect the original condition of the product inside the packaging, the essential function of the trade mark as a guarantee of origin is safeguarded. Thus the consumer or end user is not misled as to the origin of the products, and does in fact receive products manufactured under the sole supervision of the trade mark owner" (para 67).

The Court went on to define these criteria in great detail, namely:
- it is shown that the repackaging cannot affect the original condition of the product inside the packaging;
- the new packaging clearly and easily visible states who repackaged the product;
- the presentation of the repackaged product does not harm the reputation of the trade mark;
- the importer gives notice to the trade mark owner before the repackaged product is put on sale.

These criteria also apply to the replacement of the trade mark, provided this is "objectively necessary".[354] Later cases were concerned with when such "objective necessity" existed.[355] The Court was satisfied that replacement was necessary in order to overcome consumer resistance against imported medicines. Merely to make a profit was, however, not enough.

---

[351] Case 102/77 Hoffmann-La Roche v Centrafarm [1978] ECR 1139.
[352] Case 3/78 Centrafarm v American Home Products [1978] ECR 1823.
[353] Joined cases C-427, 429 + 436/93 Bristol-Meyers Squibb *et al* v Paranova [1996] ECR I-3457.
[354] Case C-379/97 Pharmacia & Upjohn v Paranova A/S [1999] ECR I-6927 at para 42, thus overruling the AHP decision, *supra* 351.
[355] Case C-143/00 Boehringer Ingelheim v Eurim Pharm [2002] ECR I-3759.

This highly contested case law is an example of judicial policy-making and is clearly aimed at protecting the consumer (and his health insurance, whether public or private) at the expense of the trade mark owner. It is questionable how far this generosity with regard to repackaging is in conformity with the control doctrine developed by the Court in *Hag II*.[356]

III. COMPETITION LAW AND INTELLECTUAL PROPERTY RIGHTS

1. *The Grundig doctrine*

Early case law also transposed to agreements between right holders and licensees or distributors the above doctrine on the limits of the exercise of intellectual property rights. This had to be measured against the competition rules. The principle which has emerged since the *Grundig* case[357] was that of a ban on absolute territorial protection. In the case at hand, the registration of the GINT (Grundig International) trade mark in France in favour of the exclusive distributor Consten:

> intended to increase the protection inherent in the disputed agreement, against the risk of parallel imports into France of Grundig products, by adding the protection deriving from the law of industrial property rights. Thus no third party could import Grundig products from other Member States of the Community for resale in France without running risks.

Even though the original starting point of the reasoning is no longer valid – the doctrine of exhaustion was developed only later and would now prevent the use of the trade mark "GINT" against parallel imports – the opposition of the Court against clauses provoking absolute territorial protection was later continued in judgments concerning licensing agreements under the competition rules. In the *Maize-Seed* case[358] it had to evaluate the extent of territorial protection in licence agreements and allowed so-called "open exclusive licences" leaving room for parallel imports, but prevented licensees from business activity beyond their territory; "closed exclusive licences" allowing absolute territorial protection are forbidden under Community law. The Court tried to strike a balance between the necessary protection of intellectual property rights and their use through licensing, in particular exclusive licensing, in order to encourage technology transfer on the one hand, and the maintenance of a balance of competition in the internal market which would allow independent distributors to

---

[356]   Cf. Reich/Micklitz, *Europäisches Verbraucherrecht*, 4. Auflage 2003 at para 5.22.
[357]   Cases 56 + 58/64 Etablissements Consten SaRL and Grundig GmbH v Commission [1966] ECR 299.
[358]   Case 258/78 L.C. Nungesser and Kurt Eisele v Commission [1982] ECR 2015.

penetrate markets. The Commission, in its later exemption practice, generalized these principles into the Technology Transfer Regulation 240/96[359], replaced by Commission Reg. No. 772/2004 of 27 April 2004.[360]

The ban on absolute territorial protection was implemented only against the free circulation of goods, not in relation to services. The Court followed a similar principle in competition as in free movement law, as can be seen in its *Coditel II* decision:[361]

> However, the mere fact that the owner of the copyright in a film has granted to a sole licensee the exclusive right to exhibit that film in the territory of a Member State and, consequently, to prohibit, during a specified period, its showing to others, is not sufficient to justify the finding that such a contract must be regarded as the purpose, the means or the result of an agreement, decision or concerted practice prohibited by the Treaty (para 15).

2. Abuse of market dominating position by intellectual property rights

The owner of an intellectual property right and, with certain limits, the beneficiary of an exclusive licence, enjoys exclusivity in protection which as the very subject matter cannot be challenged under EC law. This is not only true with regard to free movement but also as to the competition rules. Therefore, the monopoly created by allocating an intellectual property right cannot as such be considered a "market dominating position" to be controlled against abuses under Art. 82. This was with some ambiguity stated by the Court in *Renault*:[362]

> It should be noted at the outset that the mere fact of securing the benefit of an exclusive right granted by law, the effect of which is to enable the manufacture and sales of protected products by unauthorised third parties to be prevented, cannot be regarded as an abusive method of eliminating competition (para 15).

Therefore, Art. 82 EC cannot be used to impose a compulsory licence on right holders.[363] On the other hand, the Court stated that an intellectual property right may be used to reinforce a potential market dominating position, and its use may under certain conditions be regarded as an abuse by restricting or distorting competition

---

[359]   [1996] *OJ* L 31/2; for a critical evaluation of the case law and Commission practice cf. Korah, *An Introductory Guide to EC Competition Law*, 7th ed. 2000.

[360]   [2004] OJ L 123, Commission guidelines [2004] OJ C 101.

[361]   Case 262/81 Coditel SA Compagnie générale pour la diffusion de la television, et al v Ciné-Vog Fils SA et al [1982] ECR 3381.

[362]   Case 53/87 Consorzio italiano componentistica di ricambio per autoveicoli and Maxicar v Regie nationale des usines Renault [1988] ECR 6039.

[363]   Case 238/87 Volvo v Veng [1988] ECR 6211 at para 8.

in the sense of Art. 82 lit a-d EC.[364] The inherent contradiction of these two principles was clearly debated in the famous *Magill* case[365], where the Court had to evaluate the practice of Irish radio and TV stations invoking their copyright to refuse the release of their programmes to independent magazines. The Court followed the Commission and the CFI against the opinion of AG Gulmann in that this practice amounted to an abuse of a dominant position of the Irish TV stations on the regional market for programme magazines:

> The appellants' refusal to provide basic information by relying on national copyright provisions thus prevented the appearance of a new product, a comprehensive weekly guide to TV programmes which the appellants did not offer and for which there was potential consumer demand... (para 54).

This sweeping pronouncement of the Court has given rise to controversies, because it seems to contradict earlier statements that the owner of an intellectual property right cannot be forced into licensing its use.[366] The Commission took this as a starting point to develop a theory of "essential facilities" whereby holders of exclusive rights could be forced to allow access to their services if this was necessary to establish competition.[367]

In the opinion of this author, the facts of the *Magill* case should not be forgotten: The copyright invoked had a low threshold, it was invoked not in the main market of the right holder, but in a derivative market that the right holders did not themselves want to service, and there was consumer demand which was not satisfied by them. These special circumstances convinced the Court that there was an abuse of a market dominating position. In *Bronner*[368] the Court defended its case law by referring to the exceptional circumstances of the *Magill* decision. It insisted in particular that the service, for which there was a demand, and which was refused by the right holders, must be in itself "indispensable to carrying out that person's business, inasmuch as there is no actual or potential substitute in existence ..." (para 41). Again, it is a matter of fact, to be proven by the competitor of the right holder, whether this is the case.

---

[364]   Case 27/76 United Brands v Commission [1978] ECR 207.

[365]   Cases C-241 + 242/91P Radio Telefis Eireann (RTE) and Independent TV Publications Ltd (ITP) v Commission [1995] ECR I-743.

[366]   Andermann, *EC Competittion Law and Intellectual Property Rights*, 2000 at 178; Schmidt, *ECLR* 2002, 210 at 215: lack of clarification of exceptional circumstances.

[367]   Doherty, *CMLRev* 2001, 38; Goyder, *EC Competition Law*, 4th ed. 2003 at 316-320.

[368]   Case C-7/97 Oscar Bronner GmbH & Co KG v Mediaprint [1998] ECR I-7791; see also case T-504/93, Tierce Ladbroke v EC Commission, [1997] ECR II-923.

The IMS case[369] concerned the refusal of a market dominating undertaking (IMS) to supply its competitor, NDC, with its copyrighted "1860 brick structure" concerning the supply of sales of pharmaceutical products in Germany. The data aggregated according to this structure are sold to German Pharmaceutical companies and are relevant for their marketing activities. The Court took the criteria as developed in *Magill* and clarified in *Bronner* to determine whether a refusal to licence its copyright constituted an abuse under Art. 82. Three criteria are decisive:

- The undertaking which requested the licence intends to offer, on the market for the supply of data in question, new products or services not offered by the copyright owner and for which there is a potential consumer demand.
- The refusal is not justified by objective considerations.
- The refusal is such as to reserve to the copyright owner the market for the supply of data on sales of pharmaceutical products in the Member States concerned by eliminating all competition on the market.

IV. TRADE MARK DIRECTIVE 89/104 – A MODEL FOR COMMUNITY INTELLECTUAL PROPERTY LAW

1. The importance of Dir. 89/104

Directive 89/104/EEC of 21 December 1988, to approximate the laws of the Member States regarding trade marks[370], does not intend a "full-scale approximation" but merely an "approximation limited to those national provisions of law which most directly affect the functioning of the internal market"[371]. It therefore sets out some fundamental requirements concerning the concept, registration, protection, exhaustion, licensing and use of trade marks registered in the Community. It has given rise to an important body of ECJ case law, which has led to a near-complete harmonization of the central elements of trade mark law in the Community. The ECJ, via the reference procedure, has become a quasi – EU "Court of Appeal" in trade mark matters, guaranteeing *uniform interpretation of trade mark law*[372] and thereby indirectly uniform protection of trade marks, but also defining its limits which have to be respected throughout the Community. The approach and interpretation of the trade mark directive seems to have become a model for a fledgling EU system of intellectual property rights – both by harmonizing Member State law and by operating as the basis

---

[369]   Case C418/01 IMS Health v NDC Health [2004] ECR I-(29.4.2004).
[370]   [1989] OJ L 40/1 of 11.2.1989.
[371]   Recital 3 of Dir. 89/104.
[372]   Case C-206/01 Arsenal Football-Club plc. v Mathew Reed [2002] ECR I-10273 at para 45.

for creating a specific Community trade mark by the later Regulation (EC) 94/40.[373] This will not be discussed in detail here. Suffice to say that the Court gave the Community broad powers to legislate intellectual property law under the internal market provision of Art. 95.[374]

Dir. 89/104 is only concerned with trade marks in the classical sense as described in Art. 2 and which can be registered. It does not exclude protection or require registration of rights of names and similar rights[375].

The Court prefers a broad concept of trade mark, including three-dimensional signs. They must not necessarily be capable of being perceived visually, but they should be capable of being represented graphically. *Graphic representation* is an indispensable requirement both for the process of registration which must be, in the words of the ECJ, "self-contained, easily accessible and intelligible", and for relevant information of third parties which must be "unequivocal and objective". Olfactory signs which cannot be represented graphically – the indication or deposition of a chemical formula is not sufficient – are therefore excluded from registration.[376] Colours *per se* can only under limited circumstances be registered as trade marks, as the Court set out in its judgment of 6.5.2003, taking into account the public interest in not unduly restricting the use of colours.[377]

2. Ambit of protection

a. Different steps of exclusivity

The ambit of protection of the trade mark which confers on the proprietor certain "exclusive rights" is described in Art. 5 and contains a four-step test involving different interventions of Member States:

– Art. 5 (1) a) allows *ex lege* protection against the use of identical signs for identical goods or services (counterfeiting in the classic sense).
– Art. 5 (1) b) protects the trade mark also *ex lege* against "any sign where, because of its identity with, or similarity to, the trade mark and the identity or similarity of the goods or services covered by the trade mark and the sign, (where) there exists

---

[373] [1994] OJ L 11/1; Implementing Commission Regulation (EC) No 2868/95 of 13.12.1995, [1995] OJ L 301/1; for an overview, see Gioia, *CMLRev* 2004, 975.
[374] Case C-377/98 Netherlands v EP and Council [2001] ECR I-7079 concerning the legality of the biotechnology directive 98/44/EC.
[375] Per Art. 4 (4) of Dir. 89/104.
[376] Case C-273/00 Ralf Sieckmann v Deutsches Patent- und Markenamt [2002] ECR I-11737; comment by Davis, *CMLRev* 2004, 1005 at 1022.
[377] Case C-104/01 Libertel groep v Benelux Merkenbureau [2003] ECR I-3793.

a likelihood of confusion on the part of the public, which includes the likelihood of association between the sign and the trade mark" (protection against confusion).

– Art. 5 (2) contains an option for Member States, similar to Art. 6 *bis* of the Paris Convention for a trade mark "which has a reputation in the Member State and where the use of that sign without due cause takes unfair advantage of, or is detrimental to, the distinctive character or the repute of the trade mark" (protection of so-called well-known or famous marks against unfair exploitation beyond confusion).

– Art. 5 (5) allows Member States to apply their unfair competition rules to "the protection against the use of a sign other than for the purposes of distinguishing goods or services, where use of that sign without due cause takes unfair advantage of, or is detrimental to, the distinctive character of the repute of the trade mark."

A developing extensive case law of the ECJ has tried to clarify these fundamental concepts. These, it should be remembered, have to be applied uniformly throughout the entire Union, including new Member States. They are also the basis for applying the EU Trade Mark Regulation 94/40.

b. Straight counterfeiting

The *Arsenal* case[378] concerned the use of the sign of a well-known football-club called "Arsenal" of the English Premier League for football souvenirs and memorabilia sold by Mr. Reed without Arsenal's consent. The question was whether this use of the sign was "trade mark use" and whether this was a precondition for an infringement action under Art. 5 (1) a). The Court insisted on the uniformity of application of Art. 5 (1) throughout the Community, on the functions of a trade mark that are an essential element in a system of undistorted competition in order to attract and retain customers by the quality of their goods or services, and on the nature of the exclusive rights allocated to its proprietor. These rights are not without limits, as Art. 6 shows, especially when used for purely descriptive purposes. In the case at hand, Mr. Reed was engaged in a commercial activity, even if he was using the sign for support of the football club, and was therefore infringing Art. 5 (1) a).

c. The concept of confusion under Community law

The concept of confusion was first brought to the attention of the ECJ in the *Sabel* case.[379] This case resulted from the ambiguity of Art. 5 (1) b) itself because it also referred to the "likelihood of association" as an element of confusion. Was this

---

[378]   *Supra* note 372.
[379]   Case C-251/95 SABEL BV v Puma AG, Rudolf Dassler Sport [1997] ECR I-6191.

"likelihood" enough to find the existence of confusion, or just an element to be taken into account by determining it? The Court gave an answer in the second direction by stating:

> That global appreciation of the visual, aural or conceptual similarity of the marks in question must be based on the overall impression given by the marks, bearing in mind, in particular, their distinctive and dominant components ... The average consumer normally perceives a mark as a whole and does not proceed to analyse its various details ... the more distinctive the earlier mark, the greater will be the likelihood of confusion ... However, ... where the earlier mark is not especially well known to the public and consists in an image with little imaginative content, the mere fact that the two marks are conceptually similar is not sufficient to give rise to a likelihood of confusion ...

As usual, the Court did not decide the case at hand concerning the motive of a "bounding feline" but seemed to be hostile to the concept of "protection of motives" (*Motivschutz*) under trade mark law.

Later cases clarified certain aspects of the concept of confusion:
– Confusion must be determined by referring to the average, sufficiently well informed consumer standard, as known in advertising law (§ 17 III).[380]
– In assessing whether a trade mark is highly distinctive and therefore easier apt to confusion, "the national court must make an overall assessment of the greater or lesser capacity of the trade mark to identify the goods or services for which it has been registered as coming from a particular undertaking, and thus to distinguish those goods or services from those of other undertakings".[381]
– The trade mark owner maintaining confusion has the onus of proof; a "*non liquet*" situation is to his disadvantage; it is not sufficient to refer to his well known mark.[382]
– Similarity may exist between goods and services; therefore, a trade mark registered for a good ("CANON" for Japanese electronic equipment) may be confused with the sign ("Cannon" registered for video services).[383]

d. Protection of well-known marks

Art. 5 (2) allows Member States to protect well known marks also against loss of reputation, even if a case of confusion cannot be established. The action is closer to

---

[380]   Case C-303/97 Verbraucherschutzverein v Sektkellerei Kessler [1999] ECR I-513.
[381]   Case C-342/97 Lloyd Schuhfabrik Meyer v Klijsen Handel BV [1999] ECR I-3819 para 22.
[382]   Case C-425/98 Marca Mode CV v Adidas AG [2000] ECR I-4861.
[383]   Case C-39/97 Canon Kabuschiki Kaisha v Metro-Goldwyn-Mayer Inc. [1998] ECR I-5507.

traditional unfair competition, than trade mark, concepts. In the *Chevy* case[384] the ECJ was asked to determine the regional market on which the mark had to be well known. The Court was satisfied that this reputation exists in a substantial part of a Member State, for example in one linguistic region in a country like Belgium, which was divided in several linguistic zones, and not in the entire Member State.

The *Adidas* case[385] insisted that for the protection of well-known trademarks it is sufficient for the degree of similarity between the mark with a reputation and the sign to have the effect that the relevant section of the public establishes a link between the sign and the mark. This is not excluded by the fact that the sign is used as an embellishment if nonetheless the public establishes a link between it and the mark. This is a matter of fact which must be established by the national court.

3. Legitimate use under trade mark law

Art. 6 of the Dir. allows certain types of use of a trade mark which are not considered an infringement, such as name, quality indication, indication of intended use for spare parts or accessories. The importance of this derogation in the generous Community law system of protection was spelled out in the *BMW* case[386]. This concerned the advertising of an independent second hand and repair shop for selling and servicing BMW cars. The Court found no trade mark infringement of BMW where a sign was used for information purposes only. This *right of and to information* is necessary in the balancing between the rules on free movement and those on protection of industrial property, and is "in accordance with honest practices in industrial or commercial matters" (para 58), a substantial restriction to unfair competition law.

The *Toshiba* case[387] concerned the use of "OEM" (original equipment manufacturer) numbers by a spare part manufacturer for Toshiba products who was accused of unfair comparative advertising. The Court implicitly denied this charge and referred to legitimate trade mark use for information purposes under the *BMW* doctrine.

The *Gillette* judgment[388] clarified the concept of "fair use" in Art. 6 (1) (c). The use of the trademark by a third party must be necessary where it consitutes the only means of providing the public with comprehensible and complete information on the intended purpose. It is not limited to accessories or spare parts. "Honest use" must

---

[384]   Case C-375/97 General Motors v Yplon SA [1999] ECR I-5421.
[385]   Case C-408/01 Adidas-Salomon AG et al. v Fitnessworld Trading Ltd. [2003] ECR I-12537.
[386]   Case C-63/97 BMW v Ronald Karel Deenink [1999] ECR I-905.
[387]   Case C-112/99 Toshiba Europe GmbH v Katun Germany GmbH [2001] ECR I-7945.
[388]   Case C-228/03 The Gillette Company et al v LA-Laboratories Ld. Oy [2005] ECR I-(17.3.2005).

be determined in accordance with honest practices in industrial and commercial matters for which the Court gives a list of (non-exhaustive) examples.

In the *Budweis* case[389], the Court extended the concept of Art. 6 (1) (a) of Dir. 89/104 of "a third party using, in the course of trade his own name or address ... in accordance with "honest practices in industrial or commercial matters" to trade names of legal persons, in contrast to a prior joint declaration of the Council and the Commission, in the case at hand to Budweis beer. These "honest practices" depend on the "legitimate interests of the trade-mark proprietor", taking into account all the relevant circumstances, especially whether there is an unfair competition with the proprietor (para 82-84). The Court further went on to say that Art. 6 (2) read together with Art. 16 TRIPS contains the principle of priority which also extends to "existing trade names" (Budweis against the registered trade mark Budweiser). Since trade names are protected without registration, such a prior registration cannot be required as basis for priority (para. 96).

4. Community or international exhaustion?

The principle of Community exhaustion had already been developed by Court practice under primary Community law. It was based on the concept of "consent" to placing a product on the internal market, and therefore limited to the territory of the Community. It did not preclude Member States from continuing their prior theories of international exhaustion, such as, for example, in Germany or in the Scandinavian countries.

The principle of exhaustion was introduced in Art. 7 (1) of the Trade Mark Dir. 89/104, but it was not clear whether this was meant as a complete harmonization, thus excluding further-reaching Member State law, or as a mere restatement of the legal situation existing prior to its enactment. The consequences of the dispute are easily understood: international exhaustion would offer a wider variety of products and services on the internal market unprotected by trade mark law and thereby increase consumer choice, while mere Community exhaustion would be favourable to the trade mark owner, who would lose protection only if having placed products and services on the internal, not the world, market. While the advisory opinion of the EFTA-Court of 3.12.1997 in the *Maglite* case[390] opted in the first direction, the ECJ in the later

---

[389] Case C-245/02 Anheuser-Busch Inc. v Budějovický Budvar národní podnik [2004] ECR I-(16.11.2004).

[390] Cited in para 43 of the opinion AG Jacobs of 29 Jan. 1998 to the Silhouette-case, *infra* note 391.

Silhouette case[391] took the second. Whereas the EFTA Court was concerned with competition and consumer choice, in contrast the ECJ focused on complete harmonization and the risks to the unity of the internal market if Member States were allowed to impose different rules on exhaustion. The strict approach of the ECJ is surprising, for two reasons. Firstly, since the concept of "complete harmonization" of Dir. 89/104 was not intended by the Community legislator, as can be seen from the recitals. Secondly, no proof existed of disruptions to the internal market by different Member State rules – usually a reason for law approximation (§ 3 II 2) but not for Court intervention.

Later case law hardened the doctrine of Community-wide exhaustion against "circumventions" by parallel importers. That, in this author's opinion, was implemented to the detriment of competition and consumer choice by unilaterally privileging trade mark owners beyond what was necessary even in order to safeguard the unity of the internal market:

- In *Dubois*[392] the Court insisted that Community exhaustion exists only for each individual item of a product, not for an entire series or batch.
- In *Davidoff*[393] the Court rejected the theory of "implied consent" as a basis for exhaustion; consent to placing the product on the internal market must be positively expressed; Member State law cannot rule to the contrary by referring to its rules on contract construction. Silence or ignorance on the part of the trader has no influence on consent.
- *Van Doren*[394] is concerned with the burden of proof. The Court first made reference to the traditional rule on the burden of proof, namely that the defendant (third party who allegedly violates the trade mark rights of the proprietor) had to show that the product was placed on the EEA/EU market with the consent of the owner, and not on a third country market where exhaustion does not take place. If, however, such a rule would lead to a partition of markets (the *Grundig* doctrine, III 1), for example the owner using an exclusive distribution system divided among countries, the traditional rule must be modified:

> Where a third party against whom proceedings have been brought succeeds in establishing that there is a real risk of partitioning of national markets if he himself bears the burden of proving that the goods were placed on the market in the EEA by the proprietor of the trade mark or with his consent, it is for the proprietor of the trade mark to establish that

---

[391]   Case C-355/96 Silhouette Int. Schmied GmbH & Co KG v Hartlauer Handelsgesellschaft [1998] ECR I-4799; cf. O'Keefe/Kean, *YEL* 2001, 139.

[392]   Case C-173/98 Sebago Inc. and Ancienne Maison Dubois v G-B Unic SA [1999] ECR I-4103.

[393]   Joined cases C-414-416/99 Zino Davidoff SA v A & G Imports, Levi Strauss & Co v Tesco Imports *et al.* [2001] ECR I-8691; comment O'Keefe/Kean, *CMLRev* 2002, 291.

[394]   Case C-244/00 Van Doren + Q GmbH v Lifestyle sports + Sportswear Handelsgesellschaft *et al.* [2003] ECR I-3051.

the products were initially placed on the market outside the EEA by him or with his consent (para 41).

5. Limits to consent

Art. 7 (2) defines the limits to consent "where there exist legitimate reasons for the proprietor to oppose further commercialisation of the goods, especially where the condition of the goods is changed or impaired after they have been put on the market". This continues to some extent the former repackaging case law, but also contains new elements that were brought to the attention of the Court in the *Dior* case.[395] The Court preferred a broad construction of the concept of "legitimate reasons" which may include the damage done to the reputation of a trade mark by later advertising of a parallel importer. Since parallel imports are, according to the *Grundig* doctrine (*supra* III 1), a legitimate means of commercialisation in the internal market:

> a balance must be struck between the legitimate interest of the trade mark owner in being protected against resellers using his trade mark for advertising in a manner which could damage the reputation of the trade mark and the reseller's legitimate interest in being able to resell the goods in question by using advertising methods which are customary in his sector of trade (para 44).

This balancing depends very much on how the reseller places the trade mark in his presentation and advertising of the products. He must respect the luxury and prestige image of the trade mark.

6. Means of protection

Dir. 89/104 is silent on means of protection, while later directives, especially Dir. 2004/48 (*supra* I 4) expressly require Member States to guarantee effective, equivalent and deterrent remedies. This requirement of effective and equivalent legal protection when Community rights are violated is already a general principle of Community law (§ 14 I). It is up to Member State courts to provide for effective remedies. In *Silhouette*[396] the Court interpreted the necessity of granting the trade mark owner a restraining order out of Art. 5 (1) of the Directive. Later cases were concerned with Art. 50 TRIPS concerning provisional measures. This is not directly effective but a means for the judge to interpret his national law (*supra* I 1). With regard to compensation and skimming-off of illegal profits reaped by counterfeiting, Art. 13 of Dir. 2000/48 requires Member States to provide such remedies, at latest from 1st of May 2006.

---

[395] Case C-337/97 Parfums Christian Dior SA and Parfums Christian Dior NV v Evora BV [1997] ECR I-6013.
[396] *Supra* note 391 at para 35.

CHAPTER III. ADEQUATE STANDARDS

Table of Contents

Selected Bibliography of §§ 11, 12, 14

L. Allkemper, *Der Rechtsschutz des Einzelnen nach dem EG-Vertrag – Möglichkeiten einer Verbesserung*, 1995; P. Altson (ed.), *The EU and Human Rights*, 1999; A. Arnull, *The EU and its Court of Justice*, 1999; A. Arnull, "Private applicants and the action for annulment since Codorniú", *CMLRev* 2001, 7; K. Athela, "The Revised Provisions on Sex Discrimination in European Law: A Critical Assessment", *ELJ* 2005, 57; M. Bell, *Anti-Discrimination Law and the EU*, 2002; B. Bercusson, *EC Employment Law*, 4th ed. 2002; M. Besson, *L'égalité horizonale: l'égalité de traitement entre particuliers*, 1999; Chr. Brown, "The Race Equality Directive: Towards Equality for All the Peoples of Europe", *Yearbook of European Law (YEL)*, 2002, 195; A. v. Bogdandy, "The EU as a Human Rights Organisation?", *CMLRev* 2000, 1307; N. Colneric, *Protection of fundamental rights through the ECJ*, RGSL Working Papers N° 14, 2003; Y. Dorf, "Zur Interpretation der Grundrechtscharta", *Juristenzeitung* 2005, 12; J. Dutail de la Rochère, "The EU and the individual: Fundamental rights in the Draft Constitutional Treaty", *CMLRev* 2004, 345; P. Eeckhout, "The EU Charter of fundamental rights and the federal questions", *CMLRev* 2002, 945; T. Eilmannsberger, "The relationship between rights and remedies in EC law: In search for the missing link", *CMLRev* 2004, 1199; U. Everling, "Will Europe Slip on Bananas?", *CMLRev* 1996, 401; A. Garcia, "The General Provisions of the Charter of Fundamental Rights of the EU", *ELJ* 2002, 492; W. van Gerven, "Of rights, remedies and procedures", *CMLRev* 2000, 501; St. Grundmann, *Europäisches Schuldvertragsrecht*, 1999, 376-411; L. Hancher, *Regulating for Competition*, 1989; T. Hervey/J. Kenner, *Economic and Social rights under the EU Charter of Fundamental Rights*, 2005; L. Krämer (ed.), *Recht und Um-welt – Essays in Honor of G. Winter*, 2003 (FS Winter); J. Kropholler, *Europäisches Zivilverfahrensrecht*, 7. A. 2002; K. Lenaerts/E. de Smijter, "A "Bill of Rights" for the EU", *CMLRev* 2001, 273; H. W. Micklitz/N. Reich (eds.), *Public Interest Litigation before European Courts*, 1996 (cited as Micklitz/Reich); M. Nettesheim, "Effektive Rechtsschutzgewährleistung im arbeitsteiligen System europäischen Rechtsschutzes", *Juristenzeitung* 2002, 928; N. A. Neuwahl/A. Rosas (eds.), *The European Union and Human Rights*, 1995; P. Nowak/H. Cremer, *Individualrechtsschutz in der EG und WTO*, 2000; J. Newton, *The Uniform Interpretation of the Brussels and Lugano Conventions*, 2002; L. Papadopoulou, "In(di)visible citizen(ship): Same sex-partners in EU", *YEL* 2002, 229; S. Prechal, "Equality of treatment, non-discrimination and social policy", *CMLRev* 2004, 533; N. Reich, "Competition between legal orders as a new paradigm of EC Law?", *CMLRev* 1992, 861; N. Reich, *Bürgerrechte in der EU*, 1999, 62-75, 212-232; N. Reich, "Judge made 'Europe a la Carte'", *EJIL* 1996, 103; N. Reich/H.-W. Micklitz, *Europäisches Verbraucherrecht*, 4. A. 2003; O. Remien, "European Private International Law, the European Community and its Emerging Area of Freedom, Security and Justice", *CMLRev* 2001, 58; M. Ruffert, "Rights and Remedies in European Community Law", *CMLRev* 1997, 307; H.G. Schermers/D. Waelbroeck, *Judicial protection in the EU*, 6th ed., 2001; D. Triantafyllou, "The European Charter of Fundamental Rights", *CMLRev* 2002, 53; T. Tridimas, *The General Principles of Community Law*, 1999; K. Vasiljeva, "1968 Brussels Convention and EU Council Regulation 44/2001: Jurisdiction in Consumer Contracts Concluded Online", *ELJ* 2004, 129; L. Waddington/Mark Bell, "More equal than others: Distinguishing European Equality Directives", *CMLRev* 2001, 587; J. Wahnfield, *Judicial Protection through the Use of Art. 288 (2)*, 2002; A. Ward, *Judicial Review and the Rights of Private Parties in EC Law*, 2000; J. Weiler, *The Constitution of Europe*, 1999.

§ 11. NON-DISCRIMINATION

I. ISSUES – IS THERE A GENERAL PRINCIPLE OF EQUALITY IN COMMUNITY LAW?

A liberal theory and practice of law, as given special status in the Community rules on free movement and competition, cannot function without defining a "level playing field" of the actors concerned. Most notably, these are Member States, and businesses. Some of these standards are already inherent in the free movement and competition rules themselves since they refer to a balancing test. That is, Member State powers under the free movement rules are not completely limited under the heading of open markets, but can be invoked for the protection of certain societal (not economic!) goals – always keeping in mind the proportionality criteria (§ 7). Even in applying the strict competition rules on undertakings, certain types of co-operation between them will remain possible in the interest of higher societal interests, more or less closely monitored by the competent authorities of the Community and its Member States (§ 9 I 2).

Therefore, a liberal system of law cannot function without a complementary, sometimes countervailing regime – of adequate standards. These standards must be developed not only by Member states, but Union-wide, in order to avoid a "race to the bottom". Active market subjects should not be allowed to opt out of certain protective standards by simple choice of jurisdiction. A "competition between legal orders" is politically legitimate and economically efficient only if certain standards are kept and implemented Union-wide.[1]

These standards can either be imposed by institutions different from the Community as such (Member States, business associations, international organizations and the like), or by Community law itself. The development of Community law has clearly pointed in the second direction, thereby limiting competition between legal orders and avoiding a "race to the bottom". Secondary legislation, as well as an extensively interpreted primary law and a developing set of "soft" and "quasi-legal regimes", enable development of Community-specific standards. These, in turn, tend to soften the impact of a radical opening of markets. To some extent, the opening of markets and the development of adequate standards for production and marketing go hand in hand, even though with a certain time and content lag. That is, the opening mission of the Community comes first, the standard-setting only in second place. It is the main argument of this book that, in a longer perspective, the one cannot do without the other.

---

[1]   For a closer development of this concept cf. Reich, *CMLRev* 1992, 861.

The most important standard that Community law has been setting is the one of *non-discrimination*. This is to some extent already inherent in the citizenship and free movement rules. That is, the State should not grant any privileges to its own nationals (including undertakings) and should not put other EU citizens and businesses in a disadvantaged position. With regard to political action of the Community, market subjects should be treated as equals if they are in a similar situation. In *Codorniú*[2], the Court voided a Community regulation forbidding Spanish producers to use the traditional term *crémant* which was reserved to French and Luxembourg producers of sparkling wine. Spanish producers were put on an unequal basis with other producers without justification. In later cases concerning regulated markets, the Court has repeatedly held that "the principle of equality (is) one of the general principles of Community law".[3]

But non-discrimination can take on a social dimension, for example with regard to discrimination based on gender, race, ethnic origin, age, disability or sexual orientation. This development is part of a more general trend concerned with fundamental rights (§ 12). This book will single out the principle of non-discrimination as the basic standard for treating actors on the internal market, because of the prevalence of detailed secondary law which complements some rather general provisions of primary Community law. These rules have been interpreted by a highly intensive and activist ECJ case law, particularly with regard to nationality and gender discrimination on the labour market. The following lines will try to develop the basic concepts and objectives, without giving a detailed case or problem analysis.

II. NON-DISCRIMINATION WITH REGARD TO NATIONALITY

1. Art. 12 as starting point

The principle of non-discrimination with regard to nationality has been in the EC Treaty from the outset, even though its importance was somewhat overshadowed by the more specific rules on free movement. As has been shown (§ 4), all of these contain a prohibition against discrimination, and another against unreasonable restrictions. Sometimes these overlap, especially in the case of indirect discrimination. As far as discriminatory measures of Member States were restricting the free flow of goods or

---

[2]   Case C-309/89 Codorniú Sa v Council [1994] ECR I-1853.
[3]   Case 15/95 EARL de Kerlast v Union régionale de coopératives agricoles (Unicopa) and Coopérative du Trieux [1997] ECR I-1961 at para 35.

services, or deprived citizens of their rights of access to employment, residence or establishment, they could easily be included under the free movement rules. There was no need to invoke the general provision on non-discrimination which, in the case law of the Court, only had a *subsidiary* function.[4]

Situations still arise where the free movement rules would not be applicable. These would include, for example, with regard to students, tourists, and non-profit associations. Whenever an activity came within the "scope of application" of the EC Treaty, that is, had something to do with EU competences even outside the catalogue of specifically granted freedoms – then it could be protected by the non-discrimination rules. As will be shown, the ECJ used a *dynamic concept* of the "scope of application of the Treaty" in the wording of Art. 12 EC (2). Discrimination in itself relates not only to direct, but also to indirect, discrimination (3). In order to avoid too rigid a mechanism of the non-discrimination concept, the Court allowed a broad number of justifications, at least for the area of indirect discrimination (4). The question of sanctions will be discussed in the chapter on "governance" (§ 19 III, 20 III).

2. Scope of application

Since the EU/EC has jurisdiction only in fields explicitly or implicitly included in the Treaties[5], the non-discrimination principle covers a limited type of activity. However, the scope of application in the sense of Art. 12 is not identical with free movement, but concerns all other –mostly economic – activities and policies the Community is pursuing.[6] Although the Community has no authority to legislate on education or health[7], none the less access to professional education and the maintenance of high health standards remain Community aims. Therefore, student access to professional training institutions including universities came under the non-discrimination principle, insofar as they provide access to a certain profession. Therefore, in *Gravier*[8] the Court held that Member States could not demand student and inscription fees from EC citizens if their own students did not have to pay such charges. While free movement of workers is in theory limited to workers themselves (and their families) and independent professionals, this does not mean that consumers and tourists do not come under the field of application of the Treaty. That is, because they receive goods or services in a cross-border activity, they are therefore indirectly protected

---

[4]   Case C-379/92 Criminal proceedings against Peralta [1994] ECR I-3453 at para 18.
[5]   Art. 5 EC.
[6]   For a recent overview cf. Eeckhout, *CMLRev* 2002, 945 at 959-962.
[7]   Arts. 140, 152EC.
[8]   Case 293/83 Gravier v City of Liege [1985] ECR 593; extended to all higher education institutions by case 24/86 Blaizot v Université of Liège [1988] ECR 379.

against discrimination based on their nationality.[9] Access to justice is a corollary to free movement, and discrimination with regard to nationality touches the field of application of Art. 12 EC.[10] Non-profit associations do not participate in the establishment rules. These, while geared to business or professional activities, also aim at supporting or protecting such activities. Therefore, they should be protected by Art. 12 against discrimination.[11]

3.   The concept of indirect discrimination

Art. 12, when strictly applied according to its wording, is opposed only to direct discrimination, for example with regard to Member State rules that base on nationality the access to a certain activity, the granting of privileges or exemptions, or the infliction of sanctions. States may also shape their rules in such a way that not nationality, but seemingly neutral criteria such as residence, type of work, and so on, are taken as a basis for a rule on differentiated treatment. However, these may have the same effect as openly discriminatory rules. Examples from Court practice concern provisions on contracting teachers of a foreign language who may enjoy less protected standards on termination than teachers of other subjects.[12] Certain wage or pension preferentials may be limited to those residing in a certain territory identical with a Member state, thereby conferring an undue reward by regularly excluding nationals from other EU states.

The concept of indirect discrimination is not easily verifiable. Intention to discriminate is not necessary, because it would be difficult to prove in any event. An *effects test* has to be used in order to verify whether indirect discrimination of a certain group of people, to be distinguished by their nationality, exists *vis-à-vis* another group. Statistical data may suffice to establish such a pattern of discriminatory effects of a certain ruling. Indirect discrimination must therefore be assessed by objective, typical fact constellations showing that other EU nationals are treated less favourably than a Member State's own nationals. In the *Groener* case[13], concerning language tests in Irish for state officials, the Court failed to find discrimination because the tests concerned Irish candidates as well as foreigners. However, it should have looked closer at the effects of such language tests, which clearly privilege Irish citizens, who enjoy

---

[9]   Case 186/87 Cowan v Trésor public [1989] ECR 195.
[10]   Case 137/84 Mutsch [1985] ECR 2681.
[11]   Case C-172/98 Commission v Belgium [1999] ECR I-3999.
[12]   Joined cases C-259/91 + 331/91 + 332/91 Pilar Allué and Carmel Mary Coonan and others v Unviersitá degli studi di Venezia and Università degli studi di Parma [1993] ECR I-4309, case C-272/92 Maria Chiara Spotti v Freistaat Bayern [1993] ECR I-5185.
[13]   Case 379/87 Groener v Minister for education and City of Dublin Vocational Committee [1989] ECR 3967, comment Micklitz, *ZEuP* 2003, 635 .

much easier access to the Irish language than citizens from other EU countries. The Court relied on the rather formal argument that, only if access to examinations and conditions for exemption were different, would this be considered a discrimination. In this case, the Court unfortunately missed the point because the admissibility of language tests that have a negative effect on other EU nationals is not a question of (indirect) discrimination but rather one of justification.

4. Justifications of indirect discrimination

While direct discrimination cannot usually be justified because it runs counter to the very principles of Community law[14], a more flexible test is used with regard to indirect discrimination. If it can be shown that differentiation between persons is based on other factors than nationality, or if this meets a certain societal need, then indirect discrimination is justified. The best example is again – language tests. Knowledge of a certain regional language for teachers may be required to maintain the cultural identity of a nation. But even in this case such requirements must meet the proportionality criteria. That is, language tests should be easily accessible to every candidate, and requirements should not be unreasonable. The Court also requires that individuals have sufficient legal protection instruments at hand to combat indirect discrimination before courts of law.

Under general principles, the party invoking a justification of indirect discrimination will need to prove that it serves a recognized societal need, and that its application meets the standard of proportionality. On the other hand, the discriminatory effect of a measure must be proven by the plaintiff. This may be difficult as far as access to statistical data is concerned.

III. NON-DISCRIMINATION WITH REGARD TO GENDER

1. Discrimination with regard to work payment: Art. 141 EC

The principle of equal pay for equal work was already contained in the original EEC Treaty[15] and transferred to the Amsterdam Treaty[16]. The wording did not make clear whether the article only contained a policy principle to be implemented by further action, or whether it could be directly applied and, if so, whether it also took direct

---

[14] Cf. Case C-415/93 ASBL v Bosman [1995] ECR I-4921.
[15] In Art. 119 EC.
[16] As Art. 141 EC.

effect among private persons, such as in contractual relations between employers and workers, or in collective bargaining between trade unions and employers organizations.

In its *Defrenne II* judgement of 1976[17], the Court found direct effect also with regard to private law relations. The Court gave a sweeping explanation of its far reaching conclusions:

> ... the fact that certain provisions of the treaty are formally addressed to the Member States does not prevent rights from being conferred at the same time on any individual who has an interest in the performance of the duties thus laid down. The very wording of Art. 119 shows that it imposes on States a duty to bring about a specific result to be mandatorily achieved within a fixed period. The effectiveness of this provision cannot be affected by the fact that the duty imposed by the Treaty has not been discharged by certain Member States and that the joint institutions have not reacted sufficiently energetically against this failure to act. To accept the contrary view would be to risk raising the violation of the right to the status of a principle of interpretation, a position the adoption of which would not be consistent with the task assigned to the Court by Art. 164 (now Art. 220, NR) ... (paras 31-34)

On the other hand, the Court limited the effects of its judgement to the future so that it could not be applied retrospectively. It also made clear that it did not apply to social benefits, but to all other forms of remuneration directly or indirectly based on the employment contract.

In *Barber*[18] it gave the following definition of pay as comprising:

> any other consideration, whether in cash or in kind, whether immediate or future, provided that the worker receives it, albeit indirectly, in respect of his employment from his employer … Accordingly, the fact that certain benefits are paid after the termination of the employment relationship does not prevent them from being in the nature of pay …

The intensive litigation that arose out of Art. 141 (1) EC (ex-119 EEC) and the implementing Directive 75/117/EEC of 10.2.1975[19] will not be treated here in detail. Later directives were concerned with discrimination in social security matters and will also not be analysed here. However, the following steps in the evolution of the case law may be worth mentioning. The Court uses a broad, *effet utile* oriented approach,

---

[17] Case 43/75 Gabrielle Defrenne v Société anonyme belge de navigation aérienne Sabena [1976] ECR 455.

[18] Case C-262/88 Douglas Harvey Barber v. Guardian Royal Exchange Assurance Group [1990] ECR I-1889.

[19] [1975] OJ L 45/19.

which aims to promote the interests of the disadvantaged sex, usually women, but in certain cases like *Barber* also men, as much as possible:

- The concept of "pay" must be broadly interpreted. It includes any type of direct or indirect benefit related to work.[20]
- It is irrelevant whether the "pay" is based on a private or public law relationship.
- The concept of "pay" must be interpreted autonomously by Community law. Member states may not define it restrictively.[21]
- Promotion systems with regard to payment are subject to the non-discrimination principle.[22]
- Pension schemes introduced by employers, even if tax-subsidized, must be regarded as pay, while social security schemes financed by a turnover or solidarity system (*Umlageverfahren*) do not fall under Art. 141. However, the distinction is sometimes difficult to draw.
- "Equal work" includes "work of equal value", a fact to be determined by national courts.

2. Discrimination with regard to access, termination and modalities of employment

The wording of Art. 141 (1) EC (ex-119 EEC) only forbids discrimination with regard to pay, not in relation to access to and termination of employment, as well as employment conditions (beyond remuneration) as such. It was only through secondary law that this type of discrimination would come under EC (at that time: EEC) jurisdiction, namely by the adoption of Directive 76/207/EEC of 9.2.1976 "on the implementation of the principle of equal treatment for men and women as regards to access to employment, vocational training and promotion, and working conditions."[23] This directive was based on the broad jurisdiction of the Community[24], since there was no other legal basis available.

The Treaty of Amsterdam added paras 3 and 4 to Art. 141, giving the Community jurisdiction to legislate with regard to the "application of the principle of equal opportunity" and allowing Member states to take so-called highly controversial "positive discrimination measures" in order to compensate for existing inequalities of women (*infra* 4a). This new competence was used by the European Parliament and

---

[20]   Case C-360/90 AWO Berlin v Bötel [1992] ECR I-3589 (indirect benefits awarded to members of a factory council).

[21]   Case C-457/93 Kuratorium für Dialyse v Lewark [1996] ECR I-243.

[22]   Case C-184/89 Nimz v Freie Hansestadt Hamburg [1991] ECR I-297.

[23]   [1976] OJ L 39/40 of 14.2.1976.

[24]   Under Art. 308 EC.

the Council in adopting Directive 2002/73/EC of 23 September 2002 amending Directive 76/207.[25]

Art. 3 (2) EC obliges the Community to "aim at eliminating inequalities, and to promote equality between men and women", a provision which has no direct effect and does not bind Member States.

This notwithstanding, in *Rinke*[26] the Court flatly stated that "compliance with the prohibition of indirect discrimination on grounds of sex is a condition governing the legality of all measures adopted by the Community."

At the time of its adoption, the original directive was justified mostly by an economic reasoning, namely to avoid distortions of competition by different employment conditions for men and women. In the abundant case law of the ECJ, the fundamental rights character of Dir. 76/207 became increasingly obvious. An ingenious Court practice has extended the sphere of application by merging the principle of equality with the right to effective judicial protection (§ 14).[27] Community law was attempting to come into line with modern developments in Member State and international non-discrimination legislation. Therefore, recitals 3 and 4 and the new amending Dir. 2002/73 refer expressly to the European Charter of Fundamental Rights (§ 13 III) and to the fundamental principle of equality between men and women.

The Court has tended to give the Directive a broad application, including access to and employment conditions in public and military office.[28] Military service reserved to men is, however, excluded; the possible negative effects of access to employment for male persons called for service are not sufficient to come into the sphere of application of Dir. 76/207. As the Court said in its *Dory* judgement:[29]

> Nevertheless, the delay in the careers of persons called up for military service is an inevitable consequence of the choice made by the Member State regarding military organisation and does not mean that that choice comes within the scope of Community law. The existence of adverse consequences for access to employment cannot, without encroaching on the competences of the Member State, have the effect of compelling the Member State in question either to extend the obligation of military service to women, thus imposing on them the same disadvantages with regard to access to employment, or to abolish compulsory military service (para 41).

---

[25]   [2002] OJ L 269/15.
[26]   Case C-25/02 Katharina Rinke v Ärztekammer Hamburg [2003] ECR I-8349.
[27]   Case C-185/97 Belinda Jane Coote v Granada Hospitality [1998] ECR I-5199 at paras 21/24.
[28]   Case C-285/98 Tanja Kreil v Federal Republic of Germany [2000] ECR I-69.
[29]   Case C-186/01 Alexander Dory v Kreiswehrersatzamt Schwäbisch-Gemünd [2003] ECR I-2479.

The following lines cannot give a complete overview of an abundant Court practice. They will explain the concept of non-discrimination as the precondition for effectively prohibiting or sanctioning measures by Member States or injured parties (3), mostly women, unless a justification can be found (4). A detailed system of remedies should assure respect for this right to non-discrimination and compensate injured parties for loss (5). In the meantime, the principle of non-discrimination has been extended to the access to and supply of goods and services (6).

3. Direct and indirect discrimination

a. Direct discrimination

Direct discrimination with regard to sex relates to rules based on biological differences between men and women, or which can be explained only by these differences, for example the fact that only women can have children. A dismissal of women or any other type of disadvantage because of pregnancy, breast-feeding, and the like, must be regarded as discrimination. This includes questioning with regard to pregnancy when entering into a contract, or negative consequences in case of silence about pregnancy. A (pregnant) woman may not be dismissed even if she obtained her job to replace another pregnant women, or again, even if she cannot work due to a (justified) prohibition of night work for pregnant women[30]. Indeed, this is a very wide extension of the non-discrimination principle and one not always working in favour of women, who may find it hard to get a job when at the age of giving birth to a child and breast-feeding it. A woman cannot be asked about a possible future pregnancy when returning to work at the end of maternity leave, even if she cannot perform her work due to her pregnancy. Financial problems incurred by the employer are no justification – a somewhat sweeping statement by the Court![31] Such rigidity may in the end work against the (re-)employment of young women and give – contrary to the original starting point of Dir. 76/207 – preference to men (especially in health care jobs) because they do not carry the "risk of pregnancy"!

Dir. 2002/73 extended discrimination to sexual harassment in the sense of Art. 2 (2) meaning:

> any form of unwanted verbal, non-verbal or physical conduct of a sexual nature ... with the purpose or effect of violating the dignity of a person, in particular when creating an intimidating, hostile, degrading, humiliating and offensive environment.

---

[30]   Case C-421/92 Habermann-Beltermann v Arbeiterwohlfahrt [1994] ECR I-1657; C-32/93 Webb v EMO Air Cargo (UK) Ltd. [1994] ECR I-3567.
[31]   Case C-320/01 W. Bush v Klinikum Nienstadt [2003] ECR I-2041.

This is a very broad and vague concept which must be filled out by later Court practice. It did however, not include victimization into the definition of discrimination.[32]

b. Indirect discrimination

The concept of indirect discrimination was first developed in *Jenkins*[33], where the Court held:

> ... if it is established that a considerably smaller percentage of women than of men perform the minimum number of weekly working hours required in order to be able to claim the full-time hourly rate of pay, the inequality in pay will be contrary to Art. 119 where, regard having had to the difficulties encountered by women in arranging to work that minimum number of hours per week, the pay policy of the undertaking in question cannot be explained by factors other than discrimination based on sex (para 13).

This case law is of particular importance with regard to *part time work* mostly done by women. That is, differentiation with regard to pay, access to employment, promotion and dismissal of part time workers could therefore easily be caught as a violation of the non-discrimination principle. The latter question was concerned with the justification of such differentiation.

Dir. 2002/73 codifies existing case law and includes a definition of indirect discrimination:

> where an apparently neutral provision, criterion or practice would put persons of one sex at a particular disadvantage compared with persons of the other sex, unless that provision, criterion or practice is objectively justified by a legitimate aim, and the means of achieving that aim are appropriate and necessary.

4. Justifications

a. Affirmative action

Certain "seemingly discriminatory" measures may be justified, because they aim at removing existing inequalities between the sexes. This operates in particular in favor of women, who usually have to take lower paid jobs and have fewer promotion opportunities, especially in the case of childbirth and breast-feeding. Art. 2 (4) of Dir. 76/207 expressly stated that:

---

[32] For a critical appraisal see Ahtela, *ELJ* 2005, 57 at 75.
[33] Case 96/80 Jenkins v Kingsgate (Clothing Productions) Ltd. [1981] ECR 911.

this directive shall be without prejudice to measures to promote equal opportunity for men and women, in particular by removing existing inequalities which affect women's opportunities...

This exception was the battleground of so-called quota regulations. These aimed to secure women a certain fixed number or percentage of job opportunities or promotions, clearly to the disadvantage of men with similar or even better qualifications. This type of "affirmative action" foreseen by some activist Member states fell foul of the Court's verdict in *Kalanke*:[34]

National rules which guarantee women absolute and unconditional priority for appointment and promotion go beyond promoting equal opportunities and overstep the limits of the exception in Art. 2 (4)... Furthermore, in so far as it seeks to achieve equal representation of men and women in all grades and levels within a department, such a system substitutes for equality of opportunity as envisaged in Art. 2 (4) the result of which is only to be arrived at by providing such equality of opportunity (paras 22-23).

Later cases made sure that only "hard quota regulations" are forbidden under Community law, not "soft quotas" allowing a certain margin of discretion to the employer in deciding about promotion.[35]

Art. 141 (4) EC of the Amsterdam Treaty consolidated existing law by prescribing that:

With a view to ensuring full equality in practice between men and women in working life, the principle of equal treatment shall not prevent any Member State from maintaining or adopting measures providing for specific advantages in order to make it easier for the under-represented sex to pursue a vocational activity or to prevent or compensate for disadvantages in professional careers.

It is still a matter of debate as to whether hard quota regimes can be justified under the provision and whether the *Kalanke* case law has implicitly been overruled by the Community legislator. The different and broader wording of Art. 141 (4) EC, as compared to Art. 2 (4) Dir. 76/207, seems to suggest the latter. However, the Court in *Abrahamsson*[36] held that rules granting automatic preference to one sex are in any case disproportionate to the aim pursued – a somewhat strange argument running counter to the legislative intention. On the other hand, recent case law shows that the Court assigns a more favourable role to affirmative action *before employment* as such, thereby also referring to the non-binding Council recommendation 84/635/EEC of

---

[34]   Case C-450/93 Kalanke v Freie Hansestadt Bremen [1995] I-3051.
[35]   Case C-409/95 Hellmut Marschall v Land Nordrhein-Westphalen [1997] ECR I-6363.
[36]   Case C-407/98 Abrahamsson and Anderson v Fogleqvist, [2000] ECR I-5539.

13 Dec. 1984 on the promotion of positive action for women.[37] The Court will allow special vocational training schemes reserving a higher percentage to women[38], and preferential rules for women on child care places in a Ministry, provided that under exceptional circumstances caring men can also have access to these places.[39]

b. Differentiation beyond gender

The rules on justification for "indirect discrimination" are different insofar as the Court allows the employer to prove that the working conditions it practices are only by their appearance discriminatory, but can in reality be explained by reasons other than gender. These might include, for example, qualifications, experience in training, age, and length of work. With regard to a differentiation between full time and part time work, the employer's action can be justified by a policy of promotion of full time work, but in this case the principle of proportionality must be respected.[40]

c. Burden of proof

The Court usually leaves it to Member State jurisdictions to decide about "justifications" for indirect discrimination in individual cases – more correctly about the fact that a working practice differently affecting men and women in reality does not amount to indirect discrimination. The concept of "justification" is not used *stricto sensu*, but to impose a rule on the burden of proof. If statistical evidence shows that a certain practice affects women more negatively than men, then there is a *prima facie* case of indirect discrimination. It is now up to the employer to demonstrate that reasons other than gender can be invoked to explain this effect. Such a justification must be transparent and accessible to the employees concerned.[41]

These rules have been codified by Dir. 97/80/EC of 15.12.1997 on the burden of proof in cases of discrimination based on sex.[42] Art. 4 (1) reads:

> Member states shall take such measures as are necessary ... to ensure that, when persons who consider themselves wronged because the principle of equal treatment has not been applied to them, establish, before a court or other competent authority, facts from which it may be presumed that there has been direct or indirect discrimination, it shall be for the respondent to prove that there has been no breach of the principle of equal treatment.

---

[37]   [1984] OJ L 331/34. For a comment cf. Waddington/Bell, *CMLRev* 2001, 587 at 612.
[38]   Case C-158/97 Badeck and others [2000] ECR I-1875.
[39]   Case C-476/99 H. Lommers v Minister van Landbouw, Natuurbeheer en Visserij [2002] ECR I-2891.
[40]   Case C-127/92 Enderby v Frenchay Health Authority [1993] ECR I-5535.
[41]   Case C-400/93 Specialarbijderforbundet i Danmark v Royal Copenhagen [1995] ECR I-1275.
[42]   [1998] OJ L 14/6, extended to the UK by Dir. 98/52 [1998] OJ L 205/66.

5. Remedies

a. Effective sanctions

Art. 6 of Dir. 76/207 contains a very open and imprecise provision on remedies:

> Member states shall introduce into their national legal systems such measures as are necessary to enable all persons who consider themselves wronged by failure to apply to them the principle of equal treatment .... to pursue their claims by judicial process after possible recourse to other competent authorities.

It was only the practice of the ECJ that "hardened and sharpened" it. The Court developed out of this general clause the principle of "effective protection". This is part of the general principle of "judicial protection" inherent to Community law (§ 14). The present section will only be concerned with specific questions relating to sex discrimination.

In *Dekker*[43] the ECJ addressed the question of whether national law could require an applicant to prove fault on the employer's part before a claim for judicial redress could succeed. The Court rejected such requirement:

> Art. 6 of the Directive recognises the existence of rights vesting in the victims of discrimination which can be pleaded in legal proceedings. Although full implementation of the Directive does not require any specific form of sanction for unlawful discrimination, it does entail that that sanction be such as to guarantee real and effective judicial protection... It must, furthermore, have a real deterrent effect on the employer (para 23).

These principles have a number of important practical consequences:
- Even though the Directive does not have direct horizontal effect (§ 2 II 3), Member State courts are under an obligation to interpret their national law "as far as possible" to provide for effective remedies, in particular adequate compensation.[44] Mere symbolic damages do not meet the principle of effective remedies.[45]
- Member States may not impose time limits, prescription periods or ceilings which are contrary to effective protection.[46] If these limits exist, their courts should not apply them, but should set them aside.[47]

---

[43] Case C-177/88 Dekker v Stichting Vormingcentrum voor Jong Volwassenen (VJV-Centrum) Plus [1990] ECR I-3941.

[44] Case 152/84 Marshall v Southampton and South-West Hampshire Area Health Authority [1986] ECR 723.

[45] Case 14/83 Von Colson and Kamann v Land Nordrhein-Westphalen [1984] ECR 1891.

[46] Case C-271/91 Marshall v Southampton and South West Hampshire Area Health Authority (Marshall II) [1993] ECR I-4367; C-180/95 Draempaehl v Urania Immoblilienservice [1997] ECR I-2195.

[47] Case C-208/90 Emmot v Minister for Social Welfare [1991] ECR I-4269.

– In case of discrimination with regard to pay, the employer must make good the difference between the wage actually earned and the wage due, including interest. The point of reference is the favourable term in a collective bargaining agreement granted to the privileged and denied to the sex discriminated against.[48]
– However, some inherent limits exist to the right of effective protection. That is, the employer cannot be forced under Community law to renew a work contract that it has breached in a discriminatory way. Indeed, such a principle would go beyond the discretion Member States enjoy with regard to remedies, always providing that these are effective and adequate with regard to compensation to the injured party.[49]
– If a benefit is judged to be discriminatory to one sex, the employer is under no obligation automatically to extend it to the other; it may simply abolish or reduce it to avoid the discrimination; there is no "levelling-up" requirement.[50]

Art. 6 has been amended by para 2 under Dir. 2002/73 to implement the above case law:

> Member states shall introduce into their national legal systems such measures as are necessary to ensure real and effective compensation or reparation as the Member states so determine for the loss and damage sustained by a person injured as result of discrimination …., in a way which is dissuasive and proportionate to the damage suffered; such compensation may not be restricted by the fixing of a prior upper limit, except in cases where the employer can prove that the only damage suffered by an applicant as a result of discrimination …. is the refusal to take his/her job application into consideration.

b. Group actions, injunctions and complementary measures

In litigation over discrimination, it is usually the injured person who takes their case to court. However, a number of legal and social mechanisms may prevent injured persons from taking action and going to court. Therefore, national law may provide for more efficient procedures, such as group actions by employee or women's interest organizations. Moreover, Community law leaves these matters to Member State legislation. Interestingly, Art. 6 (3) now contains a provision on the possibility of group actions for enforcement of obligations under this directive, provided they have the approval of the complainant. This seems to be a provision for a Community type of class action, although with an opt-in version.[51]

---

[48] Case C-184/89 Nimz v Freie und Hansestadt Hamburg [1991] ECR I-297.
[49] Case 14/83 Von Colson *supra* note 45.
[50] Case C-200/91 Coloroll Pension Trustees Ltd. v James Richard Russel et al. [1994] ECR I-4389.
[51] Cf. the critique by Waddington/Bell, *CMLRev* 2001, 587 at 607.

The new Art. 8a-8d put forward a whole new set of new Community law requirements for effective protection. These must be implemented by Member States before 5 Oct. 2005. They include:

– establishing or designing bodies or agencies to handle equal treatment matters, support victims and conduct surveys concerning discrimination;
– promoting and encouraging social dialogue, plans and agreements on equal treatment;
– disseminating information on discrimination matters;
– encouraging dialogue with NGOs.

6. Equal treatment in the access to and supply of goods and services

On 5.11.2003, the Commission proposed a "Council Directive implementing the principle of equal treatment between women and men in the access to and supply of goods and services".[52] It would not allow different insurance tariffs for men and women, e.g. in life and sickness insurance. The proposal has been severely criticised for invading into the freedom to contract and in making realistic calculations in insurance policies impossible, which may lead to higher premiums in general.

In the meantime, Directive 2004/113/EC of the Council of 13 December 2004[53] has been adopted. It must be implemented by 21 December 2007. Art. 3 (2) and recital 14 expressly guarantee freedom to choose a contractual partner, unless this is not based on that person's sex. The rules concerning insurance contracts have somewhat been modified to allow to a limited and transparant extent the use of actuarial factors for different risks of men and women in insurance policies, with the exception of pregnancy and motherhood, where measures may be delayed till 21 Dec. 2009. The non-discrimination principle of the directive is limited, according to Art. 3 (1) to goods and services "available to the public irrespective of the person". There are certain exceptions, e.g. private and family life, education, media. Differentiations may still be justified by objective reasons within the limits of the principle of proportionality, Art. 4(5). According to recital 16, this may include rules of private associations allowing access only to one sex – a somewhat problematic exception which may easily allow possibilities of circumvention.

---

[52]   COM (2003) 657 final.
[53]   [2004] OJ L 373/37.

IV. NON-DISCRIMINATION WITH REGARD TO RACE, ETHNIC ORIGIN, SEXUAL ORIENTATION, AGE

1. Conceptual and statutory development

Combating discrimination based on factors other than gender has long been on the human rights agenda, but has only recently found its way into Community law. The first extension happened in the *P/S* case[54], where the Court held that the dismissal of a transsexual concerned a discrimination because of sex. It also referred to human rights arguments, in particular the principle of equality "which is one of the fundamental principles of Community law".

The later *Grant* case[55] made clear the limits of the Community principle of equality. This concerned a rule of a British train operator whereby privilege tickets granted to a married member of the staff were refused to the partner of a lesbian couple. Even though recognizing new trends in modern human rights law to forbid discrimination based on sexual orientation, the Court, against the opinion of AG Elmer, did not find sufficient authority in existing Community law to give a ruling equating "ordinary sex discrimination" with discrimination based on sexual orientation. It referred the case to the Community legislator.

The Community has taken up the problem by introducing Art. 13 EC into the Treaty of Amsterdam. This gives power to the Council, acting unanimously upon proposal by the Commission and after consulting the European Parliament, to:

> take appropriate action to combat discrimination based on sex, racial or ethnic origin, religion or belief, disability, age or sexual orientation.

The wording and the place of Art. 13 make clear that it *has no direct effect*, in contrast to Art. 12 and Art. 141 (1) EC. On the other hand, the power of the Council is very wide. It is not restricted to workplace discrimination, but may be extended to self employed persons, and to the sphere of consumption insofar as this is "within the powers conferred ... upon the Community". It does not limit the addressees of a possible ban on discrimination, whether they be private or public persons. It was therefore up to the Council to define the conditions, limits and remedies of the types of discrimination described in Art. 13. This happened by the two directives which will be analysed in the following.

---

[54]   Case C-13/94 P v S and Cornwall County Council [1996] ECR I-2143 at para 17.
[55]   C-249/96 Lisa Jacqueline Grant v South-West Trains Ltd. [1998] ECR I-621.

2. Racial and ethnic discrimination

The Race Directive 2000/43/EC of 29.6.2000[56], based on Art. 13 EC, addresses discrimination based on racial or ethnic origin. It relates mostly to employment relations, but also covers social and consumer protection, including social security and healthcare; social advantages; education. Particularly interesting is the reference to education. This will put on a critical stand the existing rather restrictive *language legislation or practice* in some new Member countries against the use of the Russian language, which is still the first language of a large group of the population. Such legislation amounts to a (direct or indirect) discrimination based on ethnic origin.[57]

Most important has been the extension to the sphere of consumption because "access to and supply of goods and services which are available to the public, including housing" are also covered, per Art. 3 (1) lit. h. The meaning of this extension is somewhat unclear and will certainly be subject to further litigation and potential clarification by the Court. Some observers fear an overstepping of Community competences and a violation of the principle of freedom of contract, inherent in EC (§ 15 IV) and Member State law.[58] There is however no *excès de pouvoir*, since the Community can legislate in the sphere of consumption (Art. 138 EC). This fear of an infringement of the fundamental freedoms is not justified, given the fact that in German practice of financial services and tourist operations, open or hidden racial or ethnic discrimination seems to be quite common and should not be allowed under the pretext of "freedom of contract".[59] The main criteria to be determined concern whether a good or a service is *"available to the public"*. The availability must be judged by eliminating potential discriminatory factors. Even if there is no duty to contract by any supplier of goods or services on the market, public advertising may make that good or service "available" to the public, so that a refusal to sell or the imposition of discriminatory conditions may be caught by Art. 3 (1) lit h).

Similar to Directive 76/207 as amended, Dir. 2000/43 forbids direct as well as indirect discrimination, and uses a similar definition. There is an exception for:

> difference of treatment based on nationality and is without prejudice to provisions and conditions relating to the entry into and residence of third-country nationals and stateless persons on the territory of Member states, and to any treatment which arises from the legal status of the third country nationals and stateless persons concerned.

---

[56] [2000] OJ L 180/22.
[57] Reich, *The European Constitution*, RGSL Working Paper No. 19, 2004, at 31.
[58] Eeckhout, *CMLRev* 2002, 945 at 986-988; Nickel, *NJW* 2001, 2041.
[59] Schieck, *Differenzierte Gerechtigkeit*, 2000 at 220 *et seq.*; Reich/Micklitz, *Europäisches Verbraucherrecht*, para 10.27 concering marketing activities.

The reason for this exception is quite obvious, because free movement rights in the EU are limited to citizens and to persons coming under the protective ambit of certain international law instruments, such as the EA agreements.[60] But as an exception it must be construed narrowly; a difference in treatment on nationality may be an indirect discrimination on grounds of racial or ethnic origin, and must be treated as such.

The directive contains broad provisions on implementation, effective remedies, group actions, positive action and social dialogue which are similar to the (new) rules on gender discrimination. It can be expected that the case law to Dir. 76/207 can be used in interpreting Dir. 2000/43, all part of an emerging "European Social Law".[61] Legal standing of associations is limited, since it requires prior approval of victims[62, 63]

3. Discrimination based on religion or belief, disability, age or sexual orientation

The so-called Framework directive 2000/78/EC of 27. 11.2000[64] covers the "left-overs" from Art. 13. Even though structure and content are similar, there are some remarkable differences:
– Social protection, social advantages and education are not included.
– The directive is not extended to the sphere of consumption.

Therefore, it is not clear whether the *Grant* case would be caught by the Directive because it forbids all discrimination on the ground of sexual orientation only with regard to "working conditions", not to "social advantages". It may be asked into what category fell the advantage sought by Ms. Grant for her partner which seem to be more related to the latter.[65]

Differentiation with regard to age is expressly excluded insofar as it is:

> objectively and reasonably justified by a legitimate aim, including legitimate employment policy, labour market and vocational training activities, and if the means of achieving that aim are appropriate and necessary[66].

The Directive goes on to enumerate certain types of age differentiation, for example with regard to access to employment, promotion, retirement and the like. However,

---

[60] Reich/Harbacevica, *Europarättslig Tidskrift* 2002, 411.
[61] Bell, ELJ 2002, 384 at 386.
[62] Per Art. 7 (2) of Dir. 2000/43.
[63] Waddington/Bell, *CMLRev* 2001 at 607.
[64] [2002] OJ L 303/16.
[65] Cf. Waddington/Bell, *CMLRev* 2001 at 590.
[66] Per Art. 6 (1) of Dir. 2000/78.

these rules must meet the *proportionality test* already mentioned, and can therefore potentially be challenged, if unreasonable age limits are imposed. They are an obvious exception to the general equality principle and should thereby be construed narrowly.[67]

The prohibition on discrimination based on age may prove to be particularly controversial. The general employment and pension schemes in Member States do not seem to meet the criteria mentioned above, and have never been scrutinized with regard to *their proportionality*. They may need differentiation with regard to the type of employment exercised by a person complaining of discrimination. Even reasons of "employment policy" must be legitimate, in that they must be transparent and reasoned.

---

[67]   Waddington/Bell *supra* at 599.

§ 12. FUNDAMENTAL RIGHTS

I. STAGES IN THE DEVELOPMENT OF FUNDAMENTAL RIGHTS IN THE COMMUNITY

This section is not concerned with human rights in the EU in general, nor with an analysis of the ECHR in particular. The question discussed here is limited to submission of Community institutions themselves or of Member States to fundamental rights in the implementation of Community rules[68]. This is possible only within the limits of Community competence; the latter has no general jurisdiction over human rights questions, unlike the Court in Strasbourg (ECtHR = European Court of Human Rights).[69]

1. Economic rights as fundamental rights?

The question first arose in litigation concerning Community policies with regard to agricultural markets and is perhaps not quite typical for classic fundamental rights problems. With the exception of the *Stauder* case[70] concerning protection of an individual's name, the main question was whether the right to property and to the exercise of a profession were protected outside the free movement rules. In a series of decisions, the Court developed the rule that Community law recognizes the protection of private property and free business activity as an individual right, but allows broad interventions in the Community interest, provided the formal criteria of legality are maintained.[71] Usually the Court, after verbally invoking the protection of economic fundamental rights, allowed the Community interest to prevail, even without compensation and transitional regimes.[72] In its *second tobacco-judgment* of 10.12.2002[73], the Court repeated that the right to property is protected by the Community legal order, but that "it is not an absolute right and must be viewed in relation to its social function.".

Contrary to the opinion of authors such as Rengeling[74], and to some extent the German Federal Constitutional Court (*Bundesverfassungsgericht,*)[75] these cases are not really

---

[68]   Case 5/88 Wachauf v Bundesamt fur Ernährung und Forstwirtschaft [1989] ECR 2609 at para 19.
[69]   Cf. very clearly Eeckhout, *CMLRev* 2002, 945 with a detailed case analysis.
[70]   Case 29/69 Erich Stauderv City of Ulm - Sozialamt [1969] ECR 419.
[71]   Case 4/73 Nold v Commission [1974] ECR 491.
[72]   The best known example of this approach is the highly contested Banana judgment, case C-280/93 Germany v Council [1994] ECR I-4973; critique Everling, *CMLRev* 1996, 401; Reich, *EJIL* 1996, 103.
[73]   Case C-491/01 The Queen and Secretary of State for Health *ex parte*: British American Tobacco (Investments) Ltd. *et al.*, [2002] ECR I-11453 at para 149.
[74]   Rengeling, *Grundrechtsschutz in der EG*, 1993.
[75]   Cf. the first "Solange" judgment of the German Bundesverfassungsgericht, [1974] CMLR 540 with the modifications by the Maastricht judgment, Brunner v the EU Treaty [1994] CMLR 57.

concerned with fundamental rights. They rather aim at a compromise between economic rights and interests of "market citizens" on the one hand with Community "public interests" on the other. These must at the end of the day be decided by a balancing test. This balancing can have different results depending on the legal anticipations (*Vorverständnisse*) one has. For example, German law has been much more active in protecting property and business activities of undertakings than Community law, which has given the legislator a wide margin of discretion. Community courts therefore prefer the use of such open concepts as proportionality, legality and competence, to control Community institutions in their law making and implementing powers. This stands in contrast to the rigid "fundamental rights-justified limitations" test, as used in the constitutional law of Germany, Italy, and Spain. At the same time, the Court was concerned that fundamental rights could not be used to challenge the supremacy of Community law.[76]

2. The second step: fundamental rights as (liberal) individual rights

A more precise definition of fundamental rights came with the reference of the ECJ to the ECHR. This in the meantime had been ratified by all Member countries in 1978. In the opinion of the Court, the human rights codified in the ECHR contained principles common to all Member States and which therefore had to be taken over and respected by Community organs themselves. Three fundamental rights turned out to be particularly important for Community law:
– Freedom of information under Art. 10 ECHR.
– Right to privacy and family under Art. 8.
– Judicial protection under Art. 6/13.

The Court, in the cases brought before it, was not so much concerned with the Community itself adhering to these rights as with Member States' obligation to defend them. This is particularly true with the (liberal principle of) freedom of information, which was merged with freedom to provide services or, recently, free movement of goods.[77] At the same time, the economic activity to distribute and transmit broad-casting services protected by Art. 49 EC was seen as an exercise of the fundamental right of Art. 10 (1) ECHR, which could only be limited under the restrictive criteria of Art. 10 (2).[78] Where this link to an economic activity[79] or to Community compe-tence was missing,[80] the Court refused the protection of the free flow of information "as such".

---

[76]   Case 11/70 Internationale Handelsgesellschaft v Einfuhr- und Vorratsstelle [1970] ECR 1125.
[77]   Case C-112/00 Eugen Schmidberger v Austria [2003] ECR I-5659.
[78]   Case C-260/89 ERT v DEP and Kouvelas [1991] ECR I-2925.
[79]   Case C-159/90 Society for the Protection of Unborn Children Ireland v Grogan [1991] ECR I-4685.
[80]   Case 229/83 Leclerc v Au Blé Vert [1985] ECR 1.

The right to privacy had some importance insofar as it stimulated and supported legislation on data protection and thereby indirectly promoted a Community law standard with the adoption of Dir. 95/46/EC of 24.10.95.[81] Although this was later extended to cover Community institutions per Art. 286 EC, it has not really been developed into a fundamental right.

In a later judgment[82] the Court derived a right of privacy also out of Art. 8 EHRC. Dir. 95/46 must therefore be interpreted in harmony with fundamental rights protection. This is particularly true of the limitations put on the processing of personal data which must be foreseeable and must be proportionate to a legitimate public interest objective. Art. I-51 and II-68 of the Draft Constitution will elevate data protection into the status of a fundamental right.

Family protection has found its recognition in a series of recent cases. These extended the protection of citizens to the (non-national) spouse as "primary carer" and to children already in education in an EC country, even though the parents had lost citizenship status (§ 4 II 5).[83]

Procedural rights under Art. 6/13 ECHR have been particularly important to the ECJ, and will be treated separately (§ 14). They have also been derived from the fundamental freedoms. That is, if the States have to guarantee free movement rights, then as a corollary they have to provide effective remedies in case of violations. These rights form part of governance and responsibility under Community law (Chap. V).

3.   Two-fold functions of fundamental rights in EU action

a.   Legitimise legislation

The result of this overview is somewhat ambiguous. That is, the EU recognized fundamental rights *de iure praetoris*, but so far did not use them as an instrument to control the legislative power exercised by Community institutions and to strengthen citizens rights therein. It referred to them in the scrutiny of legislative acts, but mostly with an intention to justify and legitimise Community intervention.[84] Reference to

---

[81]   [1995] OJ L 281/31.
[82]   Joined cases C-465/00 Rechnungshof et al. v Österreichischer Rundfunk et al. [2003] ECR I-4989.
[83]   For details, Reich/Harbacevica, *CMLRev* 2003, 615 at 632.
[84]   Cases 46/87 and 227/88 Hoechst v Commission [1989] ECR 2859 at para 18 concerning the highly contested (non-)protection of business premises under a fundamental rights standard. The ECtHR later took a broader view to the protection of premises than the ECJ, including business premises, Dorf, *JZ* 2005, 126 at 129! Cf. Craig/de Búrca at 335. See also joined cases C-20 + 64/00. Booker Aqua culture Ltd v Hydro Seafood GSP Ltd/The Scottish Minister [2003] ECR I-7411.

fundamental rights by the ECJ in the context of free movement served to strengthen the latter *vis-à-vis* Member States, but not to control or even invalidate action by the Community. When the Court was expressly called upon to scrutinize Community action on the basis of a fundamental rights test, it either allowed broad powers of Community intervention (banana litigation), or relied on a competence argument into which elements of a balancing test were indirectly introduced (tobacco-litigation, *supra* § 3 II).

b. Control of administrative action

Cases involving *administrative action* by Community institutions, most notably the Commission in its powers under the competition rules, show a different picture. There, a set of innovative fundamental rights requirements were developed. These were later taken over into secondary legislation:
- confidentiality between lawyer and client;[85]
- right to a fair hearing;[86]
- minimum requirements of legality for investigative measures, especially for search of business premises.[87]

In staff cases, fundamental rights protection was frequently invoked but will not be followed up in detail here.

In order to make the Community more accountable beyond existing practice under a fundamental rights test, two courses for future action are possible and under discussion:
- adherence to the ECHR (II);
- adoption of a Community Charter of Fundamental Rights (III).

II. THE EXPLICIT REFERENCE OF THE UNION TREATY TO THE ECHR AND THE REJECTION OF FORMAL ADHERENCE

The case law of the ECJ had paved the way for another innovation of the Maastricht Treaty, namely the adoption of Art. F, now Art. 6 of the Union Treaty. Para 1 is concerned with principles, para 2 with rights, and Art. 46 lit. (d) EU with implementation. Art. 6 (2) EU reads:

---

[85]   Case 155/79 AM & S Europe Ltd. v Commission [1982] ECR 1575 at para 21.
[86]   Case C-49/88 Al-Jubail Fertiliser v Commission [1991] ECR I-3187 at para 16.
[87]   Cases 46/87 and 227/88 Hoechst at para 19.

The Union shall respect fundamental rights, as guaranteed by the European Convention for the Protection of Human Rights and Fundamental Freedoms signed in Rome on 4 November 1950 and as they result from the constitutional traditions common to the Member States, as general principles of Community law.

Art. 46 (d) concerns the powers of the Court. These include:

Art. 6 (2) EC with regard to action of the institutions, insofar as the Court has jurisdiction

...

These articles make clear that "respect" for fundamental rights creates no additional remedies under the existing rules of judicial protection (§ 14 III/IV). The state of substantive law can be summarized as follows:

1.   Competence to adhere to the ECHR?

In its opinion 2/94[88], the Court was asked by the Council whether the Community, by using its legislative powers under the Treaty, could adhere to the ECHR. In recognizing respect for human rights as one of the fundamental principles of Community law, it referred to the case law where this had found recognition:

Respect for human rights is therefore a condition of the lawfulness of Community acts (para 34).

However, it denied Community competence to accede to the Convention based on the "implied competences" of Art. 235 (now Art. 308 EC):

Accession to the Convention would, however, entail a substantial change in the present Community system for the protection of human rights in that it would entail the entry of the Community into a distinct international institutional system as well as integration of all the provisions of the Convention into the Community legal order. Such a modification of the system for the protection of human rights in the Community, with equally institutional implications for the Community and Member States, would be of constitutional significance and would therefore be such as to go beyond the scope of Art. 235. It could be brought about only by way of Treaty amendment (paras 34-35).

The result of the judgment seems to contradict the Court's explicit recognition of the importance of fundamental rights for Community action. However, the question of adherence is not really one of fundamental rights, nor one of subordination of one

---

[88]   Opinion 2/94 [1996] ECR I-1759.

Court to another. It is a question of distribution of competences and of pursuing different objectives:

- The Strasbourg Court is concerned with human rights *"per se"*, and thereby imposes limitations on sovereign powers of states. It must take a more *static* approach to defend citizens against an overspill of state power.
- The Luxembourg Court has been established to control actors with limited powers, each (the Community, Member States, undertakings) in a primary economic context. This was later extended to cover broader questions relating to citizenship and personal rights. Therefore, the *dynamic function* of the Community must be reflected by the ECJ. Fundamental rights questions are merely "ancillary" in this context, and must be resolved by a functional approach.

And so, the ECJ was right to invoke a mandate of the Member States as "Masters of the Treaty" if they want to change this structural difference and merge the two functionally different jurisdictions. They would have to review their role in the Community *and* their place in the ECHR at the same time. This goes beyond the scope allowed for secondary legislation under Art. 308 (§ 3 III 2).

Art. I-9 of the Draft Constitution will contain a paragraph (2) allowing adherence of the Union to the EHRC. It will read once adopted and ratified by the Member States:

> The Union shall accede to the European Convention for the Protection of Human Rights and Fundamental Freedoms. Such accession to that Convention shall not affect the Union's competences as defined in this Constitution.

2. *"Respect" for the ECHR by Community institutions*

Maastricht, and later Amsterdam, have chosen a "soft law" formulation on the relationship between Community law and the ECHR. There is no formal adherence and therefore no "submission" of the EU/EC to the ECHR, but rather a legal bond based on common values, constitutional traditions and mutual acceptance of standards. The reference to "respect" continues the previous case law of the ECJ and makes it part of the *acquis communautaire*. It also implies a willingness to take into consideration the case law of the Court of Human Rights without giving it the character of precedent. The ECJ cites – albeit selectively – important cases of the ECtHR and thereby indicates its respect.[89] However, it will not discuss decisions with which it does not agree, instead avoiding possible conflicts by limiting its jurisdiction.[90]

---

[89] Cf. the Grant case C-249/96 *supra* note 55 at paras 33-34; also case C-368/95 Vereinigte Familiapress Zeitungsverlags und -vertriebs GmbH v Heinrich Bauer-Verlag [1997] ECR I-3689 citing the ECtHR case Informationsverein Lentia v Austria A No. 276 (1993).

[90] Cf. the Grogan case *supra* at note 79 at para 31.

The Amsterdam Treaty even went a step further by inserting Art. 46 (d) EU, whereby the ECJ, insofar as it has jurisdiction under the EC and the EU Treaties, reviews the actions of the institutions for their compatibility with fundamental rights as they are referred to in Art. 6 (2) EU. The ECJ (and the CFI) may therefore annul an act of Community institutions if it violates fundamental rights. But this competence is restricted insofar as the ECJ has jurisdiction at all. This implies:

- Access to European jurisdictions depends on the procedures available under Community law (§ 14 III and IV).
- There is no special "EU constitutional complaint" against legislative acts, even if fundamental rights are said to have been violated.
- In the so-called "Third Pillar" (§ 1 III 4), access to the ECJ depends on the discretion of Member States.[91]

3. Compliance by Member States with the ECHR when applying Community law

A problem in fundamental rights protection may emerge when Member States are on the one hand bound by Community law, but when the implementation of these rules contradicts the ECHR before the forum of the ECtHR. Such a conflict arose in *Mathews*[92], where the UK denied voting rights in Gibraltar for elections to the EP, but the actual denial and therefore violation of Art. 3 of the Protocol No. 1 to the ECHR resulted from a Decision of constitutional importance by the Council,[93] that is, all Member States, concerning EP elections. The ECtHR wrote:

> The Court (of Human Rights) observes that acts of the EC as such cannot be challenged before the Court because the EC is not a Contracting Party. The Convention (of Human Rights) does not exclude the transfer of competences to international organisations provided that Convention rights are "secured". Member States' responsibility therefore continues even after such a transfer.... The Court reiterates that Art. 3 of Protocol No. 1 enshrines a characteristic of an effective political democracy.... (T)o accept the (British) Government's contention that the sphere of activities of the European parliament falls outside the scope of Art. 3 of Protocol No. 1 would risk undermining one of the fundamental tools by which "effective political democracy" can be assured (para 32, 42-43).

The case shows an actual area of conflict when EU law and ECHR application leads to differing results, particularly when diverging levels of fundamental rights protection are at issue. Since the EU is not a party to the ECHR, the conflict can only be resolved by referring it back to Member States. These on the one hand must respect the supremacy doctrine under their duty to co-operate (§ 3 I 3), but on the other hand

---

91   Per Art. 35 EU.
92   Case Matthews v UK App. No. 24833/94, Report of Judgements and Decisions 1999-I-305.
93   Decision 76/787 [1976] OJ L 278.

have pledged to fully acknowledge the jurisdiction of the ECtHR in the area of its competence. Recent litigation is trying to lodge applications against the Member States if the protection of fundamental rights afforded by the European Court of Justice lags behind the guarantees of the ECHR. Such applications should be regarded as inadmissible, as had already been decided by the European Commission on Human rights in 1990:[94]

> The transfer of powers to an international organisation is not incompatible with the Convention provided that within that organisation fundamental rights will receive equivalent protection...

III.   THE CHARTER OF FUNDAMENTAL RIGHTS OF THE EU

The latest step in the development of a body of fundamental rights has been the solemn proclamation by the European Parliament, the Council and the Commission of the Charter of Fundamental Rights of the EU ("the Charter") in Nice on 7 December 2000.[95] In the following we will comment briefly on the origin, the contents, the legal status, and the minimum protection of the Charter, which has been discussed extensively in legal literature.[96]

1. Origin

The Charter had not been prepared by the classic instrument of a governmental conference under Art. 48 EU, but by a "Convention". This was called by the European Council in Cologne in 1999 to comprise members of the European Parliament (16) as well as Member State Parliaments (30), together with officials from Member State governments (15) and from the Commission (1). Observers from the ECJ and the Council of Europe also participated.[97] The draft was worked out by a consensus procedure aiming to be as open and transparent as possible, thereby following new patterns of governance (§ 18 II). It was not submitted to any formal voting procedure, either before national parliaments or before the European Parliament. In the preamble attached to the solemn proclamation, it was said:

---

[94]   Case M v Germany App. No. 13258/87. See Colneric, *Protection of Fundamental rights through the ECJ*, 2003 at 10-11.

[95]   Charter of Fundamental Rights of the European Union OJ C 364 v. 18.12.2000.

[96]   Lenaerts/de Smijter, *CMLRev* 2001, 273; Triantafyllou *CMLRev* 2002, 53; Dorf, *JZ* 2005, 126; Barriga, *Die Entstehung der Charta der Grundrechte der EU*, 2003.

[97]   de Búrca, *ELRev* 2001, 126 at 131.

This Charter reaffirms, with due respect for the powers and tasks of the Community and the Union and the principle of subsidiarity, the rights as they result, in particular, from the constitutional traditions and international obligations common to the Member States, the Treaty on European Union, the Community Treaty, the European Convention for the Protection of Human Rights and Fundamental Freedoms, the Social Charter adopted by the Community and by the Council of Europe and the case law of the ECJ and the ECtHR...

2. Contents

The statement cited from the preamble makes it clear that the Charter is not intended to innovate the fundamental rights debate in the EU, but rather to codify and to consolidate it. However, a closer look at structure and contents reveals some remarkable innovations parallel to well known principles either of traditional human rights law or of Community law.

The Charter is divided into 6 chapters entitled:
– Dignity.
– Freedoms.
– Equality.
– Solidarity.
– Citizen's rights.
– Justice.

The most striking feature of the Charter is that many of the fundamental rights proclaimed go far beyond Community competence, for example in the chapter on dignity, in family and criminal matters. Other rights, especially in the chapter on "freedoms", "equality" and "citizen's rights", expressly refer to the *acquis*. Certain rights are formulated so as to confer subjective rights on *all* persons, others are limited to (EU) citizens, while still others are merely "institutional guarantees" with no protective ambit *vis-à-vis* individuals. The Charter demonstrates to some extent the character of a menu card drawn from different sources and squeezed into a single document.

The innovations particularly concern the chapter on "*solidarity*". This aims to ensure that the Union is not merely an economic community, but has a broader mission, that is:
– Art. 27: Worker's right to information and consultation with the undertaking;
– Art. 28: Right of collective bargaining and action.
– Art. 29: Right of access to placement services.
– Art. 30: Protection in the event of unjustified dismissal.
– Art. 31: Fair and just working conditions.

- Art. 32: Protection of child labour and protection of young people at work.
- Art. 33: Family and professional life.
- Art. 34: Social security and social assistance.
- Art. 35: Health care.
- Art. 36: Access to services of general economic interest.
- Art. 37: Environmental protection.
- Art. 38: Consumer protection.

Clearly, these "fundamental rights" have not been – and cannot be – granted as subjective rights, but must be concretised by the Community and Member States within the framework of existing competences. But they show a direction and confirm the principle of a "socially committed market economy" of the EU which goes beyond a radical market-only liberalism.

3. Legal Status

The Charter is not a legally binding act. It neither amends the EU or EC Treaties, nor is it an act of secondary legislation in the sense of Art. 249 EC. This, however, does not mean that it has no legal meaning at all.

a. The concept of "respect"

The general provisions of Art. 51 *et seq.* are rather ambiguous with regard to its legal character. Art. 51 (2) makes it clear that the Charter does not establish "any new power or task" for the Community or the Union, nor does it modify powers and tasks defined by the Treaties. On the other hand, Art. 51 (1) provides that the Charter is addressed to the institutions and bodies of the Union and to the Member States when they are implementing Union law:

> They shall therefore respect the rights, observe the principles and promote the application thereof in accordance with their respective powers.

The formula of "respect" corresponds to the one used in Art. 6 (2) EU. This indicates that the Charter has the same legal importance for the Union/ Community as both the ECHR and the constitutional traditions of the Member States. As Lenaerts/de Smijter[98] rightly observe, the Charter is "thus part of the *acquis communautaire*, even if it is not yet part of the Treaties on which the Union is founded."

---

[98]   *CMLRev* 2001, 273 at 299.

This "indirect" binding character of the Charter has already been recognized by the Court of First Instance and by the opinions of several AGs. The CFI, in its *max.mobil Telecommuncation Service* case[99], recognized the legal effects of Art. 41 on the "Right to good administration" and of Art. 47 on the "Right to an effective remedy and to a fair trial" in reviewing Commission measures in competition matters, but did not find support by the ECJ. AG Tizzano in his opinion of 8 Feb. 2001[100] concluded that "the Charter provides us with the most reliable and definitive confirmation of the fact that the right to paid annual leave constitutes a fundamental right." Similar references can be found in opinions by AG Jacobs[101], AG Léger[102] and other AGs.[103]

b. Limited scope of applicability

The Charter need only be "respected" by the institutions of the Community itself, and by Member States when implementing Union law. This formula takes over existing case law and considerably narrows the scope of application of the Charter. To some extent, the ambitious and broad pronouncements of the Charter as mentioned above are reduced to fit within the limits of Union/Community competences. The general rule on equality in Art. 20 of the Charter can therefore not be invoked before European courts if the matter has no relation to Community law, or if this relationship – such as imprisonment of a citizen resulting in a restriction of their free movement right – is only hypothetical.[104]

The same is true with regard to procedures protecting fundamental rights, either against the Community or against Member States implementing Community law. Art. 52 (2) makes clear that:

> (r)ights recognised by this Charter which are based on the EC or the EU shall be exercised under the conditions and within the limits defined within those Treaties.

The Charter does not establish any type of judicial or extra-judicial complaint procedure, despite the somewhat ambitious pronouncement in Art. 47 of a "right" to an effective remedy. This is particularly problematic in the area of the "third pillar", where the competence of European courts is only optional[105].

---

[99]   Case T-54/99 Max.mobil Telekommunikation Service GmbH v Commission [2002] ECR II-313, set aside by Case C-142/02P [2005] ECR I-(22.2.2005).
[100] Case C-173/99 BECTU v. Secretary of State for Trade and Industry [2001] ECR I-4881.
[101] Case C-270/99P, Z v European Parliament [2001] ECR I-9197.
[102] Case C-309/99 J.C.Wouters v Algemene Raad van der Nederlandse Orde van Advocaten [2002] ECR I-1577.
[103] For an overview cf. Eeckhout *supra* note 69 at 947 fn 10.
[104] Cf. case C-299/95 Kremzow v Austria [1997] ECR I-2629 discussed by Eeckhout at 968.
[105] Art. 39 EU.

4. Minimal protection

Arts. 52 and 53 of the Charter address the scope of protection, and the relation to other instruments, especially the ECHR. Despite the somewhat ambiguous and unclear wording, a potential conflict is decided in favour of the norm guaranteeing the highest protection.[106]

There is also argument that the Charter has officially recognized the case law of the ECtHR as part of EC law. Art. 52 (3) provides for an identity of meaning of rights under the Charter and the ECHR. But again, this broad formula is limited by mere "respect" for the Charter and the ECHR by European jurisdictions, thereby always allowing a deviation from existing case law of the ECtHR: Lenaerts/De Smijter are probably exaggerating in flatly postulating that the "Court of Justice will therefore be obliged to take over the interpretation given by the ECtHR to corresponding rights guaranteed by the ECHR."[107]

5. The future of the Charter

The Nice conference deliberately left open the final legal status of the Charter. This has been taken up by the Constitutional Convention, and will eventually have to be decided by the traditional procedures of amending the Treaty, namely Art. 48 EU. It has been proposed that the Charter will become integrated into Community law. To some extent this has already been done by the new Council Reg. EC (No) 1/2003 implementing the competition rules (§ 9 I). This reads in recital 37:

> This Regulation respects the fundamental rights and observes the principles recognised in particular by the Charter of Fundamental Rights of the EU. Accordingly, this Regulation should be interpreted and applied with respect to those rights and principles.

However, such a full legal integration of the Charter into the *acquis* would not change its ambit of protection. The limitations on protection of fundamental rights in Arts. 51-53 will continue to exist, and the wording of the Charter therefore remains much broader than its actual legal content and application. It promises more rights than it can possibly implement, because fundamental rights protection is limited to areas where the Community has competence as such or where Member States apply Community law, for example in the area of the fundamental freedoms.

---

[106]   Lenaerts/de Smijter at 294.
[107]   Lenaerts/de Smijter at 296; see also Dorf, JZ 2005, 126 at 128.

The Draft Constitution of 29 October 2004 will include in its part two *"The Charter of Fundamental Rights of the Union"* with its Preamble and the relevant articles unchanged. Once ratified, this may result in certain articles taking direct effect under the general criteria of Community law (§ 2 II), subject of course to the limitations spelled out in Art. II-111-114.

§ 13. LEGITIMATE EXPECTATIONS

Selected bibliography of § 13

H. Abbott/M. Tyler, *Safer by Design*, 2nd ed. 1997; H. Beale/G. Howells, "EC Harmonisation of Consumer Sales Law – A Missed Opportunity?", *Journal of Contract Law* 1997, 21; M.C. Bianca/St. Grundmann (eds.), *EU Sales Directive – Commentary*, 2002; R. Bradgate/Chr. Twigg-Flessner, "Expanding the Boundaries of Liability for Defective Products", *JCP* 2002, 345.; J. Calais-Auloy/F. Steinmetz, *Droit de la consommation*, 6ème éd. 2003; V. Christianos/F. Picod, *Consommateurs – répertoire communautaire Dalloz*, 2003, P. Davies (ed.), *EC Labour Law: Principles and Perspectives*, 1996; C. Ehlermann, "The internal market following the Single Act", *CMLRev* 1987, 361; J. Falke, "The Community System for the Rapid Exchange of Information on Dangers Arising from the Use of Consumer Products", in: Micklitz/Roethe/Weatherill, *Federalism and Responsibility*, 1994; A. Garde, "Recent developments in the laws relating to transfer of undertakings", *CMLRev* 2002, 523; De Groot, "The Council Directive on the safeguarding of employees' rights in the event of transfers of undertakings", *CMLRev* 1998, 707; St. Grundmann/Medicus/Rolland (Hrsg.), "Europäisches Gewährleistungsrecht: Reform und Internationalisierung des deutschen Schuldrechts", Hallesche Schriften zum Recht, Bd. 13, 2000; L. Hancher, *Regulating for Competition*, 1989; D. Harland, "Legal Aspects of the Export of Dangerous Products", *JCP* 1985, 209; T.Harvey, *European Social Law and Policy*, 1998; G. Howells, *Consumer Product Safety*, 1998; G. Howells/ Th. Wilhelmsson, *EC Consumer Law*, 1997; R. Howse, "Democracy, Science and Free trade: Risk regulation on Trial at the WTO", *MichLRev* 2000, 2329; Ch. Joerges, "The New Approach to Technical Harmonisation and the Interests of Consumers", in: Bieber/Pinder/ Weiler (eds.), *1992 – One European Market*, 1988; Ch. Joerges/J. Falke/H.-W. Micklitz/G. Brüggemeier, *Die Sicherheit von Konsumgutern und die Entwicklung der Gemeinschaft*, 1988; K. H. Ladeur, "The introduction of the precautionary principle into EU-Law", *CMLRev* 2003, 1455 (with a comment by Wolf, *CMLRev* 2004, 1175); F. Maniet, "La transposition de la directive 92/59/CE relative à la sécurité générale des produits dans les Etats membres de l'union européenne", *REDC* 1997, 176; H. W. Micklitz, "Principles of Justice in Private Law", in : E. Paasavirta/K. Rissanen (eds.), *Principles of Justice and the Law of the EU*, 1995, 259; H.-W. Micklitz, *Internationales Produktsicherheitsrecht*, 1995; H.-W. Micklitz (ed.), *Post Market Control of Consumer Goods*, 1990; H.-W. Micklitz, "EC product safety regulation – a still uncompleted project", *Consumer Law Journal* 1997, 48; H. W. Micklitz, "Organizational Structures of Product Safety Regulation", in: Stauder (Hrsg.), *La sécurité des produits de consommation*, 1992, 49; H.-W. Micklitz/Th. Roethe/St. Weatherill, *Federalism and Responsibility*, 1994; H.-W. Micklitz, N. Reich & St. Weatherill, "EU Treaty Revision and Consumer Protection", *JCP* 2004, 367; S. O'Leary, *Employment Law at the ECJ*,

2002; J. Pelkmans, *Market Integration in the EC – Theory and Practice*, 1984; D. Oughton/Chr. Willet, "Quality Regulation in European Private Law", *JCP* 2002, 299; N. Reich, *The European Economic Constitution*, 1996; N. Reich, "Competition between legal orders – a new paradigm", *CMLRev* 1992, 861; N. Reich, "Die Umsetzung der EG-Richtlinie 1999/44/EG in das deutsche Recht", NJW 1999, 2397; N. Reich, *Bürgerrechte in der EU*, 1999; N. Reich/H. W. Micklitz, *Europäisches Verbraucherrecht*, 4. A. 2003; P. Rott, "Minimum harmonisation for the completion of the internal market? The example of consumer sales law", *CMLRev* 2003, 1107; D. Schiek, *Differenzierte Gerechtigkeit*, 2000; A. Schnyder/R. M. Straub, "Das EG-Grünbuch über Verbrauchsgütergarantien und Kundendienst – Erster Schritt zu einem einheitlichen EG-Kaufrecht", *ZEuP* 1996, 8; M. W. Schröter, "Lebensmittelrechtliche Vorsorge als Rechtsprinzip – nationale, europäische und welthandelsrechtliche Aspekte", *ZERP/dp* 4/2002; M. Tenreiro, "La proposition de directive sur la vente et les garanties des biens de consommation", *Revue Européenne de Droit de la Consommation* 1996, 187; D. Trubek, "The European employment strategy and the future of EU governance", *RGSL Working papers* No. 10, 2003; Ch. Twigg-Flessner, "The EC-Directive on Certain Aspects of the Sale of Consumer Goods and Associated Guarantees", *Consumer Law Journal* (1999) 7, 177; Ch. Twigg-Flesner/R. Bradgate, "The EC-Directive on Certain Aspects of the Sale of Consumer Goods and Associated Guarantees – all Talk and No Do?", (2000) 2 *Web JCLI*, 1; E. Vos, *Institutional Frameworks of Community Health and Safety Regulation*, 1999; E. Vos, "EU Food Safety Regulation in the Aftermath of the BSE Crisis", *JCP* 2000, 227.

I. OVERVIEW OF THE CONCEPT OF "LEGITIMATE EXPECTATIONS"

The protection of "legitimate expectations" is part of the general principles that Community law adheres to.[108] They are an inherent element of the principle of *legal certainty* (*Rechtssicherheit*) which is characteristic for a government of laws[109]. It was originally developed as part of Community administrative law, for example concerning retroactivity of legal acts and reliance of market citizens on representations by EC institutions.[110] Its applicability usually depends very much on the facts of the case. In *Mulder*,[111] the Court wrote:

> It must be conceded that the producer who has voluntarily ceased production for a certain period cannot legitimately expect to be able to resume production under the same

---

[108] Schermers/Waehlbroeck, *Judicial protection in the EU*, 2001, 79-83.
[109] Scott-Douglas, *EU Constitutional Law*, 2002 at 374.
[110] Craig/de Búrca at 382-387.
[111] Case 120/86 Mulder v Minister van Landbouw en Visserij [1988] ECR 2321.

conditions as those which previously applied and not be subject to any rules of market or structural policy adopted in the meantime. The fact remains that where such a producer, as in the present case, has been encouraged by a Community measure to suspend marketing for a limited period in the general interest and against payment of a premium he may legitimately expect not to be subject, upon the expiry of his undertaking, to restrictions which specifically affect him precisely because he availed himself of the possibilities offered by the Community provisions (paras 22/23).

This paragraph will broaden the concept of legitimate expectations to cover expectations not just of market citizens, but of *all EU citizens and residents*.[112] To some extent this more political than legal concept supplements the theory of fundamental rights, but without necessarily giving its beneficiaries subjective rights. The ambit and content of these legitimate expectations of citizens (in a broad sense!) is already included in primary EC Law after the Maastricht and Amsterdam amendments. These have considerably widened the fields of Community activity. The Nice Treaty has brought an extension of majority voting in some fields of social policy. Legitimate expectations will usually need concretising by secondary law, which will be selectively cited. The following areas will be considered as examples:

- Questions of *product safety* mentioned in the Treaty[113], as a corollary to the free movement of goods rules and liberalizing secondary law (§§ 7 II, 8 II), by establishing rules on so called "post marketing control"[114].
- *Health policy*, which is part of many EC provisions[115], insisting on a "high level of protection" but without the EC having a genuine legislative competence here (§ 3 III). This will be exemplified by reference to the so-called "precautionary principle" as developed in connection with the BSE crisis.
- Protection of *consumers' economic interests* beyond information (§ 17), for example by adequate standards in consumer contracts. An impressive amount of consumer law already exists.[116] The section will be limited to discussing the Consumer Goods and Guarantees Directive.[117]
- Protection of *workers* in the case of transfer of undertakings as part of Community social policy commitment.[118]

---

[112] Micklitz, in Paasavirta/Rissanen, *Principles of justice and the law of the EU*, 1995 at 259.
[113] Art. 95 (3) and 153 (1) EC.
[114] Micklitz (ed.), *Post market control of consumer goods*, 1995.
[115] E.g. Art. 19, 30, 39 (3), 46, 95 (3), 137, 152, 153 (1), 174 (1) EC.
[116] This is discussed in detail in Reich/Micklitz, *Europäisches Verbraucherrecht*, 4th ed., 2003; Christianos/Picod, *Consommation*, 2003; the book by Howells/Wilhelmsson, *EC Consumer Law*, 1997 is somewhat dated.
[117] Council Directive 1999/44/EC [1999] OJ 171/12.
[118] Per Art. 136 EC.

II. CONSUMER PRODUCT SAFETY: POST MARKET CONTROL OF CONSUMER GOODS

1. Directive 92/59

Free movement of goods, as one of the leading principles of Community law, may provoke safety risks to European consumers. That is:
– if certain dangers inherent in products are not discovered and communicated in time,
– if the safety standards of Member countries differ considerably, or
– if certain risks become apparent only later.

The fear exists of a "race to the bottom" as a consequence of liberalizing the access of products to markets. Therefore, free movement in the internal market must be supplemented by a Community-wide system of post market control. This might include, for example, a mechanism ensuring that once a product has legally been put on the internal market, the consumer can legitimately expect that risks will be treated effectively and as far as possible uniformly in the entire EU. Therefore, the Commission proposed and the Council adopted Dir. 92/59/EEC of 29.6.1992 on General Product Safety[119]. Although to some extent a corollary to the product liability directive (§ 20 III 2), it is concerned with responsibilities of the Member States and the Community with regard to unsafe products, and not with civil liability of the producer and other persons in the chain of distribution.

The Directive only applies to consumer products, not to products for industrial use, nor to services. It includes both new and used products. The Directive makes it an obligation of producers and – to a lesser extent – also suppliers to market only *safe products*[120]. It contains a definition of the concept of "safety", which is to some extent similar to the product liability directive[121].

Member States have an obligation to supervise the safety of products, and are empowered to take specific measures. These are listed in the directive and include, for example, issuing warnings, withdrawing products, and so on. In its original version it did not allow the possibility for Member States to order the *recall* of a product, that is, to eliminate from the market products already in the hands of end users and consumers. It also installed certain notification requirements of Member States *vis-à-vis* the Commission.

---

[119]   [1992] OJ L 228/24.
[120]   Art. 3 of Dir. 92/59.
[121]   Art. 2 lit b) of Dir. 92/59.

Finally, as a novelty it introduced a Community-wide system of withdrawal of products in case of urgency. This, however, was very narrowly construed:
- The Commission enjoyed no right of initiative of its own, but had to wait for an application by one Member State.
- The other Member States had to be consulted.
- The Commission could only then direct Member States to take provisional measures. This so far only happened once (softeners in child's toys[122]), by consulting a management committee containing representatives of both the Community and Member States.

There was some debate on the competence of the EC to adopt such an authorization for Community-wide action regarding product safety. This arose because the directive does not directly ease the free movement of goods, but rather imposes restrictions for safety reasons. In the *Germany v. Council* litigation,[123] the Court upheld the legality of the Directive with the following words:

> Such action is not contrary to Art. [95(1) EC]. The measures which the Council is empowered to take under that provision are aimed at "the establishment and functioning of the internal market." In certain fields, and particularly of product safety, the approximation of general laws alone may not be sufficient to ensure the unity of the market. Consequently, the concept of "measures for the approximation" of legislation must be interpreted as encompassing the Council's power to lay down measures relating to a specific product or class of products and, if necessary, individual measures concerning these products.

2. Directive 2001/95

Directive 92/59 was a relatively weak instrument, whose deficits quickly became known in practice. Therefore, the Commission proposed and Parliament and Council adopted Dir. 2001/95/EC of 3 December 2001 on "general product safety"[124]. This had to be implemented by Member States by 15.1.2004. Recital (1) describes the objective of the new Directive:

> It is necessary to amend Dir. 92/59 in several respects, in order to complete, reinforce or clarify some of its provisions in the light of experience as well as new and relevant developments on consumer product safety, together with the changes made to the Treaty ..., and in the light of the precautionary principle ...

---

[122]   Commission decision 1999/815/EC of 7.12.1999, *OJ* L 315/46 of 9.12.1999.
[123]   Case C-359/92 Germany v Council [1994] ECR I-3681 at para 37.
[124]   [2002] OJ L 11/4.

It contains several improvements in comparison to Dir. 92/59:

- The concept of "safe product" has now been defined by reference to European standards, similar to the free movement directives (§ 8 II).
- Member States are entitled to issue *recall* orders; however, the modalities, costs, and the like, are not defined.[125]
- The public has a right to be informed about unsafe products.
- The Commission can propose emergency measures on its own initiative, to be directed to the Member States; the criteria are now more open to Community action[126].
- The system of information exchange about unsafe products will be improved.

III. PROTECTION OF HEALTH: THE PRECAUTIONARY PRINCIPLE

1. The BSE crisis

Several articles of primary Community law refer to the objective of attaining a "high level of heath protection" in the Union. However, genuine legislative powers in health matters are very limited (§ 3 II 1). The Community must use its internal market powers, as well as workplace, consumer and environmental protection powers, indirectly to achieve this objective. The Court has also recognized that the competence of the Community to regulate agricultural markets[127] includes measures to attain health objectives, including human (consumer) and animal health.[128]

A controversial question arose, in the context of the BSE crisis. That is, on what basis could restrictive Community measures banning certain agricultural products from being marketed in the EU be taken under health policy aspects? It is quite clear that a conflict exists between the principle of open markets on the one hand, and the power of the Member State to regulate public health matters within the limits of the proportionality principle.[129]

Similar principles apply to Community measures themselves. The Community is itself bound by the fundamental freedoms, but must at the same time allow for a high level of health protection. What are the relevant criteria for balancing these two somewhat contradictory requirements? Is it necessary for a certain risk to have already

---

[125]   Cf. the discussion in Reich/Micklitz, *Europäisches Verbraucherrecht*, para 25.47.
[126]   Art. 13 of Dir. 2001/95.
[127]   Under Art. 34/37 EC.
[128]   Case C-180/96 UK v Commission[1998] ECR I-2269 (re BSE crisis) at para 97.
[129]   Per Art. 30 EC.

materialized before the Community intervenes? Or can the Community act preventively to avoid such risks? In the first case, the Community would have to wait for some serious incident – a policy certainly not acceptable on the principle of a "high level of health protection" and, moreover, against legitimate consumer expectations to be protected from potential dangers to health. If the Community had to choose the second option (which it did in the BSE crisis[130]), then the following question had to be decided. That is, what degree of scientific evidence was necessary to take restrictive measures concerning the internal market? Should there be "hard" scientific proof of the risk? Was "soft evidence" enough? Or could the Community act even in cases of irrational and non-justified fears of the consuming public? What type of "legitimate expectations" was the Community to protect in an environment which no longer allows risk-free consumption?[131]

The discussion centred around the so-called "precautionary principle"[132]. This principle, first developed in environmental law per Art. 174 (2) EC, allows the responsible institutions to take preliminary measures. These include restricting the marketing of potentially hazardous (food) products to avoid risks before they have materialized and even, in cases of doubt, as to whether these risks will ever occur. In the BSE case, the United Kingdom sought to annul the ban on the export of British beef and bovine products that the Commission had imposed in March 1996.[133] According to the British government, these products presented no danger to human health. The underlying purpose of the ban was more of an economic nature. That is, stabilizing the situation, reassuring consumers, and safeguarding the beef industry. In its *BSE* decision[134] the Court rejected the arguments of the British government and wrote:

> At the time when the contested decision was adopted, there was great uncertainty as to the risks posed by live animals, bovine meat and derived products. Where there is uncertainty as to the existence or extent of risks to human health, the institutions may take protective measures without having to wait until the reality and seriousness of those risks become fully apparent.

This is an implicit recognition of the precautionary principle. That, for the Court, was part of the proportionality principle. Later cases[135] confirmed the precautionary principle with regard to food additives with the following words:

---

[130] 96/239/EC; Commission decision of 27 March 1996, OJ L 78/47 which was attacked by the UK in the above mentioned case C-180/96.

[131] Case C-465/98 Verein gegen Unwesen in Handel v A. Darbo [2000] ECR I-2297 at para 27 concerning residues in foodstuffs.

[132] O'Riordon/J. Cameron (eds.), *Interpreting the precautionary principle*, 1994.

[133] Vos, *JCP* 2000, 227 at 240.

[134] Case C-180/96 *supra* note 128 at paras 98/99.

[135] Case C-192-02 Commission v Denmark [2003] ECR I-9693.

Where it proves to be impossible to determine with certainty the existence or extent of the alleged risk because of the insuffiency, inconclusiveness or impression of the results of studies conducted, but the likelihood of real harm to public health persists should the risk materialise, the precautionary principle justifies the adoption of restrictive measues ... Such measures must not be allowed unless they are non-discriminatory and objective (paras. 52/53).

And that principle must be respected by all Community actions (§ 3 III 4). Indeed, it was officially recognized by the Community legislator in Art. 7 of Food Regulation (EC) No. 178/2002 of 28.1.2002,[136] where the attempts of the Community to balance the two requirements of free trade and a high level of health protection are put on trial:[137]

In specific circumstances where, following an assessment of available information, the possibility of harmful effects on health is identified but scientific uncertainty persists, provisional risk management measures necessary to ensure the high level of health protection chosen in the Community may be adopted ...

The responsible Community institutions must strictly adhere to the proportionality principle.

2. State of WTO Law

The same conflict is inherent in the WTO rules on free trade on the one hand and the protection of human health by Art. XX GATT.[138] To a limited extent, the precautionary principle found its way into the WTO dispute resolution mechanism when the Appellate Body in its decision of January 1998 on hormones in animal feed wrote, overturning a more liberal report of the Panel of 18.8.1997:[139]

It is essential to bear in mind that the risk that is to be evaluated in a risk assessment ... is not only risk ascertainable in a science laboratory, but also risk in human societies as they actually exist, in other words, the actual potential for adverse effects on human health in the real world where people live and work and die.[140]

It seems to be that the legitimate expectations of consumers with regard to health may go beyond what science has elaborated under "hard scientific evidence rules". Only

---

[136]   [2002] OJ L 31.
[137]   Schröter, ZERP dp 4/2002 at 29.
[138]   Micklitz, Internationales Produktsicherheitsrecht, 1995 at 267; Vos, Institutional Frameworks of Health and Safety Regulation, 1999 at 102; Howse, MichLRev 2000, 2329.
[139]   Schröter at 33-47.
[140]   Cited by Schröter at 44.

such an approach is sufficient in taking into consideration the place in Community law of a "high level of health protection". The precautionary principle comes closest to fulfilling consumers' legitimate expectations within a comprehensive health policy in the Union, even at some sacrifice to the principle of "open markets".

IV. LEGITIMATE EXPECTATIONS IN CONSUMER CONTRACTING: THE EXAMPLE OF DIRECTIVE 99/44

1. The extraordinary history of Dir. 99/44

Harmonization of consumer sales law was originally not on the Community agenda. Indeed, one may question why the Community should take action in this area at all. For example, in the US – which has a much more developed internal market – there is no federal sales legislation, but the Uniform Commercial Code is a model law that has been taken over by most of the states. The internal market in the US seems to function without a uniform sales law. As a result, cross-border disputes are resolved by conflict rules. This includes those between B2C arising out of different standards. However, the Community legislator was not satisfied with the functioning of the conflict rules of the Rome Convention, because these only protect the passive consumer, not the active consumer shopping around in the internal market for the best offers (§ 16 III).

When the Commission proposed a directive on unfair contract terms in 1992,[141] it had blacklisted certain exemption clauses, for example in sales contracts. However, in order to make them effective it "smuggled" some provisions on guarantees and warranties in consumer sales contracts into the proposed directive. These could not be contracted out of. This approach was rejected by the Council when adopting Dir. 93/13 "on unfair terms in consumer contracts" (§ 17 II). However, at the same time the Commission was charged with preparing a proposal on a consumer sales directive. The Commission first published a Green Paper on 15.11.1993[142] where it discussed the issues of harmonizing and reforming the law of guarantees of consumer goods and after-sales service. It vigorously put forward the concept of legitimate expectations of consumers regarding product quality. These would allow liability to fall not only on the seller, but also subsidiarily on the producer – in the case of selling a product in a chain of distribution – for quality defects. The result would be to severely restrict the privity of contract doctrine, which governed sales law in all Member States – with the exception of the French-inspired *action directe*[143].

---

[141]   [1992] OJ C 73/7.
[142]   Com (1993) 509 final.
[143]   For a description Calais-Auloy/Steinmetz, *Droit de la consommation*, 6ème éd. 2003, at 265-267.

However, the Commission proposal for a Directive on consumer sales and guarantees did not take up the more ambitious proposals of the Green Paper.[144] In the result, this was a classic privity of contract proposal, inspired in its main concepts by the United Nations' CISG,[145] made to fit the special needs of consumer protection. It did so, for example, by forbidding a contracting out of the sellers' obligations, and by giving the consumer a bundle of remedies against the seller in case of non-conformity of the product. With regard to guarantees, the Commission made clear that it wanted to regulate only commercial guarantees, not "legal guarantees", that is, only those given voluntarily by the seller or the producer. The concept of legitimate expectations was watered down, but can be found in the (limited) liability of the seller for representations of the producer – an innovation that was particularly controversial in Germany.[146]

2. Legitimate expectations of the consumer concerning product quality

The proposal was with some minor changes adopted by Parliament and Council as Directive 1999/44 of 25 May 1999 "on the sale of consumer goods and associated guarantees".[147] In comparison with existing Member State law, it contains the following innovations:

–   The seller is liable for "conformity" of the product with contractual arrangements. The older concepts of "defect" (German law), *"vice caché"* (French law) or "merchantable quality" (common law) are replaced by a more modern concept taken from Art. 35 *et seq.* of the CISG. Delivery of a product conforming to the contract protects the legitimate quality expectations of the consumer. In the case of breach, a set of remedies is available to the consumer. These come in two stages. The first is the right to repair or to delivery of a conforming product. The second is a right to reduce the purchase price or to cancel the contract altogether if the first stage was not satisfactory to the consumer, subject to some additional conditions as far as cancellation is concerned.

–   The seller is liable not only for its own representations but also for "any public statements of the specific characteristics of the goods made about them …. by the producer or his representatives, particularly in advertising or on labelling". The directive aims to protect the legitimate expectations of the consumer concerning the quality marketing of the products to which the seller adheres. The seller has certain defences, for example if he did not know or could not "reasonably have been aware of the statement in question".[148]

---

[144]   Com (1995) 520 final.
[145]   UN Convention on Contracts for the International Sale of Goods (1980).
[146]   Micklitz, *JCP* 2002, 379.
[147]   *Supra* note 117.
[148]   Art. 2 (2) d) and (4) of Dir. 1999/44.

- The directive is applicable to the sale and – to some extent – also to the "supply" of "consumer goods" to the consumer, referring to all movables including used goods. It excludes real estate property, electricity, water and gas where they are not put up for sale in a limited volume or in a set quantity, and the purchase of "rights", such as financial securities.
- The time limit for liability for lack of conformity has been extended to two years minimum, which is considerably longer than in traditional German law (6 months). A lack of conformity that becomes apparent within 6 months of delivery of the goods is presumed to have existed at the time of delivery. It can be shortened to 1 year in case of used goods.[149]
- The directive follows the classic privity concept, for example, it does not allow for a direct action against the producer if he is not the seller, unlike product liability law. But the seller has a right of recourse against his own seller in the chain of distribution.[150] Recital 9 seems to suggest that this right to recourse cannot be contracted out of in general contract terms, but only if "he has renounced that entitlement", thus referring to an individual transaction exempting the producer or previous seller from liability or reducing it *vis-à-vis* the final seller. This remedy of recourse of the final seller against his previous seller or the producer/importer of the consumer good is justified by the fact that the final seller would otherwise be caught in between the far reaching remedies of the consumer which cannot be contracted out of,[151] on the one hand, and his contractual relations in the chain of distribution where the producer or other partners in the chain may introduce an exemption clause concerning their liability towards the final seller or make it subject to very short limitation periods and other restrictive conditions.
- Commercial guarantees are voluntary instruments of marketing, which must meet certain transparency requirements (§ 17 II 2).

V. SOCIAL POLICY AND TRANSFER OF UNDERTAKINGS: DIR. 77/187 AS CODIFIED BY DIR. 2001/23

1. Overview of the protective ambit

Social policy only plays a limited role in Community law. The most important examples are contained in the law on workplace discrimination analysed above (§ 11 III/IV). The Member States in their different economic and social structures are

---

[149] Art. 5 of Dir. 1999/44. Member States are allowed to introduce a 2 months obligation of the consumer to inform the seller of the lack of conformity.
[150] Art. 4 of Dir. 1999/44.
[151] Per Art. 7 of Dir. 1999/44.

responsible for guaranteeing an adequate level of social policy and for protecting the legitimate expectations of their citizens with regard to social rights. But law and practice, for example with regard to unfair dismissal, vary greatly between Member States. This means that different cost structures are imposed on undertakings, and different sets of rights are granted to workers depending on where they work. As a result, distortions of competition are created. These disturb the good functioning of the internal market.

The Community indirectly engaged in this area with the adoption of the Community Charter of Social Rights in 1989, not signed by the UK. This has no binding force upon social partners or Member States, but has been used by European institutions in order to legitimise actions, especially directives with the aim of protecting workers' rights. The Court has referred to such "soft law instruments" in interpreting Community law.[152] The European Charter of Fundamental Rights contains an entire chapter on "solidarity" (§ 12 III 3).

While this may be used as an interpretative guideline, it has no direct effect in favor of its beneficiaries, namely workers.

It was only the Maastricht Treaty that pushed forward the idea of a "social Europe". Because of British opposition, the relevant document was first included in a special Protocol binding only 11 out of the then 12 Member States. This instrument later became integrated into EU Law by the Amsterdam Treaty, after the UK had withdrawn its opposition. The basic objectives of social policy in the EU are as follows[153]:
– promotion of employment,
– improved living and working conditions so as to make possible their harmoniza- tion while the improvement is being maintained,
– proper social protection,
– combat exclusion, and
– dialogue between management and labour.

However, it should be noted that these have no direct effect. Certain areas are expressly excluded. These include pay, collective bargaining, the right to strike and to impose lock-outs.

---

[152]   Case C-67/96 Albany International BV v Stichting Bedrijfspensioenfonds Textielindustrie [1999] ECR I-5751 at para 57 in determining the limits of competition law vis-à-vis collective bargaining.
[153]   Art. 136/137 EC. Its importance for employment policy is discussed in Trubek, *The European employment strategy and the future of EU governance*, 2003.

Even before this official recognition of social policy as part of Community objectives within the limits of the subsidiarity principle, the Community legislator adopted a number of important directives aimed at protecting specific legitimate expectations of employees. These were regarded as close enough to the functioning of the common – later the internal – market to justify Community action, and could be included under the broad harmonization competences[154] requiring unanimity in the Council. This work will not give a complete account of existing legislation and case-law, but rather will analyse the most important – and at the same time most controversial – piece of legislation. That is, the transfer of undertakings directive, which in Court practice has given rise to intensive litigation.[155]

2. Objectives of the transfer directives

Directive 77/187 of 14 Feb. 1977 is concerned with the "approximation of the laws of the Member States relating to the safeguarding of employees' rights in the event of transfer of undertakings".[156] It was amended once[157] and codified by Dir. 2001/23/EC of 12 March 2001[158] in order to consolidate and clarify the law.

The directive, according to recital 2 (recital 3 in the codified version) aims to "provide for the protection of employees in the event of a change of employer, in particular to ensure that their rights are safeguarded." It touches upon a highly sensitive area of social policy:

– to protect employees' legitimate expectations not to see their "social *acquis*" diminished or taken away by the fact that they have a new employer because of a transaction upon which they have no influence (the transfer of "their" under-taking or "parts" of it);
– to guarantee economic efficiency and competitiveness, as well as contractual freedom to undertakings wanting to change ownership or to restructure business, which is protected by EU law, too.

The Directive clearly aims at balancing these sometimes conflicting interests. It does not intend a general protection against dismissals, nor make restructuring of undertakings impossible because of unintended and unknown costs of taking over social burdens in case of transfers of undertakings. However, it must on the other hand

---

[154] Either Art. 94 EC or 308 EC.
[155] For an excellent overview of the recent case law cf. O'Leary, *Employment Law before the ECJ*, 2002, 241-292; Garde, *CMLRev* 2002 at 523 lists 31 references and 3 direct actions till 2002.
[156] [1977] OJ L 61/26.
[157] Council Directive 98/50/EC [1998] *OJ* L 201/58.
[158] [2001] OJ L 82/16.

be an effective instrument to protect employees' rights, and not a mere symbolic law without any legal force behind it.

The original directive did not contain a definition of "employee". Art. 2 (1) (d) states that "'employee' shall mean any person who, in the Member State concerned, is protected as an employee under national employment law". Unlike in other areas of Community law, the legislator seems to avoid an autonomous definition of employee (§ 2 III 3), but refers to existing Member State law and therefore accepts its differences. This was changed by later amendments:[159]

> Member States shall not exclude from the scope of the Directive contracts of employment or employment relationships solely because:
> (a) the number of working hours performed or to be performed
> (b) they are in employment relationships governed by a fixed-duration contract of employment …or
> (c) they are temporary employment relationships…

This amendment makes clear that part-time and other atypical workers cannot be discriminated against by being excluded from the scope of the Directive:

> They benefit from the same rights under the Directive as full-time employees, irrespective of what national law may provide in their respect.[160]

3.   The controversial concept of "transfer of undertaking"

a.   Different approaches particularly to outsourcing

The concept of "transfer" is decisive in enabling protection of employees' rights against their new employer or transferee. The transfer of a "part of an undertaking or business to another employer" is sufficient. This has considerably varied in the case law of the Court. In *Spijkers*[161], the decisive criterion was whether there is an "economic entity that retains its identity". This rather narrow definition does not cover cases of outsourcing or separating certain activities from the undertaking to another entity. Therefore, in *Christel Schmidt*[162], the Court was satisfied with the *similarity of activity*. In the case at hand, a cleaning activity done by Mrs. Schmidt for the savings bank Bordesholm in Germany was separated and outsourced to a company called

---

[159]   Dir. 98/50 introduced Art. 2 (2) second para.
[160]   Garde *supra* note 155 at 527, referring to recital 9 and the Community Charter on Social Rights of 9 Dec. 1989 which is mentioned in recital (5) of the codified version.
[161]   Case 24/85 Spijkers v Gebroeders [1986] ECR 1119.
[162]   Case C-392/92 Schmidt v Spar- und Leihkasse der fruheren Amter Bordesholm, Kiel und Cronshagen [1994] ECR I-1311 at para 17.

"Spiegelblank" but continued by the same person (!). Clearly the Court wanted to protect Mrs. Schmidt against a unilateral worsening of her social position. Even if the result seems to be acceptable, it is hard to define the mere transfer of a relatively minor activity as a "transfer of a part of an undertaking". The decision therefore found strong opposition, most notably in Germany and France.[163]

In the later case of *Süzen*[164], the Court came back to a more traditional concept of "transfer", which can be effected in two ways:
– transfer of significant assets, or
– in labour intensive business, transfer of a major part of the workforce, in terms of either number (quantitative criteria) or skills (qualitative criteria) as the case may be.

The Court insisted that:

> (t)he decisive criterion for establishing the existence of a transfer within the meaning of the directive is whether the entity in question retains its identity, as indicated inter alia by the fact that its operation is actually continued or resumed ... (para 10).

The Court implicitly overruled the broader definition of "similarity" of activity in *Christel Schmidt*. It is a matter for the national court to find whether these criteria are fulfilled. Later amendments attempted to define the phrase "transfer of an under-taking[165]":

> there is a transfer within the meaning of this Directive where there is a transfer of an economic entity which retains its identity, meaning an organised grouping of resources which has the objective of pursuing an economic activity, whether or not that activity is central or ancillary.

It is quite clear that this definition narrows down the sphere of application of Dir. 77/187. It seems that the mere outsourcing of specific activities can no longer be included under the definition of "transfer of undertaking or part of an undertaking". This considerably weakens the protection of workers, and allows a certain "collusion" between transferor and transferee in order to exclude the applicability of the Directive.[166]

---

[163] Garde at 524.
[164] Case C-13/95 Süzen v Zehnacker Gebäudereinigung [1997] ECR I-1259.
[165] Directive 98/50 added a subparagraph (b) to Art. (1) (1) of the Dir. 77/187.
[166] Garde at 530; O'Leary, *Employment Law at the ECJ*, 2002, at 266.

The problems of a more restrictive interpretation of the transfer directive can clearly be seen by looking at the *Oy Liikenne* case.[167] The operation of local bus routes formerly serviced by Hakunilan Liikenne was awarded, following the Community procurement procedure for public services (*supra* § 8 IV)[168], to Oy Liikenne. No vehicles or other assets were transferred. Oy Liikenne rehired 33 of the 45 bus drivers dismissed by Hakunilan. Two of them claimed the applicability of Dir. 77/187 because their former working conditions were better than those offered by Oy. The Court rejected the applicability of the protective provisions of Dir. 77/187, since operating bus services is not labour intensive and the transfer of the majority of the workforce alone could not trigger a "transfer of undertaking", because no major assets (buses, service stations etc.) had been transferred to Oy.

b. Transfer of undertakings and insolvency proceedings

In its original version, the directive contained no specific rules on the transfer of undertakings as a consequence of insolvency proceedings. Applying Dir. 77/187 in these cases might frustrate its very objective. That is, instead of trying to preserve the insolvent undertaking or parts of it by finding a new owner, such efforts would be thwarted if this new owner would have to face the risk of taking over all the obligations arising out of social rights of employees. Moreover, a restructuring of the undertaking would probably be impossible, thereby ruling out the objective of modern insolvency law.

As early as in *Abels*[169], the Court decided to interpret the directive restrictively, and to exclude its application in case of transfer of undertakings in insolvency proceedings. The Court argued with the (negative) *effet utile* of the directive to avoid a loss of jobs if imposed upon the transferee of an insolvent undertaking.

However, this restrictive interpretation does not apply to pre-insolvency proceedings. The matter was clarified in *Dethier*[170]. The distinction was justified on the basis of the different types of proceedings. That is, genuine insolvency proceedings took place under the supervision of a court with the administrator as an independent organ, while a voluntary winding up cannot be compared to an insolvency procedure, in that the

---

[167] Case C-172/99 Oy Liikene Ab v Pekka Liskojarvi and Pentti Juntunden [2001] ECR I-745.

[168] The Court made clear that Dir. 92/50 does not *per se* exclude the application of Dir. 77/187, cf. Garde at 536-538.

[169] Case 135/83 Abels v Bedrijfsvereniging voor de Metaalindustrie en de Elektrotechnische Industrie [1985] ECR 469.

[170] Case C-319/94 Jules Dethier Equipment SA v Jules Dassy and Sovam SPRL [1998] ECR-1061.

liquidator is an organ of the company, which retains full control of the winding-up. This case law was taken over by the 1998 amendment of the directive[171]:

> Art. 3 and 4 of the directive shall not apply to any transfer of an undertaking … where the transferor is the subject of bankruptcy proceedings or any analogous insolvency proceedings which have been instituted with a view to the liquidation of the assets of the transferor and which are under the supervision of a competent public authority (which may be an insolvency practitioner authorised by a competent public authority).

4. Rights and remedies under the directive

The Directive grants three kinds of rights to the employees it covers:
- employment contracts or employment relationships are transferred automatically under the same terms and conditions (Art. 3).
- dismissals by reason of the transfer alone are prohibited (Art. 4).
- employees' representatives have the right to be informed and consulted on a transfer (Art. 7).

In any case, employees may object to their transfer. They cannot be forced against their will into a new contract.[172] A dismissal against the provisions of the directive is "unlawful".[173] The directive provides for Member States to allow employees to pursue their claims by judicial process. However, it does not provide for any specific remedies. According to the general case law of the Court, Member States have a certain freedom of choice, but must provide for effective and equivalent remedies.[174]

---

[171]   Now Art. 5 (1) of Dir. 2001/23.
[172]   Cases C 171 +172/94 Merckx + Neuhuys v Ford Motors Belgium [1996] ECR I-1253.
[173]   Case C-319/94 *supra* note 170.
[174]   Case C-382/92 Commission v UK [1994] ECR I-2435.

§ 14. JUDICIAL PROTECTION

I. THE PRINCIPLE OF "EFFECTIVE JUDICIAL PROTECTION AND CONTROL"

1. Rights, remedies and procedures

"Ubi ius – ibi remedium" – where there is a right there is a remedy.[175] This important principle of any government of law is true for Community law, too. Where Community law grants rights to a person as Union or market citizen, it must assure that these rights can be effectively protected. This is due to its direct effect, especially in the area of fundamental freedoms and competition.

The ECJ developed this principle of "effective judicial control" or, more broadly, effective judicial protection in its early case law, and has continuously refined and specified it.[176] Many cases are linked to the *effet utile* of Community law, especially its fundamental freedoms. As the Court said in *Heylens:*[177]

> Since free access to employment is a fundamental right which the Treaty confers individually on each worker in the Community, the existence of a remedy of a judicial nature against any decision of a national authority refusing the benefit of that right is essential in order to secure for the individual effective protection for his right…. Effective judicial review, which must be able to cover the legality of the reasons for the contested decision, presupposes in general that the court to which the matter is referred may require the competent authority to notify its reasons… (paras 14-15)

The guarantee of these freedoms consists of both a substantive and a remedial and procedural element. Direct effect is voided of any sense if the beneficiary cannot enforce it by effective remedies, or if procedures necessary for enforcement are unavailable. As a consequence, the Court developed the principles of *effectiveness* and *equivalence:*[178]
- Effectiveness means that a remedy should not only compensate the victim for a potential loss of or injury to a right, but also deter potential wrongdoers from violating it in the first place.

---

[175]   V. Gerven, *CMLRev* 2000, 501 at 521.
[176]   An excellent overview of the development of the case law is given by Tridimas, *The General Principles of Community Law*, 1999 at 279-290.
[177]   Case 222/86 Union nationale des entraîneurs et cadres techniques professionnels du football (Unectef) v Georges Heylens and others [1987] ECR 4097.
[178]   For details cf. Tridimas at 279-290.

– Equivalence means that the protection of Community law rights should be equivalent in strength and scope to the protection of similar rights granted under national law. In other terms: nobody should suffer from a lower standard of protection for the simple reason that the right to be protected has its origin in Community rather than in national law.

Case law has also based these principles on Art. 6 of the ECHR. Although this does not have direct effect upon Community law, it must at least be respected as an expression of the common constitutional heritage of the Member States. In *Johnston*,[179] the Court said:

> The requirement of judicial control ... reflects a general principle of law which underlies the constitutional traditions common to the Member States. That principle is also laid down in Art. 6 and 13 of the European Convention for the Protection of Human Rights and Fundamental Freedoms of 4 November 1950. As the European Parliament, Council and Commission recognized in their Joint Declaration of 5 April 1977 ... and as the Court has recognized in its decisions, the principles on which that Convention is based must be taken into consideration in Community law (para 18).

Art. 6 (2) EU transferred this case law into Union law (§ 12 II). A further step was taken by Art. 47 of the EchFR, now Art. II-107 Draft Constitution, which reads:

> Everyone whose rights and freedoms guaranteed by the law of the Union are violated has the right to an effective remedy before a tribunal ...

Many Community law directives, especially those concerned with preventing discrimination (§ 11)[180] and those protecting legitimate expectations (§ 13)[181], contain detailed *obligations de moyens* on effective legal protection. These include rights to compensation, collective interest actions, access to tribunals of law, and the like. Although earlier case law of the ECJ stressed that "the Treaty ... was not intended to create new remedies in the national courts to ensure the observance of Community law other than already laid down by national law,"[182] the notion of practical possibility was later replaced by requirements of adequacy and effectiveness. If Member State law fails to acknowledge the appropriate remedies, courts are obliged to provide for them, as the Court said in *Borelli*[183]:

---

[179]   Case 222/84 Marguerite Johnston v Chief Constable of Royal Ulster Constabulary [1986] ECR 1651.
[180]   Case C-185/97 Belinda Jane Coote v Granada Hospitality Ltd. [1998] ECR I-5199.
[181]   Case C-361/88 Commission v Germany, [1991] ECR I-2567 concerning environmental protection.
[182]   Case C-158/80 Rewe-Handelsgesellschaft Nord mbH et Rewe-Markt Steffen v Hauptzollamt Kiel, [1981] ECR 1805.
[183]   Case C-97/91 Oleificio Borelli SpA v Commission [1992] I-6313.

Accordingly, it is for the national courts .... to rule on the lawfulness of the national measure at issue on the same terms on which they review any definitive measure adopted by the same national authority which is capable of adversely affecting third parties and, consequently, to regard an action brought for that purpose as admissible even if the domestic rules of procedure do not provide for this in such a case (para 13).

Clearly, these general principles and broad *obligations de moyens* are of little help to the individual who complains about an injury to their Community law rights. A system of effective protection needs to answer a number of questions. These have to be resolved by the Court as well as by Member State jurisdictions:
–   What are the effective remedies to be chosen? Will they consist of granting an injunction, in allowing for compensation, in ordering restitution?[184] Are they limited to traditional civil law remedies, or do they do require action under administrative or even criminal law?
–   What are the procedures to be chosen for effective enforcement of remedies attached to a violation of Community law rights?
–   Which injuries should be treated by the Community, and which by national jurisdictions? How can they be linked together? How does the duty of co-operation under Art. 10 EC actually work?
–   How can the principle of effective judicial protection as a right under Community law be harmonized with the "procedural autonomy" of Member States? The latter has been recognized by the Court in several judgments, for example with regard to the characteristics of civil litigation, where it is up the parties themselves to present evidence and defend their case.[185]

2. Distribution of responsibilities

In order to understand the Community system of protection of rights, it is useful to follow the distinction developed by the former AG Van Gerven.[186] According to him, this protection works in several ways:
–   If a Community law right is violated, the victim should have an effective remedy against the perpetrator, be it a private person, a Member State or one of its bodies, or the Community institutions themselves. The basic contents of the remedy are shaped by Community law. Unreasonable restrictions on remedies, as for example by unforeseeable limitation periods,[187] or a procedural rule which prohibits the national court, on expiry of a limitation period, from finding of its own motion

---

[184]   Cf. the discussion in v. Gerven at 509-521.
[185]   Cases C-430-432/93 Van Schijndel and Van Veen v Stichting Pensioenfonds [1995] ECR I-4705 at para 21.
[186]   Van Gerven, *loc. cit.*, 526-533.
[187]   Case C-327/00 Santex SpA v Unità Socio Sanitaria Locale [2003] ECR I-1877.

or following a plea raised by a consumer that a term sought to be enforced by a seller or supplier is unfair,[188] must be disapplied by national courts. On the other hand, the Court has been rather generous towards Member States when they impose time-limits or other procedural restrictions on bringing claims for violation of Community rights, and has left its appropriateness to be decided by the national court.[189] Inversely, the potential responsibility of the violator is part of a Community system of governance. This will be developed later (§§ 18-21).

- These Community-specific remedies should be enforced by legal means, in the very end if necessary by courts of law. Member States, not the Community, have to establish a system of effective procedures. Their procedural autonomy is supplemented by the *effet utile* of Community law, as the Court has clearly shown in *Borelli*.
- Community involvement in procedures – a matter for Member States – becomes deeper in cross-border conflicts of a civil and commercial law nature (II) and in cases involving the interpretation and validity of Community law measures (III).
- Procedures allowing direct access to Community jurisdictions – the Court of First Instance (CFI) and, upon appeal, the Court of Justice (ECJ) – are only available in very limited cases, namely where an individual is directly and individually concerned by a Community measure (sub IV).

Finally, in 2003, Council Directive 2002/8/EC of 27 January 2003 concerning legal aid in cross-border litigation has been adopted.[190] It contains minimum standards of legal aid in cross-border litigation which must be put on an equal footing with national litigation.

3. Protection against jurisdiction clauses in pre-formulated contracts

Jurisdiction clauses are quite common in standard form contracts, especially those concluded with consumers. They usually impose on the weaker party a jurisdiction away from its place of residence and thereby unilaterally favour the other side, mostly business. EC law has two instruments to cope with them:
- In cross-border litigation, Reg. 44/2001 is applicable and will be studied in the next section.
- In internal relations, this depends on the "procedural autonomy" of the Member State discussed above, although this is limited by Dir. 93/13/EC of 5.4. 1993 on "Unfair Terms in Consumer Contracts".[191]

---

[188] Case C-473/00 Cofidis v Jean-Louis Fredout [2002] ECR I-10875.
[189] Case C-261/95 Palmisani v INPS [1997] ECR I-4025; comments by Craig-de Búrca, loc. cit. at p. 269/270.
[190] [2003] OJ L 26/41.
[191] [1993] OJ L 95/29.

The latter problem was raised in *Oceano*.[192] Several Spanish clients were sued by a book-club company at its place of business but not at their residence, because a jurisdiction clause was inserted in the standard contract form. The Spanish judge was not sure whether he could raise the issue of his territorial incompetence *ex officio* because he regarded the jurisdiction clause to be unfair under Art. 3 (2) of Dir. 93/13 and Nr. 1 lit q) of the so called indicative list of the Annex. The Court gave a somewhat unclear answer:

> a jurisdiction clause must be regarded as unfair within the meaning of Art. 3 of the Dir. (93/13) *in so far as*[193] it causes contrary to the requirement of good faith, a significant imbalance in the parties' rights and obligations existing under the contract to the detriment of the consumer.

The Court insisted on the protective ambit of Dir. 93/13. This means that the judge should be able to raise *ex officio* the potential unfairness of the jurisdiction clause, and that he should apply and interpret his national law in conformity with Community law. However, the Court did not completely condemn the jurisdiction clause, but left this to the national judge, depending on the circumstances of the case. There is, though, great likelihood that such unilateral clauses are unfair because they contradict the principle of effective judicial protection.

II.   CROSS-BORDER JUDICIAL PROTECTION: BRUSSELS CONVENTION AND REGULATION 44/2001

1.   The Brussels Convention of 1968 as amended

Judicial protection presumes that a party subject to a dispute should be able to bring legal proceedings in a court of law (or other body responsible for resolving legal disputes), knowing that the decision taken by such a body will be recognized and enforced. Sometimes this should be done in a State other than the State where the claimant is established or domiciled. Therefore, questions on jurisdiction, recognition and enforcement of judgments throughout the Community are crucial to ensure effective protection of rights derived from Community law. These also form part of an effective internal market presupposing a "free flow of judgments", at least in civil and commercial matters.

---

[192]   Joined cases C-240-244/98 Oceano Grupo editorial v Rocio Murciano Quintero *et al.* [2000] ECR I-4491; comment Stuyck, *CMLRev* 2001, 719.

[193]   Micklitz in: Reich/Micklitz, *Europäisches Verbraucherrecht*, para 13.22 insists that the words in italics were not translated in the German version and caused some confusion about the ambit and scope of the judgment.

Within the EU, the above-mentioned questions have been regulated primarily by the 1968 Brussels Convention on Jurisdiction and the Enforcement of Judgments in Civil and Commercial Matters.[194] The original EEC Treaty was mostly concerned with the establishment of the Common Market and contained virtually nothing about private international law and jurisdiction, except for Art. 220 EEC (now Art. 293 EC) stating that:

> Member States shall, so far as is necessary, enter into negotiations with each other with a view to securing for the benefit of their nationals ... the simplification of formalities governing the reciprocal recognition and enforcement of judgments of courts or tribunals and of arbitration awards.

The only instrument that could be adopted under these provisions was an international treaty. Therefore, the Brussels Convention was adopted as an international law instrument and ratified by all Member States. Many legal scholars characterized the Convention as a success in the process of European integration:

> [It was] a well-known success. It went even further than the relevant Treaty provision, because it established a system of direct rules for the jurisdiction of European Member state courts in international cases and did not simply provide for a "simplification of formalities governing the reciprocal recognition and enforcement of judgments" – thus the expert drafters of the Convention were forerunning the diplomatic drafters of Art. 65 EC by almost 30 years.[195]

As stated above, the Convention provides a set of uniform and directly applicable rules. These form part of the law of every State – party to the Convention. The courts of those States are under an obligation to apply these rules while considering issues on jurisdiction. Moreover, they should give virtually automatic recognition and enforcement of judgments in civil and commercial matters issued in other States – parties to the Convention, after some formal requirements have been met.

Not only is it the national courts of Member states of the European Union that applied the Convention on a regular basis. Indeed, the European Court of Justice has also delivered preliminary rulings on interpreting the Convention. This right was conferred upon the Court by the 1971 Protocol[196], thus promoting a more uniform application and autonomous interpretation of the Convention throughout Member States. A substantial body of case law exists on the Brussels Convention, from references by the original six Contracting States to the ECJ, and more recently from references from

---

[194] [1998] OJ C 27/1 (consolidated version).
[195] O. Remien, *CMLRev* 2001 at 55.
[196] Protocol on the interpretation of the 1968 Convention by the Court of Justice [1998] OJ C 27/28.

other Contracting States. The Convention takes supremacy over national law and must be applied uniformly.[197] The Court stressed its interpretative role of the Convention in the recent *HWS* case:[198]

> Only such (autonomous, NR) interpretation (of the concepts of contract and tort in Art. 5 (1) and (3) of the Brussels Convention, NR) is capable of ensuring the uniform application of the Brussels Convention, which is intended in particular to lay down common rules on jurisdiction for the courts of the Contracting States and to strengthen the legal protection of persons established in the Community by enabling the claimant to identify easily the court in which he may sue and the defendant reasonably to foresee in which court he may be sued … (para 20)

The principal objectives of the Convention may be traced through the substantial amount of ECJ case law interpreting the Convention. These include:
– determination of international jurisdiction of (national) courts in the European Community;[199]
– simplification of formalities governing reciprocal enforcement of judgments;[200]
– procedural provisions for these purposes;[201]
– avoidance of multiplicity of jurisdictions;[202]
– prohibition of the English doctrine of "*forum non conveniens*" where the case has a closer connection with the courts of a non-Member country, or the practice to issue "anti-suit injunctions" against alleged frivolous litigation in other Member countries;[203]
– the need to strengthen the legal protection of the rights of defendants;[204]
– protection of socially or economically weaker parties.[205]

The provisions of the Brussels Convention were repeated in the Lugano Convention concluded between the EEC countries and members of the European Free Trade Association.

---

[197] Case 288/82 Ferdinand M. J.J. Duijnstee v Lodewijk Goderbauer [1983] ECR 3663.
[198] Case C-334/00 Fonderie Officine Meccaniche Tacconi SpA v Heinrich Wagner Sinto Maschinenfabrik (HWS) [2002] ECR I-7357.
[199] Case 14/76 A. De Bloos, SPRL v Société en comandidte par actions Boyer [1976] ECR 1497.
[200] Case 133/78 Gourdian v Nadler [1979] ECR 733 at para. 3.
[201] Case 48/84 Spitzley v Sommer Exploitation SA [1985] ECR 787 at para. 21.
[202] Case 14/76 *supra* note 196.
[203] Case C-281/02 Andrew Owusu v N.B. Jackson et al. [2005] ECR I-(1.3.2005), Case C-159/02 Gregory Paul Turner v Felix Fareed Ismail Grovit et al. [2004] ECR I-(27.4.2004).
[204] Case 125/79 Denilauer v SNC Couchet Frères [1980] ECR 1553 at para. 13.
[205] Case 150/77 Bertrand v Paul Ott KG [1978] ECR 1431 at para 21; 201/82 Gerling Konzern Speziale Kreditversicherungs-AG v Amministrazione del Tesoro dello Stato [1983] ECR 2503 at para. 17.

The well-known international law rule *actor sequitur forum rei* is the general principle of jurisdiction of the Brussels Convention Art. 2. This means that a person should be sued in the court of the place where he is domiciled. This rule may be derogated from and a person may be sued in the courts of other States – parties to the Convention only by virtue of the rules on "special jurisdiction" stated in the Convention. These rules state that person may also be sued:
– in the courts of the state where the contract obligation was performed, Art. 5 (1),
– where a harmful event has occurred (in matters related to delict), Art. 5 (3),
– where a branch or agency is situated (in matters related to operations of a branch, Art. 5 (5).

In the *Kronhofer* case[206] the Court insisted on a narrow interpretation of Art. 5 (3) as an exeption to the general rule of Art. 2 Brussels Convention. In tort actions regarding the marketing of financial services, the mere fact that the claimant had its business seat or its assets in one Member country is not sufficient to constitute the "place where the harmful event occurred".

If the defendant is not domiciled in any of the States – parties to the Convention, the national rules of the plaintiff state will apply. In addition, parties to the contract may enter into an agreement on jurisdiction, subject to provisions of Section 6 of the Convention.

The Convention also determines the rules on "exclusive jurisdiction". This, contrary to general and special jurisdiction, is linked not to the courts of the State where the party is domiciled but where immovable property is situated, where the company has its seat, or where the public register is kept, Art. 16. The courts, which have exclusive jurisdiction under the Convention, cannot be excluded from the proceedings by an agreement on jurisdiction.

The Convention finally contains some rules on protective jurisdiction, under which economically weaker parties, such as consumers or employees, may sue in the courts of their domicile:
– With regard to consumers, the Convention provides for a set of criteria enabling these persons to enjoy protective provisions, but usually limits them to so-called *passive consumers.* They have been subject to intensive case law concerning "consumer contracts" in Art. 13 *et seq.*[207]

---

[206] Case C-168/02 Rudolf Kronhofer v Marianne Maier et al. [2004] ECR I-(10.06.2004).
[207] For a recent case C-96/00 Gabriel [2002] ECR I-6367; for details Reich/Micklitz, *Europäisches Verbraucherrecht,* paras 31.2-31.14.

- Two judgements of 20 Jan. 2005[208] continue earlier case law insisting on a strict interpretation of the special jurisdiction of Art. 13 as an exception to the general rule "*actor sequitur forum rei*". In the case of so-called "mixed contracts", the Court will apply Art. 13 only in cases where the professional activity to which the contract is related is only marginal and ancillary. Should the consumer deceive the other side on the true character of the contract – he pretends the contract to be part of a professional activity even when this is only minor – he has waived his protection and the good-faith contract partner is not subject to the special jurisdiction of Art. 13/14. Art. 13 (1) para (3) always requires that a contract is *concluded* for the supply of goods or services. This is not the case, in difference to *Gabriel*, if the trader awards to the consumer a "prize" allegedly won by him without being subject to the ordering of goods.
- With regard to contracts of employment, a special section was added to Art. 5 (1) on the occasion of the accession of Spain and Portugal to the Convention. The Court referred to the place where the work is actually performed by the employee as the place where (active or passive) litigation arising out of the employment contract should take place, including posted workers. If work is done in several places, then the central point of performance should be decisive.[209]

Prorogation of jurisdiction by agreement is subject to stricter requirements aimed at the protection of the weaker party.

It should be noted that, despite its success, the Convention had one inherent flaw. That is, with every round of accession, it had to be ratified again by all Member States. This ratification has become ever more time consuming. As an example, Austria, Finland and Sweden acceded to the European Union in 1996. And as late as in July 1999 the Commission pointed out that the "Brussels Convention, as amended following the accession negotiations with Austria, Finland and Sweden, has not yet entered into force for all the Member states as only a minority of them have ratified it."[210]

2. Brussels Regulation 44/2001

a. Overview

However, such legislation through an international convention remained the only possible way until the Amsterdam Treaty introduced Art. 65 (b) EC, which now contains provisions on:

---

[208] C-464/01 Johann Gruber v Bay Wa AG and C-27/02 Petra Engler v Janus Versand GmbH [2005] ECR I-(000); critique Reich, *EuZW* 2005, 244.
[209] Cf. Case C-383/95 Petrus Wilhelmus Rutten v Cross Medical Ltd. [1997] ECR I-57.
[210] COM (1999) 348 final of 14 July 1999 at 2.1.

measures in the field of judicial cooperation in civil matters having cross-border implications, to be taken ... promoting the compatibility of the rules applicable in the Member States concerning the conflict of laws and of jurisdiction.

Hence, the private international law and jurisdiction rules in the European Union were brought into the context of the First Pillar. This article was used as a basis for adoption of Council Regulation (EC) No 44/2001 of 22 December 2000 on jurisdiction and the recognition and enforcement of judgments in civil and commercial matters (in the following: Reg. 44/2001).[211] The Regulation replaced the Convention as of March 1, 2002, for the 14 states – Members of the EU. Art. 68 of Reg. 44/2001 provides:

> [The] Regulation shall, as between the Member States, supersede the Brussels Convention. ... In so far as this Regulation replaces the provisions of the Brussels Convention between Member States, any reference to the Convention shall be understood as a reference to this Regulation.

However, the Brussels Convention continues to apply in relations between Denmark and the Member States that are bound by the Regulation (recital 21), and to the territories of the Member States that fall within the territorial scope of the Convention and which are excluded from this Regulation pursuant to Art. 299 of the Treaty (recital 22).

Despite the fact that the Convention ceased to regulate relations between most of the Member States, it will remain important for the purpose of uniform interpretation and application of the Regulation, since "[c]ontinuity between the Brussels Convention and this Regulation should be ensured."[212] The case law of the ECJ, interpreting provisions of the Brussels Convention that were transferred unchanged into the Regulation, should remain a valid source for interpreting the provisions of the Regulation. For this reason, the case law of the ECJ[213] as well as the Official Reports on the Convention[214] have retained their importance.

---

[211]   [2002] OJ L 12/1.

[212]   Recital 19 of the Regulation.

[213]   For a recent example cf. case C-167/00 Verein für Konsumenteninformation v Karl Heinz Henkel [2002] ECR I-8111 concerning the question on whether Art. 5 (3) is also applicable to injunctions to prevent an illegal act, which the ECJ answered in the affirmative by referring to the amended text in Art. 5(3) of Reg. 44/2001.

[214]   Schlosser Report, [1979] OJ C 59, Jenard Report [1979] OJ C 59; the Evrigenis and Kerameus Report [1986] OJ C 298; The Almeida Cruz, Desanes Real, Jenard Report [1990] OJ C 189.

b. Consumer contracts

The Regulation for the most part follows both the structure and the provisions of the Brussels Convention. One of the key changes in the Regulation compared to the Convention is the new approach towards marketing activities in B2C (business to consumer) relations. According to Art. 13 (1) lit. c) of the Convention, the right of the consumer to sue the supplier in the consumer's country of domicile was subject to the existence of advertising or a specific invitation addressed to the consumer. Moreover, the consumer should have taken the necessary steps to conclude the contract in that state. Art. 15 (1) lit c) of Regulation 44/2001 replaced these two conditions with one: the consumer may sue the company if the company:

> by any means, directs such activities to that Member State or several States including that Member State.

This provision has aroused intense debate with regard to e-commerce, since it may be interpreted in such a way that the mere accessibility of the website of a company situated in one Member State by a consumer domiciled in another Member State may give such consumer the right to sue the company in the consumer's domicile – a result which makes marketing in e-commerce subject to different and diverging jurisdictions. Such a rule may on the other hand encourage the establishment of alternative dispute settlement (ADR) mechanisms, which is one of the aims of the directive on electronic commerce (§ 8 III 2, § 17 II 2). As a compromise solution, the direction of the activity of the trader can be inferred from several circumstances, e.g. prior advertising, language used, exclusion of certain countries etc.[215]

c. Employment contracts

With regard to employment contracts, a new section 5 contains special rules on jurisdiction.[216] This gives the employee the choice to sue the employer:[217]
- in the courts of domicile of the employer;
- in the courts for the place where the employee habitually carries out his work or in the courts for the last place where he did so;
- if the employee does not or did not habitually carry out his work in any one country, in the courts for the place where the business which engaged the employee is or was situated.

---

[215] Reich/Micklitz, *Europäisches Verbraucherrecht*, 4. A. at paras 31.5; 32.12; Vasiljeva, *ELJ* 2004, 123 at 133.
[216] Art. 18 of the Regulation.
[217] Art. 19 of the Regulation.

On the other hand, an employer may bring proceedings only in the courts of the Member State where the employee is domiciled.[218]

d. Other issues

Art. 60 of Reg. 44/2001 provides for an autonomous definition of the seat of legal persons, whereas the Convention had left this issue to be determined by the rules of the court in which jurisdiction is exercised. The Regulation provides three alternative criteria to define domicile of legal persons:
- the statutory seat,
- the central administration, or
- the principal place of business.

These criteria correspond to those listed in the Chapter of the EC Treaty concerned with the right of establishment of companies in the European Community.[219]

Another important change gives an autonomous definition to the place of performance of the contract. Art. 5 (1) lit b) of Reg. 44/2001 provides that in the case of sale of goods this place is the place where the goods were delivered or should have been delivered; and in the case of provision of services – the place where the services were provided or should have been provided. The purpose of this modification is, similarly as described above, "to remedy the shortcomings of applying the rules of private international law of the State whose courts are seized."[220] However, problems may still remain for the claimant in proving the place where services, such as consultancy services, should have been provided.

The Regulation has amended the rule on jurisdiction in tort claims. The defendant may be sued not only in the courts of the place where the harmful event has already occurred, but also of the place where it *may occur*. Thus, litigants are given a right to sue for preventive measures via injunctions. This was first recognized in the *Henkel* case concerning cross-border group actions.[221]

Art. 6 of Reg. 44/2001 provides that an action may be brought against a defendant in the court of a co-defendant only in cases when the claims are so closely connected that

---

[218] Art. 20 (1) of the Regulation.
[219] Art. 48 EC.
[220] Proposal for a Council Regulation (EC) on Jurisdiction and the Recognition and Enforcement of Judgments in Civil and Commercial Matters, [1999] *OJ* C 376 (1999) at p. 17.
[221] Case C-167/00, *supra* note 212 which comes to the same result under the Brussels Convention, thus minimising the changes brought about by Reg. 44/2001.

separate proceedings would risk irreconcilable judgments. Thus, the ruling of the ECJ in the *Kalfelis* case[222] was transposed into a legislative provision.

An important innovation is made to Section 7 related to prorogation of jurisdiction. An agreement on jurisdiction may be concluded in electronic form.[223] However, the restrictive rules on jurisdiction clauses in consumer contracts have not been changed[224]. The question remains how they can be coordinated with the case law of the ECJ on jurisdiction clauses in standard contract terms (*supra* I 3). In *Oceano*[225], the Court did not even mention this problem.

Rules on recognition and enforcement of judgments have been changed so as to make recognition virtually automatic, and simplifying the obtaining of an enforcement declaration. Courts asking for enforcement declarations will no longer be able to raise grounds for non-recognition on their own motion.[226] However, the claimant still has to comply with national procedure rules in order to obtain a declaration that the judgment is enforceable. Thus, the value of automatic recognition may be reduced.

III. INDIRECT PROTECTION VIA THE REFERENCE PROCEDURE

1. *Original objective: uniformity of Community law*

The most important element in protecting individual rights and insisting on adequate remedies has been the reference procedure[227] even though, paradoxically, this does not allow direct access of individuals to European courts. It was originally meant to be an interim procedure by which courts of law of the Member countries could ask the ECJ for preliminary rulings on questions of validity and interpretation of Community law. With the exception of courts against whose decisions there is no remedy under national law – which have an obligation to refer[228] – the national court has complete discretion whether to use the reference procedure or not. Therefore, it was not individual protection but uniformity of Community law that was the original objective of the reference procedure.

---

[222] See Case 189/97 Kalfelis v. Banque Schröder ECR [1988] 5565.
[223] Art. 23 of the Regulation.
[224] Art. 17 of the Regulation.
[225] Cases C-240-244/98, *supra* note 192; comment by Pfeiffer, *ZEuP* 2003, 141 at 153.
[226] Art. 33 of the Regulation.
[227] Under Art. 234 EC.
[228] Para 3 of Art. 234 EC.

This perspective can be seen by looking at two important decisions of the eighties. In *CILFIT*[229] the ECJ wrote that Art. 177:

> does not constitute a means of redress available to the parties (para 9).

The Court insisted that the reference procedure is based on cooperation. The national courts[230] enjoy full discretion as to whether to refer a case to the ECJ. Where the outcome of a case does not depend on an interpretation of Community law, where there has already been a ruling of the ECJ, or where the meaning of Community law is clear (*acte clair* doctrine), there is no obligation to refer. But the Court made an important qualification: *acte clair* does not depend on the discretion of the *judex a quo*, but it:

> must be convinced that the matter is equally obvious to the courts of the other Member States and to the Court of Justice (para 16).

This later requirement is of course difficult to fulfil, especially with now 25 jurisdictions. The Court added several criteria on when this possibility would theoretically exist, always keeping in mind the peculiarity of Community law and its concepts, the different languages used which have equal force of law, and the context in which Community law must be interpreted (§ 3). These requirements effectively limit frequent application of the *acte clair* doctrine and insist on the priority of the ECJ in interpreting Community law.

A similar spirit of "exclusivity" can be seen in the later *Foto Frost* case[231]. The preliminary question concerned the power of a national court to invalidate a Community measure. The Court insisted that Member State courts may judge on the validity of a Community act in a positive way, but they:

> do not have the power to declare acts of the Community institutions invalid (para 15).

This is due to the "necessary coherence of the system of judicial protection established by the Treaty", which is based upon a clear division of powers and competences. Later case law has clarified the scope of the reference procedure in the interest of uniformity and coherence of Community law:

---

[229] Case 283/81 Srl CILFIT and Lanificio di Gavardo SpA v Ministry of Health, [1982] ECR 3415.
[230] Including those mentioned in para 3 of Art. 234 EC.
[231] Case 314/85 Foto-Frost v HZA Lübeck Ost [1987] ECR 4199.

- Only courts of law, and not (private) arbitration, or consumer complaint tribunals whose jurisdiction is not mandatory, may refer a case to the ECJ;[232] however, if the arbitration award is subject to judicial scrutiny on public policy grounds, the reference procedure is available.[233]
- The court must fulfil judicial, not administrative, functions, as in cases concerning the registration of a company or a commercial agent.[234]
- The questions put forward must not merely be hypothetical but have a genuine relevance to the case at hand.[235]

In general, the ECJ allows a broad margin of discretion to Member State courts to decide on the relevance, on the questions posed, and on the potential application to the specific case at hand. It is not necessary that the date for implementation of the directive should have lapsed. Indeed, early reference may even be necessary in order to allow adequate judicial protection, which is not possible by a direct action challenging the directive.[236] The national courts may even ask preliminary questions in cases where the applicable law has not been enacted, in doing so fulfilling a duty of implementation, but using the same or at least similar terminology in the interest of harmonization of national with Community law.[237]

These cases make clear that the Court insists on its final say to interpret and its monopoly to invalidate Community law in the interest of its uniform application. Its decisions in the reference procedure therefore have a *de facto stare decisis* authority. It is only the Court itself (or the Community legislator) that can "overrule" an interpretation given by the Court (§ 2 II).

2. *The new function of the reference procedure: (indirect) individual rights protection*

In the meantime, the second function of the reference procedure has become clearer, owing to limited direct access by individuals to European courts (*infra* IV). The basic

---

[232] Case 102/81 Nordsee Deutsche Hochseefischerei GmbH v Reederei Mond Hochseefischerei Nordstern AG & Co. KG [1982] ECR 1095; C-125/04 Guy Denuit et al. v Transorient – Mosaique Voyages et Culture SA, [2005] ECR I-(27.1.2005).
[233] Case C-126/97 Eco Swiss China Time Ltd v Benetton International NV. [1999] ECR I-3055.
[234] Case C-111/94 Job Centre Coop. ARL. [1995] ECR I-3361 at para 11.
[235] Case 244/80 Pasquale Foglia v Mariella Novello [1981] ECR 3045 at para 16.
[236] Case C-491/01 The Queen v Secretary of State for health *ex parte*: British American Tobacco (Investments) Ltd. *et al.* [2002] ECR I-11453 at para 40.
[237] Cases C-297/88 + 197/89 Dzodzi v Belgium [1990] ECR I-3763 at para 36; C-7/97 Oscar Bronner GmbH & Co. KG v Mediaprint Zeitungs- und Zeitschriftenverlag GmbH & Co. KG.[1998] ECR I-7791.

approach, as recognized by the Court, describes a decentralized *three step procedure* of judicial protection of individual rights in the Union:

- The first and decisive step is taken by the national court system. This must meet the requirements of effective protection, as defined by the Court. It includes the grant of effective remedies as *obligation de moyens*.
- The Court may – and, in those instances against whose decisions there is no judicial remedy, must – be asked to give a binding ruling on the interpretation or validity of a question of Community law, insofar as it is relevant for the decision of the case; merely "hypothetical" questions should not be referred to the ECJ.
- In a third step, the procedure is turned back to the national *judex a quo*, which has to apply the Court ruling to the individual case before it; the ECJ is not allowed to decide the particular case, even though it has given such precise rulings in some cases that the national court could not decide otherwise.[238]

In this decentralized system, it is really the national judge, and not the ECJ or the CFI, which protects Community rights under equal conditions as national rights. The national judge becomes the *European judge*.

These two functions of the reference procedure may conflict in cases where a speedy remedy is sought. If the Court of Justice has exclusive authority to annul a Community act that forms the basis for a Member State measure, a final decision on the validity of the contested Community measure under the reference procedure would now take about 2 years. Thus, no speedy remedy would then be possible.[239] On the other hand, if the national court were allowed to set aside the application of the Community measure, this would infringe the division of competences as defined in *Foto Frost*, and the uniformity of Community law, to the unilateral benefit of individual rights protection. In *Zuckerfabrik*[240], the Court was asked to balance the interests of a party to proceedings in rapid protection against a presumably illegal Community measure violating its rights, with the interests of the Community in coherence and uniform application of EC law under the final responsibility of the ECJ. The Court allowed the national court to suspend enforcement in order to protect individual rights under the following conditions:

- The national court must have serious doubts as to the validity of the Community regulation on which the contested administrative measure is based.

---

[238]   Cf. as an example case C-470/93 Verein gegen Unwesen in Handel und Gewerbe Köln e.V. v Mars GmbH [1995] ECR I-1923.
[239]   An expedited procedure is now available in urgent and exceptional cases under Art. 104a of the Rules of Procedure of the Court, OJ L 122/43 of 2000.
[240]   Joined cases C-143/88 and 92/89 Zuckerfabrik Süderdithmarschen AG v Hauptzollamt Ithehoe and Zuckerfabrik Soest GmbH v Hauptzollamt Paderborn [1991] ECR I-415.

- The national court must refer the question of validity of the Community regulation at issue to the ECJ.
- The grant of relief must be subject to uniform conditions in all Member States; therefore, a balancing test is required between the Community interest in maintaining the regulation and the individual interest in suspending it.
- The national court must take due account of ECJ case law.[241]

However, the national court is not empowered to order positive measures that only a Community institution may take.[242]

It is the reference procedure through which the "great developments" of Community law – such as direct effect, supremacy, proportionality, state liability for infringement of Community rights – have been transformed from an imperfect and incomplete legal order to a coherent system of judicial protection and control. This simple fact shows its inherent potential for the protection of individual rights, even though the individual is in fact denied an independent right of standing. A violation of the duty to refer may therefore provoke state liability if the breach has been sufficiently serious and a causal link can be shown between the violation of the duty to refer and the damage (§ 19 II 3).[243]

3. Protection against directives

It is not yet clear how the *Zuckerfabrik* doctrine functions in cases involving protection against directives. Under Community law, directives may take vertical direct effect against the State in favour of individuals, but may not impose obligations upon individuals (§ 3 II). However, directives may be used for interpretation purposes, thereby indirectly extending existing obligations, or even imposing new ones. Yet from a formal point of view, only the implementing state measures will have a mandatory effect on the individual. On the other hand, the Member State is bound by Community law to enforce a directive under the conditions set out therein, in order to avoid state liability under the governance rules (§ 19 II). The mere existence of a directive to be implemented within a specified time frame will have a certain anticipatory effect on the legal position of the individual, on their business strategies, opportunities, and operational planning. Does the individual or undertaking fearing an infringement of its supposed rights by a foreseeable implementation of a directive have a remedy

---

[241]   Case C-465/93 Atlanta Fruchthandelsgesellschaft *et al.* v Bundesamt für Ernährung und Forstwirtschaft [1995] ECR I-3761 at para 46.

[242]   Case C-68/95 T. Port GmbH & Co. KG v Bundesanstalt für Landwirtschaft und Ernährung [1996] ECR I-6065.

[243]   Cf. opinion of AG Leger of 8.4.2003 in case C-224/01 G. Köbler v. Republic of Austria [2003] ECR I-10239.

against the directive itself, or does it have to wait until an implementing measure (such as administrative or criminal proceedings) is directed against it, only then contesting the validity of the directive under the conditions of *Foto Frost* via a reference procedure?

Since, as we shall see, the individual has no direct access to Community jurisdiction for the protection of their rights, even if they have a fundamental rights quality, it is up to the national courts to allow for adequate protection before implementation of the directive. The English courts have construed preventive action against the threat of an implementing measure if the national legislator or regulator had no choice of action.[244] A similar remedy does not seem to exist in other jurisdictions.

It can be argued that the national courts are under a requirement to extend standing under their obligation to provide effective remedies. Their "procedural autonomy" is subject to the principle of effective judicial protection and control. This includes the creation of new remedies which so far had not existed under national law.[245]

IV. LIMITED DIRECT ACCESS TO EUROPEAN JURISDICTIONS: ART. 230 (4) EC

1. Absence of a constitutional complaint in EU law against legislative acts

Such a distribution of responsibilities as described explains why specific Community law procedures are only available if individuals are *directly and individually* concerned by Community measures.[246] The wording seems to exclude any protection against legislative measures of the Community, be they regulations or directives. The individual has to seek protection of its alleged rights before national courts. In matters of Community law these act, as we have seen, as Community courts and may eventually have to refer a case to the ECJ via the reference procedure.

This is true even in cases where the individual claims a violation of fundamental rights. For Community law, unlike many Member State laws, has not yet developed a constitutional complaint system against legislative measures. In this way, it is far behind the standard of European human rights law and the constitutional traditions common to many Member States (with the exception of some countries, such as the

---

[244] Case C-74/99 The Queen v Secretary of State for Health and others, *ex parte* Imperial Tobacco Ltd and Others [2000] ECR I-8599 re tobacco litigation.
[245] Van Gerven at 522-526.
[246] Per Art. 230 (4) EC.

256

UK, France, and Sweden). Art. 46 lit. d) EU allows protection of fundamental rights under Art. 6 (2) EU against actions of Community institutions only "insofar as the Court has jurisdiction" (§ 12 II 2).

The Charter of Fundamental Rights of the EU has not changed this distribution of competences. It does not establish any new powers or tasks for the Community or the Union, nor does it modify the powers and tasks defined by the Treaties.[247] This amounts to a refusal to grant new judicial remedies against violations of the Charter.

2. The limited scope of direct actions under Community law

Art. 230 (4) EC – as the basic norm for direct actions of individuals – distinguishes three types of Community measures that may be contested before Community jurisdictions. These are now the Court of First Instance, with possible appeal to the ECJ:
– a decision addressed to a (natural or legal) person;
– a decision not addressed to that person but to another person and which is of direct and individual concern to that person;
– a decision in the form of a regulation being of direct and individual concern to another person.

This *numerus clausus* of Community measures against which direct action by an individual is possible has a number of ambiguities. These have given rise to an abundant and somewhat conflicting case law.[248] As a starting point it should be kept in mind that direct action under Community law has the character of *an administrative law remedy*. It seems completely to exclude actions against general, namely legislative, measures. Only under the qualified circumstances of direct and individual concern may a regulation – which according to the wording of the Treaty must be regarded in substance as a decision – be challenged. Directives seem to be completely excluded from Community jurisdiction.[249] A brief look at Court practice will be concerned with only whether individual, or also group or general interest actions, are allowed under Community law.

3. Regulations of direct and individual concern

Regulations under Community law are hybrid measures. According to Art. 249 (2) they have "general application" and are "directly applicable". General application

---

[247] According to Art. 51 Charter = Art. II-111 of the Draft Constitution.
[248] For details cf. Arnull, *CMLRev* 2001, 7; Reich, in: Micklitz/Reich, *Public Interest Litigation*, 1996 at 12-16.
[249] Under Art. 230 (4) EC.

seems to indicate their legislative character, thereby excluding individual concern, even if they are able to directly confer rights and impose obligations on individuals.

The case law of the Court was thus concerned with singling out those regulations that are of individual concern to persons directly subjected to them. The formula which had been developed by the famous *Plaumann* case of 1963[250] demands that the measure in question affects natural or legal persons:

> by reason of certain attributes which are peculiar to them or by reason of legal or factual circumstances in which they are differentiated from all other persons and by virtue of these factors distinguishes them individually just as in the case of the person addressed.

The Court seems to use a test based on *equal treatment*. That is, in normal circumstances, a measure of legislative character, like a regulation, treats all potential addressees similarly. Since everybody in the sense of "*quivis ex populo*" is concerned, nobody is entitled to contest the measure[251] because of its general applicability. However, there may be cases – due to legal or factual circumstances – where one individual is singled out from the general public. Then this individual – and only that individual – is entitled to direct action. It is not important whether the legislative measure poses a particular hardship on him. Later case law was concerned with defining certain types of situations where this individual concern could be established under equality criteria:

- EC law may require that the effects of a measure to certain persons be particularly taken into account. That is, even if the measure is of general character in the form of a regulation, it is still of individual concern to those persons whom Community law aims to protect, such as importers or exporters of agricultural products forming a "closed class".[252]
- A Community regulation is only adopted after certain persons or groups have had their right to a hearing, in particular in anti-dumping proceedings, but these rights have been violated.[253]
- Certain factual situations are of specific concern to individuals, for example to independent importers of products that have to pay a particular anti-dumping tariff,[254] or to the proprietor of a graphic trade mark taken away by a Community regulation.[255]

---

[250] Case 25/62 Plaumann & Co v Commission [1963].
[251] Under Art. 230 (4) EC.
[252] Case 11/82 SA Piraiki-Patraiki and others v Commission [1985] 207; C-152/88 Sofimport SARL v Commission [1990] ECR I-2477; C-451/98 Antillean Rice Mills NV v Council of the European Union [2001] ECR I-8949; for further details Arnull at 31-41.
[253] Case 264/82 Timex Corporation v Council and Commission of the European Communities [1985] ECR 849.
[254] Case C-358/89 Extramet Industrie SA v Council of the European Communities [1991] ECR I-2501.
[255] Case C-309/89 Codorniú v Council of the European Union [1994] ECR I-1853.

It appears from this overview that Community courts enjoy a certain amount of discretion whether to admit an action or not, a fact that makes any prediction as to the admissibility of an action difficult. Such legal insecurity violates the principle of effective judicial protection.

The situation is particularly unsatisfactory with regard to group actions, which Community law prescribes the Member States to accept in several areas such as non-discrimination (§ 11 III 5b), but does not seem to be willing to allow its own plaintiffs. The Court has repeatedly insisted that for a group action to be admissible it is not sufficient that the members of the group are individually concerned:[256]

> ... moreover one cannot accept the principle that an association, in its capacity as the representative of a category of businessmen, could be individually concerned by a measure affecting the general interests of that category. Such a principle would result in the grouping, under the heading of a single legal person, of the interests properly attributed to the members of a category, who have been affected as individuals by genuine regulations, and would derogate from the system of the treaty which allows applications for annulment by private individuals only of decisions which have been addressed to them or of acts which affect them in a similar matter.

Only if the group itself (for example, a producers' or consumers' association) is individually concerned does it have a right to action.[257] This may be the case if their "procedural participation right" has been violated.[258] But in general the Court has been hostile to group actions.[259]

Community jurisdictions have discussed whether standing should be extended in particular by having regard to fundamental rights developments. In its *Jégo-Quéré* judgment of 3.5.2002,[260] the Court of First Instance referred to Art. 47 of the Charter of Fundamental Rights, which grants the right to an effective legal remedy. As discussed above, the existing system of Community law remedies, in particular the reference procedure, does not allow an effective remedy. The same is true of the potentiality of

---

[256] Case 16 + 17/62 Confédération nationale des producteurs de fruits et légumes and others v Council of the European Economic Community [1962] 471 at 477.

[257] Under Art. 230 (4) EC.

[258] Reich in: Micklitz/Reich at p. 15.

[259] Case 246/81 Nicholas William, Lord Bethell, v Commission [1982] ECR 2277; C-321/95P Stichting Greenpeace Council (Greenpeace International) and Others v Commission [1998] I-1651; for a broader discussion cf. the contributions of Reich, Micklitz, Dauses, Gormley, Weatherill, Wenig, Nettesheim, Krämer, Betlem and Christianos, in: Micklitz/Reich *passim*.

[260] Case T-177/01 Jégo-Quéré & Cie SA v Commission [2002] ECR II-2365. The ECJ set aside the Jégo-Quéré-judgment of the CFI, case C-263/02P [2004] ECR I-(1.4.2004) because "such an interpretation has the effect of removing all meaning from the requirement of individual concern set out in the fourth paragraph of Art. 230 EC" (para 37).

the injured individual to receive compensation[261] (§ 18 II). Therefore, the requirement of "individual concern" should be widened to cases where a Community law provision directly curtails rights or imposes obligations (para 51 of judgment).

In his opinion of 21 March 2002[262] on *Union de pequeños agricultores* (UPA), concerning a group action of an association of small agricultural producers challenging a regulation which substantially reduced their production quotas of olive oil, AG Jacobs critically analysed existing case law and proposed a more open and flexible solution to the criteria of "individual concern". He argued for the constitutional importance of effective judicial protection and on the evolution of Community law in the direction of governance and democratic legitimacy. He also referred to prior case law of the ECJ, acknowledging an evolutionary interpretation of Art. 230 (4) EC. The criteria proposed by him suggest that an:

> applicant is individually concerned by a Community measure where the measure has, or is liable to have, a *substantial adverse effect* (italics NR) on his interest (paras 60, 102).

However, it must be doubted whether the new criterion of *substantiality* instead of equality is of much help to Community courts and their parties in determining admissibility of an action. Only after having reviewed the substance of a case will one know whether or not a party is substantially concerned by a Community regulation. Substantiality can thereby only be determined *ex post,* not *ex ante.*

In its decision of 25 July 2002, the Court was not convinced of the new criteria proposed by AG Jacobs. It insisted on the one hand on the right of effective judicial protection, but on the other hand made the Member States responsible for granting it (para 41). Member States, in their duty of loyal co-operation under Art. 10 EC are:

> required, so far as possible, to interpret and apply national procedural rules governing the exercise of rights of action in a way that enables natural and legal persons to challenge before the courts the legality of any decision or other national measure relative to the application to them of a Community act of general application, by pleading the invalidity of such an act (para 42).

The Court no more and no less requires Member States to institute a quasi-constitutional complaint mechanism against Community legislative acts, always keeping in mind that the final decision as to illegality remains within Community

---

[261]   Under Art. 288 (2) EC.
[262]   Case C-50/00P Unión de pequeños agricultores v Council [2002] ECR I-6677.

jurisdiction. Within such a system of judicial control, the Court will review the constitutionality of a Community measure.[263]

The Court found no justification for extending standing beyond existing case law. It referred this question to the Member States as "Masters of the Treaty". In turn, they are only entitled to reform the system currently in force by amending the Treaty.

The judgment of the Court can be seen as an attempt to put the responsibility for effective judicial protection back to the Member States. They – not the Community – have to extend their judicial mechanisms. Direct action will remain as before a mainly administrative remedy. The quasi-constitutional remedy against legislative acts is to be provided by Member States within the framework of the reference procedure.

Unfortunately, however, this shifting back of responsibilities does not settle the main problem posed by the Court in its insistence on division of responsibilities between Community and Member State courts, and its exclusive power to annul Community acts. That is, Member State courts are competent to decide on Community law only indirectly via implementing Community measures, and not directly via allowing an action against a Community regulation or decision, as has been correctly pointed out by AG Jacobs.[264] In cases where a regulation or decision with substantial effects on third persons is self-executing and does not require additional Member State implementation measures, judicial protection is in effect denied, contrary to the principles declared by the Court.

4. Protection against directives

Directives are not mentioned among the acts to be challenged under Art. 230 (4). Therefore, by *argumentum e contrario* the Court has persistently held that there is no direct action against them.[265] As has been held by the Court of First Instance and upheld on appeal by the ECJ:

> (T)he justification for that exclusion (of directives from judicial review – NR) lies in the fact that, in the case of directives, the judicial protection of individuals is duly and sufficiently assured by the national courts, which review the transposition of directives into the domestic law of the various Member States.

---

[263]   According to Art. 46 lit. d) EU.
[264]   Paras 41-48 of his opinion.
[265]   Case T-99/94 Asociación Española de Empresas de la Carne v Council [1994] ECR II-871, upheld on appeal Case C-10/95P [1995] ECR I-4149.

Furthermore, even supposing that it were possible – contrary to the wording of the fourth paragraph of Art. 173 of the Treaty (now Art. 230 EC, NR) – to treat directives as regulations in order to allow proceedings against a decision "in the form of" a directive, the directive at issue neither constitutes a "disguised" decision nor contains any specific provision which has the character of an individual decision. On the contrary, it is a normative measure of general application (paras 17-18).

This rather formal argument could be supported by the fact that directives do not allow for a direct imposition of duties upon individuals. Therefore, they cannot be of "direct concern" to them. As a result, it not necessary to question their "individual" concern.

However, this argument can be challenged from two directions:
- Certain directives leave to Member States such a narrow margin of discretion that they impose *de facto* obligations upon individuals even before enactment of implementing measures; individuals have to adopt their business plans and legal action in expectation of implementation.
- Other directives may in reality be disguised decisions[266] just like regulations, and therefore fulfil the criteria of direct and individual concern.

In the actions brought by tobacco manufacturers and advertisers against Dir. 98/43,[267] the CFI was not convinced of their direct and individual concern. It insisted on a formal reading of direct effect, which by definition is not possible with regard to imposing obligations upon individuals. Again it is left to the Member States to provide for adequate remedies. The individual injured by a measure implementing a (potentially illegal) directive may claim compensation as a remedy of last resort.[268] However, such a conclusion is not satisfactory, because it does not take into account the preventive effect of judicial protection, and gives a remedy only when "it is too late".[269]

5. New proposals to extend standing in the Draft Constitution

The Draft Constitution has proposed an Art. III-365 (4), which will read:

> Any natural or legal person may, under the same conditions, institute proceedings against an act addressed to that person or which is of direct and individual concern to him or her,

---

[266] In the sense of Art. 230 (4) EC.

[267] For details cf. Reich, FS Winter, 2003, 152.

[268] Case T-172, 175-177/98 Salamander AG, Una Film "City Revue" GmbH, Alma Media Group Advertising SA & Co. Partnership, Panel Two and Four Advertising SA & Co, Rythmos Outdoor Advertising SA, Media Center Advertising SA, Zino Davidoff SA and Davidoff & Cie SA v European Parliament and Council [2000] ECR II-2487 at para 78.

[269] Cf. the critique by Arnull at 50; Nettesheim, *Juristenzeitung* 2002, 928 at 934.

and against a regulatory act which is of direct concern to him or her and does not entail implementing procedures (italics NR).

This amendment will solve the problem left by the *UPA case* where a regulation or some other Community act did not need implementing measures and therefore could not be attacked before a national court. The decisive criteria will be *direct* concern; individual concern is not necessary anymore. Therefore, it will not be applicable in direct actions against directives which in the case-law of the Court, cannot impose obligations upon individuals (§ 2 II 3).

CHAPTER IV. AUTONOMY

Table of Contents

Selected Bibliography

J. Basedow, "A Common Contract Law for the Common Market", *CMLRev* 1995,
1169; H. Beale/O. Lando (eds.), *Principles of European Contract Law*, I + II, III, 2000,
2003 (Principles); H.E. Brander/P. Ulmer, "The Community Directive on Unfair
Terms in Consumer Contracts", *CMLRev* 1991, 647; J. M. Broekman, *A Philosophy
of European Union law*, 1999; D. Friedmann/D. Barak-Erez (eds.), *Human rights in
Private Law*, 2001; W. van Gerven, "Codifying European private law? Yes, if... !",
ELRev. 2002, 156; W. van Gerven, "Harmonisation of private law: Do we need it?",
CMLRev 2004, 505; St. Grundmann, *Europäisches Schuldvertragsrecht*, 1999; St.
Grundmann, "Information, Party Autonomy and Economic Agents in European
Contract Law", *CMLRev* 2002, 269; St. Grundmann/W. Kerber/St. Weatherill (eds.),

Party Autonomy and the Role of Information in the Internal Market, 2001 (cited Grundmann *et al.*); St. Grundmann/J. Stuyck (eds.), *An Academic Green Paper on European Contract Law,* 2002 (Grundmann/Stuyck); A. Hartkamp *et al.* (eds.), *Towards a European Civil Code,* 1998, 2nd ed. 2001; J. Karsten/ A.R. Sinai, "The Action Plan on European Contract Law: Perspectives for the Future of European Contract Law and EC Consumer Law", *JCP* 2003, 159; M. Kenny, "The 2003 Action Plan on European Contract Law: is the Commission Running Wild? *EL Rev* 2003, 538; E.M. Kieninger, *Wettbewerb der Privatrechtsordnungen im Europäischen Binnenmarkt,* 2002; M. Kiikeri, *Comparative Legal reasoning and European Law,* 2001; St. Leible (Hrsg.), *Das Grünbuch zum Internationalen Vertragsrecht,* 2004; B. Lurger, *Grundfragen der Vereinheitlichung des Vertragsrechts in der EU,* 2002; H.-W. Micklitz, "Perspektiven eines Europäischen Privatechts", *ZEuP* 1998, 253; H.-W. Micklitz, "The Principles of European Contract Law and the Protection of the Weaker Party", *JCP* 2004, 339; J. Ramberg, *International Commercial Transaction,* 3rd ed. 2004; M. Radeideh, *Fair Trading in EC Law – Information and Consumer Choice in the Internal Market,* 2005; N. Reich, *Sozialismus und Zivilrecht,* 1972; N. Reich/S. Harbacevica, "The Stony Road to Brussels", *Europarättslig Tijdskrift* 20002, 411; N. Reich/ A. Halfmeier, "Consumer protection in the Global Village", *Dickinson Law Review* 2001, 111; N. Reich, "The tripartite function of modern contract law in Europe: Enablement, regulation, information", in: Werro/Probst, *Das schweizerische Privatrecht im Lichte des europäischen Gemeinschaftsrechts,* 2004, 145; N. Reich, *Transformation of Contract law and civil justice in new EU member countries,* RGSL Working papers 21, 204; O. Remien, *Zwingendes Vertragsrecht und Grundfreiheiten des EG-Vertrages,* 2003; J. Smits (ed.), *The Need for a European Contract Law,* 2005; J. Smits, *The Making of European Private Law,* 2002; D. Staudenmayer, "The Commission Action Plan on European Contract Law", *ERPrL* 2003, 113; D. Staudenmayer, "The Place of Consumer Contract Law within the Process on European Contract Law", *JCP* 2004, 269; E. Steindorff, *EG-Vertrag und Privatrecht,* 1996; Study Group, "Social Justice in European Contract Law: Manifesto", *ELJ* 2004, 653; G. Wagner, "The Economics of Harmonisation: The Case of Contract Law", *ERA-Forum* 2002, 77; St. Weatherill, "The European Commission's Green Paper on European Contract Law: Context, Content and Constitutionality", *Journal of Consumer Policy* 2001, 339; Th. Wilhelmsson, *European Contract Law and Social Values,* 1995; Th. Wilhelmsson, "Private Law in the EU: Harmonised or Fragmented Europeanisation?", *ERPL* 2002, 77; Th. Wilhelmsson, "The Abuse of the 'Confident Consumer' as a Justification for EC Consumer Law", *JCP* 2004, 317; Th. Wilhelmsson, "Varieties of Welfarism in European Contract Law", *ELJ* 2004, 712.

§ 15. FUNDAMENTAL FREEDOMS, COMPETITION AND AUTONOMY

I. FREEDOMS WITHIN THE LAW

Primary Community law presupposes the autonomy of economic actors, but does not in itself guarantee it expressly.[1] On the other hand, every liberal legal order has autonomy as its basic philosophy. Open market economy only exists if actors can freely decide what markets to enter – and which not. *Vice-versa*, on the demand side potential clients – whether business or consumer – should be free to choose the products, services, and suppliers they prefer. *Freedom of decision* for active market citizens and *freedom of choice* for consumers and clients is one of its governing principles.

These freedoms are supplemented by the *freedom of contract* both in a positive and a negative sense:
– *Positive* insofar as it implies the freedom to choose partners with whom to enter into contractual negotiations, freedom of content such as price and quality of products and services offered and purchased, freedom of conditions that determine performance.
– *Negative* insofar as – in contrast to former socialist economy[2] – nobody can be forced to enter into any contract, parties may opt out of (non-mandatory) Member State contract law by choice of law and jurisdiction-clauses, and nobody will have the content of their contract prescribed by the state or other third party.

If a party breaching a contract is forced by law to perform specific performance or to pay compensation, this consequence is not determined by an imposed rule, but is the logical result of the free will of the parties. Therefore, *pacta sunt servanda* as a fundamental rule of contract law is the realization of the free will of the parties themselves.

Freedom of contract is complemented by *freedom of association*. Economic actors may decide to co-operate by pooling resources, or entering the market by founding a new entity in order to combine their financial and intellectual resources, Member State law provides for institutions and rules on how this freedom of association can be realized. Since the forms of co-operation by association are more complex and longer

---

[1] Müller-Graff, in: Grundmann *et al.*, Party autonomy and the role of information in the internal market, 2001 at 135-150.
[2] For a discussion in the historical perspective cf. Reich, *Sozialismus und Zivilrecht*, 1972; for an analysis of developments after the "fall of socialism" see Reich, *Transformation of contract law in new Member countries*, 2004; Remien, *Zwingendes Vertragsrecht und Grundfreiheiten des EG-Vertrages*, 2003.

lasting than those by contract, legal rules may be more stringent and not allow the same amount of freedom as in contract law. This applies both between the cooperating parties themselves (rules on capital, conditions and terms) and between them and third parties (rules on protection of employees or creditors). But again, these limits on the freedom of association do not contradict the liberal model, but only make its realization possible. Law has a supporting function where the free will of the associates is not sufficient to realize the goals upon which they have agreed. Since the association usually involves third parties to a greater extent than a simple contract, mandatory rules of law may be more frequent here. But again: this depends on Member State law. Primary Community law is silent on these matters.

II. FUNDAMENTAL FREEDOMS AND AUTONOMY

1. Free movement of goods and freedom of contract

As has been seen, Art. 28 EC is one of the fundamental rules of the European economic constitution in imposing the principle of open markets for products against unreasonable and disproportionate Member State restrictions (§ 7 II). It says nothing about freedom of contract. It takes it for granted. Freedom of contract is a precondition for the free movement of goods. If an economic actor were not free to choose contractual partners in another Member State, if he could not negotiate the contents of the contract or the terms of the agreement, and the applicable law and jurisdiction in case of disputes, then there would be no free movement of goods purchased under any contract. Goods – even if called "movables" – do not move by themselves but through the instrument of contract. Community law is therefore hostile to any restrictions on the contractual freedom of the parties, provided that these restrictions come into the sphere of application of the EC.

On the other hand, the ECJ has denied the applicability of the free movement rules where commercial partners can avoid Member State law restricting their freedom. In the *Alsthom* case, the Court was concerned with the question of whether the French rules on strict liability of a seller with regard to defects in a product in the chain of distribution amount to a restriction on free movement in the sense of Arts. 28 and 29 EC. The Court insisted that "the parties in an international contract are generally free to determine the law applicable to their contractual relations and can thus avoid being subject to French Law."[3] This amounts to an implicit recognition of the parties' freedom to contract. If a party is free to avoid a Member State rule restricting its

---

[3]   Case C-339/89 Alsthom Atlantique v Compagnie de construction mécanique Sulzer SA [1991] ECR
I- 107 at para 17.

freedom to contract with regard to applicable terms, there is no need for Community law intervention. On the other hand, where Member State law imposes mandatory rules which cannot be avoided by choice of a more liberal law, there may be a conflict with the free movement rules. One example would be restrictions imposed on the sale of certain goods.

2. Freedom to provide services

The Community law rules on the freedom to provide services (§ 7 III) are closer to the general principle of freedom of contract because the contents of a service, especially with regard to financial services, are usually determined by the contract itself. The only requirement of Community law is that the service be provided against remuneration,[4] while it is not necessary that this remuneration be part of the contract itself if a third party is financing the service.[5] If Member State law contains mandatory rules on the contents of certain services, if it restricts the provision of or access to certain services cross-border wise, if it imposes requirements on the qualification of service providers such as prior authorization, then this amounts both to a restriction on the free provision of services according to Art. 49 EC[6] and to a restriction of freedom to contract usually governed by Member State law. The rules on open markets and on freedom to contract coincide, always provided that an economic activity is concerned. Since the freedom to provide services is not only granted in the objective interest of establishing an internal market, but also as a subjective right to the economic actors themselves, Community law therefore contains an indirect yet powerful tool to recognize freedom of and to contract.

3. Free movement of capital

The original EEC Treaty did not contain the principle of free movement of capital as a directly applicable rule.[7] On the other hand, the Court recognized the *freedom of payment* as a corollary to the free movement of goods and services.[8] This is of course in line with the general yet implicit recognition of freedom of contract: If one party is free to offer its goods and services for "sale" and to agree to their contractual performance, the other party is not only free to accept (or reject) these at a negotiated price, but must also be able to actually pay the negotiated price. Free movement of goods and services would be paralysed if not supplemented by freedom of payment.

---

[4]   Case C-159/90 The society for the Protection of Unborn Children v Grogan [1991] ECR I-4685.
[5]   Case 352/88 Bond van Adverteerders v The Netherland's State [1988] ECR I-2085.
[6]   Case C-275/92 HM Customs and Exercise Service v Schindler [1994] ECR I-1039 concerning lotteries; these restrictions may however be justified by public policy reasons.
[7]   Case 203/80 Casati [1981] ECR 2595.
[8]   Cases 26 + 286/83 Luisi and Carbone v Ministero del Tesoro [1984] ECR 377.

Member State restrictions on the free flow of payments in order to fulfil cross-border transactions are contrary to the free movement rules themselves. But this ancillary freedom is only concerned with the execution of prior contracts, not the free flow of capital as such for investment and/or speculation purposes.

It was only through the Maastricht Treaty that Art. 73b, now Art. 56 EC was reformulated so as to introduce directly applicable rules on the free movement of capital (§ 7 IV). This includes all investment and monetary transactions on the capital markets.[9] It also implies the freedom to purchase real estate property in any Member State[10] unless certain restrictions are particularly allowed by the Treaty. An example would be the Protocol concerning the purchase of vacation homes in Denmark.[11] The Accession Treaties with the new Member countries contain restrictions on the acquisition of agricultural land.

4. Free movement of persons, freedom of contract and freedom of association

The guarantee of free movement to citizens of the Union (cf. § 4) implies the right to enter into any contractual relationship in order to make this freedom effective. Inversely, it forbids all discrimination based on nationality, even if imposed by collective agreements based on private law.[12] The main area of this freedom is concerned with labour contracts, but it can be extended to ancillary agreements such as on housing, maintenance, and education. If a Member State or a collective agreement imposes a language requirement on employment candidates, they cannot force these candidates to take the language test only through an institution accredited in that state.[13] This case shows very clearly the close link between open markets, freedom of choice, and freedom of contract.

5. Establishment and freedom of association

Freedom of association is inherent in the freedom of establishment, as guaranteed in Art. 43 and expressly extended to setting up companies or firms in Art. 48 EC:

> The right to form a company in accordance with the law of a Member State and to set up branches in other Member States is inherent in the exercise, in a single market, of the freedom of establishment guaranteed by the Treaty.

---

[9] Case C-478/98 Commission v Belgium [2000] ECR I-7587.
[10] Case C-423/98 Albore [2000] ECR I-5965.
[11] Protocol Nr. 1 attached to the Maastricht Treaty.
[12] Case C-415/93 ABSL v Bosman [1995] ECR I-4921.
[13] Case C-281/98 Roman Angonese v Casa di Risparmio di Bolzano [2000] I-4139.

This statement was pronounced by the Court in its seminal *Centros* judgment.[14] The Court refused to accept a Danish regulation on minimum capital requirements for a private limited company in order that its branch be registered. According to the facts of the case, the main office of the company was registered in the UK, which had hardly any requirements of minimum capital, but business was conducted in Denmark. In his opinion, AG La Pergola went even further in arguing that:

> the right of establishment is essential to the achievement of the objectives set in the Treaty, the purpose of which is to guarantee to all Community citizens alike the freedom to engage in business activities through the instruments provided by national law, thus giving them the *chance* to enter the market, irrespective of the motives that may actually have prompted the person concerned. In other words, it is the *opportunity* to exercise business activities that is protected, and with it the *contractual freedom* to make use of the instruments provided for that purpose in the legal systems of the Member States.[15]

However, this radical liberal position was not taken up by the Court. It is therefore still a debated question as to how far companies are free to opt for the most favourable law to their statutory regimes, notwithstanding mandatory rules on jurisdiction and applicable law.[16] The later *Überseering* case[17] referred to the different theories advanced in the international private law of Member States, namely the incorporation principle vs. the company seat principle. However, it avoided any clear answer on what theory is more in conformity with Community law. The Court seems to prefer a case-by-case approach, judging potential Member State conflict rules with regard to their restrictive effects and possible justifications. It insisted that freedom of establishment includes the right of a company not to lose judicial protection because of transfer of its business seat (§ 7 V).

Freedom of establishment includes the freedom to open up branches or agencies in any EU country. Therefore, directors of a company may not be excluded from a national sickness insurance benefit scheme for the sole reason that it does its business through a subsidiary in another Member State.[18] EC law leaves it to the free decision of economic actors where and in what form they want to organize their activities. The

---

[14] Case C-212/97, Centros Ltd v Erhvervs- og Selskabsstyrelsen [1999] ECR I-1459 at para 27.
[15] At 1477; italics La Pergola.
[16] For conflicting positions cf. Halbhuber, *CMLRev* 2001, 1385 (1395 ff.).
[17] Case C-208/00 Überseering v Nordic Construction Company Baumanagement (NCC) [2002] ECR I-9919 at paras 87 *et seq.*; in its sequel decision of 13.3.2003 the German Bundesgerichtshof rejected the traditional seat theory and opted for the incorporation theory in cases of change of the administrative seat of the foreign company.
[18] Case 79/85 D.H.M. Segers v Bestuur van de Bedrijfsvereniging [1986] ECR 2375.

only requirement for the applicability of the establishment rules is a certain permanent integration into the economic life of the chosen jurisdiction.[19]

Freedom of establishment has been extended to candidate countries by the Europe Agreements. It includes the right of free movement of leading personnel.[20]

6. Limitations to the guarantee of autonomy under primary Community law

Primary Community law is mostly concerned with the economic, not with the personal and philosophical aspects, of autonomy.[21] But it can be shown that the broad interpretation of Community freedoms also contain a personal element. Behind this, an individualistic concept of law – not just an economic one – can be discerned.[22] The right of Union citizens to free movement contains an implicit recognition of contractual autonomy without which this right would be worthless. Restrictions of this right need a specific justification under Community law.

This autonomy is not only guaranteed in B2B (business to business) relations, but also in B2C (business to consumer) and B2L (business to labour) relations. It is mostly concerned with cross-border transactions and therefore usually does not apply to "purely internal situations".[23] But it is hardly conceivable that Member States would deny their own citizens the autonomy which they are obliged to guarantee to EU citizens, even if so called "reverse discrimination" with some exceptions[24] does not come into the sphere of application of Community law.[25]

Autonomy is usually limited to Union citizens but may be extended to residents not being citizens in the traditional sense (§ 6), or third-country nationals by primary Community law, or by Association Agreements. This is true with regard to social partners who may conclude collective agreements[26], and with regard to consumers who may form consumer associations[27].

---

[19]   Case C-55/94 Gebhard v Consiglio dell'Ordine degli Avvocati e Procuratori di Milano [1995] ECR I-4165.
[20]   For a detailed account cf. Reich/Harbacevica, *Europarättslig Tidskrift* 2002, 411.
[21]   Broeckman at 106 ff.
[22]   Reich, Bürgerrechte at 158 ff.
[23]   Case C-332/90 Steen v Deutsche Bundespost [1992] ECR I-341.
[24]   For an overview Schermers/Waelbroeck, *Judicial protection*, 2001, at 91-93.
[25]   Case 14/68 Walt Wilhelm and others v Bundeskartellamt [1969] ECR 1; case 355/85 Driancourt v M. Cognet [1986] ECR 3231 at para 10.
[26]   Per Art. 139.
[27]   Per Art. 153 EC.

The movement and establishment provisions of the Europe Agreements concluded with future Member States have been regarded by the ECJ as being directly applicable.[28] These freedoms imply the guarantee of contractual autonomy within their sphere of application.

III.   COMPETITION LAW AND AUTONOMY

1. Provisions against restrictions of competition by contract

Art. 81 (1) EC is the fundamental rule on the protection of competition. If this rule has been violated by restrictive agreements, concerted practices or decisions of groups of undertakings, any contract with this objective or effect is regarded to be "automatically void"'[29]. Inversely, contracts promoting competition, for example by co-operation agreements, are valid. The competition rules thereby contain an implicit recognition of the autonomy principle insofar as concerns the enforceability of contracts not serving anti-competitive purposes.

In limiting the effects of the ban on anti-competitive contracts to a merely partial nullity[30], the ECJ tries as much as possible to respect the contractual will of the parties. Therefore, all consequential contracts concluded on the basis of anti-competitive agreements are valid. EC law interferes as little as possible in the contractual freedom of the parties and in the principles of *pacta sunt servanda*.

EC law also protects freedom of contract of economic partners, as can be seen from the reasoning in the *Courage* case:[31] The English rule banning partners in an anti-competitive agreement from claiming damages was set aside in the dispute between a brewery and a pub house which was bound by a tying agreement because this would limit effective enforcement of Community competition rules (§ 20 I 2). This right to damages of the smaller partner of an anti-competitive agreement is at the same time a tool protecting their freedom of contract. It re-establishes the contractual balance destroyed by the unilateral imposition of the tying agreement.

---

[28]   Cases C-63/99 R v Secretary of State for the Home Dpt. ex parte Wieslaw and Elzbieta Gloszcuk [2001] ECR I-6369; C-162/00 Land Nordrhein-Westphalen v Beata Pokrzeptowicz-Meyer [2002] ECR I-1049.

[29]   Art. 81 (2).

[30]   Case 56/65 Société Technique Minière v Maschinenbau Ulm [1996] ECR 235; C-234/89 Delimitis v Henninger-Bräu [1991] ECR I-935 at para 40.

[31]   Case C-453/99 Courage Ltd. v Bernard Crehan [2001] ECR I-6297.

2. Enforcing co-operation agreements as a precondition of competition

Competition law not only takes a negative role *vis-à-vis* contracts restraining competition, but either indirectly or directly exempts certain horizontal or vertical co-operation agreements from the competition rules. The ECJ has been rather generous in granting an implicit exemption to so-called franchise agreements by postulating that "such a system which allows the franchisor to profit from his success, does not in itself interfere with competition.[32]" On the other hand, the Court was hostile to restrictions impairing a franchisee's freedom to determine its own retail prices. Vertical price restraints as a limitation of the freedom to contract of a dealer or franchisee have ever since been regarded as anti-competitive.

The express or implied exemption of co-operation agreements from the competition rules has been ongoing for some time and cannot be analysed in detail here. Not only is a new economic reasoning as mentioned above (§ 9) responsible for this paradigm shift, but also a new understanding of autonomy: That is, economic actors are given more freedom in regulating their relations themselves, even if this provokes some anti-competitive effects, while competition law is not seen as a limit on autonomy but as a "long stop" against certain practices where freedoms are clearly used against public or third party interests. Therefore, modern competition law is restricted to fighting certain "hard-core restrictions" (§ 9 IV) such as price fixing and market separation. At the same time, it leaves to the parties the freedom to determine their co-operation forms themselves by autonomously limiting their freedom of action through anti-competition and exclusivity clauses. A good example is self-limitations imposed on lawyers by a (Dutch) lawyer's association statute concerning co-operation with accountants: Here, the agreement has anti-competitive effects but may be justified by professional considerations.[33]

Finally, abolition of the prior notification system of Reg. 17/62 by the new Reg. 1/2003 (§ 9 I) and the direct effect of Art. 81 (3) EC strengthen the autonomy of economic actors (undertakings). It also puts them at some risk, because the party invoking direct effect of Art. 81 (3) has the burden of proof.

3. The limited sphere of application of the competition rules

The competition rules only apply in B2B, not in B2C or B2L relations. State activities may come under the competition rules if they can be regarded as stemming from an

---

[32] Case 161/84 Pronuptia de Paris GmbH v Pronuptia de Paris Irmgard Schillgalis [1986] ECR 353 at para 15.

[33] Case C-309/99 J.C.J. Wouters, J.W. Savelbergh, Price Waterhouse Belastingadviseurs BV v Algemene Raad van de Nederlandse Orde van Advocaten [2002] ECR I-1577.

undertaking in the sense of Art. 81 or 82 EC, especially when it exercises a certain monopoly power on a (potential) market for goods or services (§ 9 IV). This is particularly true where a State enterprise has been vested with exclusive or special rights implicitly limiting the freedom of contract of its potential partners.[34]

Even when the competition rules apply against anti-competitive behavior, the principle of freedom of contract is still respected. In the *Bronner* case[35] the ECJ insisted that even market dominating enterprises are free to choose their methods of distribution and may therefore exclude competitors from access to their system.

4. Competition law and collective autonomy

Another field where the interplay between autonomy and competition has been discussed has been the limits of collective bargaining. The *Albany*[36] case concerned the question whether a compulsory affiliation to a sectoral pension scheme was compatible with the competition rules. In his carefully researched opinion based on comparative law, AG Jacobs argued that there is no general exemption for collective agreements from the competition rules. However, due to the social nature of such an agreement it is immune under certain circumstances, namely if it:
– was made in the general framework of the collective bargaining,
– was built on good faith,
– remained in the hard core of the traditional subject matter of collective agreement, and
– had no immediate effect on third parties.

The Court is somewhat broader in its respect for collective autonomy. Under an interpretation of the Treaty:

> as a whole which is both effective and consistent ... agreements concluded in the context of collective negotiation between management and labour in pursuit of such (i.e. social policy, NR) objectives must, by virtue of their nature and purpose, be regarded as falling outside the scope of Art. 81... (para. 46).

The Court implicitly recognized the priority of collective autonomy over the competition rules, albeit within certain limits.[37] The later *Pavlov* case[38] makes it clear

---

[34]   Case C-41/90 Höfner und Elser v Macroton [1991] ECR I-1979.
[35]   Case C-7/97 Oscar Bronner GmbH & Co. KG v Mediaprint [1998] ECR I-7791, also with reference to the controversial "essential facilities doctrine", § 10 III 2.
[36]   C-67/96 Albany Int. BV v Stichting Bedrijfspensioenfonds Textielindustrie [1999] ECR I-5751.
[37]   For a discussion cf. Kiikeri, *Comparative legal reasoning*, 2001 at 222-241.
[38]   Joined cases C-180-185/98 Pavel Pavlov and Others v Stichting Pensioenfonds Medische Specialisten [2000] ECR I-6451.

that this immunity relates only to collective bargaining in the traditional sense, not to rules by professional associations having anti-competitive effects.

IV. FREEDOM OF CONTRACT AS A FUNDAMENTAL RIGHT?

1. The implicit yet limited recognition of freedom of contract as a fundamental right

There has been a debate over whether the principle of freedom of contract can be regarded as a fundamental right in the sense of Art. 6 (2) EU. The ECHR does not expressly mention freedom of contract and therefore has had little impact on contract law theory.[39] However, it protects property in its Protocol Nr. 1. In doing so, it implicitly regards a contractual disposition of ownership as the normal legal way to acquire and use property. Property is not merely protected in a static sense, but also in the dynamic form of its acquisition and use by contract. There would be no protection of property if the contractual engagements undertaken in relationship to property were not respected.

2. The EU Charter of Fundamental Rights

Chapter II of the EU Charter (§ 12 III) is concerned with "Freedom" and guarantees freedom of association[40], the freedom to choose an occupation and right to engage in work[41], the freedom to conduct a business[42], and the right to property[43]. All these freedoms are exercised by contractual engagements. Contracts are the dynamic form of putting to work the freedoms of economic and civil actors, whether they use their right to association, to engage in work, to conduct a business, or to possess and use property.

Particularly interesting in this respect is the broad guarantee of the right to property which gives "everybody ... the right to own, use, dispose of and bequeath his or her lawfully acquired possessions". This right would be worthless without the dynamic element inherent in the freedom of contract as freedom to acquire goods and immovables, freedom to dispose of them by contract, freedom to enter into contracts

---

[39]   Elger & Brownswood in: Friedmann/Barak-Erez 2001 at 161, 181; Remien, *supra* note 2 at 172-177.
[40]   Charter of fundamental rights of the European Union [2000] OJ C 364/1 per Art. 12, now integrated into the Draft Constitution, Art. II-72.
[41]   Per Art. 15 of the Charter = Art. II-75.
[42]   Per Art. 16 of the Charter = Art. II-76.
[43]   Per Art. 17 of the Charter = Art II-77.

and to refuse to contract with any person at the will of the owner. Expropriation, that is, the taking of property without contract, is strictly regulated and limited by a public-interest test subject to fair compensation.

§ 16. AUTONOMY IN SECONDARY LAW INSTRUMENTS AND DOCUMENTS

I. SECONDARY LAW AS FACILITATOR AND CONTROLLER OF AUTONOMY

1. Absence of general recognition

Similar to primary law, secondary Community law and related instruments contain no express recognition of autonomy of parties in contractual relations. Autonomy is – with the exception of the Rome Convention (*infra* III) – presupposed, but not guaranteed. But it should be remembered that in the sphere of application of the EU fundamental freedom and competition rules, autonomy exercises a spill-over effect into secondary law. This, therefore, should not be restrictive beyond necessity, but should rather facilitate the use of the freedoms and avoid distortions of competition. In its *Tobacco-advertising* judgment, the Court annulled a Community directive which imposed a general ban on advertising and sponsoring of tobacco products and thereby indirectly disabled contractual relations, for example of producers and advertisers, in seeking optimal marketing arrangements for their products and services:

> By imposing a wide-ranging prohibition on the advertising of tobacco-products, the Directive would in the future generalise that restriction of forms of competition by limiting, in all Member States, the means available for economic operators to enter or remain in the market.[44]

In the meantime, Art. 3 (2) of Dir. 2004/113/EC of 13.12.2004 implementing the principle of equal treatment between men and women in the access to and supply of goods and services (§ 11 III 6) expressly states that it does not "prejudice the individual's freedom to choose a contractual partner as long as an individual's choice ... is not based on that person's sex".

2. Mandatory law as an exception

Community directives imposing certain standards on contractual relations with consumers or employees to protect their legitimate expectations (cf. § 13 IV/V) usually contain a mandatory law clause. This means that Member States, in transposing a directive, have to make sure that the standard introduced Community-wide by the directive cannot be contracted out of. Since the approach of the directive is fragmented

---

[44]   Case C-376/98 Germany v European Parliament and Council [2000] ECR I-8419 at para 113.

and sectoral, Community law thereby indirectly recognizes the freedom of contractual relations in areas not covered by the directive. This is particularly true in commercial relations which – with some exceptions – are not covered by Community law at all.

The Member States, by way of a minimal harmonization provision in a directive (*supra* § 3 III), may impose stricter limitations on contractual freedoms, but must always make sure that these rules comply with primary Community law. They should not make impossible the working of the fundamental freedoms. It is a debated and still undecided question how far they may go in this respect.

II. SECONDARY COMMUNITY LAW CONTAINING EXPRESS GUARANTEES OF AUTONOMY

1. *The Unfair terms directive*

The Unfair Terms Directive[45] (§ 13 IV 1) is the only Community law instrument which attempts a horizontal approach at contractual autonomy. This section is not so much concerned with its informative ambit by recognizing the transparency principle which will be discussed later (§ 17 II). Here, attention focuses onto Art. 4 (2) which reads:

> Assessment of the unfair nature of the terms shall relate neither to the definition of the main subject matter of the contract nor to the adequacy of the price and remuneration, on the one hand, as against the services or goods supplied in exchange, on the other, insofar as these terms are in plain intelligible language.

This is repeated somewhat more extensively in the recitals and extended to insurance contracts, which are not expressly covered by the wording of the directive as such:

> Whereas, for the purposes of this directive, assessment of the unfair character shall not be made of terms which describe the main subject matter of the contract nor the quality/price ratio of the goods or services supplied; whereas the main subject matter of the contract and the price/quality ratio may nevertheless be taken into account in assessing the fairness of other terms; whereas it follows, inter alia, that in insurance contracts, the terms which clearly define or circumscribe the insured risk and the insurer's liability shall not be subject to such assessment since these restrictions are taken into account in calculating the premium paid by the consumer.

This principle is far reaching and has been criticized by some authors.[46] Community law will respect the contractual freedom of parties with regard to the main subject

---

[45]   Council Directive 93/13/EC of 5. April 1993 on unfair terms in consumer contracts [1993] OJ L 95/29.
[46]   Howells/Wilhelmsson, *EC Consumer Law*, 1997 at 88-115.

matter of the contract. This is of particular importance in the area of financial services, as the reference to insurance contracts shows. The adequacy of the price/quality relation can usually only be determined by taking an overall look at the contractual clauses. It is therefore difficult to distinguish between those clauses which have a primary influence on the price/quality ratio, and those which only have a secondary importance. But the philosophy of Community law is clear: it does not aim to interfere in the autonomy of parties, even in pre-formulated consumer contracts, with regard to the main subject matter of the contract – the bargain itself.

A similar approach can be discerned with regard to the concept of unfairness of a term as such. Art. 3 (2) makes clear that only pre-formulated terms come under the unfairness test of the directive. This would include, for example, a term not individually negotiated "which has been drafted in advance and the consumer has therefore not been able to influence the substance of the term, particularly in the context of a standard contract". This formula stands in clear contrast to the earlier proposal by the Commission, which wanted also to submit individually negotiated terms to a fairness test. This, however, was worded somewhat differently. After criticism of this proposal[47], the present formulation was found. In doing so, it indirectly recognized contractual freedom with regard to terms, provided that these have been negotiated individually. That is, on the basis that contractual freedom can work effectively and is sufficient to avoid abuses by one party against the other. Where autonomy can be shown to work, Community law does not need to interfere. Member States may, under the minimal harmonization principle, go beyond this ban on controlling contractual terms. However, Community law seems to rely on autonomy and contractual freedom more than national law does.

In the *Freiburger Kommunalbauten*[48] case the Court insisted that it can only "interpret general criteria used by the Community legislature in order to define the concept of unfair terms. However, it should not rule on the application of these general criteria to a particular term, which must be considered in the light of the particular circumstances of the case in question" (para. 22). This implies a certain non-interference of Community law into Member State assessment of unfairness, an approach which strengthens both party and state autonomy.

---

[47] Ulmer/Brander *CMLRev* 1991, 647.
[48] Case C-237/02 Freiburger Kommunalbauten GmbH Baugesellschaft & Co KG v Ludger Hofstetter und Ulrike Hofstetter [2004] ECR I-(1.4.2004).

2. Brussels Convention resp. Regulation 44/2001

An important element of autonomy in contractual agreements is the freedom of the parties to choose the jurisdiction where they want to litigate their case. Procedural matters are usually left to Member State competence (§ 14 I). However, in cross-border litigation in civil and commercial matters which has a relationship to the Union, the former Brussels Convention (resp. the Lugano-Convention with regard to EFTA-countries) and now, from 1 March 2002 on, Regulation 44/2001[49] are applicable (§ 14 II 2). With the exception of consumer and labour contracts, these allow for a rather generous and liberal recognition of jurisdiction clauses.

Art. 17 of the Convention, and now Art. 23 of the Regulation, are the starting point for the conditions of – and limitations to – jurisdiction clauses in EU law. A valid jurisdiction clause takes away jurisdiction of the courts that would otherwise have the competence to hear the case. The only requirement is that these stipulations be in writing or, in international trade or commerce, in "a form which accords with practices in that trade or commerce of which the parties are or ought to have been aware." In the *MSG* case[50], the Court had to decide whether unilateral confirmation of conditions of contract imposed by one side on its partner are sufficient to fulfil the conditions laid down in Art. 17, third alternative. The Court stressed the need for consensus because "the weaker party to the contract should be protected by avoiding jurisdiction clauses incorporated in a contract by one party alone going unnoticed" (para 17). At the same time the Court wanted to ensure "non-formalism, simplicity and speed" in international trade or commerce, and therefore only required that commercial practices exist in this branch and ought to be known to the parties. This ruling is a clear compromise between a strict theory of contractual consensus, on the one hand, and commercial practices on the other. This may imply agreement to a jurisdiction clause by mere behavior according to certain standards or usages in trade.

The Court also considered the question of whether the clause could be upheld as a (valid oral) agreement as to the place where the person liable is actually to perform their obligations (the so-called abstract clause on performance). The Court was hostile to such fictitious prorogation clauses, and insisted that they be governed by the requirements of Art. 17 of the Convention.

It should be kept in mind that this case-law, which sees freedom of contract not in isolation but within a certain business practice, cannot be transferred to other

---

[49] Council Regulation (EC) No 44/2001 of 22 December 2000 on jurisdiction and the recognition and enforcement of judgments in civil and commercial matters [2001] OJ L 12/1.

[50] Case C-106/95 Mainschiffahrts-Genossenschaft v Gravieres Rhenanes Sarl [1997] ECR I-911.

transactions where no such link can be shown. The element of autonomy and consensus as its natural result cannot be completely eliminated from jurisdiction clauses under the Brussels Convention.

This approach has been taken over by Art. 23 of Reg. 44/2001. Para 2 makes it clear that the agreement can also be made in electronic form (§ 14 II 2). Para 1 c), in implementing the *Transporti Castelletti* case,[51] adds the following elements to commercial practice as being relevant for usage leading to prorogation:
- it must be widely known;
- it must be regularly observed;
- the parties to the contract must be of the type involved in the particular trade or commerce.

3. Commercial arbitration and Community law

Community law respects international agreements and national legislation on commercial arbitration, especially the New York Convention of 1958 to which all Member States adhere. Arbitration is expressly excluded from the applicability of the Brussels Convention resp. Regulation, including the question of whether the arbitration agreement itself is valid.[52]

It thereby respects the autonomy of parties in business transactions to submit their conflicts to a non-state type of decision making. Enforcement of arbitration awards duly handed down in respecting the New York rules is an obligation of the States party to the Convention, and can usually be refused – except for some procedural matters – only on grounds of national "public policy". The arbitrator itself is thereby indirectly bound to respect them.

In the *ECO-Swiss* case[53], the Court was concerned with the question of how this public policy proviso is to be interpreted by national courts if an arbitration award is said to violate the Community competition rules. The Court bluntly stated that Art. 81 EC, because of its imperative character, is part of (Community) public policy, and therefore has to be respected *ex officio* in recognition proceedings before a national court.

---

[51] Case C-159/97 Transporti Castelletti Spedizioni International SpA v Hugo Trumpy SpA [1999] ECR I-1597.

[52] Case C-190/89 Marc Rich and Co AG v. Societa Italiana Impianti PA [1991]ECR I-3855.

[53] Case C-126/97 ECO-Swiss v Benetton [1999] ECR I-3055.

.... Art. 81 (1) constitutes a fundamental provision which is essential for the accomplishment of the tasks entrusted to the Community and, in particular, for the functioning of the internal market (para 36).

This ruling of the Court conforms to our interpretation of the relationship between competition law and autonomy: Competition is based on autonomy of economic actors, but limits this autonomy where it is used for anti-competitive purposes. Parties to a commercial contract cannot avoid this consequence by referring their differences to arbitration, even though international and Community law respect autonomy of parties in commercial transactions. Community law only functions as a "long stop": it influences not the arbitration proceedings themselves, which are left to the complete autonomy of the parties, but the later recognition proceedings before national courts, which are under the duty of Art. 10 EC (§ 3 I 3).

III. FREEDOM OF CHOICE OF LAW UNDER THE ROME CONVENTION AND ITS LIMITS

1. The principle of Art. 3

The Rome Convention on the law applicable to obligations arising out of contracts[54] is not an instrument of Community law. Moreover, the ECJ as yet has no authority to interpret it. It is, however, closely attached to the (old) Member States of the Community, all of which are signatories of the Convention. This is demonstrated by publication of the consolidated version of the Rome Convention and its two protocols in the Official Journal of the EC, albeit series C. The report of the working group, headed by Professors Giuliano and Lagarde, was also published in the *OJ* series C and can be used for interpretation purposes.[55] Art. 18 requires uniform interpretation without, however, providing for a mechanism to ensure it. Art. 20 contains the principle that Community law, including Community directives, take supremacy over the Convention.

The Convention enjoys universal application, in contrast to the Brussels Convention and Regulation, which require a close tie to the Community. It excludes certain types

---

[54]   1980 Rome Convention on the law applicable to contractual obligations (consolidated version) [1998] *OJ* C 27/34, cf. Green Paper on the conversion of the Rome Convention into a Community instrument, Com (2002) 654, final.

[55]   Giuliano/Lagarde report, [1980] *OJ* C 282/1.

of contract, such as insurance contracts where the risk is situated within the Community, which follow special rules.[56]

Its main principle is laid down in Art. 3 (1), namely the principle of free choice and autonomy of applicable law by the parties themselves:

> a contract shall be governed by the law chosen by the parties.

The Giuliano-Lagarde report justifies this broad principle because "it simply reaffirms a rule in the private international law of the Member States and of most other countries." Its Community law importance has been recognized by the Court in the *Alsthom* case already mentioned (§ 15 II 1).

There is hardly any rule imaginable giving parties to a contract more autonomy, even though it clearly has some qualifications and limitations. By their choice, the parties can select the law applicable to the whole or a part only of the contract. This means that so-called "dépeçage" is expressly allowed. The law chosen must not necessarily be that of a certain state; it can also be *lex mercatoria*, commercial usage or some non-official codification such as the "European principles of contract law" or the "Unidroit principles" (IV 1). Choice of law also includes its counterpart, namely choice of "no-law".

Modifications and variations of choice are possible, provided that third party rights are not adversely affected. The parties can even choose the law of a country which has no relation at all with the contract. However, they may not contract out of the mandatory rules of the country with which all other elements of the contract are connected. Freedom of choice also includes labor and consumer contracts. However, this is limited by a ban on contracting out of certain mandatory rules to be excluded when the requirements of Art. 5 and 6 are met (*infra* 3).

The choice may be express or inferred. Moreover, it need not to be in writing, unlike jurisdiction clauses under the Brussels Convention or Regulation. The Giuliano/Lagarde report provides a number of examples of situations where a court may draw an inference as to the parties' intentions:
– a jurisdiction or arbitration clause,
– the place of conclusion or performance of the contract,
– previous contracting, or
– parties' domicile or business seat.

---

[56] Smulders/Glazener, *CMLRev* 1992, 775; Micklitz/Reich, *Europäisches Verbraucherrecht*, 4. Auflage 2003, paras 23.16-22.

Issues in relation to validity and existence of consent are, however, determined in accordance with special rules relating to formal validity and incapacity, Art. 3(4).

2. Making choice effective under Art. 8

Material validity is determined by Art. 8. This contains a two tier test:
- Usually, it is determined by the law hypothetically chosen, para 1.
- Para 2 contains a safeguard clause:

> ... that he (i.e. the party whose law of habitual residence is contracted out) did not consent if it appears from the circumstances that it would not be reasonable to determine the effect of his conduct (in accordance with the law hypothetically chosen).

Art. 8 gives rise to a number of interpretation questions, which make the theory of autonomy somewhat difficult to apply here. According to the Giuliano/Lagarde report, this:

> provision is also applicable with regard to the existence and validity of the parties' consent as to choice of the law applicable.

Such a far reaching rule is not without problems, for example, when only one party maintains that the contract contains a choice-of-law clause while the other rejects it. This may be particularly true in a standard form contract in which such a clause was inserted but which was not known to the other party. Para 2 only concerns cases where consent is missing, without referring to validity. Why should the law hypothetically chosen determine consent if there is a question of the existence of choice at all? In our opinion, there must at least be fulfilment of some minimum requirements on choice in a formal sense before the mechanism of Art. 8 can be effective. We will discuss this problem in connection with the transparency principle in standard form contracts (§ 17 II).

3. Limitations to autonomy under the conflict rules

Autonomy is not unlimited, and the Rome Convention contains four limitations of freedom of choice. These, however, aim to restrict party autonomy as little as possible but, rather, to make sure that certain mandatory provisions of the forum state cannot be contracted out of. The other parts of the clause, particularly on the law chosen as such, remain valid:

- Art. 3 (2) disallows contracting out of mandatory provisions of the forum state if "all the other elements relevant to the situation at the time of the choice are connected with one country only" (exorbitant choice of law clauses).[57]
- Art. 5 (1) provides in favour of the so-called *passive consumer*, that is, the consumer solicited into the contract by "specific invitation addressed to him or by advertising" at his place of residence,[58] that a choice of law made by the parties should not result in depriving the consumer of the protection afforded to him by the mandatory rules of the law of the country in which he has his habitual residence". The importance of this concept for e-commerce is not yet clear.[59]
- There is no established practice in Member state conflict of laws how this concept is to be applied to so-called "mixed contracts", that is contracts which relate both to the professional and the non-professional activity of a private person. It is questionable whether the recent case law of the ECJ on the interpretation of Art. 13 of the Brussels Convention, as developed in the *Gruber* case (§ 14 II 2), can be applied here, because the two instruments – the Brussels and the Rome Convention – have different ambits and objectives of protection.
- Art. 6 concerns individual employment contracts and in any case imposes in favor of the worker the protection of the law of the country in which he habitually carries out his work.
- Art. 7 (2) forbids a contracting out of the so-called (internationally) mandatory provisions of the forum state. There is considerable debate on this concept in legal writing. In its *Ingmar* case[60], the ECJ concluded that protective provisions in EC directives[61], adopted to avoid distortions in the internal market, belong to this category, if the contract – in the case at hand: a commercial agent residing in the EU – had close connections to the EU. This decision has broad and controversial consequences[62]!

The Court wrote:

> It must therefore be held that it is essential for the Community legal order that a principal established in a non-member country, whose commercial agent carries on his activity within the Community, cannot evade those provisions by the simple expedient of a choice of law clause ... (para 25).

---

[57]   Lando, *CMLRev* 1987, n157.
[58]   A good example of this concept is the ECJ case C-96/00 Gabriel [2002] ECR I-6367 which, though decided under the Brussels Convention, has repercussions for interpretation of the Rome Convention, in particular since the Court cites from the materials of the Rome Convention to support its interpretation of the Brussels Convention, at para 46.
[59]   Reich/Halfmeier, *Dickinson Law Rev* 2001, 111.
[60]   Case C-381/98 Ingmar GB Ltd. v Eaton Leonard Technologies Inc. [2000] ECR I-9305.
[61]   The case concerned Dir. 86/653 of 18.12.86 on commercial agents, *OJ* L [1986] 382/17.
[62]   Cf. the critique by Roth, *CMLRev* 2002, 371 against Reich, *EuZW* 2001, 51.

IV. EUROPEAN INITIATIVES FOR A COMMON CONTRACT LAW: THE FUTURE OF AUTONOMY

1. The case "for" a "European contract law"?

Contractual autonomy, as we have shown, is present in primary and secondary Community law, but has never been codified expressly. If such a codification could be attained it would lead to a truly European – or Community – contract law. "Ideally" it would be able to overcome the present system of 25 contract laws which must be co-ordinated by the mechanisms of private international law, in particular the Rome Convention, itself based on party autonomy.

It has been argued, particularly by Basedow[63], that such a European contract law would serve the purposes of the internal market and thereby fall into the competence of the Community:
- It would create uniform conditions for marketing in Europe.
- It would avoid risks by choosing or being submitted to an unknown legal order.
- It would save transaction costs to parties contracting cross-border wise.

Basedow has even advocated the possibility of a Community contract regulation which would be applicable if the parties had not expressly contracted out of it. In contrast to the existing bits and pieces of existing mandatory contract law in the Community, it would allow the parties freedom of choice and would only apply if no other legal regime had been chosen. It must be regarded, under this concept, as a hypothetical prolongation of the free will of the parties: what reasonable legal order would they have agreed on to settle their potential conflicts?

2. Private initiatives: The European Principles

The ideas of Basedow and other supporters of a European contract law have not so much been taken up by political institutions of the Community as by private initiatives. The best known were elaborated by a study group under the chairmanship of Professor Ole Lando.[64] Three volumes of principles have been published so far and have led to an intense discussion.

---

[63]   CMLRev 1995, 1169.
[64]   Lando/Beale (eds.), *Principles of European Contract Law*, Vol. I & II, 2000; Lando et al. (eds.), Vol III, 2003; see Micklitz, JCP 2004, 339 concerning (non-)protection of the weaker party; Remien *supra* note 2 at 91-99.

We will not take up this discussion, but simply refer to the leading articles of the " Principles". Art. 1 :102 expressly recognises the principle of freedom of contract. It is limited only by

- the principle of good faith;
- fairness in commercial transactions[65];
- mandatory provisions as far as recognised by the principles[66];
- the principle of co-operation in order to make the contract effective[67]: *pacta sunt servanda.*

The principles can be applied either by express agreement or if the parties refer to "general principles", *lex mercatoria* or similar rules, or if they have not chosen any law at all. Their application is not limited to cross-border transactions. The principles function as a supplementary legal order if the applicable law does not contain adequate rules[68].

The true area of application of the principles – should they become of any legal importance in the future – will however be cross-border commercial transactions in the EU. They do not suit consumer and labour contracts because of the substantial amount of mandatory law that the Community has adopted in order to avoid discrimination based on nationality, gender, and other factors (§ 11), or to allow for adequate protection of legitimate expectations of workers and consumers, as shown above (§ 13).

3. The Commission communication of 2001

The Community so far has not made any proposals in the direction of codifying contractual autonomy in a European civil code or some similar instrument. The European Parliament has on several occasions adopted resolutions encouraging or even urging Community institutions to pave the way towards a European contract law or even a Civil Code. The work done by private working groups, and the publication of the "European Principles" in particular, has greatly encouraged this work.

The Commission published a Communication on 11 July 2001[69] on European Contract Law. This Communication aroused lively comment and controversy among the

---

[65]   Art. 1 :201 of the Principles.
[66]   Art. 1 :103 of the Principles.
[67]   Art. 1 :102 of the Principles.
[68]   Art. 1 :101 of the Principles.
[69]   Communication from the Commission to the Council and the European Parliament on european contract law Com (2001) 398 final; cf. v. Gerven, *ELRev* 2002, 156.

research community, which can be read in a publication edited by Grundmann and Stuyck.[70] In May 2002, the Commission reported on the reactions to its Communication and made known its intention to publish a Green or White paper summarising proposals for future action.[71]

The Commission communication of July 2001 did not present a European contract theory, nor any suggestion as to how to proceed under the existing legal basis. It merely referred to the principles of "subsidiarity" and "proportionality":

> Moreover, legislation should be effective and should not impose any excessive constraints on national, regional or local authorities or on the private sector, including civil society.

It summarised the existing *acquis* in private law (not only contract law) and put forward four options for action, namely:
1. No action.
2. Promote the development of common contract law principles leading to greater convergence of national laws.
3. Improve the quality of legislation already in place.
4. Adopt new comprehensive legislation at EC level.

The communication then goes on to discuss the *pros* and *cons* of the different options, without making clear suggestions as to what direction to follow.

Later discussion concentrated on the methodology of the communication and on the viability of the options suggested. There seemed to be agreement that option 1 is not feasible and is not really an option.[72] Option II is already under way with the several private initiatives on a European contract law. It remains to be discussed whether option III or option IV is preferable:
– Option III would concentrate on existing mandatory law, for example, in consumer and labour law. It would to some extent contradict the concept of autonomy and follow more the philosophy of "adequate protection".
– Option IV is more in line with ideas on autonomy merged into general principles of contract law, already present in particular in the Rome Convention and indirectly in the fundamental freedoms.

---

[70] An Academic Green Paper on European Contract Law, 2002.
[71] Reactions to the Communication on European Contract Law, http://europa.eu.int/comm/consumers/cons_int/safe_shop/fair_bus_pract/cont_law/index_en.htm.
[72] Cf. Reich, in: Grundmann/Stuyck at 279.

The Communication of May 2002 defined the next steps to be taken, namely:

- To identify areas in which the diversity of national legislation in the field of contract law may undermine the proper functioning of the internal market and the uniform application of Community law.
- To describe in more detail the option(s) for action in the area of contract law which have the Commissions' preference in the light of the results of the consultation. In this context, the improvement of existing EC legislation will be pursued and the Commission intends to honour the requests to put forward legislative proposals to consolidate existing EC law in a number of areas.
- To develop an action plan for the chronological implementation of the Commission's policy conclusions.

The question remains as to the feasibility of the path chosen by the Commission. As Wilhelmsson[73] writes:

> One may ... question this starting point. Does European identity really require unified systems of law – or unified social and cultural structures in general? Is not the prevailing European identity the opposite one?

This criticism can be rephrased in accordance with the concept of autonomy as developed here: Does autonomy not imply that the parties themselves take care of the law they want to govern their contractual relationships? And do the fundamental freedoms as such not impose a decentralised contract law? Protection can either be left to secondary legislation, or to conflict rules.

4. New action plan of 12.2.2003

In the meantime the Commission has proposed a new action plan.[74] This aims at a combination of options II and III. It plans to establish a mix of non-regulatory and regulatory measures to attain more coherence in European contract law. In addition to sector-specific interventions, this should include measures:

- To increase the coherence of the Community *acquis* in the area of contract law.
- To promote elaboration of EU-wide general contract terms.
- To examine further whether problems in the European contract law area may require non sector-specific solutions, such as an optional instrument.

---

[73] *ERPL* 2002, 77 at 90.
[74] Communication from the Commission to the European Parliament and the Council - A more coherent European contract law - An action plan Com (2003) 68 Final [2003] *OJ* C 63/1; critique Kenny, *EL Rev* 2003, 538. Follow-up by communication of 11.10.2004, Com (2004) 651 final; Staudenmayer, *ERPL* 2005, 95.

Most importantly, it proposes a common frame of reference for terms frequently used in European directives, such as "damage", "conclusion" and "non-performance" of a contract, to avoid the inconsistencies that result from the divergent use of concepts in different directives.

In such a project, the concept of autonomy and its limits will have to be defined more clearly than in the somewhat haphazard approach of today's incremental law-making process.

5. Is there really a need for a "European contract law"?

The Commission's work on the action plan of 2003 has shown first results insofar as it has greatly encouraged comparative legal studies in the EU which now have to be extended to the new Member countries.[75] The most ambitous part of this work is concerned with elaborating a "common frame of reference" (CFR). The EU Commission is generously funding research in this direction and hopes that results will be available by 2007.

The status of such a CFR (if it is ever elaborated!) is however not yet clear. Is it meant to be the core of a common EU contract law (perhaps extended to some aspects of security interests in movables)? Will it only be applicable to cross-border transactions, or is it meant to substitute or at least to supplement the existing national codifications resp. contract laws? How will it relate to international law instruments like the 1980 UN Convention on the International Sale of Goods (CISG), which has been ratified by most Member countries (with the exception of the UK and of Portugal)?[76] Does the EU have any competence to adopt a general European contract law on the basis of its internal market jurisdiction (Art. 95 EC, see § 3 I)?[77]

Even more problematic is the relationship between the general rules of a European contract law and specific protective directives setting, *inter alia*, standards for consumer protection.[78] Many authors fear that the consumer *acquis* will be sacrificed on the altar of European law harmonization.[79] Others worry that the protection of the "weak" in contract law may get lost.[80]

---

[75] See Reich, *Transformation of contract law in new Member countries*, 2004 (with accounts of the development in the Baltic states, in Poland and Hungary).

[76] For an overview, see Ramberg, *International Commercial Transactions*, 3rd ed. 2004 at pp. 25 et seq.

[77] Weatherill, *JCP* 2001, 339.

[78] Karsten/Sinai, *JCP* 2003, 159.

[79] Wilhelmsson, *ELJ* 2004, 712; Study Group, Manifesto, *ELJ* 2004, 653.

[80] See the contributions in the special issue of *JCP* 2004/3 by Hondius, Hartlief, Staudenmayer, Wilhelmsson, and Micklitz.

At the time of writing a definite judgment on the future of European contract law is premature. This author would support a separate codification of EU consumer or labour law part of the general project on improving the existing *acquis*. Since this is based on directives already adopted and is mostly mandatory in character, it should not be subject to doubt as to whether EU competence exists. With regard to non-mandatory law, EU law generously grants and safeguards, as has been shown, autonomy to parties to a transaction, particularly in B2B relations. There is really no need for any further activity of the Community under the principles of subsidiarity and proportionality.

§ 17. INFORMATION AND AUTONOMY

I. THE INFORMATION MODEL IN COMMUNITY LAW

Autonomy requires actors who are informed about their rights and duties. In traditional legal concepts, it is usually left to the actors themselves to acquire the necessary information that makes their freedom of action possible and effective. *Caveat emptor* as the general rule of autonomous transactions includes responsibility to inform oneself. Autonomy is thus reduced to a formal concept based on the fiction that actors either have or can get the information needed to make decisions. Eventually they will have to "buy" and pay for it if they do not want to rely on information conveyed through advertising. A market exists for information supplementing the market for goods and services.

Community law as a basically liberal order also started from this principle. However, it has increasingly recognized that autonomy in a substantive sense must be supplemented by adequate information provisions. The first impact of this new insight has paradoxically come from the case law developing the proportionality principle (§ 3 II) as a test for justifying or rejecting Member State restrictions on free movement. That is, where it can be shown that it can be replaced by simple information requirements which may attain the envisaged goal of public policy with less restrictive means. This concept was developed by the Court in the seminal *Cassis* case as early as 1979[81]:

> ... to regard the mandatory fixing of minimum alcohol contents as being an essential guarantee of the fairness of commercial transactions (is not justified), since it is a simple matter to ensure that suitable information is conveyed to the purchaser by requiring the display of an indication of origin and of the alcohol content on the packaging of products (para 13).

In a later case the Court stated that:

> under Community law concerning consumer protection the provision of information to the consumer is considered one of the principal requirements.[82]

The philosophy behind this concept is simply that actors, when making their choices about products and services, should rely on (truthful, not misleading) information and need not be over-protected by more restrictive rules limiting market access as such.

---

[81]   Case 120/78 Rewe-Zentral AG v Bundesmonopolverwaltung für Branntwein [1979] ECR 649.
[82]   Case C-362/88 GB-INNO-BM v Confédération du commerce luxembourgeois [1990] I-667.

Information is not a supplement but an instrument of regulation on its own, thus respecting the autonomy principle. It has been said that the information rule, even "if mandatory .. is an instrument fostering party autonomy."[83] It is part of a general principle of "fair trading" in the internal market.[84]

The free flow of information is also protected by Art. 10 of the Human Rights Convention. Via Art. 6 (2) EU, it becomes part of the *acquis* of the Union which both Member States[85] and the Community[86] must respect.

This proportionality principle is binding on actions of the Community itself, as laid down in Art. 5 EC and the Protocol on Subsidiarity. It may be exercised in controlling the legality of Community measures with regard to information[87]. Its importance so far has been limited, since the Court was mostly concerned with striking down Member State measures restricting fundamental freedoms.

In the meantime, information requirements *vis-à-vis* citizens have become part of primary Community law itself, namely:
- Art. 153 (1) contains the consumer's right to information.
- Art. 255 establishes a right of access to Community documents of every Union citizen and each natural and legal person residing in a Member State, in the meantime implemented by Regulation (EC) No. 1049/2001.[88]

II. SECONDARY LAW: THE TRANSPARENCY PRINCIPLE

1. The Unfair terms directive

The transparency principle has found its express inclusion in Art. 4 and 5 of the Unfair Terms Directive 93/13:
- Terms on the price/quality ratio are only excluded from control when being "in plain intelligible language".

---

[83] Grundmann/Kerber/Weatherill in: Grundmann *et al.* at 7.
[84] Radeideh, *Fair Trading in EC Law*, 2005, at 242. With reference to the proposed Directive on "Unfair Commercial Marketing Practices" at 290.
[85] Case C-260/89 ERT v DEP and Kouvelas [1991] ECR I-2925.
[86] Cf. the discussion of AG Fenelly in Case C-376/98 Germany v European Parliament and Council [2000] I-8419 at paras 152 *et sequ.*; the Court has not taken up this line of argument.
[87] Cf. case C-51/93 Meyhui v Schott Zwiesel Glaswerke AG [1994] ECR I-3879; C-491/01R v Secretary of State *ex parte* British American Tobacco (Investments) [2002] ECR I-11453.
[88] Regulation (EC) No 1049/2001 of the European Parliament and of the Council of 30 May 2001 regarding public access to European Parliament, Council and Commission documents [2001] *OJ* L 145/43; for a critique Craig/de Búrca at 394; Krämer, in: FS Winter, 2003 at p. 153. concerning pre-trial documents in infringement proceedings against Member States according to Art. 226 EC.

- Written terms proposed to the consumer (one should add: terms in electronic form) must always be drafted "in plain intelligible language."

The importance of the transparency principle has been stressed by the Court in the litigation against the Netherlands[89] for incorrect implementation of the Directive. Since Arts. 3, 4 and 5 are intended to grant rights to the consumer, it is essential that the legal situation resulting from national implementing measures be sufficiently precise and clear and that individuals be made fully aware of their rights so that, where appropriate, they may rely on them before national courts.

> ... even where the settled case-law of a Member State interprets the provisions of national law in a manner deemed to satisfy the requirement of a directive, this cannot achieve the clarity and precision needed to meet the requirement of legal certainty ... (para 21)

The transparency principle in contract law needs to be implemented by the legislator himself, and not just be a matter of court practice. Transparency requires a two-layer approach to implementation: the first layer is concerned with contract law as such, the second with implementing state regulations.[90]

2. Specific directives

The Distance selling directive 97/7/EC of 20.5.1997[91] contains detailed information requirements which, according to Art. 4 (2), "shall be provided in a clear and comprehensible manner in any way appropriate to the means of distance communication used..." A similar formulation can be found in Art. 3 (2) of the new Directive 2002/65 of 23.9.2002[92] on distance selling of financial services. In contrast to Dir. 97/7, the financial services directive is also concerned with language questions because the provider must indicate the languages in which to communicate with the consumer during the term of the contract.

Directive 1999/44/EC on consumer goods and guarantees (§ 13 IV) does not impose a duty on the seller or producer of consumer goods to give a guarantee to the consumer with regard to the durability or quality of the product sold. Art. 6 as a minimum requirement provides that, should such a guarantee be given, it must:

---

[89] Case C-144/99 Commission v Netherlands [2001] ECR I-3541.
[90] As to the limits cf. case C-478/99 Commission v Sweden [2002] I-4147.
[91] Directive 97/7/EC of the European Parliament and of the Council of 20 May 1997 on the protection of consumers in respect of distance contracts [1997]OJ L 144/19.
[92] Directive 2002/65/EC of the European Parliament and of the Council of 23 September 2002 concerning the distance marketing of consumer financial services and amending Council Directive 90/619/EEC and Directives 97/7/EC and 98/27/EC [2002] OJ L 271/16.

- state that the consumer has legal rights under applicable national legislation, and make clear that those rights are not affected by the guarantee;
- set out in plain intelligible language the contents of the guarantee and the essential particulars necessary for making claims under the guarantee, notably the duration and territorial scope of the guarantee as well as the name and address of the guarantor.

Transparency is not just a principle of consumer law, but of contracting and marketing practices rules in general. Art. 10 (1) of the E-Commerce Directive 2000/31 (*supra* § 8 III 2) provides that information requirements should be given by the provider "clearly, comprehensively and unambiguously". This transparency rule is not limited to consumers, but is a general principle which is particularly important in e-commerce. A similar broad rule can be found in Annex III of the Life Assurance Directive 2002/83/EC.[93]

III.   THE CONCEPT OF THE "INFORMED CONSUMER" AND THE STANDARD OF DECEPTION

Autonomy presupposes that deception is absent from the market. Advertising, marketing practices, and pre-contractual information by the supplier should not be misleading.

A number of Community law instruments contain this principle of non-deception as a basis for autonomous decision-making of market actors. The question debated in literature and case-law has not been the justification of this principle, but the standard of deception. It may not always be easy to determine whether an advertising message must be said to be really misleading, especially if it contains implicit statements, double language, incomplete or ambiguous messages, if it is directed at different audiences or language groups. The addressee of an advertising message should not be over-protected. Some amount of deception must be tolerated on markets – otherwise there would be no advertising at all. In the "*naturally pure*" case[94], the Court insisted that consumers know of minimal toxic residues in fruits, and that there is a only a negligible risk of deception under existing environmental conditions. Consumers are able to learn, and the internal market in itself is a mechanism to change

---

[93]   Directive 2002/83 EC of the EP and the Council of 5 November 2002 concerning life assurance, [2002] OJ L 345/1.
[94]   Case C-465/98 Verein gegen Unwesen in Handel und Gewerbe Köln v A. Darbo [2000]ECR I-2297 at para 27.

old consumption habits, which therefore cannot be made a yardstick for deception.[95] Autonomy as the basic standard of market actions implies that the consumer itself will usually detect when a message is simply overstating without necessarily being misleading. In the words of the Court in the *Mars* case[96]:

> Reasonably circumspect consumers are supposed to know that there is not necessarily a link between the size of publicity markings relating to an increase in a product's quantity and the size of that increase (para 24).

In Community law the question has been debated as to whether there is a common standard of deception in the internal market, or whether it is left to Member States, under the minimum harmonization principle, to define deception themselves. In this way, they would be taking into account potential distortions of competition, because cross-border advertising will be subjected to different standards of assessment, and no uniform cross-border campaign is possible.

After some hesitation, the European Court of Justice has developed the "informed consumer standard" as the yardstick by which to measure deception. In the *Gut Springenheide* judgment[97] it was said:

> ... in order to determine whether .... the statement in question was liable to mislead the purchaser, the Court took into account the presumed expectations of an average consumer who is reasonable well-informed and reasonably observant.... (para 31)

However, in the *Lifting* case the Court accepted that:

> social, cultural or linguistic factors may justify the term "lifting", used in connection with a firming cream, mean(s) something different to the German consumer as opposed to consumers in other Member States.... (para 29).[98]

It thereby recognizes that no uniform standard of the "informed consumer" exists in the Community, and that the concept of deception may be interpreted differently as between Member States, despite the need to have a uniform regulation of advertising. However, different rules may exist where Community law aims at total harmonization,

---

[95] Case 178/84 Commission v Germany [1987] ECR 1227 at para 32 concerning German beer purity laws.
[96] Case C-470/93 Verein gegen Unwesen in Handel und Gewerbe Köln v Mars GmbH. [1995] ECR I-1923.
[97] Case C-210/96 Gut Springenheide v Oberkreisdirektor Steinfurt [1998] ECR I-4657 at para 31.
[98] Case C-220/98 Estée Lauder Cosmetics v Lancaster Group [2000] ECR I-117.

as for example in the cosmetics sector via Dir. 76/768/EWG.[99] Therefore, German law may not forbid the denomination of the cosmetic *Clinique* if this is legally used in the country of origin, under the pretext that the (German) consumer may be misled as to the therapeutic quality of the product.[100] A similar country of origin concept has been introduced into the E-Commerce-Directive 2000/31 (§ 8 III 2b).

IV. EXPRESS INFORMATION OBLIGATIONS IN SECONDARY COMMUNITY LAW

1. The case "for" information

Secondary Community law contains a wide plethora of information rights, of which it is impossible to give a detailed account here. With increased commitment of the Community in the area of trade practices, contract, tort and environmental law, these information obligations on the part of traders or governments have been increased and deepened. In some areas, especially product liability and environmental regulation, information is aimed at giving citizens the necessary instruments to defend themselves and to decide about risk taking. It may allow them to organize collectively, and to participate in decision making, which is particularly important in environmental law.

The philosophy behind these is always autonomous decision making. This is most obvious in contract law, where to some extent it supplements mandatory protection rules. In other areas it helps to describe the main subject matter of a contract – notably in financial services.[101]

An example of these information obligations can be found in the new broad Directive 2002/65/EC of the EC and the Council of 23.9.2002 on the distance marketing of financial services[102]. Arts. 3-6 contain detailed pre-contractual information obligations of the consumer concerning such factors as
- the supplier;
- the financial service;
- the distance contract;

---

[99] Council Directive 76/768/EEC of 27 July 1976 on the approximation of the laws of the Member States relating to cosmetic products OJ L 262/169 and later amendments; cf. Reich/Micklitz, *Europäisches Verbraucherrecht*, para 25.25.
[100] Case C-315/92 Verband Sozialer Wettbewerb v Clinique [1994] ECR I-317.
[101] Grundmann, *CMLRev* 2002, 269 at 273.
[102] Directive 2002/65/EC of the European Parliament and of the Council of 23 September 2002 concerning the distance marketing of consumer financial services and amending Council Directive 90/619/EEC and Directives 97/7/EC and 98/27/EC [2002] *OJ* L 271/16.

- redress;
- special rules on information obligations in case of telephone communications;
- communication of the contractual terms;
- right of withdrawal.

The Directive on electronic commerce 2000/31 has extended information requirements to protect every potential client, whether consumer or not, with regard to name, geographic address, and details of the service provider. This is necessary to identify the contractual partner, which should not be left uncertain in electronic commerce.

2. Consequences of non-respect

Usually, Community law does not regulate the consequences of failure to respect its provisions. It leaves it to Member States to find effective and non-discriminatory instruments in case of breach, unless otherwise specified in secondary Community law. They have to include both individual protection and collective remedies. The remedies stand at the interface between contract law *stricto sensu*, and trade practices law in general. They aim at both prevention and reparation. While the type of remedy is prescribed by Community law as an "*obligation de moyens*", the concrete procedural instruments must be determined by national law (§ 14 I).

Art. 5 of the Unfair Terms Directive is an exception insofar as it expressly prescribes the *contra proferentem* rule in case of non-respect of the transparency principle. It is an open question whether a violation of the transparency principle also involves consequences under Art. 6 of the directive, namely that intransparent terms should not be binding upon the consumer. This would be the case if an intransparant term could be qualified as an unfair term in the sense of Art. 3 (2). Good argument exists for such an interrelation between the transparency and the fairness principles, in that an intransparent term which cannot be understood by the consumer should be regarded as unfair in a formal sense. If the supplier can show that the term does not indeed violate the principles of good faith within the meaning of Art. 3 (2), then the consequence of Art. 6 (1) whereby an unfair term is not binding on the consumer, would not be justified. A presumption of unfairness exists in case of intransparent terms.[103]

Another case concerned a doorstep contract where the provider failed to inform the consumer about its right of withdrawal according to Dir. 85/577/EEC of 20.12.1985.[104]

---

[103] Reich, *ERPL* 1997, 165 at 169.
[104] Council Directive 85/577/EEC of 20 December 1985 to protect the consumer in respect of contracts negotiated away from business premises [1985] *OJ* L 372/31.

The ECJ, in its *Heininger* judgment of 13.12.2001, flatly stated that in this case the right to withdraw does not lapse. The consumer has a Community right to be informed of the contractual right to information; any violation entitles the consumer to renounce the contract indefinitely (!?) and without time limits, even if national legislation provides for a time limit.[105] One may argue that this amounts to overprotection because it is contrary to the principle of legal certainty that a contract which has already been performed in full by both parties can still be avoided.

3.   Information requirements: realization of autonomy or excuse for non-regulation?

The to some extent parallel development of autonomy and information requirements in Community law should not make us forget the fundamental question behind it: Does it start from an ideal-type model of autonomy which is not corroborated by practical experiences, or is it a normative principle rooted in the liberal philosophy of law itself?

Wilhelmsson, in his careful analysis of Community law, criticizes the "radical transparency principle..." introduced through Community law, particularly in contractual relations. He fears that it may be and has been used "in a negative manner, to prevent or slow down the creation of content-oriented rules".[106] This may not be the only direction, but the economic rational choice model seems to be inherent in Community (contract) law – a model, in his opinion, which is not sufficient to fulfil the needs of a truly social contract law and which does not conform to the contract model of his own jurisdiction (the so-called Nordic model).

On the other hand, this direction is expressly welcomed in a recent contribution by Grundmann, Kerber and Weatherill:[107]

> ... even in European re-regulation, there are strong mechanisms against unduly heavy restrictions on party autonomy. This is even a general characteristic of European contract law ... there is an important difference between mandatory information rules and mandatory substantive rules. The latter reduce variety – to one possibility only or to a smaller range of possibilities ... Reducing variety means reducing offers which match individual preferences. Individual preferences, however, are nowadays the basic point of reference for economic theory building (normative individualism). Substantive mandatory rules can be justified only if an information rule cannot remedy the market failure. This is so because

---

[105]   Case C-481/99 Georg und Helga Heininger v Bayr. Hypo- und Vereinsbank [2001] ECR I-9945, note Reich/Rörig, [2002] *EuZW* 87.
[106]   *Social Contract Law and European Integration*, 1995 at 145 f.
[107]   Grundmann *et al.* (eds.), *Party autonomy and the role of information in the internal market*, 2001 at 7.

information rules may be mandatory by construction – the duty to disclose is not subject to party autonomy –, but they are always aimed at enabling the parties to take an autonomous decisions in substance.

The opinion suggested in this context has to be a differentiated one. There are certain cases where an information type remedy as suggested by Grundmann may be sufficient to achieve the envisaged objectives, particularly in financial services. But there may also be cases where mere information is not enough, as has been well debated in unfair terms legislation: even drastic warning clauses in large print will not eliminate unfair exemption clauses which, therefore, have to be controlled by substantive law rules, as in Art. 7 of the Consumer Sales Directive 1999/44 (§ 13 IV). This is also an economically efficient solution because it saves transaction costs, negotiations about individual contract terms, and the like.

Against Grundmann, a mere information type remedy cannot achieve this result. As a result of this discussion it can be said that information is a necessary, but not as such sufficient, prerequisite to achieve autonomy.

CHAPTER V. GOVERNANCE AND ACCOUNTABILITY

Table of Contents

Selected Literature

G. Anagnostars, "State Liability and Alternative Courses of Action: How Independent Can an Autonomous Remedy be?", *YEL* 2002, 355; K. Armstrong, "Rediscovering Civil Society: The EU and the White Paper on Governance", *ELR* 2002, 102; A. Arnull/D. Wincott (eds.), *Accountability and Legitimacy in the EU*, 1992; U. Bernitz/D. Bergelius (eds.), *General principles of EC Law*, 2000; A. Böcker, "The Establishment Provisions of the Europe Agreements", *ZERP/dp* 1/2002; G. de Búrca/J. Scott (eds.), *Constitutional Change in the EU: From Uniformity to Flexibility*, 2000; G. de Burca/J. Scott (eds.), *New Governance and Constitutionalism in Europe and the US*, 2005; A. Couret, "Mondialisiation et droit des sociétés (corporate governance)", *RIDE* 2002, 339; Th. Eilmannsberger, *Rechtsfolgen und subjektives Recht im Gemeinschaftsrecht*, 1997; D. Curtin, "Citizen's fundamental right of access to EU information", *CMLRev* 2000,7; Th. Eilmannsberger, "The relationship between rights and remedies in EC-Law: In search of the missing link", *CMLRev* 2004, 1198; G. Falkner, "Innovative Regelungsformen im EG-Arbeitsrecht", *ZEuP* 2002, 222; G. Falkner, *EU Social Policy in the 1990: Toward a corporatist policy community*, 1998; G. Ferrari/K. Hopt/E. Wymeersch (eds.), *Capital markets in the Age of the Euro*, 2002; W. van Gerven, "Of rights, remedies and procedures", *CMLRev* 2000, 501; W. van Gerven, "Bridging the Unbridgeable: Community and National Tort Laws after Francovich and Brasserie", *ICLQ* 1996, 507; W. van Gerven, "Substantive Remedies for the Private Enforcement of EC Anti-Trust Rules before National Courts", in: Stuyck/Gilliams (eds.), *Modernisation of European Competition Law*, 2002, 93; J. Greenwood, *Representing Interest in the EU*, 1997; T. Heukels/A. McDonnell, *Action for Damages in Community Law*, 1997; Chr. Joerges/R. Dehousse (eds.), *Good Governance in Europe's Integrated Market*, 2002; Chr. Joerges/Y. Meny/J.H.H. Weiler (eds.), *Montain or molehole, A Critical Appraisal of the Commission White Paper on Governance*, 2002; Chr. Jones, *Private Enforcement of Anti-Trust Law in the EU, the UK and USA*, 1999; L. Krämer, "On the interrelation between consumer and environmental policies", *Journal of Consumer Policy* 1993, 455; L. Krämer (ed.), *Liber amicorum G. Winter*, 2003; L. Krämer, *EC Environmental Law*, 5th ed. 2005; P. Oliver (with M. Jarvis), *Free Movement of Goods in the EC*, 4th ed. 2003; N. Reich, "The 'Courage'-doctrine: Encouraging or discouraging compensation for antitrust injuries?", *CMLRev* 2005, 35; N. Reich/ R. Heine-Mernik (Hrg.), *Umweltverfassung und nachhaltige Entwicklung in der EU*, 1997; N. Reich/H.W. Micklitz, *Europäisches Verbraucherrecht*, 4. A. 2003; S. Regent, "The Open Method of Coordination: A New Supranational Form of Governance?", *ELJ* 2003, 190; J. Shaw, "Citizenship of the Union: Towards Post-national Membership", in: European University Institute (ed.), *Collected Coures of the Academy*, Vol VI-I, 1998, 237; H. G. Schermers/D. Waelbroeck, *Judical Protection in the EU*, 6th ed., 2001; J. Scott/D. Trubek, "Mind the Gap: Law and New Approaches to Governance in the ERU", *ELJ* 2002, 1; C. Stenaou/H. Xanthaki, *A Legal and Political Interpretation of Art. 288(2) EC – The Individual strikes back*, 2000; T. Tridimas, *The General Principles of EC Law*, 1999; T. Tridimas, "Liability for Breach of Community Law", *CMLRev* 2001, 301; D. Triantafyllou, "L'interdiction des abus de droit en tant que principe général du droit communautaire", Cahiers de droit européen 2002, 611; J. Wahnfield, *Judicial Protection through the use of Art. 288 (2)*, 2002; J. Weiler, *The Constitution of Europe*, 1999; St. Weatherill, "Compulsory notification of Draft technical regulations: the contribution of Dir. 83/189 to the management of the internal market", *YEL* 1996, 19; Th. Wilhelmsson, "Consumer Law and the Environment: from Consumer to Citizen", *Journal of Consumer Policy* 1999, 45; J. Wouters, "European Company Law: Quo vadis?", *CMLRev* 2000, 257; H. Weyer, "Schadenersatzanprüche gegen Private kraft Gemeinschaftsrecht", *ZeuP* 2003, 318.

§ 18.   GOVERNANCE AND ACCOUNTABILITY IN THE COMMUNITY LEGAL ORDER

I.   GOVERNANCE AS A BALANCE TO AUTONOMY

The concept of governance is the liberal corollary of autonomy. As shown in Chapter IV, Community law has been generous in granting and extending autonomy to economic actors, particularly undertakings. Citizens also enjoy widespread autonomy in their actions. Citizenship gives them a status of their own and a bundle of extensive rights. Information imposed by Community rules and to be provided on the market helps their autonomous decision making.

Such a concept of autonomy presupposes coordinating and limiting mechanisms in order to avoid clashes of interest. The autonomy of one restricts the autonomy of others. Autonomy can only work if its inherent limitations are put on the agenda of policy and law. Even more importantly, autonomy carries with it the risk of abuse. Sometimes it is particularly difficult to define the circumstances under which the use of autonomy is abusive – and vice versa. Law has to develop criteria to distinguish use from abuse. Law should find mechanisms in order to hold those acting abusively responsible. Governance is concerned with achieving this balance between legitimate and illegitimate use of autonomy. It aims to supplement – not substitute – a system of rights with one of duties and responsibilities.

In Community law, governance is a relatively new topic. At the outset, law was mostly concerned with the opening of markets and with the granting of autonomy. Its primary agenda has been and still is a liberal one. However, the more successful Community law became in attaining its primary objectives, the more urgent it became to develop the two neighbouring concepts of adequate standards with regard to open markets, and of governance with regard to autonomy. The concept of governance is still very much in its infancy. It is only developing. At this stage of evolution, one can distinguish two trends, one political, the other legal.

II.   THE POLITICAL AND THE LEGAL CONCEPTS OF GOVERNANCE

1.   The political concept and the Commission White Paper of 2001

The political concept of governance is concerned with justifying and limiting political action. It is invoked *before* action is taken. It is particularly important in cases where a democratic deficit of actors can be found. Illustrations might include Community legislation not backed up by a system of Parliamentary democracy, or economic activities not controlled by competition. Governance becomes a substitute for democracy or competition. Art. 253 EC can be seen as a necessary element of governance, in that regulations, directives and decisions of Community institutions, that is, both legislative and administrative measures, must "state the reasons on which they are based..." This requirement for "giving reasons" is an important element of legitimacy of action.[1] But it rests upon the "classic methods of Community action". That is, issuing *binding measures* initiated or implemented by the Commission and approved in proceedings that involve the Council, the European Parliament and eventually other bodies with different voting procedures and majority requirements. The question remains whether at Community level other, more flexible forms of governance are conceivable, in particular ones that rely less on binding acts and involve more actors of civil society.

Scott/Trubek distinguish these "new types of action" as "new, old governance" (NOG) and "open method of co-ordination" (OMC).[2] The first allows Member States more flexibility in implementation, for example via framework directives, while the second involves the actors concerned, via "social dialogue". They define as characteristics of "new governance":
– Participation and power-sharing.
– Multi-level integration.
– Diversity and decentralization.
– Deliberation.
– Flexibility and revisability.
– Experimentation and knowledge creation.

In its White Paper on governance of 25 July 2001,[3] the Commission, after extensive consultations with representatives from politics, academia and civil society, defined the principles of good governance as "openness, participation, accountability, effectiveness, and coherence". It proposed a number of measures in this direction. These included better structured relations to "civil society"[4] by involving NGOs, although without questioning the "Community method of action" as a "top-down" way to achieve integration. It was quite critical toward OMC methods of governance:

---

[1] Kadelbach, "European Administrative Law", in: Joerges/Dehousse, *Good Governance*, 2002 at 190.
[2] Scott/Trubek, *ELJ* 2002 at 2-6.
[3] Com (2001) 428.
[4] Cf. the excellent paper by Armstrong, *ELJ* 2002, 102.

(I)t (OMC, NR) must not dilute the achievement of common objectives in the Treaty or the political responsibility of the Institutions. It should not be used when legislative action under the Community method is possible.[5]

The lively debate that followed pointed to some of the shortcomings of the Commission paper, most of which were concerned with political decision making in the Union.[6] Eriksen[7] pointed to the legitimacy gap in the EU. Scharpf[8] found a "remarkable lack of concern about the real challenges confronting the Union and its Member States." Scott/Trubek[9] offered the criticism that the EU has not really begun to confront the legitimacy challenge it is facing. European courts, in their opinion, have "tended to ignore, or distort, new governance, in order that new governance can be accommodated by the premises of a traditional, positivist concept of law."

This author's view toward the White Paper is less critical than that of the above mentioned authors. In reality, governance in the Union will have to use both the traditional "Community method" and new methods like NOG and OMC. Particularly important seem to be NOG forms of law making. In this way it will be possible to try out new forms of *co- and self-regulation* with the participation of those involved. An example has been rules on decision making in the area of Social Policy[10] where the social partners (organizations of public and private employers together with trade unions) agree on measures to be taken. These may then be transposed into law by Community institutions. The decisive question is then one of the representativeness of the participants, carefully scrutinized by the Court of First Instance in its *UEAPME* decision.[11] Similar initiatives can be found in the area of environmental policy[12], where "environmental agreements" are envisaged. They are also to be found in the area of consumer policy, where a combined approach[13] is favoured to combat unfair trade practices. This consists of a framework directive, to be combined with self-regulation. The new discrimination directives (§ 11 III 5b, 6, IV 2/3) have introduced, alongside

---

[5]   At 22 of the White Paper.
[6]   Cf. the discussion papers assembled in Joerges/ Meny & Weiler (eds.), *Mountain or Molehole, A Critical Appraisal of the Commission White Paper on Governance*, European governance: Common Concerns vs. the Challenge of Diversity. http:/www/jeanmonnetprogram.org/ papers/01/010701.html
[7]   "Democratic or technocratic Governance?", in: Joerges/Meny/Weiler at 61-72.
[8]   *European Governance: Common concerns v. the challenge of diversity, ibid.* at 1-11.
[9]   *Supra* note 2 at 16.
[10]   Art. 137/139 EC.
[11]   Case T-135/96 UEAPME v Council [1998] ECR II-2335, unfortunately not decided on the merits.
[12]   Cf. Communication from the Commission to the Council, the European Parliament, the Economic and Social Committee and the Committee of the Regions On the sixth environment action programme of the European Community "Environment 2010: Our future, Our choice" – The Sixth Environment Action Programme, Com (2002) 31 final of 24.1.2002, p. 17; a sceptical view has been voiced by Krämer, *EC Environmental Law*, 5th edition 2003 at p. 59.
[13]   Commission Green Paper on European Union Consumer Protection, Com (2001) 531 of 2.10.2001, p. 13. Cf. the discussion at Reich/Micklitz, *Europäisches Verbraucherrecht*, para 11.21.

classic remedies referring to judicial protection (§ 14), instruments such as social dialogue, co-operation with NGOs and other "soft mechanisms" to ensure good governance with the goals of the directives.

Transparency of decision making is another issue to which the debate turned. This had influenced recent Community regulations and court decisions allowing broader access to documents and requiring a reasoned opinion if this access was denied. One of the results of this debate has been Regulation (EC) No. 1049/2001 of the EC and the Council of 30 May 2001 regarding public access to EP, Council and Commission documents.[14] This has now been elevated to the status of a fundamental right according to Art. II-102 of the Draft Constitution.

The importance of the debate cannot be underestimated, since it concerns the way the Union/Community would act in the future. However, the NOC/OMC types of regulation as more broadly used instruments for Community governance are not without problems. That is, they could change the existing *acquis* whereby Community legislation is meant to be of binding force to the addressees concerned and should give rights to those protected, followed by duties of those who have to implement them (§ 2 II: theory of direct effect). This legal effect can be reached to a lesser extent by NOC instruments, and not at all by OMC methods, even if it may be more effective in the short run. If different types of self-regulation, agreements with stakeholders and similar instruments are proposed, the participation of relevant NGOs must be assured. This is an area that the Commission has often addressed in environmental and consumer matters, although without so far having developed satisfactory instruments. As social legislation shows, the problem of representation of participating business organizations and NGOs becomes urgent in this type of *quasi* legislation. Thus, despite the optimism and apparent approval of Scott/Trubek, extreme caution needs to be exercised in placing new governance "outside of the courts".[15]

Therefore, a more traditional legal theory of governance will be advocated here. This promotes one of the fundamental functions of law, namely to establish *a balance sheet of rights and duties*. Similar to the discrimination legislation, it can be supplemented but not substituted by OMC-type instruments.

---

[14]   Regulation (EC) No 1049/2001 of the European Parliament and of the Council of 30 May 2001 regarding public access to European Parliament, Council and Commission documents [2001] *OJ* L 145/43. The ECJ has meanwhile recognised a right to partial access to documents when only certain parts are protected, Case C-353/99 Council v Hautala [2001] ECR I-9565.

[15]   *Supra* note 2 at 8.

2. The (narrower) legal concept of governance: accountability via enforceable duties

The legal concept of governance is narrower than the one used in policy making. It is not so much concerned with the legitimacy of political action, but rather with controlling its consequences. It acts primarily as an *ex-post* mechanism to make accountable for misuse of autonomy those to whom these consequences can be imputed. It may – and perhaps should – also function as an *ex-ante* mechanism to prevent abuse, but there is no certainty about this. The *ex-ante* limits of action are rather defined by adequate standards as developed in Chapter III. The *ex-post* allocation of risks should be achieved by a system of governance. EU law is no exception; the following principles should be applicable here, too.

Governance as a corollary to autonomy functions by defining enforceable duties. These, in the case of non-performance, may eventually give rise to liability or other forms of responsibility. Wrongful acts must be sanctioned, and those injured must be compensated. They can possibly be avoided, for example through injunctions against wrongful acts about to be committed. Remedies may focus on cash compensation, but also on prevention. At the same time, law should not establish over-strict rules that stifle action and curb autonomy. Certain risks are inherent in autonomy, which relies on freedom of action and avoids over-regulation. A permanent balance must be struck between autonomy and governance. The proportionality test should be applicable here, too (§ 3 II 4). Law must provide for a case-by-case balancing of interests. Strict general rules may be counterproductive. On the other hand, actors will have to live with a "certain uncertainty". Law cannot tell them with absolute precision whether their actions will be regarded as an autonomous expression of free will or as abusive behavior. Broad principles and standards, as opposed to narrowly defined rules, define governance in a legal sense. At the end of the day, courts of law will have to decide from broad principles what the rules of behavior are. The criticism of "hindsight" will be difficult to avoid.

3. The flawed distinction between public and private, contract and tort

The traditional concept of accountability in a broad sense, from which liability may arise, will be the basis of this chapter. It usually distinguishes between public and private actors. The main public actor is the state with its many institutions on different power and competence levels. These, in the traditional theory of the state, do not enjoy autonomy but only power legitimised by law, for example by democratic mandate. Sidestepping this authorization and other *ultra vires* acts would therefore give rise to liability in favour of those whom the law wanted to protect. Liability of the state will, according to the jurisdictions involved, often be restricted by certain other criteria such as the type of actor (excluding the legislature or judiciary in some jurisdictions), seriousness of the wrongful act, causation, proximity, negligence, assumption of risk, and the like.

Accountability and, potentially, liability of private actors is subject to substantially different criteria. In contractual relations, it follows directly from the autonomous act of contracting. That is, if a person has the right to enter freely into a contract, it must obviously carry the consequences of any breach. Liberal contract theory is unthinkable without liability for breach.

With regard to liability in tort, the justification is somewhat different. Liability is not the consequence of the free will of the parties, but of freedom of action allowed to an undefined group of persons the limits of which are defined by law. Any breach of this general legal obligation – which may be supplemented by customary, judiciary or moral norms – carries with it the liability for wrongful acts towards those the law wants to protect against such actions.

This somewhat simplified "classic" concept of accountability, channelled into liability, no longer corresponds to today's reality. The public-private and contract-tort distinctions are historic ones, and should not be used for developing a modern concept of governance and responsibility in EU law. The state in its many facets may today act like a private undertaking, for example in the exploitation of a monopoly or an exclusive right. It may therefore be subject to the competition rules (§ 9 VI).

A private actor, such as a dominating undertaking or oligopoly, may enjoy state-like powers in a certain market. Contracts can be entered into by both public and private actors. Even in private law, the distinction between contract and tort liability becomes blurred, such as when a defective product or service injures consumers: is it the specific contractual situation that gives rise to liability, or an abuse of the autonomous marketing decision by an undertaking placing defective products or services on the market? How far does the line of responsibility extend to third persons?

4. Accountability as a form of governance of autonomous action in EU law

The theory of accountability advocated in this context will define it as *a corollary to autonomy*. It sanctions duties inherent in law as the other side of granting autonomy and rights. As long as actors enjoy autonomy, any transgression of this autonomy should be governed, if possible prevented, and eventually sanctioned by rules on responsibility. It is not important what legal entity is abusing its freedom of or duty to action, nor does it matter in what type of relation it stands with the injured party.

With regard to actors traditionally coming under public law, their power of action is usually granted and at the same time limited by laws defining their competence. Therefore, an act committed within the scope of competence of a public entity usually does not give rise to liability, unless a social policy rule creates other reasons for victim compensation,[16] or if economic operators suffer unusual damage exceeding the economic risk inherent in operating in the sector concerned (special damage).[17]

Only *illegal acts* give rise to responsibility that may result in civil, administrative and/or criminal liability. In the following, the discussion advanced here will mostly be concerned with *civil liability*. It will also consider injunctions as a measure to prevent injury. In the Community context, such a theory of civil liability and of preventive measures must respect the complexity of the "European multi-level system of governance".[18] This is due to the fact that, if states transfer part of their powers to a supra-national entity, responsibility structures will shift, and liability rules will have to be reshaped. States can no longer be considered as the only trustees and guarantors of Community action; the Community itself should take over liability and not hide behind states.

Private actors, in a liberal system of competition based on autonomy, must in particular respect the rules of competition itself, namely the prohibition of restrictive agreements and of abuse of market dominating power. Third parties, whether competitors or consumers, injured by anti-competitive behavior should be able to prevent such action or, if not successful, claim compensation.

There may be other abuses of autonomy by undertakings. An example taken over by Community law concerns the marketing of defective products, not services that may give rise to strict liability. As a new problem area, externalities to the environment created by hazardous activities may give rise to creating regimes of compensation. Finally, "corporate governance" has yet to be put on the agenda of Community law, thereby setting certain enforceable rules on the responsibility of officers of a commercial company *vis-à-vis* its share- and stakeholders (§ 20 III 4). Special problems exist in cross-border situations which must be managed by conflict rules (§ 20 IV).

Finally, private actors – citizens in the broad terminology used here – cannot expect simply to enjoy autonomy without being held accountable for their actions. This is particularly true with regard to actions not directed against other individuals, usually

---

[16] Tridimas. *CMLRev* 2001 at 321; cf. ECJ-case 186/87 Cowan v Tresor public [1989] ECR 195 concerning the compensation of victims to a criminal attack that was extended to all EU nationals.

[17] Case T-184/95 Dorsch Consult Ingenieursgesellschaft v Council and Commission [1998] ECR II-667 at para 80, upheld on appeal C-237/98 P [2000] ECR I-4549.

[18] Cf. the title of the paper by Joerges, in: Joerges/Dehousse (eds.), *Good Governance*, 2002 at 7.

caught by Member State rules on liability in contract or tort, but which may injure a diffuse multitude of citizens. Here, an example would be in environmental relations: waste management is a good illustration.[19] Another problem area is individual abuses of rights that inflict no direct harm on other individuals but externalise costs on the public at large: Who answers for these costs to the community?

5. The deficits of the Community law theory and practice of governance

The discussion presented so far should allow development of a theory of governance and accountability of the four main actors in the Union context, namely:
- *Community institutions* acting wrongfully despite their duty to guarantee and protect the autonomy enjoyed by undertakings and citizens under Community law.
- *Member States*, with regard to wrongful acts performed in a similar position.
- *Undertakings* abusing their market freedom, for example by restricting competition, by placing defective products on the market, or by degrading bio-diversity.
- *Citizens* in misusing their freedom of action by environmentally harmful behavior or by producing unnecessary costs to the general public.

As will be shown in the following sections, Community law is a long way from having a consistent theory and practice of governance and accountability that would correspond to its liberal approach to autonomy. The following general observations may suffice and will be developed in more detail later:
- Responsibility of public bodies for illegal acts is better developed than that of private actors.
- Art. 288 EC provides for a specific Community liability system for wrongful acts of Community organs, referring to the general principles of Member State law. At the same time, the case law of the ECJ paradoxically shows a widening up and a narrowing down of Community liability (III).
- Member State liability for violating obligations under Community law *vis-à-vis* individuals did not exist in the original Treaty, nor was it added by the many amendments. The duty to loyalty and co-operation[20] is worded as a *lex imperfecta*. Only by judicial intervention has a sophisticated system of state liability been developed as a *judge-made* instrument of governance (§ 19 II).
- A liability system for private actors is emerging from a rather haphazard potpourri of *leges imperfectae*, supplementing the unsatisfactory state of Member State law. As for primary Community law, its rules have direct effect between private parties, for example in the area of competition and, to a lesser extent, of free movement.

---

[19]   Glinski, in: Reich/Micklitz, *Europäisches Verbraucherrecht*, § 26.
[20]   In Art. 10 EC.

Secondary law has established liability rules addressed to private actors, but excludes horizontal direct effect. The case law of the court must fill the gaps that primary and secondary Community law have left (§ 20).
– Citizens' accountability is still a blind spot in Community law, even though Art. 17 EC mentions rights *and duties* of Union citizens (§ 21).

III. PRINCIPLES OF COMMUNITY LIABILITY

1. Compensation according to Art. 288 (2) EC

Art. 288 (2) EC provides that the Community must make good any damage caused by its institutions or by its servants in the performance of their duties "in accordance with the general principles common to the laws of the Member States." However, this broad provision on Community liability requires concretising through case law – as has occurred. This study will not undertake a comprehensive case analysis here. Instead, it will underline some basic principles that support or challenge our theory on governance through liability rules. Some remarks on the development of litigation under Art. 288 (2) may be helpful to illustrate our point:
– Typically, the liability question did not arise in areas where the Community's mission was to open markets, but rather in the context of its sectoral policies aimed at closing markets, especially in the field of agriculture – in contradiction to its own self-governing liberal principles.[21]
– In its seminal *Schöppenstedt* judgment[22] the Court extended liability to legislative acts – a principle not common to the 6 Member States then existing.
– This extension of liability was limited in the same judgment by the principle that the legislator, with regard to measures of economic policy, enjoyed a wide margin of discretion. The Community does not incur liability for damage suffered by individuals "unless a sufficiently flagrant violation of a superior rule of law for the protection of the individual has occurred".
– Such a "superior rule of law" would be violated if the Commission abolished "with immediate effect and without warning the application of compensatory amounts in a specific sector without adopting transitional measures...."[23]
– Recent case law seems to have abandoned the requirement of violation of a "superior rule of law". Similar to Member State liability (*infra* § 19 II 3) this norm

---

[21] Cf. joined cases 5,7 and 13-24/66 Kampfmeyer *et al.* v Commission [1967] ECR 331.
[22] Case 5/71 Zuckerfabrik Schöppenstedt v Council [1971] ECR 975 .
[23] Case 74/74 Comptoir national technique agricole (CNTA) v Commission [1975] ECR 533 at para 43.

- including international law – must have as its objective the protection of the interests of those injured.[24]
- In the later *HNL* judgment[25] the Court held that in legislative acts where the exercise of wide discretion is essential for the implementation of a Community policy, it may not "incur liability unless the institution concerned has gravely and manifestly disregarded the limits on the exercise of power".
- Even if a Community regulation has been voided by the Court, this will not necessarily imply liability *vis-à-vis* injured individuals under Art. 288 (2).[26]
- The Community will not incur liability where action to avoid injury to consumers (in the case at hand: elimination of contaminated wine from the market) is primarily imposed on Member States, rather than on Community institutions. Unfortunately, the substantive and procedural issues of a joint and several liability of the EC and Member States in case of multiple causation have not yet been settled.[27]
- In the *Adams* case[28] the ECJ allowed compensation in favour of a "whistleblower" in competition matters where the Commission violated the confidentiality of the information and the person suffered severe personal damage due to persecution in the country of the wrongdoer (Hoffmann-la Roche with regard to Switzerland[29]).
- Later cases have allowed an award of damages where legitimate expectations were violated by Community measures.[30]
- Under certain circumstances, the Court (of First Instance) may grant provisional damages by way of interim measures.[31]
- AG Alber extends Community liability if the Council, against a decision of the Dispute Settlement Panel of the WTO, has not remedied the illegal import restriction on hormone beef for a considerable time and an importer has suffered substantial loss.
- The Court denied compensation for inaction of the Council to fulfil a decision of the WTO Dispute Settlement Board in the hormone case because the plaintiff could not prove its damage. It did not answer the decisive question of the direct effect of decisions of the WTO Board.[32]

---

[24]   Case C-352/98 P Bergaderm and Groupil v Commission [2000] ECR I-5291 at para 62.
[25]   Joined cases 83 and 94/76, 4,15 and 40/77 HNL v Council and Commission [1978] ECR 1209.
[26]   Cf. the so-called Isoglucose cases 116 + 124/77 Amylum v Council and Commission [1979] ECR 3497.
[27]   Joined cases 326/86 and 66/88 Francesconi *et al.* v Commission [1989] ECR 2087; for a discussion cf. Craig/de Búrca at 571-576.
[28]   Case 145/83 Stanley George Adams v Commission [1985] ECR 3539 at para 37.
[29]   The information of Adams lead to the prosecution of Hoffmann-la Roche that resulted in the vitamin case 85/76 Hoffmann-La Roche & Co. AG v Commission [1979] ECR 461.
[30]   Case C-152/88 Sofrimport v Commission [1990] ECR I-2477.
[31]   Case C-393/96 P (R) Antonissen v Council and Commission [1997] ECR I-441.
[32]   Case C-93/02 P Etablissements Biret/Council [2003] ECR I-10497.

This case law is an impressive example of balancing. On the one hand, there is the autonomy of action enjoyed by Community institutions, most importantly by the legislator that frequently acts "in the shadow of the law". On the other, principles of governance and accountability are emerging. Despite some highlights, there seems to be the impression that, as far as concerns the breach of a general principle of law deriving from the laws of Member States, the action in many of these cases has been dismissed.[33] With regard to the *seriousness of the breach*, the Court insists that the damage alleged by the applicants must go beyond the bounds of the economic risks inherent in the activities in the sector concerned.[34] This is a rather flexible rule giving the Court a great margin of discretion on when to impose liability and when not. It contradicts to some extent the principle of strict liability for wrongful acts by the Community.

As a result of this overview, the autonomy of action of Community institutions has only to a limited extent been held accountable by liability rules. This might have been justified at a time when the Community enjoyed very limited powers, mainly in the field of agricultural and competition policy. Now, when Community law affects all areas of economy and society, such a narrow approach is no longer justified. The Community should face liability for all its wrongful acts causing damage to its citizens. Clearly, the other criteria for liability, such as causation and proximity, must be fulfilled.

If the rules on compensation are so narrowly interpreted, the following question is justified: Can these *lacunae* in governance of Community institutions be overcome by injunctions and enforcement actions?

2. Injunctions and enforcement actions

A theoretically easy way to enforce governance against Community institutions would be the issue of Court injunctions against wrongful acts or, in the case of non-action, allowing enforcement action to make the Community act in a positive way in the interest of the individual applicant or group of applicants concerned. Here, however, the present state of Community law is quite unsatisfactory.

a. Injunctions by Community courts

Community law allows injunctions against acts by Community institutions, but under certain restrictive conditions. There is no automatic suspending effect of an action

---

[33]   Tridimas, *supra* note 16 at p. 316.
[34]   Joined cases C-104/89 and C-37/90 Mulder v Council and Commission [1992] ECR I-3061.

against a Community measure before the CFI. The following requirements must be met:

- The applicant must have standing under the narrow principles of Art. 230 (4), that is, must be directly and individually concerned by the challenged Community act.
- Under existing Community law, this will not be the case in challenging the legality of directives[35], but only of decisions and decision-like regulations (cf. § 14 IV).
- Applicants must fulfil the criteria for individual and direct concern to allow for standing. This usually excludes public interest litigants,[36] unless they have participated in the decision making process.[37]
- In allowing injunctions for interim relief, the Court usually does a balancing test[38] between the interest of the Community in exercising its functions on the one hand, and, on the other, the interest of the individual in suspending the overtly illegal act giving rise to losses that cannot later be reclaimed by a damages action.
- Preliminary judicial protection requires two elements, one legal and one factual. The applicant is required to substantiate the urgency to avoid grave and irreparable harm, and the necessity to suspend the contested act. With respect to legal requirements, the EU courts undertake a preliminary evaluation of the action on merit.[39]

b. Injunctions by national courts

Since the European Courts have exclusive power to annul Community acts[40], national courts that decide on Community law issues are barred from granting interim relief against manifestly illegal Community acts. In order to make its prerogative more flexible, the Court has allowed national courts to grant interim relief according to the criteria developed in *Zuckerfabrik*[41] under certain limiting conditions (for details cf. § 14 III 2).

Injunctions under Community law are not shaped as a remedy to ensure governance, but rather as interim relief granted to individuals coming within the ambit of the narrow procedural standing requirements of Community law. The approach towards

---

[35] Case C-10/95P Asocarne v Council [1995] ECR I-4149.
[36] For an overview cf. Reich/Micklitz, *Public Interest Litigation before European Courts*, 1996.
[37] Case T-122/96 Federolio v Commission [1997] ECR-II 1559 contrasting case C-321/95 P Stichting Greenpeace v Commission [1997] I-1651. For a recent narrowing of this criteria cf. case T-598/97 BSC Footwear Supplies v Council, [2002] II-1155.
[38] According to Art. 242 and 243 EC.
[39] Kadelbach in: Joerges/Dehousse (eds.), *Good Governance*, 2002 at 191; for a recent case C-156/03 PR Commission v Les Laboratoires Servier, order of 20 June 2003 [2003] ECR I-6575.
[40] Case 314/85 Foto-Frost v Hauptzollamt Lübeck-Ost [1987] ECR 4199.
[41] Joined cases 143/88 and C-92/89 Zuckerfabrik Süderdithmarschen and Zuckerfabrik Soest v Hauptzollamt [1991] ECR I-415.

governance and judicial protection is strictly individualistic. How far this individual also acts in the public interest to ensure governance of Community institutions is a matter of secondary concern, similar to damages actions. In contrast to liberal thinking, the Community legislator does not trust the individual to act to ensure governance of its institutions.

c. Enforcement actions

Enforcement actions may be included under Art. 232, but the same strict criteria apply here as for annulment actions. There has only been one case where a public interest group (a user's organization) has tried to force the Commission into action. However, this was dismissed.[42]

As far as the Commission has the power to enforce actions for the opening of markets, such as in the internal market and competition fields, in the view of the Court its powers are purely discretionary. Therefore, a citizen or an undertaking cannot force the Commission to take action under infringement proceedings against Member States, or under the competition rules against undertakings.[43] They do not even have access to the documents of the Commission in preparing infringement proceedings.[44] Therefore, private actions to enforce these rules without having to wait for Community action become particularly important and may substitute Commission inaction.

A similar ruling holds true with regard to reference proceedings. Where an individual wants to challenge a Community measure before a national court, it is under an obligation to refer the case to the ECJ if it acts as a court of last instance. However, under Community law this duty to refer cases to the ECJ cannot be enforced. National law may offer certain remedies, but these do not exist Community-wide.

3. Results: leges imperfectae to be overcome by activating the Charter

As a result of this short overview, the beginnings of rules assuring governance of Community institutions do exist, but they take a too narrow, namely individualistic approach, or are still constructed as *leges imperfectae* that cannot be enforced by those concerned. Governance of Member States has been much more developed by Community law – an interesting shift of responsibilities to be discussed in the following.

---

[42] Case 246/81 Lord Bethell v Commission [1982] ECR 2277.
[43] Case C-196/96 P Intertronic F. Cornelis v Commission [1998] ECR I-199.
[44] This is criticised by Krämer in: *FS G. Winter*, 2003 at p. 153.

A new approach may be possible under Art. 41 and 47 of the EU Charter on Fundamental Rights, now Art. II-101 and 107 of the Draft Constitution (§ 12 III) where the "Right to good administration" and the "Right to an effective remedy" are laid down. New case law of the Court of First Instance is taking steps in this direction. In its *max.mobil* judgment of 30.1.2002[45] the Court insisted that "diligent and impartial treatment of a complaint is associated with the right to sound administration" (para 48), and that "such judicial review is also one of the general principles that are observed in a State governed by the rule of law and are common to the constitutional traditions of the Member States" (para 57), referring to Art. 41 and 47 of the Charter – an opinion which however was not taken up by the ECJ. This case law may have far reaching consequences for the way citizens' complaints are handled by Community institutions in areas where they have jurisdiction of their own. That is, the citizen is entitled to impartial and careful treatment of their problems, should have access to relevant documents within the limits of Reg. 1049/2001, and has the right to go the Court of First Instance if their matter has not been handled properly.

---

[45] Case T-54/99 max.mobil Telekommunikation Service GmbH v Commission [2002] ECR I-313, set aside in case C-141/02 P [2005] ECR I-(22.2.2005).

§ 19. GOVERNANCE AND ACCOUNTABILITY OF MEMBER STATES

I. MEMBER STATES AS THE KEY FIGURES OF GOVERNANCE

The discussion on Community governance has shown a contradictory result: On the one hand, the Court and secondary legislation have made considerable efforts to impose on Community institutions governance – in the shape of transparency, due diligence, and liability – that to some extent did not (yet) exist in Member State jurisdictions. On the other hand, it was concerned not to impair Community policy making activities by seemingly too stringent rules. Administrative efficiency and legislative discretion are elements that limit traditional forms of governance.[46] This is particularly true with regard to liability rules, which are usually a means of last resort in case of obvious and serious abuse of powers, rather than an instrument to control everyday behavior of Community institutions. Although other instruments such as injunctions or enforcement action may safeguard individual interests, these have not developed into a means of securing governance.

The situation *vis-à-vis* Member States is quite different. Here, the Court has developed a comprehensive theory of governance of Member States with regard to fulfilling their duties under Community law and safeguarding autonomy of other actors, in particular undertakings, but also citizens. Member States, in the liberal philosophy of European law, are the corner stones of safeguarding rights and assuring governance at the Community level. From autonomous, sovereign subjects of international law they have become *agents* in the pursuit of overriding Community interests.

This change in the role of Member States will be analysed on different levels. The most striking of these is the development of state liability as a remedy in its own right in case of non-fulfilment of Community obligations. This is the so-called *Francovich* doctrine (II). The second example concerns the duty on Member States to assure that private actors do not violate Community law obligations (III 1). The third is stand-still obligations, especially under Directive 83/189 as amended (III 2). The fourth contains the obligation of Member States regarding remedies in case of enforcing Community law rights (IV).

---

[46]   Kadelbach, in: Joerges/Dehousse, *supra* note 1 at 181-192.

We will briefly discuss these different paths to assuring governance of Member States *vis-à-vis* the Community and its citizens. These to some extent have supplemented the classic instrument of infringement action[47].

II. THE *FRANCOVICH* DOCTRINE

1. The lex imperfectae character of Art. 10

Art. 10 EC is explicit in defining Member State duties *vis-à-vis* the Community. There is both a positive and a negative element. The positive element can be described as a duty to loyalty and co-operation, the negative element as a duty to abstain from all acts contrary to Community interests. These general provisions supplement the specific duties that Member States owe in particular with regard to the internal market. The duties not only lie upon the central state, but – in federal systems – also on regional and local authorities, if they exercise public power. They are not limited to the executive branch, but include the legislature and the judiciary. They should be regarded as "*obligation de resultat*", "*Erfolgshaftung*" or result-oriented duties not allowing – or at least severely restricting – the classic defences of *force majeure*, internal difficulties, non-negligence, and the like.[48] The Member State is liable even if it did not have any influence on the concrete decision made by an independent self-governing, regional, or local body. Even a reference to its constitutional principles, including fundamental rights, cannot excuse a Member State's violation of its Community law duties. These do not depend on reciprocity.[49]

But what happens if Member States do not fulfil their duties? How can governance be assured either by Community institutions or by undertakings and individuals whose rights under Community law are violated by Member States? Art. 10 EC does not answer this question – it is, as many other Community law rules, a *lex imperfecta*. The Treaty does not contain a corollary to Art. 288 concerning liability of Member States. In its *Rewe v. Hauptzollamt Kiel* judgment of 1981[50] the Court insisted that the Treaty "was not intended to create new remedies".

---

[47] Under Art. 226 EC.
[48] Case 7/61 Commission v Italy [1961] ECR 317; C-1/00 Commission v France [2001] ECR-9989 at para 131: force majeure limited to period necessary to resolve difficulties.
[49] For an account cf. Gormley, in: Bernitz/Nergelius, *General Principles*, 2000, 113; from the abundant case law cf. case C-5/94 R v Ministry of Agriculture, Fisheries and Food *ex parte* Hedley Lomas (Ireland) [1996] ECR I-2553.
[50] Case 158/80 Rewe-Handelsgesellschaft Nord mbH et Rewe-Markt Steffen v Hauptzollamt Kiel [1981] ECR 1805 at para 4.

The traditional remedies in case of breach would lie either upon the Commission or upon Member State courts. The Commission can use its powers as watchdog of the Treaty, putting Member States on guard via protracted proceedings. These, as mentioned, are completely in its discretion and cannot be initiated or monitored by individuals. The Commission can only obtain a judgment stating a breach by Member States, but without putting legal consequences upon them. This stands in contrast to the ECHR, where the Human Rights Court can condemn Member States to pay compensation. The judgement does not automatically set aside Member State rules that violate Community law, but only pronounces an obligation of Member States to do everything needed for compliance. If they have not done so, another action may be brought and they may even be condemned to pay fines[51, 52]

As far as the individual is concerned, it has to use the procedures available under its competent jurisdiction. This may or may not allow for compensation in case of breach. But the principles are quite different among Member States and may exclude such remedies in case of legislative acts[53]. The reference procedure available to national courts will not necessarily help, because it is not in the competence of the European court to develop remedies under national law. That is, it may only remove obstacles to such potential remedies if they contradict Community law (*infra* IV).

2. The Francovich doctrine

This was in brief the state of law when the *Francovich* proceedings were initiated before the Court. The case at hand concerned the non-implementation of Dir. 80/987/EEC of 20.10.1980 on compensation of workers in case of bankruptcy of their employer[54]. Italy had already been condemned for non-implementation of this directive but had done nothing to implement the judgment of the Court. Therefore, the second case was concerned with the issue of whether the State should be directly liable for breach.

In his very carefully worded opinion, AG Mischo developed a theory of direct Community liability based on general principles of the law[55]. Comparative law studies and a reference to Art. 288 (2) EC convinced him that some sort of general idea of state liability for wrongful acts already existed, and was implicit in earlier case law of the Court.

---

[51] Art. 228 EC.
[52] The first case has been against Greece C-387/97 Commission v Greece [2000] ECR I-5047.
[53] Cf. the account of AG Leger in Hedley Lomas, case C-5/94 at note 49.
[54] Council Directive 80/987/EEC of 20 October 1980 on the approximation of the laws of the Member States relating to the protection of employees in the event of the insolvency of their employer [1980] *OJ* L 283/23.
[55] Art. 220 EC.

The Court followed suit, after having correctly stated that direct effect of the directive would not help the complainants, since it did not nominate a debtor. Who should pay bankruptcy compensation for workers in cases where no fund or insurance to cover this risk was established? The only conceivable debtor was the state. The Court then went on to say that:

> The full effectiveness of Community rules would be impaired and the protection of the rights that they grant would be weakened if individuals were unable to obtain redress when their rights are infringed by a breach of Community law for which a Member State can be held responsible. The possibility of obtaining redress from a Member State is particularly indispensable where, as in this case, the full effectiveness of Community rules is subject to prior action on the part of the State and where, in the absence of such action, individuals cannot enforce before the national courts the rights conferred upon them by Community law. It follows that the principle whereby the State must be held liable for loss and damage caused to individuals as a result of breaches of Community law for which the State can the held responsible is inherent in the system of the Treaty (paras 33-35).[56]

The last sentence is somewhat surprising, since the Treaty excluded Member State liability[57], and the logical consequence according to traditional legal reasoning would have been an *argumentum e contrario*. The argument of the Court is a legal policy argument containing two branches:
- The first is concerned with the *protection of individual rights*, in the case at hand worker's rights to compensation in case of bankruptcy of their employer.[58]
- The second argument of *"full effectiveness"* of Community law (§ 2 III 5) has to do with our topic of governance: state liability is a means to ensure compliance and to make wrongdoers – the Member State – pay for their illegal acts.

The following will be concerned with the second part of the argument, even though this is closely intertwined with the first.

3. Conditions of liability and their importance for Member State governance

Later case law was concerned with making more precise the conditions for liability that were pronounced rather broadly couched in legal policy terms in *Francovich*. The basic result of this discussion is that the Court wanted to realign state liability to

---

[56]   Joined cases C-6 + 9/90 Francovich v Italy [1991] ECR I-5357 at paras 33-5.

[57]   In Art. 288 (2).

[58]   That, in case C-479/93 Francovich (II) v. Italy [1995] ECR I-3843 was denied for formal reasons! Cf. van Gerven, *ICLQ* 1996, 507: A victory for Community law but not for the victims!

Community liability[59]. The later case of *Brasserie du Pêcheur*[60] therefore named three conditions of liability:

- The Community act that was not implemented intended to give rights to individuals; direct effect is not necessary; these rights must be identifiable with sufficient precision.[61]
- The breach by the Member State must be "sufficiently serious".
- A direct causal link must exist between the breach and the damage.

The requirement of a "sufficiently serious breach" was put into effect in the later *Dillenkofer* decision[62]. That is, where the Member State has "manifestly and gravely" disregarded its Community obligations by simple non-implementation of a directive, it should be held liable for damages to persons supposedly protected by the directive. Any organ of the Member State that commits such serious breach can provoke state liability. This might include the legislator, and possibly the highest judiciary for disregarding its duty to refer a case to the ECJ. In *Köbler*,[63] the Court confirmed the principle of state liability in case of a "manifest breach" of Community law by a highest court of a Member State. Such breach had to be established by considering a number of factors like the "degree of clarity and precision of the rule infringed, whether the infringement was intentional, whether the error of law was excusable or inexcusable, the position taken, where applicable, by a Community institution and compliance by the court in question with its obligation to make a reference for a preliminary ruling under Art. 234 (3) EC" (para 55). The infringement will be sufficiently serious "where the decision concerned was made in manifest breach of the case-law of the Court in the matter" (para 56).

If the Member State had only a considerably reduced, or even no, discretion, then a mere infringement of Community law may be sufficient to establish the existence of a sufficiently serious breach[64]. On the other hand, cases where a directive leaves room for interpretation, and the exact meaning can only be determined by the Court, will usually not result in success for a damages action against the Member State that had a different interpretation in implementing the directive.[65]

---

[59] As developed under Art. 288 (2).

[60] Joined cases C-46 and C-48/93 Brasserie du Pêcheur v Germany and R v Secretary of State for Transport *ex parte* Factortame Ltd. [1996] ECR I-1029; confirmed by case C-352/98P Bergaderm v Commission [2000] ECR I-5291.

[61] Case C-140/97 Rechberger *et al.* v Austria [1999] ECR I-3499 para 22-23.

[62] Joined cases C-178/94 Dillenkofer *et al.* v Germany [1996] ECR I-4845.

[63] Case C-224/01 G. Köbler v Austria [2003] ECR I-10239.

[64] Case C-5/94 R v Ministry of Agriculture, Fisheries and Food, *ex parte* Hedley Lomas (Ireland) Ltd. [1996] ECR I-2553 at para 28.

[65] Case C-392/93 R v H.M. Treasury *ex parte* British Telecommunications, [1996] ECR I-1631; joined cases C-283, C-291 and C-292/94 Denkavit Int. BV and others v Bundesamt für Finanzen [1996] ECR I-5063.

The element of (direct) causation has not yet been clarified by the Court. Guidance can be drawn from case law of the ECJ concerning the liability of Community institutions (§ 18 III) where it was held that causality must be "direct, immediate and exclusive". This is only the case if the damages arise directly from the conduct of the institutions, and do not depend on the intervention of other causes.[66] According to *Brinkmann*,[67] there will be no causal link between the breach and the damage where this damage would have occured even when correctly implementing EU law.

Even though the starting point of the case law is the protection of individual rights, later practice clearly shows that state liability has become an important element of governance. This is particularly true in cases where Community law provides for some kind of scheme to protect tourists (*Dillenkofer),* workers (*Francovich*), bank clients and investors (Directives 94/19/EEC[68] and 97/9/EC[69]) against bankruptcy of their contract partner, for example the tour operator, the employer or the bank. If the Member State is not able effectively to implement the requirement of setting up a fund or granting insurance coverage, it will have to step in itself. This means a considerable financial and – it should be added – political burden. Therefore, state liability is an effective instrument of governance, but it is not without limits. By judgment of 12 October 2004, the Court held that the EU banking directives do not preclude a Member State from ruling that the functions of the national authority responsible for supervising credit institutions are to be fulfilled only in the public interest, which excludes individual claims in compensation for damage resulting from defective supervision on the part of the authority. These directives do not confer rights on depositors in the event that their deposits are unavailable as a result of defective supervision, a supervision which is directed at safeguarding the stability of financial markets.[70]

This argument on governance is not necessarily valid with regard to directives giving rights to individual citizens. This is especially so in contractual relations, where Community law gives the consumer a right of withdrawal[71] or allows defences in third-party credit relations[72]. The financial consequences of failure to implement such a

---

[66]   Toth, in: Heukels/McDonnell (eds.), *The Action for Damages in Community Law*, 1997, 179-198.
[67]   Case C-319/96 Brinkmann Tabakfabriken v Skatteministeriet [1998] ECR I-5255, critique by Tridimas *supra* note 16 at 305.
[68]   Directive 94/19/EC of the European Parliament and of the Council of 30 May 1994 on deposit-guarantee schemes [1994] *OJ* L 135/5; cf. case C-233/94 Germany v European Parliament and Council [1997] ECR I-2405.
[69]   Directive 97/9/EC of the European Parliament and of the Council of 3 March 1997 on investor-compensation schemes [1997] *OJ* L 84/22.
[70]   Case C-222/02 Peter Paul et al. v Federal Republic [2004] ECR I-(12.10.2004).
[71]   Case C-91/92 Faccini Dori v Recreb [1994] ECR I-3325.
[72]   Case 192/94 El Corte Inglés v Rivero [1996] ECR I-1281.

directive are not such as to be an instrument of governance. The same is true, to a somewhat lesser extent, if the state breaches its obligations under primary Community law, especially the free movement rules.[73] They are even more inefficient in case of breaches of environmental obligations, where no concrete injured persons can be found because "diffuse interests" are at stake. Does "nature" have a claim against a non-complying state? Other types of remedy may be necessary, such as injunctions and enforcement actions.

III. GETTING THE MEMBER STATE TO ACT OR NOT TO ACT

1. French road blockages and ecologists' demonstration on the Brenner motorway

The Commission enjoys broad powers to enforce compliance of Member States with Community law, thereby assuring their governance with Community policies and law. However, it may not force action as such upon the state but, rather, may obtain a pronouncement by the Court that the state should have acted to avoid non-compliance, and that therefore those injured can claim damages for breach. A state can therefore be condemned for infringement, even if having taken a mere passive role in not avoiding breaches of Community law by third parties. Under such a theory, the state becomes a *guarantor* for the fulfilment of Community law.

Such a setting happened in the case of *Commission v. France (road blockages)*[74], where the Commission complained that the French government had not done everything it could to prevent road blockages by French farmers against Spanish producers of tomatoes passing through France. These road blockages in fact violated the free movement rules, and even if they had no direct effect against private parties, Member States must ensure that grave and illegal disruptions do not occur:

> Art. 30 (now 28 EC, NR) therefore requires Member States not merely themselves to abstain from adopting measures or engaging in conduct liable to constitute an obstacle to trade but also, when read with Art. 5 (now Art. 10 EC)... , to take all the necessary and appropriate measures to ensure that that fundamental freedom is respected on their territory (para 32).

This duty also to guarantee free movement against actions by private parties, including in industrial conflicts, puts a considerable burden upon the state, as the circumstances

---

[73] Cf. the aftermath of the Brasserie and Factortame-judgments, Tridimas, *supra* note 16 at 342-347.
[74] Case C-265/95 Commission v France [1997] ECR I-6959.

surrounding the French road blockades clearly show. The state would have to mobilize the police to comply with its Community obligations, even though breaches were committed by private parties. The state, even though it is only in the position of a guarantor, becomes primarily responsible in relation to the Community. On the other hand, the Community cannot be held responsible because it does not enjoy territorial powers in the same way as a state, nor does it have its own "police" to secure compliance with Community law.

The limits of this theory were clearly shown in the *Schmidberger* case[75] concerning an authorized 30 hour closure of the Brenner motorway to allow a demonstration by ecologists against pollution caused by heavy truck driving in the Alps. The Court invoked the fundamental rights argument (§ 12 II 3) and the proportionality principle to justify the impediment to free movement causing damage to German freight forwarders. The action for compensation against the Republic of Austria was therefore dismissed. The Court argued in para 85 of its judgment of 12 June 2003:

> … because of the presence of demonstrators on the Brenner motorway, traffic by road was obstructed on a single route, on a single occasion and during a period of almost 30 hours..[T]he obstacle to the free movement of goods resulting from that demonstration was limited by comparison with both the geographic scale and the intrinsic seriousness of the disruption caused in the case (concerning the French road blockages, NR).

It remains to be seen how other disruptions of free movement, for example by wildcat strikes of air traffic controllers or deliberately slow work by custom's officers on EU border control points, will be judged by the Court.

2. The duty not to act: stand-still obligations

Another means of assuring compliance of Member States with Community law is the duty *not* to act. In some cases this stand-still obligation follows directly out of Art. 10 EC. More important has been Dir. 83/189/EEC on technical standards[76], consolidated by Dir. 94/34/EC[77] and later amended by Dir. 98/48/EC to include standards of information society services.[78] It obliges Member States to inform the Commission

---

[75] C-112/00 Eugen Schmidberger v Austria [2003] ECR I-5659.
[76] Council Directive 83/189/EEC of 28 March 1983 laying down a procedure for the provision of information in the field of technical standards and regulations [1983] *OJ* L 109/8.
[77] Directive 98/34/EC of the European Parliament and of the Council of 22 June 1998 laying down a procedure for the provision of information in the field of technical standards and regulations [1998] OJ L 204/37.
[78] Directive 98/48/EC of the European Parliament and of the Council of 20 July 1998 amending Directive 98/34/EC laying down a procedure for the provision of information in the field of technical standards and regulations [1998] OJ L 217/18.

of the introduction of new technical regulations and standards that might impede the free movement of products on the internal market. The Commission may impose a stand-still obligation on a Member State not to implement the standard before a Community solution has been found, in order to avoid impediments to free movement. However, the Directive does not specify the consequences of failure to comply with the information obligation. Again, the Community legislator had created a *lex imperfecta*, and it fell to the Court to find a sanction in the interest of governance.

In its judgment in *CIA Security International v. Signalson*[79], the Court held that the new standard could not be invoked by the state against individuals who had not complied with it. The breach of the duty of the Member State to act (information obligation), or its failure to comply with the stand-still obligation, made the standard unenforceable. This is to some extent also true with regard to private law relations (§ 2 II 3c), as the later *Unilever* case[80] shows. However, it will not prevent criminal proceedings concerning driving under the influence of alcohol, where the specifications of the new breath-analysis apparatus used by the police were not notified to the Commission.[81]

In these cases – similar as in state aid matters (§ 7 V 4) – individual litigants are used as agents for enforcing Community law against Member States, also indirectly against private parties. It clearly depends upon procedures available under national law how this remedy is used and, thereby, governance of Member States enforced.

IV. THE DUTY TO PROVIDE ADEQUATE REMEDIES: *UBI IUS, IBI REMEDIUM*

Another important direction to ensure governance by Member States has been their obligation to provide for adequate remedies, and to remove obstacles to effective enforcement. This is part of the rules on judicial protection and has been treated in this context (§ 14). It has now been written into Art. I-29(1) of the Draft Constitution. The special remedies in case of violation of the EC procurements rules have been mentioned (§ 8 IV). These contain far reaching and detailed *"obligations de resultat"* of Member States, that in case of non-compliance may lead to *Francovich* liability of the state itself.

---

[79]   Case C-194/94 CIA Security International SA v Signalson SA and Securitel SPRL [1996] ECR I-2201.
[80]   Case C-443/98 Unilever Italia SpA v Central Food SpA [2000] I-7535.
[81]   Case C-226/97 Criminal proceedings against Lemmens [1998] ECR I-3711; for an overview P. Oliver, *Free Movement of goods*, 4th ed., at 482-490.

§ 20. GOVERNANCE AND RESPONSIBILITY OF UNDERTAKINGS

I. PRIMARY COMMUNITY LAW: RULES ON COMPETITION

1. Direct effect of competition rules

The most important rules on governance of undertakings are concerned with competition. This is a direct result of the insistence of EC law on open markets, which protects not just competition as an institution but also competitors themselves (§ 9 I). The following principle may be deduced:

> Thou (undertaking) shalt not act against your competitors in a manner such as to distort competition.

Although autonomy of undertakings is a basic value of Community law and indirectly guaranteed by the competition rules – it should not, however, be abused by undertakings co-operating through anti-competitive agreements or by abusing their market dominating position (§ 15 III). The sanctioning system of this fundamental principle of Community law is twofold:

- Primary Community law provides that anti-competitive agreements are void *ex lege* and cannot be enforced in actions before courts of law or in recognition proceedings of international arbitration awards.[82]
- Regulation 1/2003 provides for administrative sanctions to be imposed either by the Commission or by national anti-trust administrations. However, it says nothing about civil sanctions such as damages, and injunctions (§ 9 I 2).

There is agreement that the Community rules on assuring governance with the competition provisions are insufficient and defective. This is particularly true with abuses of dominant positions. These are forbidden but, under primary Community law, do not as such entail civil law consequences, in particular an action for damages. The Commission is empowered to impose considerable fines or take administrative measures, but these instruments do not provide for adequate compensation to injured competitors or to businesses up- or down-stream who have suffered loss due to anti-competitive behavior. This is not to mention consumers or purchasers (in the case of public procurement) who have paid excessive prices due to restrictive practices.

---

[82]   Cf. case C-126/97 Eco Swiss China Time v Benetton International NV [1999] ECR I-3055; details are discussed by van Gerven, in: Stuyck/Gilliams, *Modernisation of European Competition Law*, 2002, at p. 93 with a proposal for a Council regulation.

It became clear to the Court in its formative years that this situation is unsatisfactory. Indeed, the Court tried to remedy it by developing three additional instruments to overcome the existing state of *lex imperfecta* of Community law:

- The competition rules enjoy *direct effect* among private parties. That is, they can be invoked not only in administrative proceedings but also in civil law disputes before national courts of law.[83]
- Member State law should provide similar sanctions against anti-competitive behavior in violation of Community law provisions as are available under national law.
- These sanctions are similar to state liability (§ 19 II 3), subject to the principles of equivalence and effectiveness.

In its early case law, later repeated by the Court of First Instance in its *Automec II* decision[84], it was made clear that these sanctions are based on *national, not Community law*. It follows that all restrictions on them can be invoked equally against Community law violations if the above mentioned principles of equivalence and effectiveness were respected. The legal situation of sanctions against anti-competitive behavior resembled very much the situation of state liability for breaches of Community law before *Francovich*.

It is clear that the traditional approach had a number of drawbacks:

- Similar violations of identical rules were treated differently according to the law that governed the violation.
- Different treatment of violations implied additional distortions of competition that Community law wanted to avoid.
- The principles of equivalence and effectiveness provided for some, but only very vague and abstract, guidance.
- Member State courts were very hesitant in private enforcement actions of the competition rules, unlike their American partners.[85]
- With the shift in Community policy to rely more on private enforcement of competition rules, the remedies available to injured parties should be more effective and give an incentive for action.

This dilemma has now been overcome by a paradigm shift *from lex imperfecta to lex perfecta* as the *leitmotif* of the new case law of the ECJ!

---

[83]   Case 127/73 BRT v SV SABAM [1974] ECR 313.
[84]   Case T-24/90 Automec Srl v Commission [1992] ECR II-2223.
[85]   Cf. the study by Jones, *Private Enforcement*, 1999.

2. New trends in competition law: The Courage doctrine

In the area of competition law, a similar change of paradigms is now being witnessed as in 1991 with respect to state liability. This was prepared by a sweeping opinion of AG van Gerven in the *Banks v. British Coal* case[86] where he said:

> ... those prohibitions (regarding anti-competitive behavior, NR) are aimed at safeguarding undistorted competition and the freedom of competition for undertakings operating in the common market, with the result that such a breach of that system must be made good in full (at p. 1260).

AG van Gerven based his opinion on the existing principles of state liability for breach of directly effective Community law provisions and applied them also to breaches of the competition rules. In his opinion, it is not the national law that determines compensation but EC law itself. This stands in stark contrast to what the CFI had previously ruled in *Automec II*[87]. The doctrine of direct effect had to be followed up by a Community system of effective compensation, possibly also of prevention. This should not depend on the different state of development of Member State law. His arguments are legal policy based, similar to the ones advanced in *Francovich*, since the Treaty itself does not give an answer, and former case law was satisfied with a simple reference to national law.

The court at the time of *Banks* did not take up this argument, because it denied direct effect of the competition rules under consideration, that is, rules of the ECSC, not the EC Treaty itself. It took a later case, *Courage*[88], to set the starting point for a still undeveloped Community doctrine of liability for breaches of competition law. The case at hand concerned a British rule of *nemo auditur propriam turpitudinem allegans* forbidding a partner to an anti-competitive agreement from claiming damages. The Court set aside this rule because it prevents the full effectiveness of Community law. It went beyond this merely negative answer and made the following sweeping statement with regard to compensation for breaches of the Community competition rules:

> It follows from the foregoing considerations that *any individual* (italics NR) can rely on a breach of Art. 85 (1) (now Art. 81 NR) ... before a national court even where he is a party to a contract that is liable to restrict or distort competition within the meaning of that provision ... Indeed, the existence of such a right strengthens the working of the Community competition rules and discourages agreements or practices, that are frequently covert, that are liable to restrict or distort competition. From that point of view, actions for damages

---

[86]   Case C-128/92 H. J. Banks & Co. Ltd. v British Coal Corporation [1994] ECR I-1209.
[87]   *Loc cit.*, note 85 at para 50.
[88]   C-453/99 Courage Ltd. v Bernhard Crehan [2001] ECR I-6297.

before the national courts can make a significant contribution to the maintenance of effective competition within the Community (paras 25-27).

The Court makes it very clear that actions for damages are an important contribution to governance of undertakings in the field of competition. This action is based directly on Community, not on national law,[89] even if the procedural features as well as the determination of the competent court are subject to national law.

3. The consequences of Courage: extent and limits of compensation

The highly general and sweeping statement of the ECJ in *Courage* must be seen as the beginning of a series of cases similar to those litigated after *Francovich*. This of course would imply that economic actors are making use of the new case law of the ECJ.

The following points still need to be clarified, without going deeply into a still very open discussion[90]:

– Due to the similarities of the liability of states and of undertakings for breaches of Community law obligations, the standards for determining a wrongful act should be the same. There needs to be a *sufficiently serious breach* to invoke a claim for compensation. Minor offences will not be sufficient, especially when the basic data on which breach is based are contested, for instance market determination. Clear and obvious breaches will be subject to an action in damages. Examples would include breaches of provisions contained in so called "black listed clauses" of exemption regulations such as horizontal or vertical price fixing agreements, market segregation, territorial restrictions, unjustified refusal to supply. The new exemption regulations 2790/1999 and 1400/2002 discussed above (§ 9 III/IV) contain "hardcore restrictions". Violations against these may give rise to damages actions by those protected by these directly applicable regulations.

– It is not yet clear who can be a plaintiff in a damages action. The Court very broadly spoke of "any individual", but this formula seems to be somewhat imprecise. In his Opinion of 22.3.2001, AG Mischo mentioned third parties as victims, most notably consumers and competitors.[91] The criteria of "direct causation" used for determining state liability may be of help in specifying compensation in a vertical chain of distribution.

– The burden of proof of a violation of Art. 81 (1) and the "hardcore restrictions" lies upon the injured plaintiff, but there may be a *prima facie* case for a violation

---

[89]   Komninos, CMLRev 2002 at 473; cf. the differing opinions of Reich/Micklitz, *Europäisches Verbraucherrecht*, at paras 4.74 and 29.12.

[90]   For details, see Reich, *CMLRev* 2005, 35.

[91]   Para 38.

by the defendant if he participated in some way in the anti-competitive behaviour of the other party to the distribution contract.[92]

– The amount of damages must be in conformity with the loss provoked by the breach, thus excluding punitive damages, but allowing the skimming off of profit. Comparative law studies could be helpful, similarly as with regard to Community or state liability, to set Community-wide thresholds for compensation.

– The defendant cannot argue that the plaintiff was able to "pass on" the damage in the downstream line of commerce, since an absolute "passing-on"-defense would frustrate the full effectiveness of Community law and therefore cannot be accepted.[93]

– It is not clear how far injunctions or positive actions are possible under Community law. Examples here would include not to refuse to conclude a contract because a denial would amount to an anti-competitive practice of the potential partner. In its *Automec II* decision the Court of First Instance left this to Member State law. However, following the trend in decentralized enforcement, Community law will have to develop its own rules here. It is submitted that injunctions should be possible against anti-competitive behavior under the principle: *ubi res ibi remedium*[94].

II. COMPENSATION FOR VIOLATIONS OF DIRECTLY APPLICABLE PROVISIONS OF PRIMARY COMMUNITY LAW

The *Courage* case was concerned only with violations of competition law. However, its logic can be extended to all rules of primary Community law that directly apply regarding private parties. In the recent case law of the Court, this is particularly true with regard to free movement of workers. In its *ASBL v. Bosman* judgment[95], the Court made this clear in regard to rules of professional soccer associations, and in *Angonese*[96] with regard to language tests by private undertakings. Moreover, in *Wouters* the Court extended this rule to all Community law provisions protecting free movement of persons against collective restrictions.[97] These rulings also apply to the freedoms guaranteed in the EA agreements, particularly on establishment and on non-

---

92   Case C-49/92 P Commission v Anic [1999] I-4125 at para 96.
93   For a detailed discussion see Reich *supra* note 90 at 45-48.
94   See now AG Jacobs, opinion of 22.5.2003 in cases C-2 + 3/01 etc. AOK-Bundesverband v Ichthyol-Gesellschaft Cordes *et al.* [2004] ECR I-(6.1.2004) at para 104.
95   Case C-415/93 ASBL v Bosman [1995] ECR I-4921.
96   Case C-281/98 Roman Angonese v Cassa di Risparmio di Bolzano SpA [2000] ECR I-4139.
97   Case C-309/99 Wouters, Savelbergh, Price Waterhouse Belastingadviseurs v Algemene Raad [2002] ECR I-1577 at para 120.

discrimination of legally employed workers because, according to the new case law of the Court, they enjoy direct effect.[98] This reasoning was upheld by AG Stix-Hackl in her opinion of 11 July 2002 and the Court in its judgment of 8 May 2003 in the *Kolpak* case that concerned discrimination against a professional handball player from Slovakia by the statutes of the German Handball association. These limited the number of third-country foreigners in professional handball matches.[99]

The reasoning of AG van Gerven in *Banks* concerning the interrelationship between directly applicable Community law rules and an action for compensation in case of "sufficiently serious breaches" is transferable here, too. Mr. Bosman therefore should be able to claim damages for his being eliminated from his career as a professional soccer player by the rules of ASBL. Mr. Angonese should get compensation for not being allowed to show language proficiency by other means than those prescribed by the Cassa di Risparmio di Bolzano. Mr. Kolpak should be compensated by the German *Handballbund* for discrimination in his career as a professional sportsman from Slovakia enjoying the protection of the EA agreement with his country.

III. VIOLATIONS OF SECONDARY LAW

1. Directives demanding effective remedies in cases of breach

In the discussion on adequate standards, several directives were analysed that provide for a level playing field in the area of labour, consumer, and financial services law. Best known is Directive 76/207 on non-discrimination in labour relations with regard to gender (§ 11 III 2).

The relevant directives are quite explicit in demanding effective sanctions in the case of violations of the obligations they contain, for example in cases of unjustified discrimination, or placing defective products on the market. Although the directives have undertakings (employers or producers) as addressees of obligations, the following factors make the legal position of those who are injured quite weak because of the character of Community directives as *leges imperfectae*:

---

[98] Cases C-63/99 R v Secretay of State for the Home Department, ex parte Wieslaw and Elzbieta Gloszczuk, [2001] I-6369; C-235/99 R v Secretary of State for the Home Department, es parte Eleanora Ivanova Kondova [2001] ECR I-6427, C-257/99; R v Secretay of State for the Home Department, ex parte Julius Barkoci and Marcel Malik, [2001] ECR-6557, C-268/99 Aldona Malgorzata Jany and Others v Staatssecretaris van Justitie [2001] ECR-8615, C-162/00 Land Nordrhein-Westfalen v Beata-Pokrzeptowicz-Meyer [2002] ECR I-1049; for an overall discussion; Reich/Harbacevica, *Europarättslig Tidskrift* 2002, 411.

[99] Case C-438/00 Deutscher Handballbund eV v Maros Kolpak [2003] ECR I-4135.

- As a ground rule, directives are directed towards Member States, not towards individuals. That is, direct effect takes place only "vertically" (against the state and similar public institutions).
- According to a relatively consistent case law, directives cannot as such impose obligations on individuals (absence of horizontal direct effect, § 2 II 3b).
- If directives are not correctly implemented, either the principle of directive conforming interpretation "as far as possible" or, in the final resort, of state liability, can be invoked to ensure, on the one hand, enforcement of citizens' rights and on the other hand governance of undertakings, § 3 IV 2.
- Recent case law is somewhat vague as to how far restrictions in Member State law on rights guaranteed in directives can be overcome by directly invoking the directive, or whether the limits put on a "*contra legem*" interpretation must be respected. So far, the Court has not given a clear answer, leaving this to Member State jurisdictions (§ 2 II 3c).

One way to overcome this dilemma would be to rewrite directives into regulations. Then a direct action of injured individuals against illegal acts by business would arise out of violations of the rights they contain. This would be the most effective way to ensure governance. But according to an overwhelming opinion in legal doctrine, this is excluded by the principle of subsidiarity (§ 3 I) – a doctrine that will not be questioned here. The focus will be on directives imposing governance on undertakings or their directors for certain of their activities. The following sections will be concerned with product safety, environmental quality, and "corporate governance".

2. The case of product liability

A free and open market based upon autonomous decisions by active market subjects – undertakings as they are called in competition law (§ 9 II 2) – must establish rules on risk allocation in case of hazardous products or services placed on the market. Therefore, a liberal theory of autonomy does not contradict rules on responsibility and liability in case of defective products, provided that certain basic requirements are met. The most important of these is that there be a clear attribution of risks. That is, a liability rule will only be effective to enforce governance if those who have caused the risk will have to answer to allow for prevention or compensation, potentially followed by insurance cover. The question of *causation* is therefore crucial.

On the other hand, and in contrast to traditional civil law theory, the recourse to negligence as a standard is not necessary. Negligence may be used with regard to liability of private persons, who are only obliged to pay compensation for an injury caused to another person if they had direct control over their individual action or could have avoided it by being more careful. For collective entities such as undertakings, this is not the decisive problem. Liability is a problem of *organization and risk management*, not of individual behavior. It is a cost, not a moral factor.

When the Community, based upon a prior draft convention of the Council of Europe, started its work on product liability in the seventies, there was no doubt that the standard should not be negligence as in most Member State jurisdictions, but *strict liability* based on placing a defective product on the market. The discussion was mostly concerned with how strict this standard should be. Should it be limited by the "state of the art", for example by the extent of scientific and technological knowledge existing about inherent risks at the time the product was placed on the market? Or should the producer and marketer also respond to defects that later knowledge discovered but that were not known, or could not possibly be discovered at the time of putting the product into circulation?

The product liability directive 85/374/EEC enacted on 25 July 1985[100] after controversy between business and consumers, chose a middle-of-the-road solution. This still seems to be acceptable today and prescribes a good standard of governance. Liability of producers of defective products undergoes a *three-step test*:
–   The defect must be first be proven to exist according to the "safety that a person is entitled to expect", including presentation, reasonable use, and time of placement of the product on the market.
–   If a defect is found under this standard, the producer is liable if the other elements have been proven to exist by the injured party, especially causation[101].
–   The state-of-the-art standard gives the producer only a defence[102]. He is excused only if he is able to prove, according to recent Court practice, that the risk has not been described in the reasonably accessible and relevant scientific or technological literature.[103]

In today's European product liability practice, the state-of-the-art defence has not played a significant role. It is accepted practice that the producer bears not only the risk of a defective product in the traditional sense as such, but also the risk that a product may become defective if the elements potentially leading to such defect can already be verified at the time of placing the product on the market. Therefore, the producer is liable not so much for defects as for *risk-taking* – a standard that seems to be quite well in harmony with the theory of governance developed here.

---

[100]   Council Directive 85/374/EEC of 25 July 1985 on the approximation of the laws, regulations and administrative provisions of the Member States concerning liablity for defective products [1985] *OJ* L 210/29.
[101]   Art. 4 of Dir. 85/374.
[102]   Art. 7 (e) of Dir. 85/374.
[103]   Case C-300/95 Commission v UK [1997]ECR I-2649.

On the other hand, it is no longer understandable why the directive takes such a narrow approach with regard to compensation. In its original version, liability for primary agricultural and fishery products had been excluded. This defence has now been eliminated by Dir. 1999/34 of 10 May 1999 as a follow-up to the BSE scandal.[104] On the other hand, compensation of personal injury does not, by Community law, include pain and suffering (non-material damage). This is left to the Member States – quite in contrast to a recent decision in the area of package holidays.[105] The Court, in product liability litigation at least, insists on "full and proper compensation" of any other bodily injury:

> A Member State cannot therefore restrict the types of material damage resulting from death or personal injury, or from damage to or destruction of an item of property that are to be made good.[106]

Compensation for damage to property has several severe limitations:
- First of all, there is a *de minimis* threshold of 500 euro for which no compensation can be claimed and that cannot be waived by Member States.[107]
- There is no compensation for property damage in B2B relations.
- Compensation is only given for consumer products if they are used by the injured person "mainly for his private use or consumption".
- There is only compensation if the damage did not occur to the defective product itself.

The effect of the product liability directive on governance has so far been negligible, and there is little case law to explain the ambit of the directive. Many concepts remain unclear, for example:
- Could *waste* be regarded as a "product" in the sense of the directive if, *e.g.*, used for recycling purposes?
- Will computer software be regarded as "product" in the sense of Art. 2, namely as "movable"? Usually, software is integrated in some "hardware", which then, as "movable" and therefore product, may be defective and cause injury in the sense of Dir. 85/377.
- Does liability under Art. 6 also extend to *non-effective* but not as such hazardous products?

---

[104] Directive 1999/34/EC of the European Parliament and of the Council of 10 May 1999 amending Council Directive 85/374/EEC on the approximation of the laws, regulations and administrative provisions of the Member States concerning liability for defective products [1999] *OJ* L 141/20.
[105] ECJ case C-168/00 Simone Leitner v TUI Deutschland [2002] ECR I-2631.
[106] Case C-203/99 Henning Veedfald v Arhus Amtscommune [2001] ECR I-3569.
[107] Case C-154/00 Commission v Greece [2002] I-3879.

- How can one distinguish defects in the product itself, that cannot be recovered from the producer, from other defects to property?
- How far does the harmonization effect of the directive go under Art. 13, whereby the directive "shall not affect any rights that an injured person may have according to the rules of law of contractual or non-contractual liability or a special liability system at the moment when this directive is notified"? In a series of cases the ECJ insisted in its judgments of 25.4.2002 that Dir. 85/374 is not a minimum directive and Member States may therefore not set higher standards for consumer protection, for example with regard to the compensation sought or the introduction of additional product monitoring duties,[108] or recently concerning the Danish rule on strict liability of suppliers who are not subsidiarily responsible in the sense of Art. 3 (3) of Dir. 85/374.[109]

3. The case of environmental liability

a. A new approach towards environmental governance

Community law, in contrast to Member State law, has not yet developed a standard for environmental liability, despite the many accidents that have happened to the environment, the numerous contaminated sites where hazardous waste had been dumped, and the overall degradation of water, air, soil, and climate caused by an ever growing flux of harmful emissions and undisposed waste.

The reasons for this absence are manifold. One was certainly that the Community, in developing its own environmental policy and law till the 6th and last action program,[110] has relied on regulation through the setting of technical standards on air and water emissions, waste management, product and processes, and especially with regard to chemicals. Later discussion sought to establish economic incentives for improving the environment or preventing harm, through environmental taxes (duties) and benefits (subsidies), tradable emission certificates, and the like.

As a result, one must say that this policy was not very successful and has not been used actively by the EU.[111] Environmental taxes need unanimity in the Council, per Art. 175 (2) EC, which is difficult to obtain. Economic incentives depend on the willingness

---

[108] Case C-52/00 Commission v France, [2002] ECR I-3827.

[109] Case C-402/03 Skov et al. v Jette Mikkelsen et al. [2005] ECR I-(per opinion of AG Geelhoed of 20.1.2005).

[110] Communication from the Commission to the Council, the European Parliament, the Economic and Social Committee and the Committee of the Regions On the sixth environment action programme, Com (2002)31 final of 24.1.2002.

[111] For a discussion cf. Krämer, *EC Environmental law*, 5th ed. 2003, 167-170.

of the actors to "play the game"; environmental taxes or emission charges cannot really implement the "polluter pays" principle, because they would have to be so high as to prohibit certain types of production altogether. This in reality would as a consequence provoke an outsourcing of these environmentally hazardous activities to less developed countries, abolishing workplaces in the EU – a highly unpopular option among Member States and the EU itself.

The 6th program is somewhat more innovative, as it proposes certain new elements:
- Stakeholders and citizens must take more ownership of efforts to protect the environment.
- Voluntary commitments and agreements to achieve clear environmental objectives should be encouraged. This could be an example of the OMC method of governance.[112]
- A Community Environmental Liability regime should be created.

b. Directive 2004/35 on environmental liability

At the beginning of 2002, the Commission finally published its long awaited proposal "on environmental liability with regard to the prevention and remedying of environmental damage".[113] This is mostly concerned with collecting funds to clean up contaminated sites, and in obtaining compensation for environmental accidents causing a serious degradation of bio-diversity.

The proposal addresses several problems, but not always in a satisfactory way:
- Similarly to the product liability directive, the main standard is *causation*, not negligence.
- The directive allows for several defences, the most important of these being that an emission or event was allowed in applicable laws and regulations, or in the authorization to the operator.
- Another defence is, quite surprisingly in a scheme based on causation, absence of fault or negligence, per Art. 8 with regard to bio-diversity damage.
- A third defence is the impossibility of establishing a causal link between the damage and the activities of certain individual operators, thereby excluding diffuse environmental damage from compensation.
- Finally, there is the state-of-the-art defence of Art. 9 (1) d) of the proposal.

---

[112] Scott/Trubek, *ELJ* 2002, 1 at 5-7.
[113] Proposal for a Directive of the European parliament and of the Council on environmental liability with regard to the prevention and remedying of environmental damage Com (2002) 17 final [2002] OJ C 151/132.

– The proposed directive does not give private parties a right of compensation for any economic loss sustained in consequence of environmental damage or of an imminent threat of such damage. It contains in reality a *cost recovery scheme*, where bio-diversity has been destroyed due to environmental pollution or accidents.

As a novelty, the directive also foresees preventive action in the sense that a "qualified entity" may request action under Art. 14. However, this entity has to furnish extensive documentation. Clearly, it cannot force the competent authority to act, but only to give reasons in case of non-action.

In the meantime, Directive 2004/35/EC of the EP and the Council of 21 April 2004 on environmental liability has been adopted.[114] The modifications with regard to the proposal are rather minor; the question of mandatory insurance has been postponed to a Commission report to be issued in 2010. Art. 3 (3) makes it clear that the directive "shall not give private parties a right of compensation as consequence of environmental damage or of an imminent threat of such damage". Causation is an element of liability, Art. 4 (5), not merely a defence. The consequences of multiple party causation have to be determined by national law, Art. 9. The defence of non-negligence on the part of the operator, combined with express authorisation of the hazardous activity or the state-of-the-art defence, is left to the Member States, Art. 8 (4). Request for action may be sought by natural or legal persons showing a sufficient interest of alleging the impairment of a right, but these concepts will be determined by the Member States. Environmental NGOs under national law will be deemed to have sufficient interest or capable of having rights which can be impaired, Art. 12 (1).

An evaluation of the Directive is too early. A critical look should be taken at the defences that the Directive allows against environmental liability. Are they in conformity with the concept of environmental governance as expressed by the "polluter pays" principle?[115] The state-of-the-art and the legal activity defences are justified only if they are interpreted narrowly. The first must be construed similarly to product liability law. That is, what risks is the polluter willing to accept, even if the activity was seemingly not risky at the time of action? In the second case, the decisive point has to do with the interpretation of an action or event being allowed or authorized; mere tolerance should not be enough.

Finally, the negligence defence is misplaced and should not be left to the discretion of Member States. It is also not clear why private parties should not be able to get compensation for damage to bio-diversity if they re-establish the former state of a site.

---

[114]   [2004] OJ L 143/56.
[115]   Per Art. 174 (2) EC.

4. *"Corporate governance"*

"Corporate governance" is a catchword to characterize the responsibility of directors of a (public) company towards its (minority) shareholders and other "stakeholders", such as creditors in the securities market. The debate originated in the US. It has only hesitantly come over to the EC as a corollary to freedom of establishment of companies[116]. This freedom is part of open markets, but may be limited (§ 7 V), as the Court said in *Überseering*,[117] by:

> overriding requirements relating to the general interest, such as the protection of the interests of creditors, minority shareholders, employees and even the taxation authorities may, in certain circumstances and subject to certain conditions, justify restrictions on freedom of establishment (para 92).

Art. 44 (2) lit g) EC gives the Community power to legislative harmonization measures:

> by coordinating to the necessary extent the safeguards that, for the protection of the interests of members and other, are required by Member States of companies.... with a view to making such safeguards equivalent throughout the Community.

The Community legislator has done so by adopting several company law directives. Their content varies and will not be described in any detail. They are very hesitant in imposing duties and obligations on directors and companies. However, there are some small examples of an emerging doctrine of legally enforceable "corporate governance" rules. The first Directive 68/151/EEC of 9.3.1968[118] requires a limited liability company to make accessible its balance sheets. German law restricted this access to shareholders, creditors and factory councils, but excluded other persons. In *Daihatsu*[119] the Court rejected this restriction and interpreted broadly the concept of "in the interest of members and others"[120], including the public, that was implicitly justified by reasons of "corporate governance":

> ...disclosure of annual accounts is primarily designed to provide information for third parties who do not know or cannot obtain sufficient knowledge of the company's

---

[116]   Per Art. 48 EC.
[117]   Case C-208/00 Überseering BV v Nordic Construction Company Baumanagement [2002] ECR I-9919.
[118]   First Council Directive 68/151/EEC of 9 March 1968 on co-ordination of safeguards which, for the protection of the interests of members and others, are required by Member States of companies within the meaning of the second paragraph of Article 58 of the Treaty, with a view to making such safeguards equivalent throughout the Community [1968] *OJ* L 65/8.
[119]   Case C-97/96 Verband deutscher Daihatsu Händer eV v Daihatsu Deutschland GmbH [1997] ECR I-6843.
[120]   In Art. 44 (2) lit g) EC.

accounting and financial situation….(This).. confirms the concern to enable any interested persons to inform themselves of these matters…(para 22).

At the same time the Court repeated that the Directive has no horizontal direct effect and can therefore not be enforced by members of the public to whom access to the balance sheet was denied.

On the other hand, the exclusion of the pre-emption right (*Bezugsrecht*) of share-holders in case of considerations in kind (*Sacheinlagen*) by German law was not seen as a violation of Art. 29 of the second Dir. 77/91/EEC of 13.12.1976[121], thus allowing a reduction in the position of minority shareholders in the company statutes.[122]

The state of EU company law in general and corporate governance in particular is generally regarded as unsatisfactory.[123] There is some discussion on referring these questions more to OMC-methods instead of the traditional harmonization by directives. Wouters[124] has made a proposal for "model rules and codes of conduct under the *aegis* of the Commission." The Court itself, if *Centros* (§ 7 V 3) is correctly interpreted, seems to favour a model of information through capital market provisions that are not necessarily sanctioned by liability rules.

On the other hand, where Community law sets certain standards with regard to corporate behavior, such as with private investors by investment service providers like brokers in Art. 11 of Directive 93/22/EC of 10.5.1993[125], it avoids any clear answer to the question how far it may be enforced by private actors. It seems to leave enforcement to the competence of public authorities. Tison[126] suggests that such a private right of action may be based upon the *effet utile* doctrine of the Court deman-ding effective judicial protection if rights of individuals are violated (§ 14 I). This author[127] has argued in a similar way, because the rules on investor protection implement a general principle inherent in the marketing of securities, namely duties of care and information of the broker. The new Commission proposal of a Directive

---

[121]   Second Council Directive 77/91/EEC of 13 December 1976 on coordination of safeguards which, for the protection of the interests of members and others, are required by Member States of companies within the meaning of the second paragraph of Article 58 of the Treaty, in respect of the formation of public limited liability companies and the maintenance and alteration of their capital, with a view to making such safeguards equivalent [1976] *OJ* L 26/1.

[122]   Case C-42/95 Siemens AG v Henry Nold [1996] ECR I-6017.

[123]   For an overview Couret, *RIDE* 2002, 339.

[124]   Wouters, *CMLRev* 2000, 257 at 298.

[125]   Council Directive 93/22/EEC of 10 May 1993 on investement services in the securities field [1993] *OJ* L 141/27.

[126]   In: Ferrari/Hopt/Wymeersch (eds.), *Capital markets in the Age of the Euro*, 2002, 65 at 76.

[127]   Reich/Micklitz, *Europäisches Verbraucherrecht*, 4. A. 2003 para 22.16.

on Investment Services of 19.11.2002[128] aims to stiffen administrative sanctions against violations of the investor protection rules, but contains no rule on civil liability. The recently adopted Directive 2004/39/EC of the EP and the Council of 21 April 2004 on markets in financial instruments[129] contains rules on investor protection in Art. 19 (information, know-your-customer-rule, exceptions for EOB [exceptions-only business], Art. 21 (best possible execution in the interest of the client), but leaves enforcement to administrative action, per Art. 25 et seq., without giving the client a direct right of compensation in case of violation. The same is true for Directive 2003/6/EC of the EP and Council of 28 Jan. 2003 on Market Abuse.[130] Enforceable "corporate governance" rules protecting private parties therefore still await implementation.

IV. CONFLICT RULES APPLICABLE TO NON-CONTRACTUAL OBLIGATIONS

On 22.7.2003, the Commission published a proposal for a Council Regulation on the "Law applicable to non-contractual obligations (Rome II)".[131] The proposal is based on the new provisions of the Amsterdam Treaty concerning judicial co-operation in civil matters, similar to the Brussels Regulation 44/2001 (supra § 14 III 2). To some extent it follows suit the Rome Convention concerning the law applicable to contractual obligations (so-called Rome I, § 16 III) with regard to conflict rules, even though the principles differ:

– Rome I is an instrument under international law, not yet integrated into the *acquis* and without authority of the ECJ to interpret it; Rome II will be a Community regulation (with Denmark opting out and the UK and Ireland able to opt in), recognising the interpretative authority of the ECJ under Art. 68 EC;

– Rome I starts from the principle of freedom of choice of law (Art. 3), while the principle of close connection (Art. 4) has a mere subsidiary function, while Rome II being concerned with non-contractual obligations takes as a basis the objective "*lex loci delicti commissi*" principle, which to some extent is already present in Art. 5 (3) of the Brussels Convention/Regulation (supra § 14 II 2d).

– While Rome I is satisfied with some specific rules on consumer and worker protection, Rome II has as its aim also victim protection in general, in whatever function the person was injured, and contains therefore elements of governance

---

[128] Com (2002) 625 final [2003] OJ C 71/62.
[129] [2004] OJ L 145/1.
[130] Directive 2003/6/EC of the European Parliament and of the Council of 28 January 2003 on insider dealing and market manipulation (market abuse) [2003] *OJ* L 96/16.
[131] Com [2003] 427 final.

and legitimate expectations. At the same time, it must make the applicable law predictable to potential tort feasors in order to allow insurance and legal certainty, which is the more necessary since most part of tort law is not harmonised. Victim choice of law and compensation must therefore be balanced with legitimate interests of business and insurers.

Rome II tries to reach this balance by spelling out the universal rule of *lex loci delicti commissi*, which refers to the country where the damage arises or is likely to arise (usually the place of residence of the victim), Art. 3 (1), with some exceptions due to the "closer connection principle". For sake of clarity and governance of undertakings, the following articles contain specific rules for certain types of injury:
- Art. 4, product liability: applicability of the law of the country of habitual residence of the victim, provided the product was marketed there. Otherwise, the law of the country of residence of the tort feasor will be applicable.
- Art. 5, unfair competition, including a violation of the collective interest of consumers: Rome II will codify the so-called "market rule", e.g. applicability of the law of the market where the competitive relations or consumer interests are affected.
- Art. 6, violations of privacy and rights relating to the personality: Rome II introduces the so-called forum of victim-rule, unless this contradicts principles of the forum on freedom of expression and information. It is irrelevant whether the publisher intended to market his product in the victim's country or not – in difference to product liability cases. The British "double actionability rule" would be abolished. Art. 6 (1) is particularly controversial given the wide differences of Member State laws with regard to defamation, protection of privacy, and freedom of press. With regard to the right of reply, the law of the country of the habitual residence of the publisher will be applicable.
- Art. 7, violation of the environment: applicability of the law of the victim's residence, with an option to an eventual more favourable law of the country of origin (seat of the company responsible of the damage to the environment). This follows the *Mines de Potasse* case law of the ECJ.[132]
- Art. 8 relates to infringements of intellectual property rights and codifies the well-established *lex loci protectionis*.
- A special rule concerning the country of origin-principle e.g. for electronic commerce (supra § 8 III 2) is reserved in Art. 23 (2). This will lead to different conflict rules with regard to unfair competition and violations of privacy, depending whether traditional media or online instruments led to the injury – a somewhat problematic privilege of online operations.

---

[132]   Case 21/76, [1976] ECR 1735.

The fate of the draft regulation is unclear. While Art. 3, 4, 5, 7 and 8 spell out well recognised principles of private international law, the proposal of Art. 6 (liability of press, broadcasting etc.) and the privilege of e-commerce in Art. 23 (2) remain extremely controversial.

§ 21. GOVERNANCE AND RESPONSIBILITY OF CITIZENS – A BLIND SPOT?

I. THE EUROPEAN CITIZEN "KING"

Citizens' rights in Member States are invariably followed by a list of citizenship duties. Shaw[133] specifies the duty to "obey lawful rules", the "defence of the country", the duty to "pay taxes" and the "duty to work". Art. 17 EC itself speaks of rights and *duties* imposed on Union citizens (§ 5 I).

Ironically enough, so far the ordinary Union citizen whose rights have been so remarkably extended has successfully escaped from such obligations.[134] This is a result of the hybrid status of the Union/Community between an international organization and a state. The duty to obey lawful rules will usually be imposed by primary Community law and regulations, but is *de facto* limited to market citizens, for example business and other economic actors. Directives, according to the case law of the Court, cannot directly impose obligations on individuals (§ 2 II 3). The duty to pay taxes, other duties and tariffs is again coupled with the position of the market citizen; the Community has no power to levy direct taxes unless by a unanimous act of the Council.

II. IS THERE A DUTY TO LOYALTY?

Can one at least speak of a duty of loyalty by the Union citizen to Union institutions and Community law? This question is usually discussed in the relationship between Community, or Union and Member State, institutions. Article 10 EC is a basis for such a mutual loyalty obligation. There is no similar duty imposed on individuals. As Shaw[135] correctly remarks:

> The tendency of any discourse of citizenship duties is to construct the figure of the citizen in the light of some conception – however vague – of moral virtue.

This "moral virtue" has not yet been transposed into a legal obligation. Moreover, it is hardly realistic that this will ever be done in the near future. Indeed, it seems to be contrary to the *liberal spirit of EC* law and Union citizenship itself, which focuses exclusively on rights and not on duties. For example, EC law has greatly extended

---

[133] Collected Courses of the Academy of European Law, 1998, Vol VI-I at 343.
[134] For a general critique, cf. Weiler, *The Constitution of Europe*, 1999, at 324-357.
[135] *Supra*, note 131 at 344.

consumer rights to legitimate expectations (§ 13) but has done little to impose corresponding environmental obligations, as Krämer and Wilhelmsson have rightly and critically pointed out.[136] As an example, the package holiday directive 90/314/EEC of the Council of 13.6.1990[137] has developed extensive tourist rights including a directly applicable safety net in case of insolvency of the tour operator[138], but no corresponding obligations relating to environmental protection. As another example, the packaging waste directive 94/62/EC of the EP and the Council of 20.12.94[139] makes it an indirect duty of the consumer/citizen to participate in waste management and prevention, for example through information about recycling systems, but does not prescribe a moral, even less a legal, obligation to limit waste. It allows Member state regulations to introduce more environmental friendly deposit and return systems for soft drinks which encourage consumers to return the used containers against receiving back their deposit, providing that consumers who have been charged a deposit when buying goods in non-reusable packing can recover the deposit even if they do not go back to the initial place of purchase.[140]

Citizens' duties are indirectly contained in EC directives on waste, such as Art. 9 of Dir. 75/439/EEC of 16 June 1975 on used oils[141] and Art. 8 of Dir. 75/442/EEC of 15 July 1975 on waste.[142] These impose obligations on Member States, which consequently have to make citizens responsible for orderly waste management. They cannot directly put duties upon citizens due to their character as *leges imperfectae*. The only exception where obligations are imposed directly on citizens is Art. 9 of Reg. 338/97 of 9 Dec. 1996 on the protection of species of wild fauna and flora by regulating their trade[143], and banning movement of certain live specimens, which also obliges private persons and is not limited – unlike Art. 8 – to commercial activities.

---

[136] In this sense the critique of Krämer, *JCP* 1993, 455; Wilhelmsson, *JCP* 1993, 45.

[137] Council Directive 90/314/EEC of 13 June 1990 on package holidays and package tours [1990] *OJ* L 158/59.

[138] This is obviously the substance of the case law of the Court, *e.g.*, joined cases C-178/94 Dillenkofer and others v Germany [1996] ECR I-4845; C-364/96 Verein für Konsumenteninformation v Österreichische Kreditversicherungs AG [1998] ECR I-2949; C-140/97 Rechberger, Greindl et al. v Austria [1999] ECR I-3499.

[139] European Parliament and Council Directive 94/62/EC of 20 December 1994 on packaging and packaging waste [1994] *OJ* L 361/10.

[140] Case C-309/02 Radlberger Getränkegesellschaft v Land Baden-Württemberg [2004] ECR I- (14.12.2004).

[141] Council Directive 75/439/EEC of 16 June 1975 on the disposal of waste oils [1975] *OJ* L 194/31.

[142] Council Directive 75/442/EEC of July 1975 on waste [1975] *OJ* 194/39.

[143] Council Regulation (EC) No 338/97 of 9 December 1996 on the protection of species of wild fauna and flora by regulating trade therein [1997] *OJ* L 61/1.

III. "ABUS DE DROIT" AND "SOCIAL FUNCTION OF RIGHTS" AS A SUBSTITUTE FOR OBLIGATIONS?

A liberal concept of citizenship and subjective rights of citizens, that is the one adhered to by the EU, should at least develop a *minimalist concept* of limiting these rights in case of obvious abuse. It would be interesting to enter into the debates of the 19th century where the concept of "*abus de droit*", supplemented by a broader theory of "social function of rights", first evolved in French law,[144] was then taken over by German and Swiss law and even introduced into revolutionary Soviet law even though abandoned during Stalinization as a "bourgeois" theory of law.[145] It imposed a certain "*socialization*" of individual, mostly property, rights in the spirit of a post-liberal theory of law and state – a concept quite close to the beginnings of a distinctive European law and polity.

The extensive grant of rights to European citizens, especially in the free movement area as the strongest pillar of EU law, should at least in a theory of "socialization of law" be protected against unilateral abuse. This *immanente Schranke* (inherent limitation) has been recognized by the Court in the *Paletta II* case, where it refers to having "consistently held that Community law cannot be relied on for purposes of abuse or fraud".[146] At the same time, the Court insisted that the defence of *abus de droit* should not rule out the exercise of Community rights. Therefore, it is up to the person alleging "abuse or fraudulent conduct" to give adequate proof that this is the case; mere allegations are not sufficient in that respect. The Court did not even try to develop objective criteria for specifying *abus de droit*, such as preventing a circumvention of protective provisions justified by fair labour conditions.

The Court repeated its rather unsatisfactory case law in its well known *Centros* judgment of 9 March 1999[147] concerning free movement of companies by establishing subsidiaries (§ 7 V 2c). While AG La Pergola gave a sweeping support of the theory

---

[144] For an account cf. Grimm, *Solidarität als Rechtsprinzip*, 1972.
[145] Cf. for a development in socialist law Reich, *Sozialismus und Zivilrecht*, 1972 at 175-186.
[146] Case C-206/94 Brennet v Paletta [1996] ECR I-2357 at para 24; cf. also AG Cosmas relying on the Roman law principle "fraus omnia corrumpit" at 2373 para 51; in case C-36/96 Günaydin v Freistaat Bayern [1997] ECR I-5143 the Court did not find "abus de droit" by Turkish migrant workers who had signed a paper agreeing on their only temporary work permit and later wanting to remain in the receiving country. Cf. also Case C-367/96 Kefalas et al v Greece [1998] ECR I-2843; critique Triantafyllou, *CMLRev* 1999, 157; Ranieri, *ZEuP* 2000, 165. For an overview cf. Schermers/Waelbroeck, *Judicial Protection in the EU*, 6th ed. 2001, at 108-112; Triantafyllou, CDE 2002, 611.
[147] Case C-212/97 Centros v Erhvers-og Selskabsstyrelsen [1999] ECR I-1459; comment Roth, *CMLRev* 2000, 147.

of "competition of legal orders"[148], the Court in a more cautious fashion referred to its earlier case law forbidding an improper circumvention of national legislation under cover of the rights created by the Treaty. As a result, the Court confirmed the opinion of the AG in holding that:

> (t)he right to form a company in accordance with the law of a Member State and to set up branches in other Member States is inherent, in a single market, of the freedom of establishment guaranteed by the Treaty (para 27).

However, this argument misses the point since the case did not concern the establishment of branches as such, but more specifically the intention of a company to do its main national business through a branch as "principal establishment", while the main office was merely chosen to avoid the more restrictive company legislation of the host country.

As a result of *Paletta II* and *Centros*, the Court verbally recognizes the possibility of *abus de droit* of Union citizens invoking their rights guaranteed by the Treaty against restrictive but still justified Member State provisions. However, the Court is not willing to flesh it out more specifically in the sense of an inherent and implied duty, as a corollary to the effective grant of free movement rights. Such a concept of citizenship may satisfy a unilateral reading of Community rights in general and Union citizenship in particular *without inherent duties and obligations*. But it is problematic to conceptualise rights without duties. In an environment characterized by a growing dependence of citizens on each other, by the evolution of elements of solidarity inherent in the concept of citizenship itself, and by the principle of "proportionality", which requires the balancing of different rights, this one sided liberal reading of citizenship provokes criticism and should be reconsidered.

It remains to be seen whether the express reference to the concept of *abuse of rights*, as used in Art. 17 EHRC, by Art. 54 of the "Charter of Fundamental Rights in the EU" – now Art. II-114 of the Draft Constitution – will provoke a change of thinking in the direction as suggested here. The case-law of the ECHR so far has treated only extreme situations where, for example, the right to freedom of expression was used by radical movements denying democratic values as such. Therefore Community law, which is much closer to everyday entitlements of citizens, needs a more focused approach on a theory of *abus de droit* that still awaits development. A first step in this direction may be seen in the new case law concerning consumer deception of the other side on the true character of the contract in order to invoke the protection of Art. 13/14 EC-Regulation 44/2001 (§ 14 II 1). This can be regarded as "abuse of rights" in the sense

---

[148]   At 1477.

of Art. II-114 of the Draft Constitution because "the individual must be regarded, in view of the impression he has given to the other party acting in good faith, as having renounced the protection afforded by those provisions".[149]

CASE REGISTER

EUROPEAN COURT OF JUSTICE

7/61 Commission v Italy [1961] ECR 3170: 322

16 + 17/62 Confédération nationale des producteurs de fruits et légumes and others v Council [1962] 471: 259

25/62 Plaumann & Co. v Commission [1963] ECR 95: 258

26/62 Van Gend en Loos v Nederlandse Administratie van Belastingen [1963] ECR 1: 6, 16

6/64 Flaminio Costa v ENEL [1964] ECR 585: v, 36

56 + 58/64 Etablissements Consten SARL and Grundig-Verkaufs GmbH v Commission [1966] ECR 299: 144, 173

56/65 Société Technique Minière v Maschinenbau Ulm [1996] ECR 235: 274

5, 7, 13-24/66 Kampfmeyer et al v Commission [1967] ECR 331: 315

14/68 Walt Wilhelm and others v Bundeskartellamt [1969] ECR 1: 274

29/69 Erich Stauder v City of Ulm - Sozialamt [1969] ECR 419: 209

45/69 AFC Boehringer Mannheim GmbH v Commission [1970] ECR 769: 150

48/69 ICI v Commission [1972] ECR 619: 150

11/70 Internationale Handelsgesellschaft GmbH v Einfuhr- und Vorratsstelle für Getreide und Futtermittel [1970] ECR 1125: 36, 38, 210

22/70 Commission v Council [1971] ECR 263: 13, 43

5/71 Zuckerfabrik Schöppenstedt v Council [1971] ECR 975: 315

6/72 Europemballage Corporation and Continental Can Inc. v Commission [1973] ECR 495: 158

4/73 Nold v Commission [1974] ECR 491: 209

6 + 7/73 Istituto Chemioterapico Italiano SpA and Commercial Solvents v Commission [1974] ECR 223: 159

127/73 BRT v SV SABAM [1974] ECR 313: 331

155/73 Sacchi [1974] ECR 409: 107, 128, 163

173/73 Italian Republic v Commission [1974] ECR 709: 119

192/73 Van Zuylen v Hag [1974] ECR 731: 169

8/74 Procureur du Roi v Dassonville [1974] ECR 837: 101

15/74 Centrafarm BV et Adriaan de Peijper v Sterling Drug Inc [1974] ECR 1147: 169

16/74 Centrafarm BV et Adriaan de Peijper v Winthrop BV [1974] ECR 1183: 169

33/74 Van Binsbergen v Bestuur van de Bedrijfsvereniging voor de Metaalnijverheid [1974] ECR 1299: 108

36/74 Walrave v Union Cycliste Int. [1974] ECR 1405: 56

41/74 Van Duyn v Home Office [1974] ECR 1337: 17

74/74 Comptoir national Tnchnique agricole (CNTA) v Commission [1975] ECR 533: 316

32/75 Christini v Société Nationale des Chemins de Fer Francais [1975] ECR 1085: 62

43/75 Gabrielle Defrenne v Société anonyme belge de navigation aérienne Sabena [1976] ECR 455 : 19, 35, 195

48/75 Royer [1976] ECR 497: 66, 81

104/75 Adriaan de Pijper [1976] ECR 613: 101

119/75 Terrapin Overseas v Terranova [1976] ECR 1039: 171

12/76 Tessili v Dunlop [1976] ECR 1473: 28

14/76 A. De Bloos, SPRL v Société en comandite par actions Boyer [1976] ECR 1497: 245

26/76 Metro-SB-Grossmärkte GmbH & Co JG v Commission [1977] ECR 1875: 142, 145

27/76 United Brands Company and United Brands Cont. BV v Commission [1978] ECR 207: 157, 158, 160, 174

83 + 94/76, 4,15 and 40/77 HNL v Council and Commission [1978] ECR 1209: 316

85/76 Hoffmann-La Roche AG v Commission [1979] ECR 461: 157, 159

13/77 GB Inno-BM v ATAB [1977] ECR 2115: 148

30/77 R v Boucherau [1977] ECR 1999: 30

102/77 Hoffmann-La Roche v Centrafarm [1978] ECR 1139: 171

106/77 Amministrazione delle Finanze v Simmenthal [1978] ECR 629: 36

116 + 124/77 Amylum v Council and Commission [1979] ECR 3497: 316

150/77 Bertrand v Paul Ott KG [1978] ECR 1431: 245

3/78 Centrafarm v American Home Products [1978] ECR 1823: 171

22/78 Hugin Kassaregister AB and Hugin Cash Register Ltd. v Commission [1979] ECR 1869: 158

110 + 111/78 ASBL v Van Wesemael [1979] ECR 35: 36

120/78 Rewe-Zentral AG v Bundesmonopolverwaltung für Branntwein (Cassis de Dijon) [1979] ECR 649: 101, 294

133/78 Gourdain v Nadler [1979] ECR 733: 245

207/78 Criminal proceedings against Even [1979] ECR 2019: 62

258/78 L.C. Nungesser KG and Kurt Eisele v Commission [1982] ECR 2015: 146, 173

16-20/79 Criminal proceedings against Danis [1979] ECR 3327: 103

52/79 Procureur du Roi v. Debauve [1980] ECR 833: 110, 129

62/79 Coditel et al v Cine-Vog Films et al [1980] ECR 881: 171

125/79 Denilauer v SNC Couchet Frères [1980] ECR 1553: 245

155/79 AM & S Europe Ltd. v Commission [1982] ECR 1575: 212

730/79 Phillip Morris Holland BV v EC Commission [1980] ECR 2671: 119

815/79 Criminal proceedings against Cremonini and Vrancovich [1980] ECR 3583: 127

55 + 57/80 Musik-Vertrieb Membran v GEMA – Gesellschaft fur musikalische Aufführungsrechte [1981] ECR 147: 168

96/80 Jenkins v Kingsgate (Clothing Productions) Ltd. [1981] ECR 911: 199

155/80 Summary proceedings against Oebel [1981] ECR 1993: 103

158/80 Rewe-Handelsgesellschaft Nord mbH et Rewe-Markt Steffen v Hauptzollamt Kiel [1981] ECR 1805: 240, 322

203/80 Criminal proceedings against Casati [1981] ECR 2595: 97, 270

244/80 Pasquale Foglia v Mariella Novello [1981] ECR 3045: 252

279/80 Criminal proceedings against Webb [1981] ECR 3305: 110

53/81 Levin v Staatssecretaris van Justitie [1982] ECR 1035: 26, 58

65/81 Reina v Landeskreditbank Baden-Württemberg [1982] ECR 33: 62

75/81 Blesgen v Belgium [1982] ECR 1211: 102

102/81 Nordsee Deutsche Hochseefischerei GmbH v Reederei Mond Hochseefischerei Nordstern AG & Co. KG [1982] ECR 1095: 252

115 + 116/81 Adoui and Cornuaille v Belgium [1982] ECR 1665: 60

246/81 Nicholas William, Lord Bethell v Commission [1982] 2277: 259, 319

249/81 Commission v Ireland [1982] ECR 4005: 100

262/81 Coditel SA Compagnie générale pour la diffusion de la television, et al v Ciné-Vog Fils SA et al [1982] ECR 3381: 174

283/81 Srl CILFIT and Lanificio di Gavardo SpA v Ministry of Health [1982] ECR 3415: 25, 251

322/81 Nederlandsche Banden-Industrie Michelin v Commission [1983] ECR 3461: 158

11/82 SA Piraiki-Patraiki and others v Commission [1985] ECR 207; C-152/88 Sofrimport SARL v Commission [1990] ECR 2477: 258

201/82 Gerling Konzern Speziale Kreditversicherungs-AG v Amministrazione del Tesoro dello Stato [1983] ECR 2503: 245

228 + 229/82 Ford v Commission [1984] ECR 1129: 150

264/82 Timex Corporation v Council and Commission [1985] ECR 849: 258

286/82 + 26/83 Luisi & Carbone v Ministerio del Tesoro [1984] ECR 377: 68, 111, 270

288/82 Ferdinand M.J.J. Duijnstee v Lodewijk Goderbauer [1983] ECR 3663: 245

14/83 Von Colson and Kamann v Land Nordrhein-Westfalen [1984] ECR 1891: 49, 203

16/83 Criminal proceedings against Prantl [1984] ECR 1299: 102

37/83 Rewe Zentrale v Landwirtschaftskammer Rheinland [1984] ECR 1229: 36

72/83 Campus Oil v Minister for Industry and Energy [1984] ECR 2727: 98

135/83 Abels v the Administrative Board of the Bedrijfsvereniging voor de Metaalindustrie en de Electrotechnische Industrie [1985] ECR 469: 237

145/83 Stanley George Adams v Commission [1985] ECR 3539: 316

229/83 Leclerc v Au Blé Vert [1985] ECR 1: 211

240/83 Procureur de la République v Association de Défense de Brûleurs de Huiles Usagers [1985] ECR 531: 9

267/83 Diatta v Land Berlin [1985] ECR 567: 64

293/83 Gravier v City of Liège [1985] ECR 593: 68, 192

18/84 Commission v France [1985] ECR 1139: 117

19/84 Pharmon BV v Hoechst AG [1985] ECR 2281: 171

48/84 Spitzley v Sommer Exploitation SA [1985] ECR 787: 245

103/84 Commission v Italy [1986] ECR 1749: 100

137/84 Criminal proceedings against Mutsch [1985] ECR 2681: 193

142 + 158/84 British American Tobacco Ltd. and R.J. Reynolds Industries v Commission [1987] ECR 4487: 150

152/84 Marshall v Southampton and Southwest Hampshire Health Authority [1986] ECR 723: 21, 204

161/84 Pronuptia de Paris GmbH v. Pronuptia de Paris Irmgard Schillgallis [1986] ECR 353: 146, 275

178/84 Commission v Germany (Beer case) [1987] ECR 1227: 104, 298

205/84 Commission v Germany [1986] ECR 3755: 107, 108

222/84 Marguerite Johnston v Chief Constable of Royal Ulster Constabulary [1986] ECR 1651: 240

311/84 Telemarketing (CBEM) v SA Compagnie luxembourgeoise de télédiffusion (CLT) and Information publicité Benelux (IPB) [1985] ECR 3261: 166

24/85 Spijkers v Gebroeders [1986] ECR 1119: 236

45/85 Verband der Sachversicherer v Commission [1987] ECR 405: 148

66/85 Lawrie-Blum v Land Baden-Würtemberg [1986] ECR 2121: 59

67/85 et al, Kwekerij Gebroeders Van der Koy BV v Commission [1988] ECR 219: 118

79/85 D.H.M. Segers v Bestuur van de Bedrijfsvereniging [1986] ECR 2375: 273

225/85 Commission v Italy [1987] ECR 2625: 60

314/85 Foto-Frost v HZA LübeckOst [1987] ECR 4199: 252, 318

316/85 Centre public d'aide sociale de Courcelles v Lebon [1987] ECR 2811: 62

352/85 Bond van Adverteerders v Netherlands [1988] ECR 2085: 107

355/85 Driancourt v M. Cognet [1986] ECR 3231: 274

2/86 Demirel v Stadt Schwäbisch Gmünd [1987] ECR 3719: 23

24/86 Blaizot v University of Liège [1988] ECR 379: 192

39/86 Lair v Universität Hannover [1988] ECR 3161: 68

62/86 Akzo Chemie BV v Commission [1991] ECR I-3359: 160

120/86 Mulder v Minister van Landbouw en Visserij [1988] ECR 2321: 223

222/86 Unctef v Heylens [1987] ECR 4097: 56, 239

263/86 Belgium v Humbel [1988] ECR 5365: 107, 161

326/86 and 66/88 Francesconi *et al* v Commission [1989] ECR 2087: 316

31/87 Gebroeders Beentjes v Netherlands [1988] ECR 4635: 136

45/87 Commission v Ireland [1988] ECR 4929: 135

46/87 and 227/88 Hoechst v Commission [1989] ECR 2859: 212

53/87 Consorzio italiano della componentistica di ricambio per autoveicoli and Maxicar v Régie nationale des usines Renault [1988] ECR 6039: 170, 174

81/87 R v Treasury and Commissioners of Inland Revenue *ex parte* Daily Mail and General Trust [1988] ECR 5483: 113

C-142/87 Re Tubemeuse: Belgium v Commission [1990] ECR I-959: 118

186/87 Cowan v Trésor public [1989] ECR 195: 67, 68, 71, 74, 193, 314

238/87 Volvo v Veng [1988] ECR 6211: 174

266/87 R. v Pharmaceutical Society ex parte API [1989] 1295: 100

C-307/87 France v Commission [1990] ECR I-307: 118, 122

379/87 Groener v Ministry of Education and the City of Dublin Vocational Committee [1989] ECR 3967: 61, 193

382/87 Buet et al v Min. Public [1989] ECR 1235: 47

5/88 Wachauf v Bundesamt für Ernährung und Forstwirtschaft [1989] ECR 2609: 209

C- 49/88 Al-Jubail Fertiliser v Council [1991] ECR I-3187: 212

103/88 Fratelli Costanzo SpA v Comune di Milano [1989] ECR 1839: 51

C-143/88 and 92/89 Zuckerfabrik Süderdithmarschen AG v Hauptzollamt Ithehoe and Zuckerfabrik Soest GmbH v Hauptzollamt Paderborn [1991] ECR I-415: 254, 319

145/88 Torfaen Borough Council v B & Q plc.[1989] ECR 3851: 104

C-152/88 Sofrimport v Commission [1990] ECR I-2477: 258, 317

C-177/88 Dekker v Stichting Vormingscentrum voor Jong Volwassenen (VJV-Centrum) Plus [1990] ECR I-3941: 203

210, 241, 242/88 Lucazeau et al v Commission [1989] ECR 2811: 160

C-262/88 Barber/GRE [1990] ECR I-1889: 35, 195

C-297/88 + 197/89 Dzodzi v Belgium [1990] ECR I-3763: 252

C-322/88 Grimaldi (Salvatore) v Fonds des maladies professionnelles [1989] ECR 4407: 14

C- 352/88 Bond van Adverteerders v The Netherlands [1988] ECR I-2085: 270

C-361/88 Commission v Germany [1991] ECR I-2567: 240

C-362/88 GB-INNO-BM v Confédération du commerce luxembourgeois [1990] I-667: 294

C-10/89 SA CNL-SUCAL NV v HAG GF AG [1990] I-3711: 169

C-23/89 Quietlynn and Richards v Southend Borough Council [1990] ECR I-3059: 103

C-104/89 and C-37/90 Mulder v Council and Commission [1992] ECR I-3061: 317

C-106/89 Marleasing SA v La Comercial Internacional de Alimentación SA [1990] ECR-4135: 49

C-113/89 Rush Portuguesa v Office national d'immigration [1990] ECR I-1417: 61, 109

C-184/89 Nimz v Freie Hansestadt Hamburg [1991] ECR I-297: 196, 204

C-188/89 Foster v British Gas [1990] I-3313: 21

C-190/89 Marc Rich and Co AG v Societa Italiana Impianti PA [1991]ECR I-3855: 283

C-192/89 Sevince v Staatssecretaris van Justitie [1990] ECR I-3461: 23

C-213/89 R v Secretary of State for Transport *ex parte* Factortame Ltd. and others [1990] ECR I-2433: 36

C-234/89 St. Delimitis v Henninger Brau [1991] ECR I-935: 151, 274

C-260/89 ERT v DEP and Kouvelas [1991] ECR I-2925: 211, 295

C-288/89 Collectieve Antennevoorziening Gouda v Commissariaat voor de Media [1991] ECR I-4007: 107

C-292/89 R v Immigration Appeal Tribunal *ex parte* Antonissen, [1991] ECR I-745: 26, 59

C-300/89 Commission v Council [1991] ECR I-2867: 9, 259

C-309/89 Codorniú Sa v Council [1994] ECR I-1853: 191, 258

C-339/89 Alsthom Atlantique v Compagnie de construction mécanique Sulzer SA [1991] ECR I-107: 269, 284

C-340/89 Vlassopoulou v Ministerium für Justiz, Bundes- und Europaangelegenheiten des Landes Baden-Würtemberg [1991] ECR I-2357: 66

C-358/89 Extramet Industrie SA v Council [1991] ECR I-2501: 258

C-361/89 Criminal proceedings against Di Pinto [1991] ECR I-1189: 47

C-1 + 176/90 Aragonesa de Publicidad v Departamento de Sanidad y Seguridad Social de la Generalitat de Cataluña [1991] ECR I-4151: 103

C-6 and 9/90 Francovich and Others v Italy [1991] ECR I-5357: 14, 31, 324

C-41/90 Höfner and Elser v Macroton [1991] ECR I-1979: 149, 161, 276

C-76/90 Säger v Dennemeyer & Co Ltd. [1991] ECR I-4221: 108

C-159/90 Society for the protection of Unborn Children (SPUC) v Stephen Grogan [1991] ECR I-4685: 105, 211, 215, 270

C-179/90 Merci Convenzionale Porto di Genova SpA v Siderurgica Gabrielle SpA [1991] ECR I-5889: 163

C-204/90 Bachmann v Belgium [1992] ECR I-249: 99

C-208/90 Emmot v Minister for Social Welfare [1991] ECR I-4269: 204

C-332/90 Steen v Deutsche Bundespost [1992] ECR I-341: 60, 273

C-354/90 Fédération nationale du commerce extérieur des produits alimentaires et Syndicat national des négotiants et transformateurs de saumon v Commission [1991] ECR I-5505: 120

C-360/90 AWO Berlin v Bötel [1992] ECR I-3589: 196

C-369/90 Micheletti v Delegación del Gobierno en Cantabria, [1992] ECR I-4239: 71

C-370/90 Secretary of State for the Home Department v Singh [1992] ECR I-4265: 65

C-2/91 Criminal proceedings againt Meng [1993] ECR I-5751: 148

C-4/91 Bleis v Ministère de l'éducation nationale [1991] ECR I-5627: 60

C-97/91 Oleificio Borelli SpA v Commission [1992] I-6313: 240

C-155/91 Commission v Council [1993] ECR I-939: 9

C-159 + 160/91 Poucet and Pistre [1993] I-637: 161

C-200/91 Coloroll Pension Trustees Ltd. v James Richard Russel et al. [1994] ECR I-4389: 204

C-241 + 242/91P Radio Telefis Eireann (RTE) and Independent TV Publications Ltd (ITP) v Commission [1995] ECR I-743: 174

C-259/91 + 331/91 + 332/91, Pilar Allué and Carmel Mary Coonan and others v Unviersitá degli studi di Venezia and Università degli studi di Parma [1993] ECR I-4309: 191

C-267 + 268/91 Bernhard Keck and Daniel Mithouard [1993] ECR I-6097: 34, 103

C-271/91 Marshall (II) v Southampton and South West Hampshire Area Health Autority [1993] ECR I-4367: 20, 21, 204

C-320/91 Procureur du Roi v Paul Corbeau [1993] ECR-2533: 163

C-19/92 Kraus v Land Baden-Württemberg [1993] ECR I-1663: 65, 66

C-49/92 P Commission v Anic [1999] I-4125: 334

C-91/92 Paola Faccini Dori v Recreb [1994] ECR I-3325: 21

C-92 + 326/92 Phil Collins v Imtrat Handelsgesellschaft mbH and Patricia Im- und Export Verwaltungsgesellschaft mbH and Leif Emanuel Kraul v EMI Electrola GmbH [1993] ECR I-5145: 170

C-93/92 CMC-Motorradcenter v Pelin Baskiciogullari [1993] ECR I-5009: 101

C-127/92 Enderby v Frenchay Health Authority [1993] ECR I-5535: 202

C-128/92 H. J. Banks & Co. Ltd v British Coal Corporation [1994] ECR I-1209: 332, 335

C-272/92 Maria Chiara Spotti v Freistaat Bayern [1993] ECR I-5185: 81, 193

C-275/92 HM Customs and Excise v Schindler [1994] ECRI- 1039: 99, 106, 270

C-292/92 Hünermund v Landesapothekerkammer Baden-Württemberg [1993] ECR I-6787: 101

C-315/92 Verband sozialer Wettbewerb v Clinique Laboratories SNC [1994] ECR I-317: 105, 299

C-359/92 Germany v Council [1994] ECR I-3681: 226

C-364/92 SAT Fluggesellschaft mbH v Eurocontrol [1994] ECR I-43: 161

C-379/92 Criminal proceedings against Peralta [1994] ECR I-3453: 192

C-382/92 Commission v UK [1994] ECR I-2435: 238

C-392/92 Christel Schmidt v Spar- und Leihkasse der früheren Ämter Bordesholm, Kiel und Cronshagen [1994] ECR I-1311: 235

C-421/92 Habermann-Beltermann v Arbeiterwohlfahrt [1994] ECR I-1657: 195

C-9/93 IHT Internationale Heiztechnik GmbH v Ideal Standard GmbH [1994] ECR I-2789: 171

C-23/93 TV 10 v Commissariaat voor de Media [1994] ECR I-4795: 108

C-32/93 Webb v EMO Air Cargo (UK) Ltd. [1994] ECR I-3567: 196

C-46 and C-48/93 Brasserie du Pêcheur v Germany and the R v Secretary of State for Transport *ex parte* Factortame Ltd. [1996] ECR I-1029: 325, 326

C-51/93 Meyhui v Schott Zwiesel Glaswerke AG [1994] ECR I-3879: 295

C-70/93 BMW v ALD Auto-Leasing [1995] ECR I-3439: 145

C-280/93 Germany v Council [1994] ECR I-4973: 37, 209

C-316/93 Vaneetveld v SA Le Foyer [1994] ECR 673 : 21

C-322/93P Peugeot v Commission [1994] ECR I-2727: 154

C-384/93 Alpine Investments BV v Minister van Financiën [1995] ECR I-1141: 110

C-392/93 R v. H.M. Treasury *ex parte* British Telecommunications, [1996] ECR I-1631: 325

C-400/93 Specialarbejderforbundet i Danmark v Royal Copenhagen [1995] ECR I-1275: 202

C-412/93 Société d'importation Edouard Leclerc-Siplec v TF1 Publicité [1995] ECR I-179: 102

C-415/93 ASBL v Bosman [1995] ECR I-4921: 19, 46, 59, 81, 194, 271, 334

C-427, 429 + 436/93 Bristol-Meyers Squibb et al v Paranova [1996] ECR I-3457: 29, 172

C-430-432/93 Van Schijndel and Van Veen v Stichting Pensioenfonds [1995] ECR I-4705: 241

C-450/93 Kalanke v Freie Hansestadt Bremen [1995] ECR I-3051: 30, 200

C-457/93 Kuratorium für Dialyse v Lewark [1996] ECR I-243: 196

C-465/93 Atlanta Fruchthandelsgesellschaft *et al* v Bundesamt für Ernährung und Forstwirtschaft [1995] ECR I-3761: 35, 255

C-470/93 Verein gegen Unwesen im Handel v Mars GmbH [1995] ECR I-1923: 104, 253, 298

C-473/93 Commission v Luxembourg [1996] ECR I-3207: 38

C-479/93 Francovich (II) v Italy [1995] ECR I-3843: 324

C-484/93 Swensson & Gustavsson v Ministère du Logement et de l'Urbanisme [1995] ECR I-3955: 111

C-5/94 R v Ministry of Agriculture, Fisheries and Food *ex parte* Hedley Lomas (Ireland) [1996] ECR I-2553: 322, 323, 325

C-13/94 P v S and Cornwall County Council [1996] ECR I-2143: 205

C-55/94 Gebhard v Consiglio dell'Ordine degli Advocati e procuratori di Milano [1995] ECR I-4165: 45, 66, 273

C-111/94 Job Centre Coop. ARL. [1995] ECR I-3361: 252

C-157/94 Commission v Netherlands [1997] ECR I-5699: 163

C-159/94 Commission v France [1997] ECR I-5815: 163

C 171 +172/94 Merckx + Neuhuys v Ford Motors Belgium [1996] ECR I-1253: 238

C-178/94 Dillenkofer *et al*. v. Germany [1996] ECR I-4845: 16, 325, 348

C-192/94 El Corte Inglés v Cristina Blásquez Rivero [1996] ECR I-1281: 22, 326

C-193/94 Criminal proceedings against Skanavi Chryssanthakopoulos [1996] ECR I-929: 73

C-194/94 CIA Security International SA v Signalson SA and Securitel SPRL [1996] ECR I-2201: 22, 329

C-206/94 Brennet v Paletta [1996] ECR I-2357: 350

C-214/94 Boukhalfa v Bundesrepublik Deutschland [1996] ECR I-2253: 73

C-233/94 Germany v European Parliament and Council [1997] ECR I-2405: 327

C-237/94 O'Flynn v Adjudication Officer [1996] ECR I-2617: 60

C-283, C-291 and C-292/94 Denkavit Int. BV and others v Bundesamt für Finanzen [1996] ECR I-5063: 325

C-319/94 Jules Dethier Équipement SA v Jules Dassy and Sovam SPRL [1998] ECR-1061: 238

C-10/95P Asocarne v Council [1995] ECR I-4149: 265

C-13/95 Süzen v Zehnacker Gebäudereinigung [1997] ECR I-1259: 256

15/95, EARL de Kerlast v Union régionale de coopératives agricoles (Unicopa) and Coopérative du Trieux [1997] ECR I-1961: 191

C-24/95 Land Rheinland-Pfalz v Alcan GmbH [1997] ECR I-1591: 118, 139

C-34-36/95 Konsumentenombudsmannen (KO) v De Agostini (Svenska) Forlag AB and TV Shop Sverige AG [1997] ECR I-3843: 105, 130

C-42/95 Siemens AG v Henry Nold [1996] ECR I-6017: 343

C-65 + 111/95 R v Secretary of State for the Home Department ex parte Shingara and Radion [1997] ECR I-3343: 73

C-68/95 T. Port GmbH & Co. KG v Bundesanstalt für Landwirtschaft und Ernährung [1996] ECR I-6065: 254

C-73/95P Viho Europe v Commission [1996] ECR I-5457: 149

C-74 + 129/95 Criminal proceedings against X [1996] ECR I-6609: 51

C-106/95 Mainschiffahrts-Genossenschaft v Gravieres Rhenanes Sarl [1997] ECR I-911: 282

C-180/95 Draehmpaehl v Urania Immobilienservice [1997] ECR I-2195: 22

C-251/95 SABEL BV v Puma AG, Rudolf Dassler Sport [1997] ECR I-6191: 178

C-261/95 Palmisani v INPS [1997] ECR I-4025: 229

C-265/95 Commision v France [1997] ECR I-6959: 38, 327

C-267+ 289/95 Merck & Co Inc. et al. v Primecrown et al [1996] ECR I-6285: 171

C-299/95 Kremzow v Austria [1997] ECR I-2629: 219

C-300/95 Commission v UK [1997] ECR I-2649: 337

C-321/95P Stichting Greenpeace Council (Greenpeace International) and Others v Commission [1998] I-1651: 259, 318

C-368/95 Vereinigte Familiapress Zeitungsverlags- und Vertriebs GmbH v Heinrich Bauer Verlag [1997] ECR I-3689: 105, 215

C-383/95 Petrus Wilhelmus Rutten v Cross Medical Ltd. [1997] ECR I-57: 72, 247

C-398/95 SETTG v Ypourgos Ergasias [1997] ECR I-3091: 98

C-409/95 Hellmut Marschall v Land Nordrhein Westfalen [1997] ECR I-6363: 201

C-35/96 Commission v Italy [1998] ECR I-385: 148

C-36/96 Günaydin v Freistaat Bayern [1997] ECR I-5143: 350

C-55/96 Job Centre coop arl. [1997] ECR I-7119: 161

C-67/96 Albany International BV v Stichting Bedrijfspensioenenfonds Textielindustrie [1999] ECR I-5751: 28, 164, 233, 276

C-85/96 Maria Martínez Sala v Freistaat Bayern [1998] ECR I-2691: 59, 73

C-97/96 Verband Deutscher Daihatsu Händler eV v Daihatsu Deutschland GmbH [1997] ECR I-6843: 21, 343

C-149/96 Portugal v Council [1999] ECR I-8395: 24

C-158/96 Kohll v Union des Caisses de Maladie [1998] ECR I-1931: 110

C-180/96 UK v Commission [1998] ECR I-2265: 227, 228

C-196/96 P Intertronic F. Cornelis v Commission [1998] ECR I-199: 319

C-210/96 Gut Springenheide v Oberkreisdirektor Steinfurt [1998] ECR I-4657: 298

C-249/96 Grant v South West Trains Ltd. [1998] ECR I-621: 34, 205, 215

C-274/96 Criminal proceedings against H.O. Bickel und U. Franz, [1998] ECR I-7637: 74

C-319/96 Brinkmann Tabakfabriken v Skatteministeriet [1998] ECR I-5255: 326

C-348/96 Criminal proceedings against Donatella Calfa [1999] ECR I-11: 74

C-355/96 Silhouette International Schmied GmbH & Co KG v Hartlauer Handelsgesellschaft GmbH [1997] ECR I-4799: 50, 182, 183

C-364/96 Verein für Konsumenteninformation v Österreichische Kreditversicherungs AG [1998] ECR I-2949: 349

C-367/96 Kefalas et al v Greece [1998] ECR I-2843: 350

C-369 + 376/96 Criminal proceedings against Arblade [1999] ECR I-8453: 108

C-393/96 P (R) Antonissen v Council and Commission [1997] ECR I-441: 317

C-395-396/96P Compagnie Maritime Belge Transports SA et al v Commission [2000] ECR I-1365 : 156

C-7/97 Oscar Bronner GmbH & Co KG v Mediaprint [1998] ECR I-7791: 175, 252, 276

C-39/97 Canon Kabushiki Kaisha v Metro-Goldwyn-Mayer Inc [1998] ECR I-5507: 179

C-63/97 Bayerische Motorenwerke (BMW) and BMW Nederland BV v Ronald Karel Dseenik [1999] ECR I-905: 51, 179

C-75/97 Belgium v Commission [1999] ECR I-3671: 118, 139

C-76/97 Tögel v Niederösterreichische Gebietskrankenkasse [1998] ECR I-5357: 136

C-114/97 Commission v Spain [1998] ECR I-6717: 60

C-124/97 Läärä, Cotswold Microsystemsand Oy Transatlantic Software v Finland [1999] ECRI-6067: 107

C-126/97 Eco Swiss China Time Ltd v Benetton International NV. [1999] ECR I-3055: 252, 283, 330

C-140/97 Rechberger et al v Austria [1999] ECR I-3499 : 325, 348

C-147+148/97 Deutsche Post AG v Gesellschaft für Zahlungssysteme and Citicorp Kartenservice [2000] ECR I-825: 164

C-158/97 Badeck and others [2000] ECR I-1875: 201

C-159/97 Transporti Castelletti Spedizioni International SpA v Hugo Trumpy SpA [1999] ECR I-1597: 282

C-185/97 Belinda Jane Coote v Granada Hospitality [1998] ECR I-5199: 32, 197, 240

189/97 Kalfelis v. Banque Schröder ECR [1988] 5565: 250

C-212/97 Centros Ltd. v Erhvervs og Selskabsstyrelsen [1999] ECR I-1459: 112, 270, 350

C-222/97 Trummer and Mayer [1999] ECR I-1661: 110

C-226/97 Criminal proceedings against Lemmens [1998] ECR I-3711: 329

C-303/97 Verbraucherschutzverein v Sektkellerei Kessler [1999] ECR I-513: 179

C-337/97 Parfums Christian Dior SA and Parfums Christian Dior NV v Evora BV [1997] ECR I-6013: 182

C-342/97 Lloyd Schuhfabrik Meyer v Klijsen Handel BV [1999] ECR I-3819: 179

C-375/97 General Motors v Yplon SA [1999] ECR I-5421: 179

C-378/97 Criminal proceedings against Florus Ariel Wijsenbeek [1999] ECR I-6207: 124

C-379/97 Pharmacia & Upjohn v Paranova A/S [1999] ECR I-6927: 172

C-387/97 Commission v Greece [2000] ECR I-5047: 74, 323

C-6/98 Arbeitsgemeinschaft Deutscher Rundfunkanstalten (ARD) v PRO Sieben Media AG [1999] ECR I-7599: 131

C-172/98 Commission v Belgium [1999] ECR I-3999: 193

C-173/98 Sebago Inc. and Ancienne Maison Dubois v G-B Unic SA [1999] ECR I-4103: 181

C-180/98 Pavlov v Stichting Pensioenfonds Medische Specialisten [2000] ECR I-6451: 151, 277

C-208/98 Berliner Kindl Brauerei AG v Andreas Siepert [2000] ECR I-1741: 30

C-220/98 Estée Lauder Cosmetics v Lancaster Group [2000} ECR I-117: 298

C-224/98 Marie-Nathalie D'Hoop v Office national de l'emploi [2002] ECR I-6191 : 76

C-240-244/98 Océano Grupo Editorial v Rocio Murciano Qintero [2000] ECR I-4941: 28, 242, 250

C-254/98 Schutzverband gegen unlauteren Wettbewerb v TK Heimdienst Sass GmbH [2000] ECR I-151: 105

C-281/98 R. Angonese v Casa di Risparmio de Bolzano [2000] ECR I-4139: 18, 80, 271, 334

C-285/98 Tanja Kreil v Germany [2000] ECR I-69: 197

C-324/98 Telaustria Verlags GmbH and Telefonadress GmbH v Telekom Austria AG [2000] ECR I-10745: 27

C-352/98 P Bergaderm and Groupil v Commission [2000] ECR I-5291: 316, 325

C-366/98 Criminal proceedings against Geoffrey [2000] ECR I-6579: 105

C-367/98 Commission v Portugal [2002] ECR I-4731: 34, 112

C-376/98 Germany v European Parliament and Council [2000] ECR I-8419: 41, 279, 295

C-377/98 Netherlands v EP and Council [2001] ECR I-7079: 176

C-379/98 PreußenElektra v Schleswag [2001] ECR I-2099: 117, 119

C-381/98 Ingmar GB Ltd. v Eaton Leonard Technologies Inc. [2000] ECR I-9305: 288

C-405/98 Konsumentenombudsmannen (KO) v Gourmet International products [2001] ECR I-1795: 106

C-407/98 Abrahamsson and Anderson v Fogelqvist, [2000] ECR I-5539: 200

C-423/98 Albore [2000] ECR I-5965: 111, 271

C-424/98 Commission v Italy [2000] ECR I-4001: 68

C-425/98 Marca Mode CV v Adidas AG [2000] ECR I-4861: 179

C-443/98 Unilever Italia SpA v Central Food SpA [2000] ECR I-7535: 22, 329

C-451/98 Antillean Rice Mills NV v Council [2001] ECR I-8949: 258

C-456/98 Centrosteel v Adipol [2000] ECR I-6007: 51

C-465/98 Verein gegen Unwesen in Handel v A. Darbo [2000] ECR I-2297: 228, 298

C-476/98 Commission v Germany [2002] ECR I-9855: 43, 98

C-478/98 Commission v. Belgium [2000] ECR I-7587: 271

C-54/99 Eglise de Scientologie v The Prime Minister [2000] ECR I-1335: 111, 321

C-63/99 R v Secretary of State for the Home Dpt. *ex parte* Wieslaw and Elzbieta Gloszczuk [2001] ECR I-6369: 24, 84, 274 , 335

C-74/99 The Queen v Secretary of State for Health and others, *ex parte* Imperial Tobacco Ltd and Others [2000] ECR I-8599: 255

C-89/99 Schieving-Nijstad v Groenveld [2001] ECR I-5851: 23, 167

C-112/99 Toshiba Europe GmbH v Katun Germany GmbH [2001] ECR I-7945: 180

C-144/99 Commission v Netherlands [2001] ECR I-3541: 51, 296

C-157/99 Geraets-Smits v Stichting Ziekenfonds et al. [2001] ECR I-5473: 99

C-172/99 Oy Liikenne Ab v Pekka Liskojärvi and Pentti Juntunen [2001] ECR I-745: 237

C-173/99 R v. Secretary of State for Trade and Industry ex parte BECTU [2001] ECR I-4881: 219

C-184/99 Rudy Grzelczyck v le Centre Public d'aide sociale d'Ottignies-Louvain-la-Neuve [2001] ECR I-6193: 75

C-192/99 R v Secretary of State for the Home Department ex parte Mangjit Kaur [2001] ECR I-1237: 71

C-203/99 Henning Veedfald v Arhus Amtscommune [2001] ECR I-3569: 338

C –235/99 R v Secretary of State for the Home Department *ex parte* Eleanora Ivanova Kondova [2001] ECR I-6427: 82, 335

C-257/99 R v Secretary of State for the Home Department *ex parte* Julius Barcosi and Marcel Malik [2001] ECR I- 6557: 30, 82, 335

C-268/99 Aldona Malgorzata Jany and others v Staatssecretaris van Justitie [2001] ECR I-8615: 82, 335

C-270/99P Z v European Parliament [2001] ECR I-9197: 219

C-309/99 J.C.J. Wouters et al v Algemene Raad van de Nederlandse Orde van Advocaten [2002] ECR I-1577: 19, 148, 219, 276, 334

C-353/99 Council v Hautala [2001] ECR I-9565: 310

C-413/99 Baumbast & R v Secretary of State for the Home Department [2002] ECR I-7091: 17, 63, 77

C-414-416/99 Zino Davidoff SA v A & G Imports, Levi Strauss & Co v Tesco Imports *et al.* [2001] ECR I-8691: 181

C-453/99 Courage Ltd v Crehan [2001] ECR I-6297: 32, 275, 332

C-459/99 MRAX v Belgium [2002] ECR I-6591: 56, 60, 62

C-476/99 H. Lommers v Minister van Landbouw, Natuurbeheer en Visserij [2002] ECR I-2891: 202

C-478/99 Commission v Sweden [2002] I- 4147: 296

C-481/99 Heininger v Bayr. Hypo und Vereinsbank [2001] ECR I-9945: 35, 280, 301

C-482/99 France v Commission [2002] ECR I-4397: 119

C-483/99 Commission v France (Stardust Marine) [2002] ECR I-4781: 111

C-503/99 Commission v Belgium [2002] ECR I-4809: 111

C-513/99 Concordia Bus Finland Oy Ab v Helsingin kaupunki and HKL-Bussiliikenne [2002] ECR I-7213: 137

C-1/00 Commission v France [2001] ECR-9989: 322

C-13/00 Commission v Ireland [2003] ECR-I 2943: 44

C-20+64/00 Booker Aquaculture Ltd and Hydro Seafood GSP Ltd v The Scottish Ministers [2003] ECR I-7411: 212

C-50/00P Unión de pequeños agricultores v Council [2002] ECR I-6677: 260

C-52/00 Commission v France [2002] ECR I-3827: 47, 339

C-53/00 Ferring SA v Agence centrale des organismes de sécurité sociale (ACOSS) [2001] ECR I-9067: 119, 120

C-60/00 Mary Carpenter v Secretary of State for the Home Department [2002] ECR I-6279: 32, 66

C-96/00 Rudolf Gabriel [2002] ECR I-6367: 28, 246, 286

C-112/00 Eugen Schmidberger v Austria [2003] ECR I-5659: 101, 210, 328

C-143/00 Boehringer Ingelheim v Eurim Pharm [2002] ECR I-3759: 172

C-154/00 Commission v Greece [2002] I-3879: 358

C-162/00 Land Nordrhein-Westphalen v Beata Pokrzeptowicz-Meyer [2002] ECR I-1049: 24, 80, 274, 335

C-167/00 Verein für Konsumenteninformation v Karl Heinz Henkel [2002] ECR I-8111: 28, 248, 250

C-168/00 Simone Leitner v TUI Deutschland [2002] ECR I-2631: 338

C-208/00 Überseering BV v Nordic Construction Company Baumanagement GmbH (NCC) [2002] ECR I-9919: 115, 272, 341

C-244/00 Van Doren + Q GmbH v Lifestyle sports + Sportswear Handelsgesellschaft *et al.* [2003] ECR I-3051: 181

C-245/00 Stichting ter Exploitatie van Naburige Rechten (SENA) v Nederlandse Omroep Stichting (NOS) [2003] ECR I-1251: 26

C-257/00 Nancy Givane and Others v Secretary of State for the Home Department [2003] ECR I-345: 25

C-273/00 Ralf Sieckmann v Deutsches Patent- und Markenamt [2002] ECR I-11737: 187

C-280/00 Altmark Trans et al v Nahverkehrsgesellschaft Altmark [2003] ECR I-7747: 118, 120

C-325/00 Commision v Germany [2002] ECR I-9977: 100

C-327/00 Santex v Unito Socio Sanitaria [2003] ECR I-1877: 139

C-334/00 Fonderie Officine Meccaniche Tacconi SpA v Heinrich Wagner Sinto Maschinenfabrik (HWS) [2002] ECR I-7357: 245

C-338/00P Volkswagen v Commission [2003] ECR I-9188: 150, 154

C-411/00 Felix Swoboda v Österreichische Nationalbank [2002] ECR I-10567: 136

C-438/00 Deutscher Handballbund v Maros Kolpak [2003] ECR I-4135: 24, 80, 81, 335

C-465/00 Rechnungshof et al. v Österreichischer Rundfunk et al [2003] ECR I-4989: 199

C-473/00 Cofidis v Jean-Louis Fredout [2002] ECR I-10875: 229

C-2 + 3/01 P Bundesverband der Arneimittel-Importeure et al v Bayer-AG [2004] ECR I-(6.1.2004): 142

C-104/01 Libertel groep v Benelux Merkenbureau [2003] ECR I-3793: 177

C-109/01 Secretary of State for the Home Department v Hacene Akrich [2003] ECR I-9607: 64

C-167/01 Kamer van Koophandel v Inspire Art [2003] ECR I-1055: 116

C-186/01 Alexander Dory v Kreiswehrersatzamt Schwäbisch Gemünd [2003] I-2479: 197

C-192/01 Commission v Denmark [2003] ECR I-9693: 220

C-206/01 Arsenal Football-Club plc. v Mathew Reed [2002] ECR I-10273: 176

C-224/01 G. Köbler v Austria [2003] ECR I-10239: 57, 254, 305, 325

C-243/01 Piergiorgio Gambelli et al [2003] ECR I-13031: 99

C-261 + 262/01 Belgische Staat v Van Calster et al [2003] ECR I-12249: 122, 138

C-264/01 AOK Bundesverband et al v Ichtyol-Ges. Cordes, Hermani & Co et al [2004] ECR I-(16.3.2004): 161

C-313/01 Christine Morgenbesser v Consiglio dell'Orinde degli avvocati di Genova [2003] ECR I-13467: 65

C-320/01 W. Bush v Klinikum Nienstadt [2003] ECR I-2041: 198

C-322/01 Deutscher Apothekenverband v Doc Morris NV and Jacques Waterval [2003] ECR I-14887: 106

C-388/01 Commission v Italy [2003] ECR I-721: 68

C-397/01 Bernhard Pfeifer et al v Deutsches Rotes Kreuz [2004] ECR I-(5.10.2004): 51

C-408/01 Adidas-Salomon AG et al v Fitnessworld Trading Ltd. [2003] ECR I-12537: 179

C-418/01 IMS Health v NDC Health [2004] ECR I-(29.4.2004): 176

C-464/01 Johann Gruber v Bay Wa AG [2005] ECR I-(20.1.2005): 208, 350

C-491/01 R v Secretary of State for Health *ex parte* British American Tobacco (Investment) Ltd. et al. [2002] ECR I-11453: 34, 41, 43, 209, 295

C-25/02 Katharina Rinke v Ärztekammer Hamburg [2003] ECR I-8349: 182, 211

C-27/02 Petra Engler v Janus Versand GmbH [2005] ECR I-(20.1.2005): 208

C-93/02P Etablissements Biret v Council [2003] ECR I-10497: 316

C-138/02 Brian Francis Collins v Secretary of State for Work and Pension [2004] ECR I-(23.3.2004): 62, 76

C-141/02P Commission v max.mobil Telecommunication Service [2005] ECR-(22.2.2005): 219, 320

C-148/02 Carlos Garcia Avello v Etat belge [2003] ECR I-11613: 77

C-157/02 Riester International Transporte GmbH v Autobahnen- und Schnellstrassen-Finanzierungs-AG (Asfinag) [2004] ECR I-(5.2.2004): 20

C-159/02 Gregory Paul Turner v Felix Fareed Ismail Grovit et al [2004] ECR I-(27.4.2004): 203

C-168/02 Rudolf Kronhofer v Marianne Maier et al. [2004] ECR I-(10.6.2004): 246

C-172/02 Streekgewest Westelijk Noord-Brabant v Staatssecretaris van Financiën [2005] ECR I-(13.1.2005): 122

C-200/02 Kungqian Catherine Zhu et al v Secretary of State for the Home Department [2004] ECR I-(19.10.2004): 77

C-222/02 Peter Paul et al v Federal Republic [2004] ECR I-(12.10.2004): 326

C-237/02 Freiburger Kommunalbauten GmbH Baugesellschaft & Co.KG v Ludger Hofstetter und Ulrike Hofstetter [2004] ECR I-(1.4.2004): 260

C-245/02 Anheuser-Busch Inc. v Budějovický Budvar národní podnik [2004] ECR I-(16.11.2004): 181

C-263/02P Jégo-Queré v Commission [2004] ECR I-(1.4.2004): 259

C-281/02 Andrew Owusu v N.B. Jackson et al [2005] ECR I-(1.3.2005): 245

C-309/02 Radlberger Getränkegesellschaft v Land Baden-Württemberg [2004] ECR I-(14.12.2004): 105, 331

C-327/02 Lili Georgieva Panatova et al v Minister voor Vreemdelingenzaken en Integratie [2004] ECR I-(16.11.2004): 82

C-377/02 Léon van Parys v BIRB [2005] ECR I-(1.3.2005): 24

C-429/02 Bacardi-France v TF1 et al [2004] ECR I-(13.7.2004): 130

C-26/03, Stadt Halle, RPL Recyclingpark Lochau GmbH v Arbeitsgemeinschaft Thermische Restabfall- und Energieverwertungsanlage TREA Leuna [2005] ECR I-(11.1.2005): 136

C-156/03 PR Commission v Les Laboratories Servier [2003] ECR I-6575: 318

C-209/03 The Queen (on application of Dany Bider) v London Borough of Ealing, Secretary of State for Education and Skills [2005] ECR I-(15.3.2005): 68, 76

C-228/03 The Gillette Company et al v LA-Laboratories Ltd. Oy. [2005] ECR I-(17.3.2005): 180

C-265/03 Igor Simutenkov v Ministerio de Educación y Cultura et al. [2005] ECR I-(12.4.2005): 24

C-402/03 Skov et al v Jette Mikkelsen et al [2005] ECR I-(per opinion of AG Geelhoed of 20.1.2005): 339

C-125/04 Guy Denuit et al v Transorient – Mosaique Voyages et Culture SA [2005] ECR I-(27.1.2005): 252

OPINIONS OF THE EUROPEAN COURT OF JUSTICE

1/94 Competence of the Community to conclude international agreements concerning services and the protection of intellectual property [1994] I-5267: 43, 166

2/94 on accession by the Community to the European Convention for the Protection of Human Rights and Fundamental Freedoms [1996] ECR I-1759: 44, 213

EUROPEAN COURT OF FIRST INSTANCE

T-30/89 Hilti v. Commission [1991] ECR II-1439 : 159

T-24/90 Automec Srl v Commission [1992] ECR II-2223 : 331

T-7/93 Langnese Iglo GmbH v Commission [1995] ECR II-1533: 151

T-504/93 Tiercé Ladbroke v Commission [1997] ECR II-923: 175

T-99/94 Asociación Española de Empresas de la Carne v Council [1994] ECR II-871: 261

T-184/95 Dorsch Consult Ingenieursgesellschaft v Council and Commission [1998] ECR II-667: 313

T-41/96 Bayer v Commission [2000] ECR II-3383 : 150

T-122/96 Federolio v Commission [1997] ECR-II 1559: 318

T-132 & 143/96 Freistaat Sachsen v Commission [1999] ECR II-3663: 120

T-135/96 UEAPME v Council [1998] ECR II-2335: 309

T-598/97 BSC Footwear Supplies v Council [2002] II-1155: 318

T-62/98 VW/Commission [1998] ECR II-2707: 154

T-172, 175-177/98 Salamander AG, Una Film "City Revue" GmbH, Alma Media Group Advertising SA & Co. Partnership, Panel Two and Four Advertising SA & Co., Rythmos Outdoor Advertising SA, Media Center Advertising SA, Zino Davidoff SA and Davidoff & Cie SA v European Parliament and Council [2000] ECR II-2487: 262

T-198/98 Micro Leader Business v Commission [1999] ECR II-3989: 175

T-54/99 Max.mobil Telekommunikation Service GmbH v Commission [2002] ECR II-313: 219, 320

T-177/01 Jégo-Quéré & Cie SA v Commission of the European Communities [2002] ECR II-2365: 259

TABLE OF SECONDARY LEGISLATION

REGULATIONS

Council Regulation No 17: First Regulation implementing Articles 85 and 86 of the Treaty Special English edition 1956-1962 at 87: 134, 276

Regulation (EEC) No 1612/68 of the Council of 15 October 1968 on freedom of movement for workers within the Community [1968] OJ L 257/2: 56, 58, 61-64, 68, 74, 84, 89

Commission Regulation (EEC) No 123/85 of 12 December 1984 on the application of Article 85 (3) of the Treaty to certain categories of motor vehicle distribution and servicing agreements [1985] OJ L 15/16: 155

Council Regulation (EEC) No 2137/85 of 25 July 1985 on the European Economic Interest Grouping (EEIG) [1985] OJ L 199/1: 116

Commission Regulation (EEC) No 4087/88 of 30 November 1988 on the application of Article 85 (3) of the Treaty to categories of franchise agreements [1998] OJ L 359/46: 146

Council Regulation (EC) No 40/94 of 20 December 1993 on the Community trade mark [1994] OJ L 11/1: 176

Commission Regulation (EC) No 1475/95 of 28 June 1995 on the application of Article 85 (3) of the Treaty to certain categories of motor vehicle distribution and servicing agreements [1995] OJ L 145/25: 154, 156

Commission Regulation (EC) No 240/96 of 31 January 1996 on the application of Article 85 (3) of the Treaty to certain categories of technology transfer agreements [1996] OJ L 31/2: 146, 173

Council Regulation (EC) No 338/97 of 9 December 1996 on the protection of species of wild fauna and flora by regulating trade therein [1997] OJ L 61/1: 348

Council Regulation (EC) No. 994/98 of 7 May 1998 on the application of Articles 92 and 93 of the Treaty to certain categories of horizontal state aid [1998] OJ L 142/1: 138

Council Regulation (EC) No 659/99 of 22 March 1999 laying down detailed rules for the application of Art. 93 (now Art. 87) of the EC Treaty [1999] OJ L 83/1: 118, 138

Commission Regulation (EC) No 2790/1999 of 22 December 1999 on the application of Article 81(3) of the Treaty to categories of vertical agreements and concerted practices [1999] OJ L 336/21: 146, 152, 154, 333

Commission Regulation (EC) No 68/2001 of 12 January 2001 on training aid [OJ] L 10/10: 138

Commission Regulation (EC) No 69/2001 of 12 January 2001 on de minimis aids [2001] OJ L 10/30: 137

Commission Regulation (EC) No 70/2001 of 12 January 2001 on aid for SMU [2001] OJ L 10/33: 138

Council Regulation (EC) No 44/2001 of 22 December 2000 on jurisdiction and the recognition and enforcement of judgments in civil and commercial matters [2001] OJ L 12/1: 9, 27, 235-250, 281, 282

Regulation (EC) No 1049/2001 of the European Parliament and of the Council of 30 May 2001 regarding public access to European Parliament, Council and Commission documents [2001] OJ L 145/43: 295, 310, 320

Council Regulation (EC) No 2157/2001 of 8 October 2001 on the Statute for a European company (SE) [2001] OJ L 294/1: 114

Council Regulation (EC) 6/2002 of 12.12.2001 on Community designs OJ L 3/1: 170

Regulation (EC) No 178/2002 of the European Parliament and of the Council of 28 January 2002 laying down the general principles and requirements of food law, establishing the European Food Safety Authority and laying down procedures in matters of food safety [2002] OJ L 31/1: 229

Commission Regulation (EC) No 1400/2002 of 31 July 2002 on the application of Article 81(3) of the Treaty to categories of vertical agreements and concerted practices in the motor vehicle sector [2002] OJ L 203/30: 154-156, 333

Commission Regulation (EC) No 2204/2002 of 23 December 2002 on aid to employment [2002] OJ L 337/3: 138

Council Regulation (EC) No 1/2003 of 16 December 2002 on the implementation of the rules on competition laid down in Articles 81 and 82 of the Treaty [2003] OJ L 1: 8, 143, 151, 155, 276, 330

Council Regulation (EC) No 139/2004 of 20 January 2004 on the control of concentrations between undertakings [2004] OJ L 24/1: 150

Commission Regulation (EC) No 364/2004 of 2 February 2004 amending Reg. (EC) No. 70/2001 as regards the extension of its scope to include aid for research and development [2004] OJ L 63/22: 138

Commission Regulation (EC) No. 772/2004 of 27 April 2004 on the application of Art. 81 (3) of the Treaty to categories of technology transfer agreements [2004] OJ L 123: 165

DIRECTIVES

First Council Directive 68/151/EEC of 9 March 1968 on co-ordination of safeguards which, for the protection of the interests of members and others, are required by Member States of companies within the meaning of the second paragraph of Article 58 of the Treaty, with a view to making such safeguards equivalent throughout the Community [1968] OJ L 65/8: 343

Council Directive 68/360/EEC of 15 October 1968 on the abolition of restrictions on movement and residence within the Community for workers of Member States and their families [1968] OJ L 257/13: 56, 62

Council Directive 71/305/EEC of 26 July 1971 concerning the co-ordination of procedures for the award of public works contracts [1971] OJ L 185/5: 135

Council Directive 73/23/EEC of 19 February 1973 on the harmonization of the laws of Member States relating to electrical equipment designed for use within certain voltage limits [1973] OJ L 77/29: 128

Council Directive 73/148/EEC of 21 May 1973 on the abolition of restrictions on movement and residence within the Community for nationals of Member States with regard to establishment and the provision of services [1973] OJ L 172/14: 66, 67

Council Directive 75/117/EEC of 10 February 1975 on the approximation of the laws of the Member States relating to the application of the principle of equal pay for men and women [1975] OJ L 45/19: 195

Council Directive 75/439/EEC of 16 June 1975 on the disposal of waste oils [1975] OJ L 194/31: 349

Council Directive 75/442/EEC of 15 July 1975 on waste [1975] OJ 194/39: 349

Council Directive 76/207/EEC of 9 February 1976 on the implementation of the principle of equal treatment for men and women as regards access to employment, vocational training and promotion, and working conditions [1976] OJ L039/40: 21, 196, 203, 335

Council Directive 76/768/EEC of 27 July 1976 on the approximation of the laws of the Member States relating to cosmetic products OJ L 262/169: 299

Council Directive 77/62/EEC of 21 December 1976 coordinating procedures for the award of public supply contracts [1977] OJ L 13/1: 135

Second Council Directive 77/91/EEC of 13 December 1976 on coordination of safeguards which, for the protection of the interests of members and others, are required by Member States of companies within the meaning of the second paragraph of Article 58 of the Treaty, in respect of the formation of public limited liability companies and the maintenance and alteration of their capital, with a view to making such safeguards equivalent [1976] OJ L 26/1: 341

Council Directive 77/187/EEC of 14 February 1977 on the approximation of the laws of the Member States relating to the safeguarding of employees' rights in the event of transfers of undertakings, businesses or parts of businesses [1977] OJ L 61/26: 234

Council Directive 80/987/EEC of 20 October 1980 on the approximation of the laws of the Member States relating to the protection of employees in the event of the insolvency of their employer [1980] OJ L 283/23: 323

Council Directive 83/189/EEC of 28 March 1983 laying down a procedure for the provision of information in the field of technical standards and regulations [1983] OJ L 109/8: 216, 328

Council Directive 84/450/EEC of 10 September 1984 relating to the approximation of the laws, regulations and administrative provisions of the Member States concerning misleading advertising [1984] OJ L 250/17: 131

Council Directive 85/374/EEC of 25 July 1985 on the approximation of the laws, regulations and administrative provisions of the Member States concerning liability for defective products [1985] L 210/29: 29, 48, 337, 339

Council Directive 85/577/EEC of 20 December 1985 to protect the consumer in respect of contracts negotiated away from business premises [1985] OJ L 372/31: 300

Council Directive 88/361/EEC of 24 June 1988 for the implementation of Article 67 of the Treaty [1988] OJ L 178/5: 97, 111

Council Directive 88/378/EEC of 3 May 1988 on the approximation of the laws of the Member States concerning the safety of toys [1988] OJ L 187/1: 127

First Council Directive 89/104/EEC of 21 December 1988 to approximate the laws of the Member States relating to trade marks [1989] OJ L 40/1: 47, 176, 180, 182

Council Directive 89/552/EEC of 3 October 1989 on the coordination of certain provisions laid down by Law, Regulation or Administrative Action in Member States concerning the pursuit of television broadcasting activities [1989] OJ L 298/23: 128-130, 133

Council Directive 89/665/EEC of 21 December 1989 on the coordination of the laws, regulations and administrative provisions relating to the application of review procedures to the award of public supply and public works contracts [1989] OJ L 395/33: 135

Council Directive 90/314/EEC of 13 June 1990 on package travel, package holidays and package tours [1990] OJ L 158/59: 343

Council Directive 90/364/EEC of 28 June 1990 on the right of residence [1990] OJ L 180/26: 60, 69

Council Directive 90/365/EEC of 28 June 1990 on the right of residence for employees and self-employed persons who have ceased their occupational activity [1990] OJ L 180/28: 60, 69

Council Directive 92/50/EEC of 18 June 1992 relating to the coordination of procedures for the award of public service contracts [1992] OJ L 209/1: 135

92/59 Council Directive 92/59/EEC of 29 June 1992 on general product safety [1992] OJ L 228/24: 225-226

Council Directive 92/100/EEC of 19 November 1992 on rental right and lending right and on certain rights related to copyright in the field of intellectual property [1992] OJ L 346/61: 27

Council Directive 93/13/EEC of 5 April 1993 on unfair terms in consumer contracts [1993] OJ L 95/29: 242, 280, 300

Council Directive 93/22/EEC of 10 May 1993 on investment services in the securities field [1993] OJ L 141/27: 344

Council Directive 93/36/EEC of 14 June 1993 coordinating procedures for the award of public supply contracts [1993] OJ L 199/1: 135

Council Directive 93/37/EEC of 14 June 1993 concerning the coordination of procedures for the award of public works contracts [1993] OJ L 199/54: 135

Council Directive 93/38/EEC of 14 June 1993 coordinating the procurement procedures of entities operating in the water, energy, transport and telecommunications sectors [1993] OJ L 199/84: 135

Council Directive 93/42/EC of 14 June 1993 concerning medical devices OJ L 169/1: 127

Council Directive 93/96/EEC of 29 October 1993 on the right of residence for students [1993] OJ 317/59: 56, 68-69, 75-77

Directive 94/19/EC of the European Parliament and of the Council of 30 May 1994 on deposit-guarantee schemes [1994] OJ L 135/5: 326

European Parliament and Council Directive 94/62/EC of 20 December 1994 on packaging and packaging waste [1994] OJ L 361/10: 348

Directive 95/46/EC of the European Parliament and of the Council of 24 October 1995 on the protection of individuals with regard to the processing of personal data and on the free movement of such data [1995] OJ L 281/31: 211

Directive 96/71/EC of the EP and the Council of 16 December 1996 concerning posted workers [1997] OJ L 18/1: 109

Directive 97/7/EC of the European Parliament and of the Council of 20 May 1997 on the protection of consumers in respect of distance contracts [1997] OJ L 144/19: 132, 296

Directive 97/9/EC of the European Parliament and of the Council of 3 March 1997 on investor-compensation schemes [1997] OJ L 84/22: 326

Directive 97/36/EC of the European Parliament and of the Council of 30 June 1997 amending Council Directive 89/552/EEC on the coordination of certain provisions laid down by law, regulation or administrative action in Member States concerning the pursuit of television broadcasting activities [1997] OJ L 202/60: 132, 134

Council Directive 97/80/EC of 15 December 197 on the burden of proof in cases of discrimination based on sex [1997] OJ L 14/6: 201

Directive 98/34/EC of the European Parliament and of the Council of 22 June 1998 laying down a procedure for the provision of information in the field of technical standards and regulations [1998] OJ L 204/37: 328

Directive 98/37/EC of the European Parliament and of the Council of 22 June 1998 on the approximation of the laws of the Member States relating to machinery [1998] OJ L 80/34: 127

Directive 98/43/EC of the European Parliament and of the Council of 6 July 1998 on the approximation of the laws, regulations and administrative provisions of the Member States relating to the advertising and sponsorship of tobacco products [1998] OJ L 213/9: 42 (annulled by case C-376/98)

Council Directive 98/50/EC of 29 June 1998 amending Directive 77/187/EEC on the approximation of the laws of the Member States relating to the safeguarding of employees' rights in the event of transfers of undertakings, businesses or parts of businesses[1998] OJ L 201/58: 234

Directive 98/71/EC of the EP and the Council of 13 October 1998 on the legal protection of designs, OJ L 289/28: 170

Directive 1999/34/EC of the European Parliament and of the Council of 10 May 1999 amending Council Directive 85/374/EEC on the approximation of the laws, regulations and administrative provisions of the Member States concerning liability for defective products[1999] OJ L 141/20: 338

Directive 1999/44/EC of the European Parliament and of the Council of 25 May 1999 on certain aspects of the sale of consumer goods and associated guarantees [1999] OJ 171/12: 224, 225, 231, 296, 302

Directive 2000/31/EC of the European Parliament and of the Council of 8 June 2000 on certain legal aspects of information society services, in particular electronic commerce, in the Internal Market ('Directive on electronic commerce') [2000] OJ L 178/1: 132-134, 297, 299-300

Council Directive 2000/43/EC of 29 June 2000 implementing the principle of equal treatment between persons irrespective of racial or ethnic origin [2000 OJ L 180/22: 206

Council Directive 2000/78/EC of 27 November 2000 establishing a general framework for equal treatment in employment and occupation [2000] OJ L 303/16: 207

Council Directive 2001/23/EC of 12 March 2001 on the approximation of the laws of the Member States relating to the safeguarding of employees' rights in the event of transfers of undertakings, businesses or parts of undertakings or businesses [2001] OJ L 82/16: 234

Directive 2001/95/EC of the European Parliament and of the Council of 3 December 2001 on general product safety [2002] OJ L 11/4: 226

Council Directive 2002/8/EC of 27 January 2003 concerning legal aid in cross-border litigation [2003] OJ 26/41: 242

Directive 2002/65/EC of the European Parliament and of the Council of 23 September 2002 concerning the distance marketing of consumer financial services and amending Council Directive 90/619/EEC and Directives 97/7/EC and 98/27/EC [2002] OJ L 271/16: 296, 299

Directive 2002/73/EC of the European Parliament and of the Council of 23 September 2002 amending Council Directive 76/207/EEC on the implementation of the principle of equal treatment for men and women as regards access to employment, vocational training and promotion, and working conditions [2002] OJ L 269/15: 197

Directive 2002/83/EC of the EP and the Council of 5 November 2002 concerning life assurance [2002] OJ L 345/1: 297

Directive 2003/6/EC of the European Parliament and of the Council of 28 January 2003 on insider dealing and market manipulation (market abuse) [2003] OJ L 96/16: 344

Council Directive 2003/86/EC of 22 September 2003 on the right to family reunion [2003] OJ L 251/12: 88

Council Directive 2003/109/EC of 25 November 2003 "concerning the status of third-country nationals who are long-term residents" [2004] OJ L 16/44: 87

Directives 2004/17 and 18/EC of the EP and the Council of 31 March 2004 on procurement procedures [2004] OJ L 134: 126

Directive 2004/35/EC of the EP and the Council of 21 April 2004 on environmental liability with regard to the prevention and remedying of environmental damage [2004] OJ L 143/56: 341

Directive 2004/38/EC of 29 April 2004 on the right of citizens of the Union and their family members to move and reside freely within the territory of the Member States [2004] OJ L 158/77: 78 with corrigendum L 229/35

Directive 2004/39/EC of the EP and the Council of 21 April 2004 on markets in financial instruments [2004] OJ L 145/1: 327

Directive 2004/48/EC of the EP and the Council of 29 April on the enforcement of intellectual property rights [2004] OJ L 157/45: 170, 183

Council Directive 2004/113/EC of 13 December 2004 implementing the principle of equal treatment between women and men in the access to and supply of goods and services [2004] OJ L 373/37: 204, 279

Comparison between the main Articles of the EU and EC Treaties in the Amsterdam/Nice versions cited in the book, with the Draft Treaty Establishing a Constitution for Europe of 29.10.2004. Institutional arrangements are omitted.

EU/EC	Subject matter	Draft Constitution	Remarks
6 (2) EU	Respect for fundamental rights	I-9 (2)	Accession to ECHR possible
43-47 EU	Enhanced cooperation	III-416-423	
Case law	Primacy of Community law	I-6	Express recognition of primacy
Case law	Principle of effective judicial protection	I-29 (1), II-107	"Member States shall provide remedies sufficient to ensure effective legal protection in the fields covered by Union law"
4/109 EC	Principle of market economy	I-3, III-177	"… a highly competitive social market economy"
5 (1) EC	Action "…within the limits of powers conferred upon it…"	I-11 (1) (2)	Principle of conferral
		I-12-17	Categories of competence (exclusive, shared, coordination, complementary action)
5 (2) EC	subsidiarity	I-11 (3)	Role of National Parliaments according to protocol
5 (3) EC	proportionality	I-11 (4)	
6/176	Environmental protection	II-97; III-119	
10	Loyalty obligation of Member States	I-5 (2)	
12	Discriminations based on nationality "in the scope of application of this Treaty…"	I-4 (2), II-81 (1)	
13	Competence to combat discriminations	II-81 (2), III-118, 124	Direct effect?
14 (2)	Internal market as an area of fee movement	I-4 (1), 130 (2)	Additional guarantee of free movement
16	Services of general economic interest	II-96, III-122	
17	Citizenship EU	I-10 (1)	

EU/EC	Subject matter	Draft Constitution	Remarks
18	Free movement of citizens	I-10 (2)(a), II-105, III-125	
19-20	Political rights of citizens	I-10(2)(c), II-99-100, III-126	
28/29	Free movement of goods	III-153	Exports and imports are on the same footing
30	Allowed restrictions	III-154	
39	Free movement of workers	II-75(2), III-133	
43	Establishment of persons	II-75(2), III-137	
46	Public policy proviso	III-140	
48	Establishment of undertakings	III-142	
49	Freedom to provide services	III-144	
56/57	Free movement of capital and payments, including third countries	III-156/157	
58	Public policy proviso	III-158	
81	Prohibition of restrictive practices between undertakings	III-161	
82	Prohibition of abuse by market dominating undertaking	III-162	
86	Special rules of public undertakings or undertakings with exclusive or special rights	III-166	
87	Prohibition of state aids	III-167	
90	Prohibition of discriminations in indirect taxation	III-170	
95	Adoption of internal market measures	III-172	
141	Principles of equal pay disregarding sex	II-83, III-214	Charter guarantees equality between men and women "in all areas", including employment, work and pay
153	Consumer protection	II-98, III-120	
194	Right of petition of "any" person	II-104	

EU/EC	Subject matter	Draft Constitution	Remarks
220	Observance of the law	I-29 (1)	
226	Infringement proceedings	III-360	
228	Fines for non-compliance	III-362	
230 (4)	Direct actions	III-365(4)	"…and against a regulatory act which is of direct concern to him or her and does not entail implementing measures."
232 (3)	Complaint for omission of an action	III-367(3)	
234	Reference procedure	III-369	"… minimum delay" in cases concerning persons in custody
242/243	Suspensory effect/interim measures	III-379	
249	Effects of regulations and directives	I-33(1), 38	Community laws and framework laws; selection of instrument on a case-by-case basis in compliance with principle of proportionality
		I-33(1), 36	Delegated European regulations – recognition of the doctrine of "essential elements" in the delegating act
253	Obligation to state reasons	I-38(2)	Extended to all "legal acts"
255	Access to EU documents of "any" citizen	II-102	"fundamental right of access…"
286	Data protection	I-51, II-68	Right to data protection
288 (2)	Non-contractual liability of EC	II-101(3), III-431(2)	
295	Respect for national property regimes	II-77, III-425	Right to property (including intellectual property)
308	"implied competences"	I-18	flexibility clause

INDEX OF SUBJECT MATTERS